Anonymous

**Wright's Directory of Green Bay and Fort Howard**

1894-95

Anonymous

**Wright's Directory of Green Bay and Fort Howard**
*1894-95*

ISBN/EAN: 9783337731830

Printed in Europe, USA, Canada, Australia, Japan

Cover: Foto ©ninafisch / pixelio.de

More available books at **www.hansebooks.com**

# JOHN L. F. JANSSEN,

## Manufacturing Jeweler,

### WATCHMAKER,

### GOLD and SILVER PLATER,

916 Main St.

GREEN BAY, - WIS.

---

## JULIUS LIEBENOW,

Successor to E. L. Hall,

## *Watchmaker and Jeweler,*

GREEN BAY, WIS.

---

## G. KÜSTERMANN,

ESTABLISHED 1870.

DEPARTMENT A.

### PIANOS, ORGANS AND MUSICAL MERCHANDISE.

DEPARTMENT B.

### BOOKS AND STATIONERY.

GREEN BAY, WIS.

GUSTAV GREEN.
CHARLES GREEN.
ROBERT ARMSTRONG.

# GREEN BROS. & CO.

## Artesian Well Contractors.

Wells drilled to any Depth and Size in Good, Workmanlike manner, on Short Notice.

ALL WORK GUARANTEED.

1215 Stuart Street.
Green Bay, - - - Wis.

---

# F. FRISQUE,

## Merchant Tailor,

CARRIES A FULL LINE OF

### FOREIGN AND DOMESTIC GOODS,

222 MAIN STREET,

Green Bay, - - - Wis.

## W. A. BRANDENSTEIN,
## MERCHANT TAILOR,
311 Cherry Street,
**GREEN BAY,** - **WISCONSIN.**

---

## J. HOPPE,
## Merchant Tailoring
219 N. ADAMS ST., GREEN BAY, WIS.

ROB. HOPPE, Cutter.

---

## WILLIAM C. MAHN,
## Artistic * Tailor,
COR. PINE AND ADAMS STS.,
**GREEN BAY,** - **WISCONSIN.**

---

**FOR BARGAINS**
—IN—
## DRY GOODS, CLOTHING
LADIES' AND GENTS' FURNISHING GOODS, HATS, CAPS, ETC.

Also a Full Line of
CROCKERY and TIN WARE at Lowest Prices.
Call at the **MAIN STREET FAIR STORE, 521 Main Street,**
JOHN BAUM, Prop.   GREEN BAY, WIS.

JOSHUA CRONE,            HENRY VAN DER STEEN,
1707 Cedar                               1164 Cherry

# CRONE & VAN DER STEEN,
## Carpenters and Contractors.

Estimates Furnished and Satisfaction Guaranteed.

**GREEN BAY,**    -   -    **WISCONSIN.**

# EUGENE LORENT
## CARPENTER-CONTRACTOR AND BUILDER.

Plans and Specifications Drawn and Estimates Made.

**445 S. Madison Street,**
**GREEN BAY, WIS.**

ERNEST W. SERVOTTE,           JOSEPH H. SERVOTTE,
1034 Walnut.                            510 S. Monroe Ave.

# E. W. & JOS. H. SERVOTTE,
## Carpenters and Contractors.

Estimates made on Plans and Specifications.

*ALL ORDERS PROMPTLY ATTENDED TO.*

**GREEN BAY, WIS.**

# CHARLES GOLUEKE,
## *Contractor and Builder*

Estimates Furnished for all kinds of Mason Work.
*Fine Pressed Brick Work.*
*All Work Guaranteed.*

**921 Cherry Street,**              **GREEN BAY, WIS.**

LOUIS FABRY,  EDWARD HENKELMANN,
330 S. Jackson.  1124 Cass.

## FABRY & HENKELMANN

DO ALL KINDS OF

# MASON WORK

330 S. Jackson St.,

GREEN BAY,  -  WISCONSIN.

## PETER MAY,
# MASON CONTRACTOR

ALL KINDS OF

### BRICK AND STONE MASONRY.

1019 WALNUT ST.  GREEN BAY, WIS.

## JOHN B. ROSE,
# MASON CONTRACTOR.

All Work Promptly Attended to.

**SATISFACTION GUARANTEED.**

1268 DAY STREET,

GREEN BAY, WIS.

## HERMAN SCHMIDT,
# MASON CONTRACTOR,

Will put up every description of

### Stone or Brick Masonry.

619 South 11th Street,  GREEN BAY, WIS.

## ADOLPH GREEN,
## CONTRACTOR AND BUILDER.

All Kinds of Work done to Order.

1019 Pine Street, GREEN BAY, WIS.

CHARLES H. GREILING.      HERMAN GREILING.

## GREILING BROS.
### *General Contractors.*

Both Mason and Carpenter Work. Churches, Schools and Residences a Specialty. Estimates Given on All Work.

P. O. BOX 1556.    -    -    GREEN BAY, WIS.

## W. F. KENDALL,
### Civil Engineer and Architect

Plans for Buildings, also Surveys for Land, Railroad, Foundations and Municipal Works.

Room 6, 320 N. Washington St., GREEN BAY, WIS.

## JOS. F. ROTHE,
PROPRIETOR
# GREEN BAY IRON & BRASS FOUNDRY

House and Sewer Work a Specialty.

Works, 318 N. Eleventh Street, South of Main St.

**GREEN BAY, WIS.**

---

## JOANNES & EDWARDS,
### GALVANIZED IRON CORNICES, SKYLIGHTS & GENERAL ROOFERS

Electric Wiring and Electric Goods of all kinds.

THE FULLER-WARREN HOT AIR HEATERS LEAD THE WORLD (will save one-third of your coal bill over any other Furnace in use).

BUILDING PAPERS OF ALL DESCRIPTIONS.

---

## Green Bay Plumbing & Heating Co.,
Successors to the J. H. CASE CO.

# PLUMBING, SEWERAGE

Hot Water, Air and Steam Heating a Specialty.

ALSO IRON, TIN, COPPER and BRASS WORKERS

All Kinds of Roofing

224 PINE STREET, - GREEN BAY, WIS.

---

## NELS SKOGG,
# Sanitary Plumbing and Sewerage

*GAS, STEAM AND HOT WATER HEATING.*

All Work Warranted.      313 Cherry Street.

## IRA KRAKE,
### PAINTER, PAPERHANGER, CALCIMINER AND MASON.

All Orders Promptly Attended to and Nicely Done.

Ask for Prices Before Contracting Elsewhere.
First-class Work Guaranteed.

N. E. Cor. 5th Ave. and 10th St.,   Ft. Howard, Wis.

---

## WUERTZ & BURKARD,
### DECORATORS.

Fresco, Sign and House Painters.

Calcimining and Paper Hanging. All Work Guaranteed.

718 and 927 Cherry St.,   GREEN BAY, WIS.

---

## JOHN H. MALLORY,
### CITY BILL POSTER
### AND
### PAPER HANGER,

Walnut St., adjoining the Bridge.   GREEN BAY, WIS.

---

## MARTIN ERICKSEN,
### Frescoer and Designer.

Artistic Paper Hanging and Decorating.  Sign Writing and General House Painting.

RESIDENCE:                           SHOP:
409 S. Monroe Ave., GREEN BAY, WIS.   335 Broadway, FORT HOWARD, WIS.

## A. L. ADAMS & CO.

DEALERS IN ALL KINDS OF **LUMBER,**

Pine Stuff, Flooring, Siding, Ceiling and Finishing Lumber.

Lumber delivered to any part of Green Bay or Ft. Howard.
Yard, South Fort Howard. - Post Office Address, Green Bay.
Telephone 110.

---

## JOHN NICK,
### DEALER IN
### Hard and Soft Wood, Cedar Posts
SAWED SHINGLES, CORD WOOD, SLABS,

Yards, Foot of N. Jackson, on E. River,
Residence, 1201 Walnut Street,
**GREEN BAY, WIS.**

---

### Howard Foundry and Machine Works.
## A. M. DUNCAN,
MANUFACTURER OF AND DEALER IN

### Steam Engines, Saw & Grist Mill
AND STEAM BOAT MACHINERY, ETC.

All Kinds of Castings Made to Order. Rail Castings a Specialty. The only First-class Foundry in the City.
**FT. HOWARD, WIS.**

---

## N. WAGNER,
DEALER AND JOBBER IN

### Wall Paper, Paints, Oils,
**PLATE GLASS AND VARNISH,**

220 Cherry Street, - - GREEN BAY, WIS.

ANY SHADE OF COLOR MIXED UPON APPLICATION.

# GREEN BAY CREAMERY CO.

Manufacturers of

## Fancy Creamery Butter

And Dealers in

## Jersey Milk and Cream.

W. H. WOODRUFF, MANAGER.

Corner Adams and Doty Streets.        GREEN BAY, WIS.

---

# E. SCHILLING,

Wholesale Dealer in

## BUTTER, EGGS AND PRODUCE.

907 MAIN STREET, GREEN BAY, WIS.

General Merchandise; also all kinds of Farm Produce,

Wequiock, Wis.

---

# J. S. JOHNSON,

WHOLESALE DEALER IN

## FRESH, SALT and SMOKED FISH

### AND OYSTERS,

1234 Main St., GREEN BAY, WIS.

---

# C. SCHILLER,

WHOLESALE DEALER IN

## Fresh, Lake and River Fish.

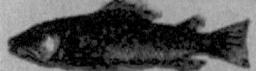

Also Salt and Smoked Fish.

TELEPHONE NO. 80.

PACKING HOUSE AND FREEZER,
Foot of N. Jefferson St.        GREEN BAY, WIS.

## J. N. HOWLETT,

DEALER IN

## Groceries and Provisions

FLOUR, FEED, ETC.

FORT HOWARD, WIS.

---

E. M. MILLER.                                      N. J. JULEY.

## MILLER & JULEY,

## The South Side Grocers

214 THIRD AVE., SOUTH SIDE.

FT. HOWARD, - - WIS.

---

L. E. NEJEDLO.        M. R. NEJEDLO.        G. J. NEJEDLO.

## NEJEDLO BROS.,

(SUCCESSORS TO L. LEFEBVRE.)

DEALERS IN

**Choice Family Groceries, Crockery, Flour, Feed,**

Provisions and Farm Produce.

FINE TEAS AND COFFEES A SPECIALTY.

321 ADAMS STREET, - GREEN BAY, WIS.

---

G. B. HESS.            H. A. WOLTER.            C. MASSEY.

## THE GEO. B. HESS CO.

MANUFACTURERS OF THE CELEBRATED

**STAR PATENT,**  **DELIGHT STRAIGHT,**

CHOICE BRANDS                        OF FLOUR.

ROLLER GROUND FEED, and Dealers in OATS, CORN, Etc.

COR. CEDAR and NORTH QUINCY.

TELEPHONE No. 100.

# JIM J. BLACK,
## Livery, Sale and Boarding Stable

FUNERALS PROMPTLY ATTENDED TO.  PRICES REASONABLE

3d Avenue, SOUTH FORT HOWARD, WIS.

---

## P. H. CARLIN,
PROPRIETOR OF

### LIVERY AND FEED STABLES,
Telephone 69.

103-105 S. WASHINGTON STREET.

---

## DOMINICK FLATLEY,
PROPRIETOR OF

### Livery and Sale Stable.

**HORSES AND CARRIAGES TO LET.**

220 N. Adams, North of the Post Office.   Residence, S. W. Cor. Main and Quincy,

### GREEN BAY, WIS.

---

## JAS. McKONE,
PROPRIETOR

### MAIN STREET LIVERY
#### HACK AND BUS LINE.

First-Class Turnouts Furnished at Quick Notice.
Telephone orders Promptly Attended to.

Telephone 77.
415-417 Main Street, 2 blocks east Beaumont House.

GREEN BAY,   -   WIS.

## MALCOLM A. SELLERS,
## Livery and Sale Stable,
First-class Turnout.   Careful Drivers.
WEST SIDE THIRD AVE., SOUTH THE SLOUGH,
FORT HOWARD, WIS.

### FRANK SNYDER'S
### First Class Livery,
215 N. Adams St.,
Opp. P. O.       GREEN BAY.

**HACK AND 'BUS LINE.**
Leave Orders with Driver, or at any First class Hotel.

TELEPHONE 54.

## McCORMICK & BATES,
## FREIGHT TRANSFER AGENTS
### AND DEALERS IN WOOD.
Special Attention Given to Moving of Household Furniture, Pianos, Safes, Etc.

TELEPHONE NO. 16.         220 S. WASHINGTON.

## W. A. SALISBURY,
MANUFACTURER OF
King of Leather
Oil for Buggy Tops,
Lotion and Salve,
Yucca Hoof Salve,
Yucca Spavin Cure,

### 273 Central Avenue
**OSHKOSH, WIS.**

## HOCHGREVE BREWING CO.

BREWERS OF

Pilsener, Bohemian, Select, and Lager **BEER**

On the Monroe Ave. Road, between Green Bay and De Pere,

Town of Allouez.          GREEN BAY, WIS.

---

## O. Van Dycke Brewing Co.

BREWERS OF THE

GREEN BAY CELEBRATED WIENER BEER,

Cor. Chicago and S. Jackson Sts.,

Telephone No. 76-3.          GREEN BAY, WIS.

---

## J. HUERTH,

MANUFACTURER OF **FINE CIGARS**

PROPRIETOR OF THE POPULAR BRANDS

"GREEN BAY BASE BALL CLUB" AND "LA VIDA,"

308 N. Washington St.,          GREEN BAY, WIS,

---

### WELL! WELL! WELL!

## L. P. WEISSMILLER,

MANUFACTURER

OF THE FINEST **CIGARS** IN THE MARKET

FAVORITE, 10 Cents.          RAZZLE DAZZLE, 5 Cents.

110 North Washington Street,   ·   GREEN BAY, WIS.

### J. P. C. SCHMIT,

WHOLESALE

## Wine and Liquor

MERCHANT,

215 N. Washington Street,

GREEN BAY, - WIS.

---

### S. BENDER,

CHOICE

## WINES, LIQUORS AND CIGARS,

220 PINE STREET, GREEN BAY, WIS.

Opera House, GREEN BAY, WIS.
............ For open dates and terms, inquire of
S. BENDER.

---

### JOHN P. JUENGER,

PROPRIETOR OF

## Saloon and Restaurant

429 Broadway, cor. of Dousman Street,

One Block from Bridge and C. & N. W. R'y Depot.

Ft. Howard, - - Wisconsin.

---

### J. F. SCHMITT,

DEALER IN CHOICE

## WINES, LIQUORS AND CIGARS

PROPRIETOR OF THE

### ST. CHARLES SALOON AND RESTAURANT.

118½ Washington St. - GREEN BAY, WIS.

Lunch Served Every Morning.

# REIS' HOTEL,

ANDREW REIS, Jr., Proprietor.

**1148 MAIN STREET, NEAR EAST RIVER BRIDGE,**

**GREEN BAY, WIS.**

Good accommodations, Reasonable Prices. Passengers carried free to and from Depots.

IN CONNECTION WITH THE HOTEL IS A

## FIRST CLASS LIVERY STABLE.

FINE HACKS AND HEARSE. CHARGES REASONABLE.

---

## PETER ROBILLARD,

PROPRIETOR OF THE

*Board by the Day or Week.* **Main Street Hotel**

Choice Wines, Liquors and Cigars,

GOOD STABLING ATTACHED.    316 MAIN STREET, GREEN BAY, WIS.

---

## SCHAUER HOTEL.

SCHAUER BROS., Proprietors.

**FIRST-CLASS ACCOMMODATIONS FOR TRAVELERS**

Most Convenient Location in the City.

FREE BUS TO AND FROM ALL TRAINS.    GOOD STABLING IN CONNECTION WITH THE HOUSE.

401 MAIN ST., COR. JEFFERSON ST.

GREEN BAY, - - - WISCONSIN.

---

# JAMES PETCKA,

## Saloon and Boarding House.

ALSO DEALER IN

### Wines, Liquors and Cigars,

322 MAIN STREET,

**GREEN BAY, WIS.**

JOS. LeROY.                              MELCHIOR THEISEN.

# Cook's Hotel.

**FIRST-CLASS HOTEL.**          **RATES, $2.00 PER DAY.**

Special Rates to Permanent Guests.

'Busses to and from all Trains.   Electric Light all through the House.

SAMPLE ROOMS IN CONNECTION ON GROUND FLOOR.

Telephone No. 49,

S. W. Cor. N. Washington and Cherry.

# Bradley House,

## D. P. BRADLEY, Prop.

**GREEN BAY,   -   WISCONSIN.**

# ADAMS ✳ HOUSE,

### GEO. SNAVELY, Prop.

This House has been thoroughly renovated and put in the best possible shape for the accommodation of the traveling public.

**Rates $1.00 per day.**     Good Stables are Connected with the House.

209 NORTH ADAMS STREET, Opposite Post Office,

**GREEN BAY,   -   WISCONSIN.**

E. K. Ansorge.                                      E. P. Parish.

## ANSORGE & PARISH,
## Fire, Life & Accident Insurance
### Real Estate and Loans,

Notaries Public, Ocean Passage, Drafts to Europe, and Collections.

**GREEN BAY, WIS.**

Telephone 101.                    Office Citizens National Bank Building.

## O. J. B. BRICE,
### BELGIAN CONSUL,
## Fire, Life, Accident Insurance

REAL ESTATE AND PASSAGE AGENCY.

LEGAL PAPERS EXECUTED BOTH IN FRENCH AND ENGLISH.

Office, Parmentier Blk., North Washington Street, cor. Main,

**GREEN BAY, WIS.**

## JOHN SHEPECK, Jr.,
## REAL ESTATE,
## INSURANCE,
## LOANS,
### PASSAGE AGENCY.

314 MAIN STREET,   -   GREEN BAY, WIS.

## MALCOLM SELLERS,
## General Commission Merchant,
### PENSION AND CLAIM AGENT,

Justice of the Peace, Notary Public and Real Estate Dealer,

FT. HOWARD,        -        -        WISCONSIN.

# WRIGHT'S
## DIRECTORY
### OF
## GREEN BAY
## FT. HOWARD
### FOR
## 1894-95

COMPRISING

AN ALPHABETICALLY ARRANGED LIST OF BUSINESS FIRMS AND
PRIVATE CITIZENS; A CLASSIFIED LIST OF ALL TRADES,
PROFESSIONS AND PURSUITS; A MISCELLANEOUS
DIRECTORY OF CITY AND COUNTY OFFICERS,
SCHOOLS, CHURCHES, BANKS, INCORPORA-
TED INSTITUTIONS, SOCIETIES, ETC.

### VOLUME III.

PRICE, THREE DOLLARS.

A. G. WRIGHT,
107 WISCONSIN STREET, MILWAUKEE, WIS.
1894.

## TABLE OF CONTENTS.

| | PAGE. | | PAGE. |
|---|---|---|---|
| Additions, Alterations, etc., opp. | 54 | General Directory | 55 |
| Asylums, Homes, etc. | 37 | Index to Advertisements | 24 |
| Banks and Incorp. Co's., Ft. H. | 60 | Parks, Ft. H. | 52 |
| " " " G. B. | 34 | " G. B. | 43 |
| Blocks, Halls, etc., Ft. H. | 53 | Post Office, Ft. H. | 50 |
| " " " G. B. | 44 | " G. B. | 32 |
| Business Directory | 259 | Public Schools, Ft. H. | 49 |
| Cemeteries, Ft. H. | 51 | " " G. B. | 27 |
| " G. B. | 38 | Railroad Distances and Fares. | 33 |
| Churches, Ft. H. | 50 | Societies and Lodges, Ft. H. | 51 |
| " G. B. | 30 | " " " G. B. | 38 |
| City Government, Ft. H. | 48 | Stages | 33 |
| " " G. B. | 25 | Street Directory, Ft. H. | 53 |
| County Government | 31 | " " G. B. | 44 |
| Fire Department, Ft. H. | 49 | United States Offices. | 32 |
| " " G. B. | 27 | | |

Copyright, 1884, by A. G. WRIGHT.

# INTRODUCTORY.

THE Publisher presents herewith his third Directory of Green Bay and Ft. Howard. He trusts it will be found of sufficient value, and of such substantial accuracy, as to justify a continuance in the future of the support accorded in the past. Many men, of varying degrees of capacity, have published Directories at this point, but the undersigned is the only one who has ever made a second effort. He will continue in the good work, and if the business men, whose patronage is necessary to make such a work a success, will exercise discrimination, and refuse support except to such as have shown the ability to produce a reliable Directory, they will be assured of good work in the future.

The canvass has shown that the cities of Green Bay and Ft. Howard have increased fully ten per cent. since the last Directory was made. No effort has been made to separate the two towns, which are practically identical in interest; and, from observation as well as experience, the Publisher will venture the prediction that when the census is taken next year the population of the settlement will be found to approximate 18,000.

The single alphabetical arrangement has been retained, the residents of Fort Howard being designated, as formerly, by "Ft. H." after the name. The sentiment was practically unanimous, among those approached on the subject, that this was the more convenient method; especially in view of the fact that the movement in favor of the union of the two cities seemed to be growing in strength.

That the consolidation may be consummated in season to enable the new city to take its proper place in the State census of 1895, is the best wish the Publisher can offer.

Very truly,

A. G. WRIGHT.

107 WISCONSIN STREET,
MILWAUKEE, WIS.

## INDEX TO ADVERTISEMENTS.

| | PAGE. |
|---|---|
| Adams A. L. & Co | 11 |
| Adams House | 19 |
| Ansorge & Parish | 20 |
| Baum J | 5 |
| Bender Sebastian | 17 |
| Black Jim J | 14 |
| Bradley House | 19 |
| Brandenstein W. A. | 5 |
| Brice O. J. B | 20 |
| Buscher Josus | 285 |
| Carlin P. H | 14 |
| Citizens' Nat. Bank | front cover |
| Clark & Fiedler | opp. 54 |
| Columbian Baking Co. | front cover |
| Cook's Hotel | 19 |
| Corbett M. J | back cover |
| Crone & Van der Sloen | 6 |
| Duncan A. M | 11 |
| Engels & Mohr | 286 |
| Erickson Martin | 10 |
| Fabry & Henkelmann | 7 |
| Flatley Dominick | 14 |
| Frisque F. | 4 |
| Green Adolph | 8 |
| Green Bros. & Co. | 4 |
| Green Bay Advocate Co | opp. 122 |
| Green Bay Business College | backbone and 2 |
| Green Bay Creamery Co. | 12 |
| Green Bay Plumbing & Heating Co. | 9 |
| Green Bay, Winona & St. Paul Ry. | 287 |
| Grelling Bros | 8 |
| Golueke Charles | 6 |
| Hagemeister L | stencil edges |
| Handlen J. J. | 285 |
| Haupt Geo. & Co | 286 |
| Hess Geo. B. Co., The | 13 |
| Hochgreve Brewing Co. | 16 |
| Hoppe J. | 5 |
| Howlett J. W | 18 |
| Huerth J | 16 |
| Janssen John L. F. | 3 |
| Joannes & Edwards | 9 |
| Johnson J. S. | 12 |
| Jorgensen-Blesch Co. | front cover |
| Juenger J. P. | 17 |
| Kellogg Nat. Bank | front cover |

| | PAGE. |
|---|---|
| Kendall W. F. | 8 |
| Kerr Jas. & Son | opp. 150 |
| King-Fowle-McGee Co. | 283 |
| Kittner E. C. | 284 |
| Krake Ira | 10 |
| Küstermann O. | 3 |
| Lehman & Robinson | opp. 162 |
| Liebenow Julius | 3 |
| Lochmann Peter J | 284 |
| Lorent Eugene | 6 |
| McCormick & Bates | 15 |
| McDonald H. | back cover |
| McKone James | 14 |
| Mallory J. H | 10 |
| Mahn Wm. C. | 5 |
| Manthey Carl | 2 |
| May Peter | 7 |
| Miller & Juley | 13 |
| Nejedlo Bros | 13 |
| Nick John | 11 |
| Oldenburg & Co. | 286 |
| Petcka James | 18 |
| Rels Andrew Jr | 18 |
| Robillard Peter | 18 |
| Rose John B | 7 |
| Rothe Jos. F. | 9 |
| St. John Mineral Water | 285 |
| Salisbury W. A. | 15 |
| Schauer Bros | 18 |
| Schiller C. | 12 |
| Schilling E | 12 |
| Schmidt Herman | 7 |
| Schmit J. P. C. | 17 |
| Schmit J. F. | 17 |
| Schmitz Paul N | 284 |
| Sellers Malcolm | 20 |
| Sellers M. A | 15 |
| Servotte E. W. & Jos. H. | 6 |
| Shepeck John Jr. | 20 |
| Simon Mathias | 284 |
| Skogg Nels | 9 |
| Smits Herman | 284 |
| Snavely George | 19 |
| Snyder Frank | 15 |
| Spuhler A. Co. The | top lines |
| Van Dycke O. Brewing Co. | 16 |
| Wagner N | 11 |
| Weisamiller L | 16 |
| Woertz & Burkard | 10 |

# WRIGHT'S
# GREEN BAY DIRECTORY
## 1894.

### MISCELLANEOUS DIRECTORY.

### CITY GOVERNMENT.

Municipal election, first Tuesday in April. City Hall, e. s. S. Washington, nr. Walnut.
Mayor, Jas. H. Elmore.
President of Council, Frank B. Desnoyers.
Clerk, X. Parmentier.
Treasurer, Porter H. Campbell.
Assessor, Xav. Martin.
Attorney, Carlton Merrill.

### Members of the Common Council.

First Ward, Frank Murphy, 1 year; Adam Spuhler, 2 years.
Second Ward, F. B. Desnoyers, 1 year; Geo. D. Nau, 2 years.
Third Ward, Wm. Rothe, 1 year; F. J. B. Duchateau, 2 years.
Fourth Ward, F. Gronnert, 1 year; John Shepeck, Jr., 2 years.
Fifth Ward, J. N. McCunn, 1 year; Max. Zilkoski, 2 years.

### COMMITTEES.

Finance—McCunn, Desnoyers, Shepeck.
Fire Department—Murphy, Duchateau, Desnoyers.
Streets and Bridges—Desnoyers, Rothe, Spuhler.
Sewers and Plumbing—Rothe, Spuhler, Gronnert.
Gas and Electric Lights—Duchateau, Murphy, Nau.
Accounts—Shepeck, Nau, McCunn.

Public Grounds—Gronnert, Zilkoski, Murphy.
Taverns and Groceries—Nau, McCunn, Zilkoski.
Ordinances—Spuhler, Gronnert, Duchateau.
Printing—Zilkoski, Shepeck, Rothe.

### Justices.

Police Justice—E. R. Smith.
Justices of the Peace—D. H. Grignon, Elie Martin.

### Board of Health.

First Ward, James Robb, F. C. Cady.
Second Ward, B. C. Brett, H. A. Straubel.
Third Ward, C. W. Streckenbach, W. J. Thomas.
Fourth Ward, Fillmore B. Smith, Philip Heavers.
Fifth Ward—Manfred Jacobi, John Nick.

### Police.

M. H. Nolan, Chief; John Bassett, Anton Cox, John Flemming, Henry Kitts, Frank Brice, John Dupont.

### Fire Wardens.

First Ward, Chas. G. LeClair, James Robb.
Second Ward, Thos. Joannes, L. C. Mohr.
Third Ward, Victor Bader, Henry F. Hagemeister.
Fourth Ward, L. E. Nejedlo, Andrew Reis, Jr.
Fifth Ward, E. W. Servotte, Frank Piske.

### Poor Board.

First Ward, Ald. Spuhler.
Second Ward, Ald. Nau.
Third Ward, Ald. Duchateau.
Fourth Ward, Ald. Shepeck.
Fifth Ward, Ald. McCunn.

### Board of Education.

President, Chas. E. Vroman; Secretary, M. H. McMahon.
Regular meetings of the Board, at the High School building, third Friday of each month, at 8 o'clock P. M.

#### COMMITTEES.

On Finance—Coms. Baker, Wagner and Bertles.
On Hiring Teachers—Coms. Hurlbut, Bertles and Findeisen.
On Visiting Schools—Coms. Joannes, Hurlbut, Baker, and Vroman, *ex-officio*.

On Text Books—Coms. Findeisen, Wagner and Baker.
On Rules—Coms. Wagner, Joannes and Hurlbut.
On Buildings—Coms. Bertles, Findeisen and Joannes.

## Schools and Teachers.

M. H. McMahon, Supt.

High School Building, n. w. cor. Webster av. and Chicago. William O. Brown, principal; Katharyn Lummis, first assistant; Elizabeth M. King, second assistant; Minnie M. Enteman, third assistant; Ellen May Smith, 8th grade; Effie A. Derby, 1st grade.

Pine Street School, s. w. cor. Webster av. and Pine. Minnie H. Kelleher, principal; Mary D. Ahearn, 6th grade; Ellen Heffernan, 5th grade; Florence M. Murray, 4th grade; Cora C. Whitesides, 3d grade; Teresa Dolan, 2d grade; Helena Bradley, 1st grade; Emma Rathman, 1st grade.

South Ward School, s. e. cor. Madison and Chicago. Jennie L. Smith, principal; Kate Gaylord, 6th grade; Sarah A. Connell, 6th grade; Elva Vosburgh, 5th grade; Carlotta Bridgman, 4th grade; Grace A. Howe, 3d grade; Rosalie Le Clair, 2d grade; Margaret Kelleher, 1st grade.

East River School, n. w. cor. 12th and Elm. Eleanor Gunn, principal; Della L. Wells, 3d grade; Lizzie D. Fox, 2d grade; Ernestine Huenger, 1st grade; Anna C. Zimmer, 1st grade.

Park School, School bet. Madison and Monroe. Josephine S. Luckenbach, principal; Hattie E. Goodell, 8th grade; Mary N. Kelleher, 2d grade; Katherine Schoemaker, 1st grade.

Mason Street School, n. e. cor. Mason and 12th. Louise A. Senn, principal.

### JANITORS.

High School, Henry Rogalski.
South Ward School, Mrs. Mary Berns.
Mason Street School, Mrs. Mary Joley.
Pine Street School, Emile LaCrosse.
East River School, Mrs. K. Ketter.
Park School, Mrs. Mary Erdmann.

## Fire Department.

William Kennedy, chief.

Hose Co. No. 1, located S. Washington, bet. Walnut and Doty. Jas. Church, captain; Wm. Johnson, pipeman; Tod. Fleming, pipeman; Bart. Lyman, driver.

Hose Co. No. 2, located Main, bet. Webster ave. and 10th. Frank Bodart, captain; A. L. Brice, pipeman; Jas. Simmon, pipeman; Peter Olson, driver.

Hook and Ladder, located S. Washington, bet. Doty and Walnut. John Bardouche, captain; A. L. Church, truckman; Gus. Delwich, truckman; John Sweeney, driver.

### FIRE ALARM SYSTEM AND BOX LOCATION.

No. of Box.
- 12—Cor. Main and Washington Sts.
- 13—Cor. Main and Jefferson Sts.
- 14—Engine House No. 1.
- 15—Cor. Doty and Jefferson Sts.
- 16—Cor. Adams and Cherry Sts.
- 21—Cor. Adams and Crooks Sts.
- 23—Cor. Jefferson and Mason Sts.
- 24—Cor. Monroe Ave. and Cass St.
- 25—Cor. Monroe Ave. and Eliza St.
- 26—Cor. Mason and Van Buren Sts.
- 31—Cor. Crooks St. and Monroe Ave.
- 32—Cor. Crooks St. and Webster Ave.
- 34—Cor. Monroe Ave. and Cherry St.
- 35—Cor. Monroe Ave. and Cedar St.
- 36—Cor. Main and Jackson Sts.
- 41—Cor. Van Buren and Walnut Sts.
- 42—Engine House No. 2.
- 43—Cor. Walnut and Eleventh Sts.
- 45—Cor. Doty and Twelfth Sts.
- 51—Cor. Harvey and Jackson Sts.
- 52—Cor. St. George and Main Sts.
- 53—Cor. Main and Pleasant Sts.
- 54—Cor. Harvey and Twelfth Sts.
- 61—Murphy Lumber Co. planing mill.
- 62—Murphy Lumber Co. office.

### WHERE KEYS ARE KEPT FOR FIRE ALARM BOXES.

No. of Key.
- No. 1. ———
- No. 2. John Zilles, cor. Main and Pleasant.
- No. 3. O. A. Kees, cor. Jefferson and Mason.
- No. 4. John Nick, cor. Walnut and 11th.
- No. 5. James H. Elmore, cor. Monroe and Cass.
- No. 6. The Beaumont, cor. Main and Washington.
- No. 7. Gust. Radelet, cor. Jefferson and Mason.
- No. 8. Capt. Hart, cor. S. Adams and Crooks.
- No. 9. Britton's Mill.
- No. 10. Ed. First, s. w. cor. Walnut and 11th.
- No. 11. Joseph Peakofski, cor. Doty and 12th.
- No. 12. A. Tennis, saloon, cor. S. Adams and Crooks.
- No. 13. Thomas Joannes, n. e. cor. Monroe and Crooks.

## MISCELLANEOUS DIRECTORY.

**KEYS TO FIRE ALARM BOXES—Continued.**

| No. of Key. | |
|---|---|
| No. 14. | Murphy Lumber Co.'s office. |
| No. 15. | J. F. Bertles, 926 S. Monroe av. |
| No. 16. | Murphy Lumber Co.'s planing mill. |
| No. 17. | Frank Reed, 124 S. Monroe av. |
| No. 18. | — |
| No. 19. | Coffeine office, n. e. cor. Cherry and Adams. |
| No. 20. | Elias Elson, 709 Harvey. |
| No. 21. | Weiss Furniture Co., cor. Harvey and Jackson. |
| No. 22. | John L. Tennis, cor. Main and Washington. |
| No. 23. | William Pickett, cor. Doty and 12th. |
| No. 24. | J. B. Schoonen, cor. Harvey and 12th. |
| No. 25. | John Brückner, cor. Harvey and 12th. |
| No. 26. | Martin Schauwell, cor. Harvey and 12th. |
| No. 27. | Mathew Zilles, cor. St. George and Main. |
| No. 28. | Post Office, n. e. cor. Cherry and Adams. |
| No. 29. | Water Works office, n. e. cor. Cherry and Adams. |
| No. 30. | Van Erman's saloon, n. e. cor. Main and Jefferson. |
| No. 31. | E. E. Britton, s. e. cor. Monroe and Cedar. |
| No. 32. | Carl Mangles, cor. Doty and 12th. |
| No. 33. | Mrs. Randall, n. w. cor. Jefferson and Mason. |
| No. 34. | Mrs. Ellis, n. w. cor. Adams and Crooks. |
| No. 35. | E. Morrow, n. e. cor. Adams and Crooks. |
| No. 36. | George Mueller, n. e. cor. Walnut and Van Buren. |
| No. 37. | Joseph Spitz, cor. Washington and Main. |
| No. 38. | Dorr Clark, n. w. cor. Monroe and Eliza. |
| No. 39. | A. Duchateau, cor. Washington and Main. |
| No. 40. | L. B. Sale, s. w. cor. Monroe and Cass. |
| No. 41. | L. E. Nejedlo, cor. Pleasant and Main. |
| No. 42. | C. Merrill, n. e. cor. Monroe and Cass. |
| No. 43. | S. Berceaux, cor. Harvey and 12th. |
| No. 44. | M. Budzis, cor. Pleasant and Main. |
| No. 45. | Andrew Reis Jr., Reis Hotel. |
| No. 46. | Joseph Mraz, cor. Jackson and Harvey. |
| No. 47. | C. Massey, n. e. cor. Cedar and Monroe. |
| No. 48. | D. W. Britton's office, Monroe av. |
| No. 49. | Engine House No. 2, Main st. |
| No. 50. | — |
| No. 51. | John Beth, s. w. cor. Monroe and Crooks. |
| No. 52. | F. W. Schneider, s. e. cor. Monroe and Crooks. |
| No. 53. | St. Joseph's Orphan Asylum, s. e. cor. Webster and Crooks. |
| No. 54. | Jules Parmentier, s. w. cor. Jefferson and Doty. |
| No. 55. | Freimann House, n. e. cor. Main and Jefferson. |
| No. 56. | Ernest Hultz, n. w. cor. Cherry and Adams. |
| No. 57. | William Schaikey, s. w. cor. Jefferson and Mason. |
| No. 58. | Joseph F. Rothe, cor. 11th and Cherry. |

| No. of Key. | KEYS TO FIRE ALARM BOXES—Continued. |
|---|---|
| No. 59. | Joseph Dave, n. w. cor. Walnut and 11th. |
| No. 60. | J. B. Baker, s. e. cor. Monroe and Eliza. |
| No. 61. | Chas. Pfotenhauer Sr., Main st. bridge, East River. |
| No. 62. | Frank Snyder, cor. Jefferson and Doty. |
| No. 63. | J. S. Johnson, cor. Main and St. George. |
| No. 64. | W. J. Abrams, s. w. cor. Webster and Crooks. |
| No. 65. | M. Resch, s. e. cor. Monroe and Cass. |
| No. 66. | Carl Mueller, s. w. cor. Doty and 12th. |
| No. 67. | C., M. & St. P. depot. |
| No. 68. | Frank Snyder's livery barn. |
| No. 69. | H. Rahr's Sons' office. |
| No. 70. | Mr. Beaumont, s. e. cor. Jefferson and Doty. |
| No. 71. | F. E. Murphy, 430 S. Webster av. |
| No. 72. | ——— |
| No. 73. | James Wall, n. e. cor. Van Buren and Walnut. |
| No. 74. | C. E. Crane or F. B. Desnoyers, n. e. cor. Monroe and Cherry. |
| No. 75. | ——— |
| No. 76. | John Bassett, police, carries in pocket. |
| No. 77. | H. C. Reber, carries in pocket. |
| No. 78. | Frank E. Murphy, carries in pocket. |
| No. 79. | ——— |
| No. 80. | Gustav Radelet, police, carries in pocket. |
| No. 81. | ——— |
| No. 82. | Anton Cox, police, carries in pocket. |
| No. 83. | Wm. Kennedy, chief of fire dept., carries in pocket. |
| No. 84. | ——— |
| No. 85. | John Fleming, police, carries in pocket. |
| No. 86. | ——— |
| No. 87. | ——— |
| No. 88. | M. H. Nolan, chief of police, carries in pocket. |
| No. 89. | { Frank E. Murphy, carries in pocket. <br> { Michael J. Evans, carries in pocket. |
| No. 90. | ——— |
| No. 91. | ——— |
| No. 92. | ——— |
| No. 93. | James H. Elmore, mayor, carries in pocket. |
| No. 94. | Murphy Lumber Co., Walter Woods, watchman, carries in pocket. |
| No. 95. | Engine House No. 1. |
| No. 96. | ——— |
| No. 97. | W. J. Lander, n. w. cor. Webster av. and Crooks. |
| No. 98. | A. A. Warren, n. w. cor. Monroe and Crooks. |
| No. 99. | Paul Fox, s. w. cor. Cherry and Monroe. |
| No. 100. | James McKone, livery, 415 Main. |

## COUNTY GOVERNMENT.

Circuit Judge—Hon. S. D. Hastings.
County Judge—Hon. H. J. Huntington.
Register in Probate—A. G. M. Masse.
Sheriff—John Bartelme.
District Attorney—P. H. Martin.
Clerk Circuit Court—Henry Watermolen.
County Treasurer—William Lueke.
County Clerk—D. H. Martin.
Register of Deeds—James T. Moran.
County Superintendent of Schools—D. S. Rice.
County Surveyor—August Brauns.
Coroner—D. H. Grignon.

### Board of Supervisors.

Allouez—Matt. Reynan.
Ashwaubenon—J. J. Rasmussen.
Bellevue—Leonard Verdigan.
De Pere—James Sherlock.
City of De Pere—1st Ward, Thos. D. Bowering; 2d Ward, John B. Heyrman; 3d Ward, Paul Scheuring; 4th Ward, Julius Rupiper.
Town of Eaton—Jerry Coleman.
City of Fort Howard—1st Ward, A. Rondou; 2d Ward, A. Williams; 3d Ward, Fred. P. Gross; 4th Ward, E. Becker; 5th Ward, M. A. Sellers; 6th Ward, J. A. Sorensen.
Town of Glenmore—John Murphy.
Town of Green Bay—Joseph Brunner.
City of Green Bay—1st Ward, Joseph Servotte; 2d Ward, Patrick Ryan; 3d Ward, Henry Hagemeister; 4th Ward, Magnus Johnson; 5th Ward, Daniel Lee.
Town of Holland—J. E. Clark.
Town of Howard—Manuel Brunette.
Town of Humboldt—Louis Schoen.
Town of Lawrence—Thomas Turriff.
Town of Morrison—G. F. Brill.
Town of New Denmark—H. D. Van Seggern.
Town of Pittsfield—Wm. Streckenbach.
Town of Preble—J. M. Hogan.
Town of Rockland—Daniel Conway.
Town of Scott—A. B. Gonion.
Town of Suamico—A. Hunter.
Town of Wrightstown—Jacob Hein.

### STANDING COMMITTEES.

Finance — Hagemeister, Heyrman, Sorenson, Brunette, Gonion.

Accounts—Scheuring, Rondon, Turriff, Hunter, Brill.

Justices, Constables and Sheriff—Ryan, Sherlock, Gross, Johnson, Lee.

Poor—Bowring, Sellers, Verdigem, Streckenbach, Rupiper.

Tax Certificates—Reynen, Becker, Schoen, Coleman, Van Seggern.

Public Buildings—Servotte, Brunner, Williams, Hein, Sellers.

Roads and Bridges—Clark, Hogan, Murphy, Conway, Van Seggern.

Printing—Verdigem, Schoen, Streckenbach, Conway, Becker.

Insane—Brunette, Reynen, Verdigem.

Equalization—1st Dist., Hagemeister, Servotte, Ryan, Brunner, Hogan; 2d Dist., Heyrman, Rondou, Hunter, Hein, Clark; at large, Sherlock.

## UNITED STATES OFFICES.

Post Office Department—Post Office, n. e. cor. N. Adams and Cherry. G. Küstermann, postmaster; C. Küstermann, asst.-postmaster. Office hours for delivery of letters 8 A. M. to 7:30 P. M.; Sundays 9 to 10 A. M.

Court Commissioner for Eastern District Wisconsin, John F. Watermolen—300 N. Washington.

United States Customs—Deputy collector, Daniel P. Bradley, 321 N. Washington.

Internal Revenue, 8th Division, 1st District—Deputy Division collector, Patrick Clifford, of Marinette, Wis.; Deputy stamp collector, John Shepeck Jr., 314 Main.

United States Weather Bureau—F. W. Conrad, observer, 17 Parmentier blk.

Rail routes—Chicago & Northwestern, from north to south ; Chicago, Milwaukee & St. Paul, from north to south ; Green Bay, Winona & St. Paul, to west; Kewaunee, Green Bay & Western, east.

### Stages.

Green Bay and Two Rivers Stage Line, Andrew Reis Jr., prop.; leaves daily except Sunday at 7:30 A. M. from Reis Hotel.

## MISCELLANEOUS DIRECTORY.

### RAILROAD DISTANCES AND FARE FROM GREEN BAY AND FORT HOWARD, WIS.

| Dist. | | Fare. | Dist. | | Fare. |
|---|---|---|---|---|---|
| 596 | Aberdeen | $17.11 | 18 | Marinette | $1.47 |
| 70 | Amherst Jc | 2.10 | 187 | Marquette | 4.94 |
| 107 | Antigo | 3.15 | 116 | Marshfield | 3.45 |
| 29 | Appleton | .80 | 37 | Menasha | .95 |
| 266 | Ashland | 7.84 | 50 | Menominee | 1.52 |
| 973 | Baltimore | 20.89 | 145 | Merrill | 4.74 |
| 242 | Bessemer | 6.77 | 113 | Milwaukee | 3.39 |
| 23 | Black Creek | .70 | 299 | Minneapolis | 8.13 |
| 1060 | Boston | 22.39 | 521 | Moorhead | 15.07 |
| 458 | Brainerd | 11.95 | 36 | Neenah | .95 |
| 574 | Buffalo | 15.39 | 175 | Negaunee | 4.44 |
| 150 | Champion | 4.44 | 39 | New London | 1.15 |
| 198 | Chicago | 5.91 | 1123 | New Orleans | 33.49 |
| 34 | Chilton | 1.04 | 984 | New York | 21.39 |
| 192 | Chippewa Falls | 5.77 | 28 | Oconto | .87 |
| 497 | Cincinnati | 13.85 | 620 | Omaha | 16.60 |
| 491 | Cleveland | 15.94 | 236 | Ontonagon | 7.83 |
| 323 | Davenport | 11.11 | 48 | Oshkosh | 1.33 |
| 1189 | Denver | 34.75 | 23 | Pensaukee | .72 |
| 354 | Detroit | 10.54 | 41 | Peshtigo | 1.27 |
| 300 | Dubuque | 9.04 | 882 | Philadelphia | 21.39 |
| 338 | Duluth | 9.97 | 58 | Plymouth | 1.73 |
| 193 | Eau Claire | 5.77 | 152 | Portage | 4.47 |
| 114 | Escanaba | 3.71 | 369 | Port Huron | 10.27 |
| 202 | Evanston | 5.58 | 152 | Racine | 4.03 |
| 66 | Fond du Lac | 1.85 | 276 | Red Wing | 7.83 |
| 132 | Ft. Atkinson | 3.82 | 141 | Republic | 4.13 |
| 95 | Grand Rapids | 2.90 | 153 | Rhinelander | 4.55 |
| 27 | Hilbert Jc | .81 | 481 | St. Louis | 13.44 |
| 250 | Hurley | 6.77 | 280 | St. Paul | 7.83 |
| 95 | Iron Mountain | 2.79 | 371 | Saginaw | 10.29 |
| 249 | Ironwood | 6.77 | 2516 | San Francisco | 65.73 |
| 178 | Ishpeming | 4.44 | 270 | St. Ste Marie | 10.29 |
| 151 | Janesville | 4.42 | 17 | Seymour | .50 |
| 126 | Jefferson | 3.65 | 74 | Sheboygan | 2.76 |
| 666 | Kansas City | 16.76 | 81 | Stevens Pt | 2.50 |
| 22 | Kaukauna | .59 | 378 | Toledo | 9.45 |
| 163 | Kenosha | 4.39 | 1014 | Washington | 20.89 |
| 34 | Kewaunee | 1.00 | 112 | Watertown | 2.54 |
| 239 | La Crosse | 7.00 | 72 | Waupaca | 3.25 |
| 18 | Luxemburg | .50 | 109 | Wausau | 3.21 |
| 148 | Madison | 4.43 | 334 | W. Superior | 9.82 |
| 49 | Manitowoc | 1.46 | 214 | Winona | 6.40 |

## Banks and Incorporated Companies.

Citizens' National Bank—Incorporated 1888; capital, $100,000; surplus, $20,000; H. S. Eldred, pres.; Jas. H. Elmore, v.-pres.; W. P. Wagner, cashier; s. e. cor. N. Washington and Cherry.

Kellogg National Bank, The—Incorporated, 1874; capital, $100,000; surplus, $50,000; Wm. J. Fisk, pres.; Fred. Hurlbut, v.-pres.; Henry B. Baker, cashier; 301 N. Washington.

Allouez Mineral Spring Co.—Incorporated, 1893; capital, $50,000; Joseph Hoeffel, pres.; Joseph P. Hoeffel, mngr.; James I. Hoeffel, sec.; s. e. cor. Chicago and S. Jackson.

Annen J. P. Candy Co.—Capital, $15,000; Edwin Van den Braak, pres.; August E. Brauns, treas.; John P. Annen, sec. and mngr.; manfg. confectioners, 109-111 N. Washington.

Brown County Horticultural and Agricultural Society—Incorporated, 1880; J. D. McAllister, pres.; Miss H. Dickey, sec. and treas.

Columbian Baking Co.—Incorporated 1893; capital, $50,000; John H. Ebeling, pres.; M. Joannes, v.-pres.; Llewellyn C. Reber, sec. and treas.; 401-411 Walnut.

Fontaine B. Hardware Co.—Capital, $20,000; B. F. Fontaine, pres.; Raphael Fontaine, sec. and treas.; 218 Main.

Fox River Electric Railway Co.—Incorporated 1894; capital, $100,000; Charles H. Holmes, pres.; W. P. Harvey, mngr.; 312-318 S. Washington.

Green Bay Advocate Co., The—Capital, $15,000; Edward Decker, pres.; David Decker, v.-pres.; W. C. Jenkins, sec.; publishers and blank book mnfrs., 216 Pine.

Green Bay Athletic Association—Incorporated 1894; F. B. Desnoyers, pres.; W. J. Thomas, v.-pres.; E. E. Grenn, sec. and treas.; n. w. cor. N. Adams and Doty.

Green Bay Business Men's Association—Fred. Hollman, pres.; J. Parmentier, v.-pres.; M. J. McCormick, sec.; H. B. Baker, treas.; meets at Business College.

Green Bay Carriage Co. The—Capital, $25,000; A. Weise, pres.; Jos. Hebert, v.-pres. and mngr.; H. B. Baker, sec. and treas.; 419 N. Adams.

Green Bay Dairy Men's Board of Trade—Incorporated 1888; H. F. Meyers, pres.; J. R. Meyers, v.-pres.; Warden Reynolds, sec. and treas.; meets 1st and 3d Thursdays in each month at American House.

Green Bay Dredging and Pile Driving Co.—Christ. Schwarz, pres.; Charles Berner, sec. and treas.; 218 N. Jefferson.

Green Bay Planing Mill Co.—Capital, $50,000; C. Schwarz, pres.; Fred. Hurlbut, v.-pres.; James Robb, sec. and treas.; N. Adams, n. e. cor. Cedar.

Green Bay Plumbing and Heating Co.—Capital, $2,000; Joseph W. Callahan, pres.; John Anderson, sec. and treas.; 212 Pine.

Green Bay Public Library—S. D. Hastings, Jr., pres.; Mrs. Ella H. Neville, v.-pres.; A. H. Reynolds, sec. and treas.; Anna H. McDonnell, librarian; P. O. Blk.

Green Bay, Winona & St. Paul R. R.—Incorporated 1866; capital, $10,000,000; Sam Sloan, pres.; Jos. Walker, Jr., v.-pres.; Wm. H. Leupp, sec. and treas.; S. W. Champion, gen. mngr.; John B. Last, gen. frt. and pass. agt.; s. e. cor. Adams and Pine.

Green Bay & Ft. Howard Gas & Electric Light Co.—Capital, $65,000; Carroll Collins, pres. and mngr.; H. B. Baker, sec. and treas.; 415 Elm.

Green Bay and Fort Howard Water Works Co.—Eli Marvin, pres.; A. C. Neville, sec.; A. B. Palmer, treas. and supt.; P. O. block.

Hagemeister Brewing Co.—Capital, $150,000; Henry F. Hagemeister, pres.; George Scholer, v.-pres. and supt.; A. Hagemeister, sec. and treas.; 310 N. Adams.

Hess George B. Co.—Capital, $25,000; H. A. Walter, pres.; Clement Massey, v.-pres.; George B. Hess, sec. and treas.; flour mills, Cedar, n. w. cor. N. Quincy.

Jorgensen-Blesch Co.—Incorporated 1886; J. L. Jorgensen, pres.; F. T. Blesch, sec. and treas.; 303-307 N. Washington.

Kewaunee, Green Bay & Western R. R.—Incorporated 1890; W. J. Abrams, pres.; S. W. Champion, gen. mngr.; s. e. cor. Adams and Pine.

Land & Abstract Co. The—Capital, $10,000; C. E. Vroman, pres.; P. R. Kendall, sec. and treas.; 301 N. Washington.

Murphy Lumber Co.—Incorporated 1888; Simon J. Murphy, pres.; Wm. H. Murphy, v.-pres.; Frank E. Murphy, sec. and treas.; lumber mnfrs., mouth of Fox River, n. city limits.

Spuhler A. Co. The—Capital, $50,000; Adam Spuhler, pres. and treas.; E. A. Arthur, sec.; dry goods, etc., 229-231 N. Washington.

Union Building, Loan and Savings Association—Capital, $2,000,000; D. W. Flatley, pres.; J. S. Chase, v.-pres.; G. L. North, sec.; W. P. Wagner, treas.; F. C. Cady, attorney; 8 Parmentier Block.

Weise-Hollman Co. The—Incorporated 1889; Albert Weise, pres.; Fred. A. Hollman, v.-pres.; Fred. L. G. Straubel, sec. and treas.; whol. crockery and glassware, 304-306 N. Washington.

## Churches.

### AMERICAN CATHOLIC.

His Eminence J. Rene Vilatte, archbishop metropolitan and primate; Very Rev. Father Kolaszewski, vicar-general; Rev. Father Kamiski, consultor; Rev. Brother Nicholas, church mngr. St. Louis Church, s. w. cor. Cass and S. 12th.

### BAPTIST.

Central Baptist Church, s. s. Moravian, bet. S. Madison and S. Monroe; Rev. Granger W. Smith, pastor. Services, 3 P. M.; Sunday-school, 2 P. M.

### CATHOLIC.

Diocese of Green Bay, Rt. Rev. Sebastian G. Messmer, D. D. bishop; Rev. J. J. Fox, vicar-general. Office and residence, n. e. cor. S. Madison and Doty.

St. Francis Xavier Cathedral, n. w. cor. S. Monroe av. and Doty; Rev. Clement Lau, rector. Services, 8 and 10 A. M. and 3 P. M.

St. John's Church, n. s. Milwaukee, bet. S. Jefferson and S. Madison; Rev. L. A. Ricklin, pastor. Services, 8 and 10 A. M. and 3 and 7 P. M. Sunday-school, 2 P. M.

St. Peter and Paul Church (English, French and German), Rev. M. T. Anderegg, pastor. Services: daily mass, 7 A. M.; Sunday, first mass, 7:30 A. M.; high mass, 9:30 A. M.; winter, first mass, 8 A. M.; high mass, 10 A. M.; daily mass, 8 A. M.; catechism, 2 P. M.; vespers, 3 P. M.

St. Wilebroeg's Church, s. e. cor. N. Adams and Doty; Rev. Wm. Roosmalen, pastor. Services: daily mass, 8 A. M.; Sunday, first mass, 8 A. M.; high mass, 10 A. M.; vespers, 3 P. M.; catechism, 2 P. M.

### EPISCOPAL.

Christ Church, n. w. cor. Cherry and N. Madison; Rev. F. R. Hath, pastor. Services, 8 and 10:30 A. M. and 7 P.M. Sunday-school, 12 M.

### EVANGELICAL.

German Evangelical Lutheran Church, n. e. cor. Cherry and N. Van Buren; Rev. Jacob Siegrist, pastor. Services, 10:30 A. M. Sunday-school, 9 A. M.

### LUTHERAN.

St. Paul's German Church, n. w. cor. S. Madison and Stuart; Rev. William Huth, pastor. Services, 10:30 A. M. Sunday-school, 9:30 A. M.

## MISCELLANEOUS DIRECTORY.

### METHODIST EPISCOPAL.

First Methodist Episcopal Church, n. e. cor. School and S. Madison; Rev. H. W. Thompson, pastor. Services, 10:30 A. M. and 7:30 P. M. Sunday-school, 12 M.

German M. E. Church, s. w. cor. Doty and S. 10th; Rev. A. M. Wieting, pastor. Sunday-school, 9:30 A. M. Services, 10:30 A. M. and 7:30 P. M. Meeting of Epworth League at 7 P. M. Prayer meeting Wednesday, 7:30 P. M.

### MORAVIAN.

Moravian Church, s. e. Moravian bet. S. Madison and S. Monroe; Rev. Herman Meinert, pastor. Services, 10:30 A. M. and 7:30 P. M. Sunday-school, 9:30 A. M.

### PRESBYTERIAN.

First Presbyterian Church, s. e. cor. S. Adams and Crooks; Rev. J. L. Hewitt, D. D. pastor. Services, 10.30 A. M. and 7.30 P. M. Sunday-school, 12 M.

French Presbyterian Church, Doty, bet. S. Adams and S. Jefferson; Rev. George C. Mosseau, pastor. Services, 11 A. M. and 7.30 P. M.; Sunday-school, 9.30 A. M., Prayer meeting every Thursday 7.30 P. M.

### SCIENTIST.

Church of Christ, Scientist; Hugh McDonald, C. S. Meets every Sunday at 10.30 A. M. at Green Bay Business College; also every Wednesday at 3 P. M. at 420 N. Jefferson.

## Parochial Schools.

Cathedral School, n. e. cor. S. Monroe av. and Doty; Rev. C. Lau, director. Conducted by the Sisters of Notre Dame.

Catholic High School, n. w. cor. Doty and S. Monroe av.; Rev. C. Lau, director. Conducted by the Sisters of Notre Dame.

German-English Lutheran School, e. s. Van Buren, bet. Cherry and Pine; P. S. Lorenzen, teacher.

St. John's School, n. e. cor. Milwaukee and S. Jefferson. Conducted by the Sisters of St. Joseph.

St. Paul's German Lutheran School, n. s. Stuart, bet. S. Jefferson and S. Madison; Rev. Wm. Huth, instructor.

St. Vincent's School, in charge of the Sisters of Notre Dame, s. s. Doty, bet. S. Adams and S. Jefferson.

## Asylums, Homes, Etc.

Allouez Villa Orphan Asylum, Sister Melania, lady superioress, e. s. De Pere Road.

Convent of Notre Dame, Sister M. Leopoldine, superioress, 139 S. Monroe av.
Foundlings Home, Mrs. Jennie E. Drake, matron, 912 S. Jackson.
Marine Hospital, service under the charge of St. Vincent's Hospital. The port of Green Bay is a relief station of second class. All seamen and mariners entitled to admittance to the hospital in case of sickness or distress and in need of assistance. Dr. A. W. Slaughter, acting assistant surgeon.
Odd Fellows' Home. Wm. Warren, supt.; Mrs. Wm. Warren, matron. For old and disabled Odd Fellows, who are unable to support themselves; also orphans of Odd Fellows; 822 Grignon.
St. Joseph's Convent, Sister Herman Joseph, conductress, 307 S. Jefferson.
St. Joseph's Orphan Asylum, 403 S. Webster av. Sister M. Melania, superioress. Branch house, Allouez Villa.
St. Vincent's Hospital, 626 S. Quincy.

### Cemeteries.

Allouez Catholic Cemetery, Town of Allouez. Henry Paul, sexton.
Woodlawn Cemetery, Peter Jacobson, sexton. City office, H. M. Reinecke, superintendent, 112 S. Jefferson.

## SECRET AND BENEVOLENT SOCIETIES.

### Masonic.

Washington Lodge No. 21, F. & A. M.—A. D. McGruen, A. M.; J. H. Leonard, sec.; C. Merrill, treas. Meets 1st and 3d Thursdays each month, Masonic Hall.
Warren Chapter No. 8, R. A. M.—L. F. Pease, H. P.; J. H. Leonard, sec.; George G. Green, treas. Meets 2d and 4th Monday each month at Masonic Hall.
Palestine Commandery No. 20—Levy Howland, E. C.; J. H. Leonard, rec.; C. W. Bliedung, treas. Meets 2d and 4th Thursday of each month at Masonic Hall.

### I. O. O. F.

Green Bay Lodge No. 19—W. E. Fairfield, N. G.; B. F. Tilton, V. G.; David Nys, sec.; Wm. H. Gibson, treas. Meets every Tuesday at Odd Fellows' Hall, Parmentier blk.
Herman Lodge No. 111—John Noffz, N. G.; Frank Burghardt, V. G.; F. Gehr, sec.; Aug. Straubel, treas. Meets every Wednesday at 212 Pine.

Green Bay Encampment No. 49—E. G. Markle, C. P.; W. A. Brandenstein, H. P.; Carl Manthey, S. W.; P. G. Wright, J. W.; Daniel T. Kies, scribe; Chas. Le Comte, treas. Meets 1st and 3d Monday in each month in Odd Fellows' Hall, Parmentier blk.

Rebecca Lodge No. 47—Mrs. M. Eastman, N. G.; Mrs. B. F. Tilton, V. G.; Mrs. W. A. Brandenstein, P. N. G.; Miss Minnie Gilger, sec.; Mrs. Jas. Harbridge, treas. Meets every 2d and 4th Wednesday of each month at Odd Fellows' Hall in Parmentier blk.

### Catholic Knights of Wisconsin.

Green Bay Branch No. 21—J. H. M. Wigman, State pres.; George Stenger, pres.; John Nick, sec.; M. Heidgen, treas. Meets every 3d Monday at their hall on Cherry opp. Court House.

### C. S. P. S.

Order Podripan No. 45, C. S. P. S.—Joseph Mraz, pres.; Martin Zahorik, v.-pres.; John Shepeck Jr., sec.; L. E. Nejedlo, treas. Meets 1st Sunday in each month at 207 N. Washington.

### Grand Army.

T. O. Howe Post No. 124—S. W. Peters, com.; H. P. Campbell, adjt.; John Looze, Q. M. Meets 2d and 4th Friday at G. A. R. Hall, 223 N. Adams.

Women's Relief Corps to T. O. Howe Post No. 124—Mrs. A. Kilmer, pres.; Mrs. —. Smith, S. V. C.; Mrs. H. H. Hubbard, J. V. C.; Mrs. Peter Miller, sec.; Miss Alice Kilmer, treas. Meets every 2d and 4th Saturdays at G. A. R. Hall.

Star Club, auxilary to W. R. C.—Miss Anna Beth, pres.; Miss Lizzie Bagley, V. C.; Miss Kate Smith, sec.; Miss Anna Weissmiller, treas. Meets 1st and 3d Wednesday at G. A. R. Hall.

Sons of Veterans, Col. Catlin Camp No. 74—Fred A. Krause, com.; William Delaporte, 1st lieut.; Charles Philips, 2d lieut.; O. B. Graves, 1st serg.; Val. J. Beth, Q. M. serg. Meets every Thursday at G. A. R. Hall.

### Knights of Honor.

Navarino Lodge, 1384—John Huerth, D. C. F. Schroeder, V. D.; J. N. Schoemaker, rep.; Joseph Gotto, treas. Meets 1st and 3d Wednesday of each month at Chapman Hall.

### Knights and Ladies of Maccabees.

Twin City Tent No. 25, K. O. T. M.—David Nys, commander; C. E. Smith, record keeper. Meets every Friday at 8 P. M. in Schumacher Bros. blk., Main St.

Star Hive, No. 7, Ladies of Maccabees—Mrs. Anna Nys, P. C.; Mrs. Nellie Coffeen, com.; Mrs. Merkel, lieut. com.; Mrs. Conrad Beth, rec.; Miss Anna Weissmiller, finance kpr. Meets every 2d and 4th Monday in each month at 314-316 Main.

### Knights of Pythias.

Pochequette Lodge, No. 26—John McCann, C. C.; Dr. H. M. Beck, K. of R. & S.; Fred. Schuette, M. of E. Meets every Tuesday evening at Knights of Pythias Hall, 224 N. Washington.

### Modern Woodmen of America.

Navarino Camp, 534—G. A. Doney, V. C.; E. J. LeMieux, W.A.; David Nys, clk.; Conrad Beth, banker. Meets every Thursday in Parmentier blk.

### Royal Arcanum.

Iron Gate Council, No. 349—W. J. Thomas, regent; Joseph Loukotka, sec.; George H. Mueller, collr. Meets every Monday at Royal Arcanum Hall, 224 N. Washington.

### Miscellaneous Societies.

Beaumont Cycle Club—J. V. De Cremer, pres.; W. C. Jenkins, v.-pres.; Wm. H. Field, sec. and treas. Regular meeting 2d Tuesday of each month at 314 Cherry.

Brewers' Benevolent Society—Aug. Joppe, pres.; Herman Schwartz, sec.; R. Fontaine, treas. Meets every 2d Sunday of each month at Zille's Hall.

Brotherhood Locomotive Engineers, Lodge No. 297—Henry Hancock, chief; J. C. Wigman, sec.; J. W. Du Bois, treas. Meets 1st and 3d Sunday of each month at Chapman blk.

Brotherhood of Locomotive Engineers, auxiliary to No. 297—Mrs. J. H. Harwin, pres.; Mrs. J. N. Crane, v.-pres.; Mrs. Charles Baker, sec.; Mrs. Charles Edwards, treas. Meets 2d and 4th Wednesdays in each month at Chapman blk.

Brotherhood of Locomotive Firemen, Baldwin Lodge No. 189—Martin Sheeby, master; Dennis Hogan, sec. and treas. Meets 1st Sunday in each month at Chapman blk.

Brotherhood of Trainmen, W. B. Woolford Lodge No. 411—F. E. Valentine, master; F. B. Beach, sec.; J. A. Schriber, financier. Meets 1st and 3d Sunday in each month at Royal Arcanum Hall.

Brown County Bar Association.—John C. Neville, pres.; E. H. Ellis, sec. Meets at call of the secretary at 201 N. Washington.

## MISCELLANEOUS DIRECTORY. 41

Brown County Medical Society—Dr. B. C. Brett, pres.; Dr. C. E. Crane, v.-pres.; Dr. F. L. Lewis, sec. Meets at call of secretary.

Carpenters' Local Union—Aug. Rogalski, pres.; J. Van der Boom, v.-pres.; Christ. Erdmann, rec. sec.; W. Wagner, fin. sec.; Chas. Photenhauer Jr., treas. Meets 2d and 4th Thursday in each month at Turner Hall.

Catholic Benevolent Legion, Green Bay Council No. 432—J. I. Hoeffel, pres.; F. J. Clark, collector; Phil. O'Connor, sec. Meets 1st and 3d Wednesday at Y. M. C. A. Hall, N. Adams.

Chevaliers of the Order of Crown of Thorns—Most Rev. Archbishop J. Reni Vilatte, Grand Master. S. w. cor. Cass and S. 12th.

Christ Church Guild—Miss Emilie Irwin, pres.; Mrs. G. W. Cowles, v.-pres.; Miss Belle Resch, sec. and treas. Meets every 2d week.

Cigarmakers' Union, No. 162—Wm. Umbehaun, pres.; James Trich, v.-pres.; Jos. Brans, fin. and cor. sec.; Peter Eggner, rec. sec.; A. Van Schyndle, treas. Meets last Thursday of each month at Royal Arcanum Hall.

Coopers' International Union of N. America, Lodge No. 13—Wm. Fischer, pres.; D. Allie, v.-pres.; F. C. Gilger, cor. sec.; John Jacobs, treas. Meets every Monday, Chapman blk.

Epworth League of 1st M. E. Church—Prof. P. F. Benton, pres.; Miss Alice Geer, sec.; Miss Carrie Tilton, treas. Meets every Sunday eve. at 6:30 P. M.

Epworth League M. E. Church (German branch)—Rev. A. M. Wieting, pres.; Miss Martha Greiser, v.-pres.; Arthur Schilke, sec.; Miss Louise Scheider, treas. Meets every Sunday at German M. E. Church at 7:30 P. M. Literary branch, at call.

Germania Kranken Unterstuetzungsverein—John Nick, pres.; Christoph Meister, v.-pres.; George Haupt, sec.; Aug. Brehme, treas. Meets 1st Sunday of each month at Turner Hall.

Green Bay Athletic Assn.—F. B. Desnoyers, pres.; W. J. Thomas, v.-pres.; E. E. Gunn, sec. and treas. Meets 1st Tuesday after 1st Monday in each month at n. w. cor. N. Adams and Doty.

Green Bay Business Men's Assn.—Fred. Hollman, pres.; J. Parmentier, v.-pres.; M. J. McCormick, sec.; H. B. Baker, treas. Meets every 2d Thursday in each month at the Business College.

Green Bay Public Library—Sam. D. Hastings Jr., pres.; Mrs. Ella H. Neville, v.-pres.; A. H. Reynolds, sec. and treas.; Anna H. McDonnell, librarian. P. O. blk.

Green Bay Shooting Society—Fred Hollman, pres.; E. K. Ansorge, sec.; F. Gehr, treas. Meets quarterly at E. K. Ansorge's office.

Green Bay Turn Verein—Gustav Küstermann, pres.; Carl Manthey, v.-pres.; George Haupt, rec. sec.; Fred Straubel, fin. sec.; Theodore Mueller, treas.; William Hills, turn teacher. Meets 1st Thursday in each month at Turner Hall.

Green Bay Turn Section, auxilary to Green Bay Turn Verin—Otto Von Goeben, pres.; Jacob Nick, v.-pres.; Otto Ansorge, sec. and treas.; William T. Hills, instructor. Meets last turning night of every month at Turner Hall.

Green Bay Yacht Club—Horace J. Conley, com.; John C. Follett, v.-com.; Walter T. Hagen, capt.; W. J. Casey, sec.; A. B. Gunderson, treas.; P. B. Benton, measurer. Meets once a month.

Jugendverein der ersten deutschen luth. Gemeinde—P. Lorenzen, pres.; Miss Elsa Hottensen, treas.; Miss Lily Hollman, sec. Meets every 2d Sunday at the Church.

Junior League of First M. E. Church—Mrs. H. W. Thompson, pres.; Miss Charlotte Geer, sec.; Miss Maud McGrath, treas. Meets every Sunday afternoon, 3 P. M.

Ladies' Aid Society of First Presbyterian Church—Mrs. H. W. Chapman, pres.; Mrs. George B. Nau, rec. sec.; Mrs. Frank Desnoyers, treas. Meets every Tuesday afternoon.

Ladies' Altar Society—Rev. M. T. Andergg, spiritual adviser. Meets quarterly in St. Peter and Paul Church, also subject to call.

Ladies' Section of the Green Bay Turnverein—Mrs. Lydia Hollman, pres.; Miss Leon Lintleman, v.-pres.; Miss Ida Buscher, sec.; Miss Valeska Halbuch, treas.; William Hills, instructor. Meets last Friday in every month at Turner Hall.

Marquette Club—Miss Minnie Kelleher, pres.; M. J. McCormick, v.-pres.; Miss Theresa Dolan, sec.; Miss Mary L. Desnoyers, treas. Meets 1st and 4th Fridays in each month in Weise's Block.

Marine Engineers' Beneficial Assn., Lodge No. 73—E. B. Kellogg, pres.; James Lucas, v.-pres.; E. D. Rasmussen, rec. sec.; H. C. Wheelock, sec. and treas. Meets every Saturday of the winter months at hall, Chapman blk.

Masons' and Bricklayers' Union—Edward Henkelmann, pres.; Peter Lagers, v.-pres.; Otto Brehme, sec.; Jacob Hansen, treas. Meets 2d and 4th Fridays in each month, Zille's Hall.

St. Bonifacius Catholic Society—John Killian, pres.; Rev. C. Lau, spir. director. Meets 1st Sunday in each month.

St. Francis Xavier Society—Peter Nick, pres.; Rev. C. Lau, spir. director. Meets 2d Sunday in each month.

St. Stanislaus Society (Polish)—Anton Slupinski, pres.; Rev. C. Lau, spir. director. Meets 3d Sunday in each month.

St. Peter and Paul Benevolent Society—Philip Simon, pres.; Peter Alsteen, sec.; Rev. M. T. Anderegg, spiritual adviser. Meets at Zille's Hall every 4th Sunday in each month.

Society of St. Aloysius of St. John's School. Meets once a month.

Sodality of the Christian Mothers of St. John's Church; Rev. Leo A. Ricklin, director. Meets 1st Sunday in each month.

Wisconsin Society for the Prevention of Cruelty to Animals—Xavier Martin, pres.; Hon. J. C. Neville, v.-pres.; Werden Reynolds, sec. Meets at the call of the president at 318 N. Washington.

Women's Christian Temperance Union—Mrs. Ida M. Cooke, pres.; Mrs. H. M. McMahon, rec. sec.; Mrs. C. E. Vroman, treas. Meets 1st Monday in each month at the president's residence.

Womans' Aid Society of Christ Church—Mrs. J. S. Baker, pres.; Mrs. N. S. Kimball, v.-pres.; Miss Hattie Irwin, treas.; Miss Abbie Robinson, sec. Meets every 2d Wednesday at the Guild room, Christ Church.

Women's Missionary Society—Mrs. James Robb, v.-pres.; Mrs. A. C. Neville, sec.; Mrs. Geo. G. Green, treas. Meets 1st Friday in every month.

Young Ladies' Sodality of St. Francis Xavier Cathedral—Rev. C. Lau, spir. director; Miss Mary Klaus, pres.; Miss Mary Heidgen, treas. Meets 1st Sunday in each month.

Young Ladies' Sodality of St. John's Church—Rev. Leo A. Recklin, director. Meets 2d Sunday in each month.

Young Men's Columbus Club—F. J. O'Conner, pres.; Edward J. Martin, v.-pres.; L. J. Engels, rec. sec.; W. T. Bates, fin. sec.; J. L. Hoeffel, treas.; J. H. Verheyden, librarian. Meets 1st and 3d Tuesday in each month at Weise blk.

Y. P. S. C. E. of 1st Pres. Church—Miss May Belle Hewitt, pres.; Miss Pauline Martin. sec.; Miss May E. Smith, treas.; Miss Addie Gardiner, cor. sec. Meets every Sunday evening at 6.30 P. M.

## Parks.

Astor Park, bet. Porlier, 11th, Eliza and Day.
Brown County Fair and Park Assn. Park, e. end Walnut.
Jackson Square, bet. S. Madison, Monroe av. School and Moravian.
St. James Park, bet. Spring, Monroe, Congress and S. Madison.
St. John's Park, bet. Milwaukee, Madison, Howard and S. Jefferson.
Washington Park, bet. Cherry, Crooks and East River.
Whitney Park, bet. Main, Pine, Van Buren and Jackson.

## Public Buildings, Halls, Etc.

Chapman Block, 228–230 Pine.
Citizens' National Bank Building, s. e. cor. Cherry and N. Washington.
City Hall, 111–113 S. Washington.
Court House, Cherry, s. w. cor. Jefferson.
Grand Army Hall, 225 N. Adams.
Green Bay Business College, n. e. cor. Adams and Walnut.
Klaus Hall, 220–224 Pine.
Knights of Maccabees Hall, 314 Main.
Masonic Hall, 309 N. Washington.
Parmentier Block, s. e. cor. Washington and Main.
Post Office Block, n. e. cor. Cherry and N. Adams.
Royal Arcanum Hall, 224 N. Washington.
Schumacher's Block, 314 Main.
Shaylor's Block, Adams, s. e. cor. Pine.
Turner Hall, Walnut, n. w. cor. Monroe av.
Zille's Hall, n. e. cor. Main and St. George.

## STREET DIRECTORY.

In numbering the city, what is known as the Philadelphia plan is used. This plan allows 100 for a block, so that on every corner a fresh hundred commences. Walnut street is the dividing line for all streets running north and south. On all streets crossing Walnut the number at that street is 100, increasing 100 for every block either north or south. All streets running north and south have "North" prefixed north of Walnut, and "South" south of that street. South of Walnut, the even numbers are on the west side and the odd numbers on the east side of streets. North of Walnut, the even numbers are east, and the odd numbers west.

For all streets running east and west, Fox River is the base line, and 100 the base number, the numbers increasing 100 for each block from the river west, the even numbers being on the south side and the odd numbers on the north side of streets.

*Adams*, from 300 Porlier n. to Elm.
*Baird*, from 1400 Crooks, s. to city limits.
*Bellevue*, in Guesnier's Addition, from Preble n.
*Cass*, from 700 S. Adams e. to East River.
*Cedar*, from 500 N. Washington e. to city limits.
*Charles*, first s. Mason-st. Bridge, from East River to Bellevue.
*Cherry*, from 200 N. Washington e. to Fair Grounds.
*Chicago*, from 500 S. Washington e. to East River.
*Clay*, from 1100 Walnut, n. and s. to city limits.

## MISCELLANEOUS DIRECTORY.    45

*Congress*, from 821 S. Madison e. to S. Monroe av.
*Crooks*, from 400 S. Washington e. to East River.
*Day*, from 900 N. Madison e. to Newberry's Addition.
*Derby* is south of city limits, and runs from Monroe av. e. to Webster av.
*Doty*, from 200 S. Washington e. to Fair Grounds.
*Eastman Av.*, from 1100 N. Madison e. to city limits.
*Eleventh*, from 1200 Walnut s. to city limits, and n. to East River and from 1200 Harvey n. to city limits.
*Eliza*, from 1000 S. Madison e. to East River.
*Ellis*, from junction Main and Forest e. to city limits.
*Elm*, from 600 N. Washington e. to Newberry's Addition.
*Farlin*, from junction Main and Grove e. to city limits.
*Forest*, from 1600 Main n. to Willow.
*George*, in Guesnier's Addition, 4th east of East River.
*Greene*, from junction Main and Newhall e.
*Grignon*, from 1200 S. Madison e. to East River.
*Grove*, from 1500 Main n. to junction Day and Farlin.
*Guesnier*, from e. end Mason-st. Bridge e. beyond limits.
*Harvey*, from 315 Day s. e. to Monroe av., and from 800 N. Monroe av. e. to city limits.
*Heyzman*, in Guesnier's Addition, from Preble to Mary, 5 e. of East River.
*Howard*, from 520 S. Jefferson e. to S. Madison, s. of St. John's Park.
*Jackson*, from 800 Walnut n. to city limits and s. to Derby.
*Jefferson*, from 400 Porlier n. to East River.
*John*, in Guesnier's Addition, from Mary to Preble, 2d e. of East River.
*Laws*, from 800 S. Adams e. to East River.
*Madison*, from 500 Grignon n. to city limits.
*Main*, from lower Fox River bridge e. and s. e. to Ellis Creek.

NUMBERS:

| | | | |
|---|---|---|---|
| Fox River | 100 | N. Van Buren | 900 |
| N. Washington | 200 | N. Webster | 1000 |
| N. Adams | 300 | N. Clay | 1100 |
| N. Jefferson | 400 | N. 11th | 1200 |
| N. Madison | 500 | N. 12th | 1300 |
| N. Monroe av | 600 | Pleasant | 1400 |
| N. Quincy | 700 | Grove | 1500 |
| N. Jackson | 800 | Forest | 1600 |

*Manitowoc Rd.*, a continuation of Main from Ellis Creek s.
*Mary*, in Guesnier's Addition, 1 n. Mason, e. bridge, from East River to Heyzman.
*Mason*, from 600 S. Adams e. to East River.

*Mill,* is from Main to Greene, 1 w. Ellis Creek.
*Milwaukee,* on n. s. St. John's Park, from 430 S. Jefferson e. to Madison.
*Monroe Av.,* from 600 Walnut n. to city limits and s. to Woodlawn cemetery.

NUMBERS:

| South: | | | North: | | |
|---|---|---|---|---|---|
| | Walnut | 100 | | Walnut | 100 |
| | Doty | 200 | | Cherry | 200 |
| | Stuart | 300 | | Pine | 300 |
| | Crooks | 400 | | Main | 400 |
| | Chicago | 500 | | Cedar | 500 |
| | Mason | 600 | | Elm | 600 |
| | Cass | 700 | | Willow | 700 |
| | Lawe | 800 | | Harvey | 800 |
| | Porlier | 900 | | Day | 900 |
| | Eliza | 1000 | | Smith | 1000 |
| | Emilie | 1100 | | Eastman av | 1100 |
| | Grignon | 1200 | | | |

*Moravian,* the south boundary of Jackson Square.
*Morrow,* from junction of Main and Grove e. to city limits.
*Newhall,* from Ellis Creek opp. Hagemeister's brewery n. to Greene.
*Pine,* from 300 N. Washington e. to East River.
*Pleasant,* from 1400 Main n. to Day.
*Porlier,* from C., M. & St. P. R. R. bridge e. to East River.
*Preble,* on south line of Guesnier's Addition from East River to Manitowoc Rd.
*Quincy,* from 700 Walnut n. and s. to city limits.
*St. Clair,* from 220 N. 11th e. to Fair Grounds.
*St. George,* from junction Harvey and 11th, s. and s. e. to East River.
*School,* the northern boundary of Jackson Square.
*Smith,* from 1000 N. Madison e. to Newberry's Addition.
*Spring,* the southern boundary of St. James Park.
*Stuart,* from 300 S. Washington e. to Fair Grounds.
*Suydam,* from junction Eliza and East River, s. to city limits.
*Twelfth,* from 1300 Walnut n. and s. to city limits.
*Van Buren,* from 900 Walnut n. to city limits and s. to Derby.
*Walnut,* from 100 Washington e. to Fair Grounds and w. to Fox River.

NUMBERS:

| Fox River | 100 | Monroe av | 600 | Clay | 1100 |
|---|---|---|---|---|---|
| Washington | 200 | Quincy | 700 | 11th | 1200 |
| Adams | 300 | Jackson | 800 | 12th | 1300 |
| Jefferson | 400 | Van Buren | 900 | Baird | 1400 |
| Madison | 500 | Webster av | 1000 | | |

## MISCELLANEOUS DIRECTORY.

*Washington*, from 200 Mason n. to Elm.

NUMBERS:

| South: | Walnut | 100 | North: | Walnut | 100 |
|---|---|---|---|---|---|
| | Doty | 200 | | Cherry | 200 |
| | Stuart | 300 | | Pine | 300 |
| | Crooks | 400 | | Main | 400 |
| | Chicago | 500 | | Cedar | 500 |
| | Mason | 600 | | Elm | 600 |

*Water*, in Guesnier's Addition, from Preble n. to Mary, 1 e. of East River.
*Webster Av.*, from 1000 Walnut, n. to city limits and s. to Woodlawn cemetery.
*Willow*, from 700 N. Adams e. beyond city limits.

# A. G. WRIGHT,
# DIRECTORY PUBLISHER,

107 Wisconsin Street,

## MILWAUKEE.

Directories of the Principal Cities of the United States are kept on file for reference.

# WRIGHT'S
# FORT HOWARD DIRECTORY
## 1894.

### MISCELLANEOUS DIRECTORY.

#### CITY OFFICERS.

Mayor, William Larsen.
Treasurer, Albert Anderson.
Assessor, John Cody.
Clerk, W. L. Kerr.
Marshal, William Driscoll.
Street Commissioner, Abe Lucas.
Attorney, L. A. Calkins.

#### Members of the Common Council.

Alderman-at-large and president of the Council, C. Schwarz.
First Ward, J. E. Shaughnessy.
Second Ward, A. Cleerman.
Third Ward, Theo. Kemnitz.
Fourth Ward, J. H. Tayler.
Fifth Ward, E. D. Rasmussen.
Sixth Ward, A. Wohlfeil.

#### STANDING COMMITTEES.

Finance—Tayler, Schwarz, Shaughnessy.
Sewers and Plumbing—Schwarz, Wohlfeil, Rasmussen.
Streets and Bridges—Kemnitz, Schwarz, Rasmussen.
Ordinances—Tayler, Cleerman, Schwarz.
Accounts—Wohlfeil, Tayler, Cleerman.
Fire Department—Shaughnessy, Rasmussen, Kemnitz.

Poor—Rasmussen, Shaughnessy, Cleerman.
Waterworks—Schwarz, Kemnitz, Tayler.
Public Grounds—Rasmussen, Kemnitz, Wohlfeil.
Printing—Cleerman, Tayler, Wohlfeil.
Taverns and Groceries—Shaughnessy, Kemnitz, Wohlfeil.

## Justices of the Peace.

Malcolm Sellers, Wm. Hood.

## Police Force.

Wm. Driscoll, marshal; Thomas Hauley, Fred. Devolder, Tor. Anderson, patrolmen.

## Fire Department.

Chief engineer, John Gross; asst. chief, A. Lucas; fireman, S. Shaughnessy; hose captain, Charles Burns; secretary, R. Henderson; treasurer, T. Leicht.

## Board of Education.

### SCHOOL COMMISSIONERS.

C. W. Lomas, commissioner at large; John Clory, 1st Ward; D. M. Burns, 2d Ward; John H. Eisman, 3d Ward; F. A. Dieckmann, 4th Ward; R. J. Black, 5th Ward; C. A. Friderici, 6th Ward.

### OFFICERS.

D. M. Burns, pres.; A. W. Burton, supt.

### STANDING COMMITTEES.

Finance—Eisman, Clory, Lomas.
Teachers and Text Books—Lomas, Dieckmann, Eisman.
Buildings and Grounds—Dieckmann, Black, Friderici.
Supplies—Black, Friederici, Clory.
Rules and Regulations—Clory, Dieckmann, Eisman.
Visiting Schools—Friderici, Eisman, Clory.

### PUBLIC SCHOOLS.

High School, n. w. cor. Cedar and Shawano. A. W. Burton, prin.; Miss Louie P. Adams, 1st asst.; Miss Clara Austin, 2d asst.; Miss Clara Schuette, 3d asst.
Fourth Ward School, same building with High School. Miss Anna Mickelsen, 8th grade; Miss Mary K. Platten, 7th grade; Miss Mary L. Shultz, 6th grade; Miss Essie W. Smith, 6th and 3d grades; Miss Elsie S. Dunlap, 3d and 2d grades; Miss Lizzie R. Clory, 1st grade.

FORT HOWARD.

Second Ward School, n. e. cor. Chestnut and Dousman. Robt. C. Faulds, prin.; Daisy Barclay, 4th grade; Ella Cusick, 3d grade; Jennie Hogan, 2d grade; Mamie Farrell, 1st grade.
Fifth Ward School, n. w. cor. 7th av. and 5th. Miss Jennie Dunn, prin.; Miss Ingebor Hansen, 4th grade; Miss Nellie Nelson, 3d grade; Miss May Salvas, 2d grade; Miss Emelia Indra, 1st grade; Miss Emma Franks, 1st grade.
Sixth Ward School, s. w. cor. 9th and 5th av. Miss Mary C. Black, 1st grade.
First Ward School, n. s. Mather w. Cedar. Miss Mary Kane, 1st grade.
Chapel School, e. s. Chapel n. Shawano rd. Miss Bessie Barclay, teacher.

### Post Office.

General delivery open daily, except Sundays and legal holidays, from 7:30 A. M. to 7:30 P. M.; Sundays and legal holidays open from 9 to 10 A. M. Money order and registry department open from 8 A. M. to 6 P. M. daily, except Sundays and legal holidays. Andrew E. Elmore, postmaster; William S. Dillon, asst.-postmaster.

### Banks and Incorporated Companies.

Fisk Land & Lumber Co. The—H. W. Fisk, pres.; W. D. Fisk, v.-pres.; W. J. Fisk, sec. and treas.; real estate and lumber, office C. & N. W. passenger depot.
Fort Howard Lumber Co.—F. Hurlbut, pres.; George Beyer, v.-pres.; F. W. Weeks, sec. and treas.; office n. w. cor. 2d av. and 10th; yards e. s. 2d av., s. of 10th.
McCartney National Bank—D. McCartney, pres.; Wm. Larsen, v.-pres.; J. H. Tayler, cashier; s. s. Main, 5 e. Chestnut, Music Hall bldg.
Voigt John M. Manufacturing Co.—Incorporated 1890; D. J. Davidson, pres.; F. A. Dieckmann, sec. and treas.; e. s. Pearl, opp. Shawano, Ft. H.

### Churches.

First Baptist Church, e. s. Chestnut, n. of Main. Rev. Granger W. Smith, pastor. Services, 10:30 A. M. and 7:30 P. M. Sunday-school, 12 M. Prayer meeting, Wednesday evening 7:30.
First Congregational Church, s. w. cor. 4th av. and 3d. Services, 7:30 P. M.
First M. E. Church, n. w. cor. Hubbard and Chestnut. Rev. John Schneider, pastor. Services, 10:30 A. M. and 7:30 P. M. Sunday-school, 12 M.

First Presbyterian Church, w. s. Chestnut bet. Main and Hubbard. Rev. J. Frank Young, pastor. Services, 10:30 A. M. and 7:30 P. M. Sunday-school after morning service.

Moravian Church, s. e. cor. 5th av. and 4th. Rev. John J. Groenfeld, pastor. Services, 10:30 A. M. Sunday-school, 9:15 A. M.

Norwegian Lutheran Church, Broadway cor. John. Rev. A. Peterson, pastor, Ft. H. Services, Sunday 10 A. M. and 7:30 P. M. Sunday-school, 8:30 A. M.

St. Patrick's (cath.) Church, n. w. cor. Cherry and Hubbard. Rev. Father Michael John O'Brien, pastor. Sunday services: mass, 8 and 10:15 A. M. Sunday-school and benediction, 3 P. M.

Seventh Day Adventists' Church, n. s. Main, 2 w. Cedar. Thos. Pringle, elder. Services, every Saturday 1 P. M. Sabbath-school, 11 A. M.

Young Men's Christian Association, n. w. cor. Main and Chestnut. C. W. Lomas, pres.; J. H. Tayler, v.-pres.; H. W. Fisk, rec. sec.; G. A. Richardson, treas.; J. P. Rawlings, sec.

### Cemeteries.

Ft. Howard Cemetery, on w. line of city, s. of Duck Creek rd.

### Societies and Lodges.

Alumni Association—Mrs. Henry Erbe, pres.; Miss Mary Platten, v.-pres.; Miss Anna Mickelsen, sec.; Edward McGinnis, treas. Meets semi-annually in May and October at High School building. Ft. H.

American Legion of Honor—August Brauns, com.; John G. Gross, v.-com.; Ed Rasmussen, sec.; Fred P. Gross, coll.; Conrad Silbersdorf, treas. Meets 1st and 3d Monday in Gross block, 213 Broadway, Ft. H.

Ancient Order United Workmen, Howard Lodge No. 72.—Wm. Gobler, M. W.; Rob. Dunn, P. M. W.; W. L. Witters, fin.; J. K. Ford, sec.; M. A. Waldo, foreman. Meets 1st and 3d Tuesdays, 7:30 P. M., at Platten Bros. Hall, Dousman, Ft. H.

Anagar Society, n. w. cor. 2d and 3d av.—Fred Madson, pres.; M. Nissen, v.-pres.; Louis Hansen, sec.; Chas. Meller, treas.; Hans Hansen, rec. sec. Meets every Wednesday, 8 P. M., at Anagar Hall, Ft. H.

Baptist Church Ladies' Aid Society—Mrs. George Ranous, pres.; Harry Fisk, v.-pres., sec. and treas. Meets every Tuesday, 2 P. M., at Baptist Church parlors.

Baptist Young People's Union—Delian Gillis, pres.; Clarence Reynolds, v.-pres.; Elsie Dunlap, sec.; Gordon Lyons, treas. Meet every Sunday 6:30 P. M. at parlors of Baptist Church.

**FORT HOWARD.**

Epworth League, M. E. Church—Miss Nellie Tayler, pres.; Rev. J. Schneider, S. A. Bell, Mrs. Ed. Challenger, v.-prests.; Miss Nellie Waldo, sec.; Rob. Hansen, treas. Meets every Sunday at 6.30 P. M. at M. E. Church, n. w. cor. Chestnut and Hubbard, Ft. H.

Ft. Howard Tennis Club—Chas. Kerr, sec.; Miss Lillie Marshall, treas.; Dr. Ringsdorf, capt.

Good Will Lodge No. 161, I. O. G. T.—Herm. Kull, C. T.; Miss Olive Braasch, V. T.; Mary Albert, sec.; Gust. Walters, treas. Meet every Tuesday 8 P. M. at s. s. 3d, bet. 4th and 5th avs., Ft. H.

Knights of Maccabees—L. R. Vandenberg, C.; J. P. Wallen, L. C.; A. N. Lucas, F. K.; W. L. Kerr, R. K.; J. Flatley, P. C.; Wm. O'Leary, S.; T. J. Shannon, M. A. A.; J. Neville, F. M. O. G.; J. P. Howlett, 2d M. O. G.; P. Nadeau, Sen.; H. Kuhaupt, piquet; A. J. Reed, chapl. Meet Royal Arcanum Hall 2d and 4th Tuesdays, 8 P. M.

Modern Woodmen of America, Ft. Howard Camp—J. P. Rawlings, V. C.; Ed. Challenger, W. A.; G. W. Fisk, W. B.; John Eisman, clk.; Gust. Walters, watchman; Fred. Martin, sentry; W. H. Fisk, escort; Dr. Slaughter, physician; G. W. Fisk, del. state con. Meet every Monday at Y. M. C. A. Hall, Ft. H.

Royal Arcanum Mystical Council No. 519—L. G. Schiller, R.; W. F. McCloskey, sec.; J. E. Shaughnessey, treas. Meets every Thursday 8 P. M. at Platten's blk., Ft. H.

Uniform Rank of the Mystical Council No. 519, R. A.—L. G. Schiller, pres.; Wm. F. McCloskey, sec.; A. G. Oldenburg, treas.; I. A. Dickey, lieut. Meets last Thursday of each month at the Royal Arcanum Hall.

Women's Auxiliary to the Ft. Howard Y. M. C. A.—Mr. D. J. Davidson, pres.; Mrs. A. L. Gray, v.-pres.; Edith Cann, sec.; Mrs. H. W. Fisk, treas. Meet 1st Tuesdays in February, May, August and November at Y. M. C. A. hall, Ft. H.

Womans' Christian Temperance Union of Ft. Howard—Mrs. Fannie Lomas, pres.; Mrs. Geo. Ranous, sec.; Mrs. M. A. Waldo, treas.; Mrs. Sarah C. Henderson, cor. sec. Meet every other Wednesday 2 P. M. at residence of members.

Young Peoples' Society of Christian Endeavor, Presbyterian Church—Fred Henderson, pres.; Ena K. Potts, v.-pres.; Mrs. J. A. Williams, sec.; John Larsen, treas.; Mrs. J. F. Young, supt. Meets every Sunday, 7 P. M., at Presbyterian Church.

**Parks.**

City Park, bet. 8th and 10th av., 3d and 5th.

## Halls.

A. L. O. H. Hall, 213 Broadway.
Ansgar Hall, 3d av. n. 2d.
Music Hall, s. e. cor. Main and Chestnut.
Platten Hall, s. s. Dousman, 1 w. Broadway.
Y. M. C. A. Hall, n. w. cor. Main and Chestnut.

## STREET GUIDE.

*Baird*, from Fox River w. to the slough, 1 s. Broadway.
*Bond*, from Broadway w. to Guesnier, bet. Elmore and Mather.
*Broadway*, from 3d av. bridge runs n. to limits, 1 w. R. R. track.
*Buchanan*, from Shawano rd. to south line of Private Claim 1, 3 w. Oak.
*Caroline*, from Oak w. to Oneida, 1 s. Shawano rd.
*Cedar*, from 6th av. bridge n. to limits, 3 w. Broadway.
*Chapel*, see Fisk.
*Cherry*, from the creek n. to limits, 2 w. Broadway.
*Chestnut*, from John n. to limits, 1 w. Broadway.
*Christiania*, bet. Willow and Hazel, parallel with and next s. Shawano rd.
*Cleveland*, from Shawano rd. to s. line of P. C. 1, 1 w. Oak.
*Division*, from Willow w., 1 n. Dousman.
*Dousman*, from lower Fox River bridge w. to limits, 2 n. Main.
*Eighth*, from Fox River w. to C. & N. W. R'y, 2 s. C. M. & St. P. R'y bridge.
*Eighth Av.*, from 1st s. to 5th, 5 w. 3d av.
*Elmore*, from C. & N. W. depot w. to limits, 2 n. Dousman.
*Fifth*, from 3d av. w. to city limits, 5th s. the creek.
*Fifth Av.*, from G. B., W. & St. P. R'y s. to 10th, 2 w. 3d av.
*Fink*, bet. Dousman and Division, 3 w. Willow.
*First*, from 3d av. to 7th av., 1 s. the slough.
*Fisk*, from Shawano av. n. to Elmore, 5 w. Willow.
*Fourth*, from 3d av. w. to 5th av., 2 n. the slough.
*Fourth Av.* from G. B., W. & St. P. R'y s. to 10th, 1 w. 3d av.
*Fox*, 4 w. Willow, bet. Dousman and Division.
*Garfield*, from Shawano rd. to s. line of P. C. 1, 2 w. Oak.
*George*, bet. Dousman and Division, 2 w. Willow.
*Grant*, from Mather to James, 5 w. Broadway.
*Guesnier*, bet. Dousman and Division, 1 w. Willow.
*Harrison*, from Mather to James, 4 w. Broadway.
*Hazel*, 1 w. Willow, runs s. from Shawano rd.
*Hubbard*, from Fox River w. to Willow, 1 n. Main.
*James*, from Cedar to McDonald, 1 n. Mather.

## FORT HOWARD.

*John,* from Fox River w. to Chestnut, 1 n. the creek.
*Kellogg,* from Broadway w. to Cedar, 1 n. of Dousman.
*Lincoln,* from Mather n. to city limits, 4 w. Cedar.
*McDonald,* from C. & N. W. R'y n., bet. Broadway and the river.
*Main,* from Walnut-st. bridge w. to Willow.
*Mather,* 4th n. Dousman, from C. & N. W. R'y w. to Lincoln, then n. w. to city limits.
*Muckwonago,* from Mather to James, 1 e. Broadway.
*Murphy's Row,* n. Hugh McDonald's lumber-yard.
*Ninth,* from 2d av. w. to city limits, 3 s. the slough.
*Ninth Av.,* from City Park n. to C., M. & St. P. shops, 6 w. 3d av.
*Oak,* from Shawano av. s., 2 w. Willow.
*Oneida,* from Shawano av. s. and s. w., 4 w. Willow.
*Pearl,* from John n., 1 e. Broadway.
*Phebe,* from Broadway to Crocker's Addition, 3 n. Mather.
*Second,* from Mason-st. bridge w. to city limits.
*Second Av.,* from the creek s. to city limits, 1 w. Fox River.
*Seventh,* from 2d av. w. to the Ry. track, 1 s. the slough.
*Seventh Av.,* from G. B., W. & St. P. R. R. s. to C., M. & St. P. shops.
*School Place,* (formerly Shawano street) from Fox River w. to the slough.
*Shawano Rd.,* from Willow w. to city limits, 1 s. Dousman.
*Sixth Av.,* from Cedar-st. bridge s. to 5th, 3 w. 3d av.
*Tenth,* the southern boundary line from 2d av. w. to city limits, 4 s. of the slough.
*Tenth Av.,* from G. B., W. & St. P. R. R. s. to 5th, 7 w. 3d av.
*Third,* from 2d av. w., 2 s. the slough.
*Third Av.,* from Broadway bridge s. to 10th, 2 w. of Fox River.
*Water,* from John n. to Hubbard, 2 e. of Broadway.
*Willow,* from the creek n. to Elmore, 4 w. of Broadway.

# ADDITIONS, REMOVALS, ETC.
### Too Late for Insertion in Alphabetical Order.

Alamine Jean B., mason, res. 1120 Walnut.
Bowes Daniel, lumberman, res. 1200 Walnut.
Bowes Tessie Miss, dressmkr, res. 1200 Walnut.
Burslem Thomas, res. n. w. cor. Main and Cedar, Ft. H.
Clark Charlotte Miss, res. n. w. cor. Main and Cedar, Ft. H.
Daniels C. H., mill-hand, res. Ferris Hotel, Ft. H.
Erdmann & Galineau (Albert Erdmann and Emery D. Galineau), barbers, 210 Main.
Forrer Edward W., res. 1367 Walnut.
Fox River Soap Co., Nicholas N. Meyer, pres.; John Nick, sec. and treas. 219 Main.
Galineau Emery D. (Erdmann & Galineau), res. 316 S. Adams.
Green Bay Leather & Harness Co., Anton F. Stiller, prop., 208 N. Adams.
Herman Nicholas, lab., res. Empire House.
McGiveran John T., ins. agent, res. The Beaumont.
Nelson Catherine, dressmkr, res. n. s. 5th, 2 e. 4th av., Ft. H.
Oliver Thomas C., conductor, res. n. w. cor. Main and Cedar, Ft. H.
Oliver Thomas J., student, res. n. w. cor. Main and Cedar, Ft. H.
Paulson Annie Miss, res. w. s. 2d av., 5 s. 9th, Ft. H.
Paulson Berndt, lab., res. w. s. 2d av., 5 s. 9th, Ft. H.
Paulson Olivia Miss, res. w. s. 2d av., 5 s. 9th, Ft. H.
Pearce Martha (wid. Henry), res. w. s. 2d av., 4 s. 7th, Ft. H.
Ramsey John E., mach., res. w. s. Guesnier, 2 n. Dousman, Ft. H.
Russmueller Florian, mach., res. 202 5th av., Ft. H.
Schacha Frank, ry.-hand, res. s. s. 9th, 1 e. r. r., Ft. H.
Schefe Martha Miss, res. 109 9th av., Ft. H.
Spencer Robert, lab., res. 640 Elmore, Ft. H.

# WRIGHT'S DIRECTORY
## OF
# GREEN BAY & FT. HOWARD
## 1894.

### ABBREVIATIONS.

| | |
|---|---|
| agt............agent | n............north |
| al............alley | n. s............north side |
| asst............assistant | opp............opposite |
| av............avenue | P. O............post office |
| bel............below | pres............president |
| bet............between | R. R............railroad |
| bds............boards | rd............road |
| bldg............building | res............residence |
| blk............block | Rev............reverend |
| clk............clerk | s............south |
| com. mercht............commission merchant | s. s............south side |
| cor............corner | sec............secretary |
| e............east | servt............servant |
| e. s............east side | supt............superintendent |
| Ft. H............Fort Howard | trav. agt............traveling agent |
| lab............laborer | treas............treasurer |
| mkr............maker | w............west |
| mnfr............manufacturer | w. s............west side |
| mnfg............manufacturing | wid............widow |
| n............near | | |

### ALPHABETICAL LIST OF NAMES.

## A

ABBOTT Alfred, boilermkr, res. 407 1st, Ft. H.
  Abbott Alfred, Jr., baggageman, res. 407 1st, Ft. H.
Abbott Nellie Miss, res. 407 1st, Ft. H.
Abrahams Samuel, cattle-dlr., res. 1441 Cedar.
Abrahams Benjamin, peddler, res. 120 S. Quincy.
Abrams William J., pres. G. B., Kewaunee & Western R. R., res. 402 S. Webster av.
Abrams Winford, fireman, res. 402 S. Webster av.
Absileus Frank, boarding-house, res. 418 N. Adams.

**ADAMS A. L. & CO.** (A. L. Adams, prop.), dealers in lumber, lath, shingles; offices n. w. cor. 2d av. and 10th, Ft. H.; yards s. s. of 2d av., nr. R. R. track.
Adams Abbot L. (A. L. Adams & Co.), res. 431 Walnut.
Adams George, conductor, res. 529 N. 12th.
**ADAMS HOUSE**, Geo. Snavely, prop., 209-213 N. Adams.
Adams Ira, sawyer, res. 411 Broadway, Ft. H.
Adams James, lab., res. 316 Main.
Adams Nicholas, gardener, res. 922 N. 12th.
Addison Charles S., cooper, res. 630 N. Madison.
Adolfs William J., fireman, res. 603 Cherry, Ft. H.
Adolph Johanna C. (wid. Theodore), res. 7 w. of 874 Dousman, Ft. H.
Adriaenssens Arsene L., jeweler, res. 1413 Harvey.
Aga Dora Miss, res. 404 5th, Ft. H.
Agamet Edward, carp., res. 1227 Day.
Ahearn Annie G. Miss, teacher, res. w. s. Cherry, 2 n. Dousman, Ft. H.
Ahearn Hannah (wid. Daniel), res. w. s. Cherry, 2 n. Dousman, Ft. H.
Ahearn John, teamster, res. 1100 Mason.
Ahearn Marie D. Miss, teacher Pine Street School, res. w. s. Cherry, 2 n. Dousman, Ft. H.
Ahearn Michael, saw-filer, res. w. s. Cherry, 2 n. Dousman, Ft. H.
Ahlstrom Charles, captain, res. 1100 Grignon.
Ahlstrom Fred., res. 1100 Grignon.
Ahrens Gustav L., hostler, res. Huffman House, Ft. H.
Ainsworth Richard W., loco. engineer, res. 216 S. Madison.
Aird Hugh, machinist, res. 614 N. Jefferson.
Aland Charles, teamster, res. 1350 Walnut.
Aland Frank, res. 1350 Walnut.
Aland John, lab., res. 420 S. Quincy.
Aland Martha Miss, res. 1350 Walnut.
Alart & McGuire, pickle mnfrs., e. s. Broadway n. Bond, Ft. H.
Albert Marie E. Miss, bkpr, res. 404 4th, Ft. H.
Albert Phoebe (wid. Jacob), res. 404 4th, Ft. H.
Alberts John, lab., res. 637 S. Adams.
Alberts Katie (wid. George), boarding, 110 S. Madison.
Albrecht Emil, butcher, res. 1411 Main.
Albrecht Emma, clk. Theo. Mueller & Co., res. 1411 Main.
Albright Frank J., agent, res. cor. Kellogg and Cedar, Ft. H.
Allair George L., loco. fireman, res. 403 Mather.
Allen Bessie Miss, res. 605 Cedar, Ft. H.
Allen Betsey (wid. Emerson) res. w. s. Pearl, 4 s. Hubbard, Ft. H.
Allen Charles, boilermkr, res. 1012 Dousman, Ft. H.

**THE A. SPUHLER CO.** *LADIES', MISSES' and CHILDREN'S* **CLOAKS, CAPES, JACKETS**
**GREEN BAY**

ALL        57        AND

Allen Charles, lab., res. s. e. cor. 12th and Day.
Allen Edward, lab., res. s. e. cor. 12th and Day.
Allen Geo. G., storekpr. C., M. & St. P. Ry., res. 528 S. Quincy.
Allen James, lab., res. w. s. Pearl 4 S. Hubbard, Ft. H.
Allen Jay B., engineer, res. 605 Cedar, Ft. H.
Allen Joseph, lab., res. s. e. cor. 12th and Day.
Allen Philip, teamster J. H. Ebeling, res. s. e. cor. 12th and Day.
**ALLEN WILLIAM B.**, saloon, 216 N. Washington, res. 337 S. Monroe av.
Allie Amos J., cooper, res. 927 Pine.
Allie Homer, cooper, res. 1149 Walnut.
Allouez Mineral Spring Co., Joseph Hoeffel, pres.; Joseph P. Hoeffel, mngr.; James I. Hoeffel, sec.; s. e. cor. Chicago and S. Jackson.
**ALLOUEZ VILLA ORPHAN ASYLUM**, Sister Melania, superioress, De Pere rd.
Alm August, section boss, res. Junction Hotel, Ft. H.
Alsteens Henry, clk. 1299 Main, res. same.
**ALSTEENS PETER J.**, general mdse., 1299 Main, res. same.
Althof Elizabeth (wid. Henry), res. 713 Walnut.
Altmeyer Lizzie (wid. Michael), janitress Citizens' Nat. Bank, res. 220 Cherry.
Altmeyer Michael P., bartender, res. 320 Main.
American Catholic Church, Most Rev. J. Rene Vilatte, Archbishop Metropolitan and Primate, n. w. cor. Cass and S. 12th.
**AMERICAN EXPRESS CO.**, W. C. Hinsdale, agent, 224 N. Adams.
**AMERICAN HOUSE**, Frank Van Kessel, prop., n. e. cor. N. Washington and Walnut.
Amlin Lulu Miss, res. n. s. St. Clair 1 e. N. 11th.
Amunson Andrew, carp., res. 102 Cherry, Ft. H.
Amunson Helena E. (wid. Alex.), res. 400 2d, Ft. H.
Amunson James, sailor, res. n. s. Bond, 2 w. Cedar, Ft. H.
Anderegg Adele H. Miss, res. 710 Pleasant.
Anderegg Adele S. (wid. Thomas), res. 710 Pleasant.
**ANDEREGG MARTIN T. REV.**, pastor St. Peter and Paul Church (Cath.), res. 710 Pleasant.
Andersen Charles, carp., res. 104 3d, Ft. H.
Andersen Iver, res. 216 Broadway, Ft. H.
Andersen Peter, res. s. e. cor. 4th av. and 9th, Ft. H.
Andersen Rasmus, com. trav., res. 1205 Cherry.
Andersen Soren, ship-carp., res. s. s. 3d, 4 w. 3d av., Ft. H.
Anderson Aaron, lab., res. s. e. cor. 2d and 11th av., Ft. H.

| AND | 58 | AND |

Anderson Adolph, tallyman, res. 704 3d av., Ft. H.
Anderson Albert, city treas., res. s. s. Baird, 2 e. Cherry, Ft. H.
Anderson Allan, carp., res. 342 S. Webster av.
Anderson Andrew, carp., res. 119 7th av., Ft. H.
Anderson Anna Miss, dressmkr 207 7th av., res. same, Ft. H.
Anderson August, lab., res. 908 3d av., Ft. H.
Anderson Axel, lab., res. 1125 Pine.
Anderson Caroline Miss, domestic 312 Cherry.
Anderson Carl, salesman Wm. Larsen, res. 104 Cherry, Ft. H.
Anderson Charles, brakeman, res. St. James Hotel.
Anderson Charles, lab., res. w. s. Oneida rd., 1 n. 9th, Ft. H.
Anderson Charles, lab., res. n. w. cor. 2d and 12th av., Ft. H.
Anderson Christian, lab., res. 117 7th av., Ft. H.
Anderson Frederick, carp., res. 104 Cherry, Ft. H.
Anderson Hans, farmer, res. s. s. 2d, 5 w. R. R. track, Ft. H.
Anderson Hans, farmer, res. w. s. Oneida rd., 1 n. 9th, Ft. H.
Anderson Hans, fisherman, res. 308 N. 11th.
Anderson Hans Jr., lab., res. w. s. Oneida rd., 1 n. 9th, Ft. H.
Anderson James R., clk., res. 342 S. Webster av.
Anderson John, boilermkr, res. 704 3d av. Ft. H.
Anderson John, sec. and treas. Green Bay Plumbing and Heating Co., res. 120 S. Webster av.
Anderson Lena Miss, res. 704 3d av., Ft. H.
Anderson Martin, carpenter-contractor, res. 606 1st, Ft. H.
Anderson Mary (wid Chas.), res. 404 3d, Ft. H.
Anderson Math., ins. canvasser, res. 1156 Walnut.
Anderson May, domestic n. e. cor. 6th av. and 3d, Ft. H.
Anderson Melvin, res. s. s. 3d, 4 w. 3d av., Ft. H.
Anderson Nels, lab., res. 201 Baird, Ft. H.
Anderson Nicholas, boilermkr, res. 704 3d av., Ft. H.
Anderson Ole, carp., res. 120 Chestnut, Ft. H.
Anderson Ole A., car-smith, res. 902 3d av., Ft. H.
Anderson Peter, lab., res. 400 5th av., Ft. H.
Anderson Ranghild, domestic 106 Chestnut, Ft. H.
Anderson Rasmus, agt., res. 210 Willow, Ft. H.
Anderson Rasmus, lab., res. 718 4th av., Ft. H.
Anderson Rena Miss, res. s. s. 3d, 4 w. 3d av., Ft. H.
Anderson Sarah (wid. Axel), res. 706 3d av., Ft. H.
Anderson Sena, domestic 621 Main.
Anderson Theodore, night police, res. 207 7th av., Ft. H.
Anderson William B. (McGrath & Anderson), res. 342 S. Webster av.
Andreason Andrew K., clk. Buengener & Bur, res. 311 6th av., Ft. H.

**THE A. SPUHLER CO., Green Bay** CARPETS, RUGS, OIL CLOTHS, Draperies and Window Shades.

Andreason Knut, painter, res. 311 6th av., Ft. H.
Andree Edward, clk., res. 538 S. Monroe av.
Andree Lambert, lab., res. 601 N. 12th.
Andressen Andrew, lab., res. 1501 Main.
Andrews Frank W., motorman, res. 227 S. Jackson.
Andrews Walter N., boilermkr, res. 208 6th av., Ft. H.
Anhauser Gertrude Miss, compositor, res. 206 S. Quincy.
Anhauser Peter, carp., res. rear 716 Main.
Anhauser Peter J., collector, res. rear 716 Main.
Anheuser Mathias (Thomas & Anheuser), res. 804 Cherry, Ft. H.
Annen J. P. Candy Co., Edwin Van den Braak, pres.; August E. Brauns, treas.; John P. Annen, sec. and mngr.; mnfg. confectioners, 109–111 N. Washington.
Annen John P., sec. and mngr. J. P. Annen Candy Co., res. 516 S. Van Buren.
Ansorge Anna C. Miss, milliner, res. 1001 Walnut.
Ansorge Clara Miss, res. 529 Pine.
Ansorge Eugene K. (Ansorge & Parish), res. 529 Pine.
Ansorge Fannie Miss, res. 1001 Walnut.
Ansorge Otto, watchmkr, res. 1001 Walnut.
Ansorge Wm. K., music teacher, 1001 Walnut, res. same.
**ANSORGE & PARISH** (Eugene K. Ansorge and Edwin P. Parish), insurance, real estate, loans and ocean passage, 126 N. Washington.
Antonnau Flora Miss, res. 1111 Pine.
Antonnau Paul, carp., res. 1111 Pine.
Antonnau Philomine (wid. Joseph), res. 1111 Pine.
Antonnau Raoul, lab., res. 1111 Pine.
Archey Sophie (wid. Theodore), res. 537 S. Monroe av.
Archibald George, lab., res. Willmar House.
Arends Jacob, farmer, res. s. w. cor. Manitowoc rd. and Bellevue.
Arkens Theodore, carp., res. 1232 Doty.
Arlington Hotel (Thomas Gaffney, prop.), 419 Broadway, Ft. H.
Armstrong Alex., brakeman, res. 732 S. Jefferson.
Armstrong James T., res. 333 S. Madison.
Armstrong John, lab., res. 735 Walnut.
Armstrong John Jr., lab., res. 735 Walnut.
Armstrong John C., tinsmith, res. 1030 Doty.
Armstrong Robert, drayman, res. 1030 Doty.
Armstrong Robert H., (Green Bros. & Co.), res. 1030 Doty.
Armstrong William, lab., res. 215 S. Webster av.
Armstrong William A., blacksmith, res. 1030 Doty.
Arndt Anna, domestic 231 Walnut.
Arndt Kate, cook Schauer Hotel.

| ARN | 60 | BAE |

Arnold Peter, engineer, res. Northwestern Hotel, Ft. H.
Arthur Everett A., sec. The A. Spuhler Co., res. 413 Pine.
Arvey Joseph J., carp., res. 447 S. Van Buren.
Aschenbrenner John, shoemkr, res. 1253 Main.
Asimont George, fishpacker, res. 417 Cedar.
Asimont Julia (wid. George), res. 815 Cherry.
Ast Charles, painter, res. 122 S. Jackson.
Ast Charles, Jr., clk. Findeisen Bros., res. 122 S. Jackson.
Astor Park, bet. Porlier and Eliza, 10th and 11th.
Atkinson Emilie Miss, res. 735 Walnut.
Atkinson Fanny, domestic 514 Walnut.
Atkinson Harry, res. 818 Cherry.
Atkinson John, res. 818 Cherry.
Atkinson John, foreman Metropolitan Lumber Co., res. Broadway House, Ft. H.
Atkinson Katie Miss, res. 818 Cherry.
Atkinson Mary (wid. Hellis), res. 109 N. Quincy.
Augustin Christoph, carp., res. s. w. cor. 2d av. and 9th, Ft. H.
Augustin George, mill hand, res. s. w. cor. 2d av. and 9th, Ft. H.
Augustin Henry, carp., res. s. w. cor. 2d av. and 9th, Ft. H.
Aul Edward, engineer, res. Pearl, s. w. cor. Bridge, Ft. H.
Austin Clara, teacher High School, res. 309 Cedar, Ft. H.
Austin Frank, farmer, res. 309 Cedar, Ft. H.
Austin Miriam Miss, milliner, res. 309 Cedar, Ft. H.
Austin Thirsa Miss, music teacher, 309 Cedar, Ft. H., res. same.
Aylward Thomas J. carp., res. 1125 Mason.

# B

BABCOCK Alson E., brakeman, res. 316 S. Webster av.
Babcock Edward W., carriagemkr, res. 316 S. Webster av.
Babcock John H., res. 316 S. Webster av.
Babcock John H., res. Odd Fellows' Home.
Babcock Stella Miss, music teacher, res. 315 S. Jackson.
Babier Louis, lab., res. n. s. St. Clair, 5 e. N. 12th.
Babier Matt, lab., res. n. s. St. Clair, 5 e. N. 12th.
Bachmeier Anton, tailor, res. Schauer Hotel.
Bacon Edwin, com. trav., res. 1036 S. Quincy.
Bacon Edwin H., com. trav., res. 534 S. Quincy.
Bacon Florence Miss, res. 1036 S. Quincy.
Bader Victor, saloon, 301 Main, res. 503 N. Jefferson.
Baeb Felix, lab., res. w. s. Rich rd., 2 s. 9th, Ft. H.
Baeb Mary (wid. Joseph), res. w. s. Rich rd., 2 s. 9th, Ft. H.
Baenen Albert, lab., res. w. s. Hazel, 1 s. Shawano rd., Ft. H.

**THE A. SPUHLER CO., GREEN BAY, WIS.** **Fine Dress Goods**
Samples Furnished on Application.

BAE     61     BAR

Baenen Frank, boilermkr, res. w. s. Hazel, 1 s. Shawano rd., Ft. H.
Baenen John, carp., res. w. s. Hazel, 1 s. Shawano rd., Ft. H.
Baenen Kate Miss, res. 138 S. Webster av.
Baenen Lucie, milliner, res. w. s. Hazel, 1 s. Shawano rd., Ft. H.
Baenen Nettie Miss, res. w. s. Hazel, 1 s. Shawano rd., Ft. H.
Baerman Otto, grocer, 300 S. Webster av., res. same.
Baetsen Henry, carp., res. 134 S. Van Buren.
Bahan Patrick, saloon, 227 Main, res. same.
Bailey Henry, wood-turner, res. 214 Chestnut, Ft. H.
Baird Park, bet. Cass and Mason, Webster av. and 10th.
Baker Anna C. (wid. Peter), res. 1174 Chicago.
Baker Charles S., loco.-engineer, res. 123 6th av., Ft. H.
Baker Coral, lab., res. s. s. Duck Creek rd., 8 w. Mather, Ft. H.
**BAKER DAVID,** millwright, res. n. s. Duck Creek rd., 8 w. Mather, Ft. H.
Baker Eliza (wid. James S.), res. 1015 S. Monroe av.
**BAKER HENRY B.,** cashier the Kellogg National Bank, res. 1015 S. Monroe av.
Baker James F., barkpr. Wm. Garner, res. 932 Main.
Baker Joseph H., dockforeman, res. 124 6th av., Ft. H.
Baker Philip E. engineer, res. Hoffmann House, Ft. H.
Bakule Joseph, lab., res. 525 St. George.
Balden Joseph, fisherman, res. w. s. McDonald, 2 s. lumber yd., Ft. H.
Baldwin Charles H., fireman C., M. & St. Ry., res. 415 Mason.
Baldwin Dymae H. (wid. Charles A.), res. 415 Mason.
Baldwin Fred. K., switchman C., M. & St. P. Ry., res. 415 Mason.
Baldwin H. Walter, dentist, Citizens' Nat. Bank bldg., res. 802 Walnut.
Baldwin John A., carp., res. 134 Chestnut, Ft. H.
Baldwin Nellie Miss, res. 134 Chestnut, Ft. H.
Ball Caleb F., engineer C., M. & St. P. Ry., res. 309 S. Adams.
Ballenger George, bkpr., res. Broadway House, Ft. H.
Bangart John, cooper, res. 1103 Pine.
Bannon Mary, domestic Northwestern Hotel, **Ft. H.**
Banquest Peter, tailor, res. American House.
Banzhaf Albert, student, res. 923 S. Quincy.
Banzhaf Edwin, student, res. 923 S. Quincy.
Banzhaf Mathilde (wid. Henry), res. 923 S. Quincy.
Barclay Daisy Miss, teacher 2d ward, res. 310 Chestnut, Ft. **H.**
Barclay Edward, clk. M. J. Corbett, res. 302 Cherry, Ft. H.
Barclay Robert, tel.-opr. C. & N. W. R'y, res. 310 Chestnut, Ft. H.

Barclay Thomas, loco. engineer, res. 302 Cherry, Ft. H.
Bardouche Annie, clk. Jorgensen, Blesch Co., res. 509 Elm.
Bardouche Henry, cooper, res. 604 N. Madison.
Bardouche John, lab., res. 1142 Stuart.
Bardouche John B, wood-dlr., N. Madison cor. **Willow, res. 509 Elm.**
Bardouche John B. Jr., capt. Truck No. 1, res. 602 N. Madison.
Bardouche Joseph, painter, res. 215 S. Jackson.
Bardouche Joseph, teamster, res. 509 Elm.
Bardouche Mary Miss, res. 509 Elm.
Bardouche Peter, painter, res. 215 S. Jackson.
Barker Edwin S., res. 418 Cherry.
Barker Ellen (wid. James), res. 445 S. Adams.
Barkhausen Henry A. (Barkhausen & Hathaway), res. 822 Pine.
**BARKHAUSEN & HATHAWAY** (Henry A. Barkhausen and Oscar C. Hathaway), coal oil, salt, grain and hay, w. end Walnut-st. bridge, Ft. H.
Barlement Eliza Mrs., res. 300 3d av., **Ft. H.**
Barlement Robert, switchman, res. s. **w. cor. 3d and 3d av.,** Ft. H.
Barlement Wm., foreman **Kellogg Stock Farm, res. Depere rd.,** 2½ miles s. city limits.
Barlow Julia (wid. James), res. 307 S. Adams.
Barnes C. A. Mrs., res. 426 S. Monroe av.
Barnes John E., loco.-engineer, res. n. w. **cor. 9th av. and 3d,** Ft. H.
Barrette Augustus G., carp., res. 1213 Day.
Bartel Christoph, lab., res. 741 S. Van Buren.
Bartel John, lab., res. 1331 Crooks.
Bartelme Frank, res. Court House.
**BARTELME JOHN,** sheriff Brown County, res. Court House.
Bartelme Minnie Miss, res. Court House.
Bartelme Nettie Miss, dressmkr, res. Court House.
Bartelme Tillie Miss, res. Court House.
Bartelme Tinie Miss, res. Court House.
Barth Alois Jr., cigar mnfr, 1109 Cherry, res. same.
Barth Amelia Miss, res. 200 S. Monroe av.
Barth Edward, whol. liquors, 103 N. Washington, res. 132 Broadway. Ft. H.
Barth Emma, clk. Jorgensen Blesch Co., res. 1009 Main.
Barth George, cigarmkr, res. 925 Walnut.
Barth Henry, clk., res. 200 S. Monroe av.
Barth Joseph, mngr. E. Barth, res. 200 S. Monroe av.

**Headquarters for Boys' Clothing** THE A. SPUHLER CO.
GREEN BAY.

Barth Joseph Jr., watchmkr, res. 200 S. Monroe av.
Barth Martin, saloon, 214 Pine, res. 1009 Main.
Barth Mary Miss, res. 200 S. Monroe av.
Bartlett Fred, painter, res. 701 Cherry.
Bartlett Hiram, filer, res. 701 Cherry.
Bartran George, physician, Jorgensen's block, res. 149 Broadway, Ft. H.
Bartran Lilly, domestic 403 Chestnut, Ft. H.
Bartran William H., physician, 307 Broadway, res. 309 Chestnut, Ft. H.
Bartran Wm. H. Jr., student, res. 309 Chestnut, Ft. H.
Basche Anton, clk. Engels & Mohr, res. 1237 Cedar.
Basche Arthur A., cigarmkr, res. 1237 Cedar.
Basche Douglas S., res. 426 S. Jefferson.
Basche Edward H., lab., res. 405 5th, Ft. H.
Basche Frank, barber, res. 1237 Cedar.
Basche Fred W., wall paper, window shades, toys and hooks, and baby carriages, 221 N. Washington, res. 426 S. Jefferson.
Basche Fred Jr., lab., res. 317 S. Adams.
Basche George, lab., res. 1237 Cedar.
Basche Harry E., tallyman, res. 405 5th, Ft. H.
Basche Maud E., clk., res. 426 S. Jefferson.
Basche Michael, carp. contr., 539 S. Jefferson, res. same.
Basche Richard, engineer, res. 539 S. Jefferson.
Basche William, ticket agt. C., M. & St. P. R. R., res. 539 S. Jefferson.
Baschinger John, brewer, res. w. s. Manitowoc rd., 3 s. Bellevue.
Baschinger Joseph, lab., res. w. s. Manitowoc rd., 3 s. Bellevue.
Baschinger Joseph A. carp., res. w. s. Manitowoc rd., 2 s. Bellevue.
Bashnier Louise Miss, res. e. s. Buchanan, 1 s. Shawano av., Ft. H.
Bashnier Samuel, lab., res. e. s. Buchanan, 1 s. Shawano av., Ft. H.
Bassett Francis, fish-packer, res. 909 Main.
Bassett John, policeman, res. 411 N. Jackson.
Basten Annie, domestic 820 S. Monroe av.
Basten Frank, barkpr., res. 225 N. Washington.
Basten Gertrude, dressmkr, 521 Main, res. same.
Basten John, mngr. Chicago Saloon, res. 225 Main.
Basten John, upholstr, res. 521 Main.
Basten Joseph, saloon, 225 N. Washington, res. same.
Basteyns Alphons, lab., res. s. s. Duck Creek rd., 3 w. Mather, Ft. H.

Bates John, drayman, res. 620 S. Jackson.
Bates Warren, asst.-engineer, res. 607 S. Adams.
Bates William, dockmaster, res. 620 S. Jackson.
Bates Zachary T. (McCormick & Bates), res. 620 S. Jackson.
Bauer Julius A., cooper, res. 727 Harvey.
**BAUM JOHN**, dry goods, 701-703 Main, res. 416 N. Quincy.
Bauman William, coachman, res. 1015 S. Monroe av.
Baumann Katie, domestic 108 S. Jefferson.
Baumgardner Charles, teamster, res. 310 S. Quincy.
**BAY CITY HOUSE**, Konrad Silbersdorf, prop., 100-104 S. Washington.
Bayer. See Beyer.
Beach Fred. B., brakeman, res. e. s. Cherry, 2 s. Dousman, Ft. H.
Beach George, barber, 1119 Main, res. Flintville.
Beach Omer, barn boss, res. 415 Main.
Beacham Charles, lab., res. 720 Main.
Beahan Bridget Miss, dressmkr, res. 118 N. Monroe av.
Beahan Johanna (wid. Christopher), res. 118 N. Monroe av.
Beahan Kate Miss, dressmkr, res. 715 Pine.
Beahan Maggie Miss, res. 118 N. Monroe av.
Bean George, watchman, res. Ferris Hotel, Ft. H.
Bean J. C. E., res. Odd Fellows' Home.
Beard George F., machinist, res. 514 Walnut.
Beattie Frank Miss, res. 117 Broadway, Ft. H.
Beattie Marguerite Miss, res. 117 Broadway, Ft. H.
Beaudwin Emma Miss, res. 901 Pine.
Beaumont Ethan A., express messenger, res. 533 S. Quincy.
Beaumont Israel G., res. 203 S. Jefferson.
Beaumont Julia Miss, teacher, res. 203 S. Jefferson.
Beaumont May Miss, res. 203 S. Jefferson.
Beaumont Sophia Miss, clk., res. 203 S. Jefferson.
**BEAUMONT THE**, Capt. A. W. Powers, prop., Main, n. e. cor. N. Washington.
Beaupre William, oculist, 121 N. Washington, res. Charles House
Bebeau Joseph, bridge carp., res. w. s. 6th av., 2 s. Bridge, Ft. H.
Becher Anna (wid. Josef), res. s. w. cor. Manitowoc rd. and Finger rd.
**BECK H. MAX**, physician and surgeon, 209 N. Washington, res. 723 Cherry.
Becker Ernst, mach., res. 147 Broadway, Ft. H.
Becker John, gardener, res. 509 Broadway, Ft. H.
Becker Mary, domestic Schauer Hotel.
Becker, see Baker.
Beerotsen Henry, grocer, 1221 Crooks, res. same.

**THE A. SPUHLER CO.** *LADIES', MISSES' and CHILDREN'S* **CLOAKS, CAPES, JACKETS**
GREEN BAY

Beerntsen Lizzie, clk., res. 1400 Mason.
Beerntsen Wm., carp. contr., n. s. Emilie, nr. Baird, res. same.
Befay Dennis, supt. mail-carriers, P. O., res. 527 School.
Befay Leona (wid. Joseph), res. 2 w. 929 Dousman, Ft. H.
Behrend Gustave, painter, res. American House.
Behrendt Adolph, stripper, res. 1132 S. Quincy.
Behrendt Albert, packer, res. 1137 S. Monroe av.
Behrendt Augusta Miss, seamstress, res. 1137 S. Monroe av.
Behrendt Charles, lab., res. 204 7th av., Ft. H.
Behrendt Charles, machinist, res. 1132 S. Quincy.
Behrendt Ernst, cabinetmkr, res. s. s. 5th, 1 w. 7th av., Ft. H.
Behrendt Ferdinand, lab., res. s. s. 5th, 1 w. 7th av., Ft. H.
Behrendt Frederick, cabinetmkr, res. s. s. 5th, 1 w. 7th av., Ft. H.
Behrendt Herman, carsmith, res. 1137 S. Monroe av.
Behrendt Otto, lab., res. 1132 S. Quincy.
Belanger Isaac, lab., res. 1284 Cedar.
Belanger Noah, res. 1168 Walnut.
Bell Horace M., supt. C., M. & St. P. Ry., res. 208 S. Adams.
Bell Marguerite (wid. William), res. 205 Chestnut, Ft. H.
Bell May, res. 224 N. Adams.
Bell Samuel A., teller The Kellogg Nat. Bank, res. 205 Chestnut, Ft. H.
Bender C. Joseph, clk., res. 724 Walnut.
Bender Elizabeth (wid. Charles J.), res. 724 Walnut.
Bender Frank C., clk. 124 S. Washington, res. 724 Walnut.
Bender Jacob, horse-shoer, res. 724 Walnut.
**BENDER SEBASTIAN**, saloon and mngr. Klaus Opera House, 226 Pine, res. 228 Pine.
Benedix Edward, teamster, res. 412 Broadway, Ft. H.
Benedix Ida Miss, res. 412 Broadway, Ft. H.
Benedix Paul, lab., res. 412 Broadway, Ft. H.
Benefiel James F., loco.-engineer, res. 215 Stuart.
**BENENG CHARLES**, whol. dlr. pure grape wines, 1115 Main, res. same.
Beneng Josie, dressmkr, 1115 Main, res. same.
Bennett Alexander, ry. hand, res. e. s. 10th av., 2 n. 3d, Ft. H.
Bennett E. P., lab., res. Bradley House.
Bennett Elizabeth (wid. Thomas), res. 840 S. Madison.
Bennett Martha Miss, res. 701 4th av., Ft. H.
Bennett Samuel W., engineer, res. 701 4th av., Ft. H.
Bense Albert, lab., res. 619 Main.
Bensel Gustave, grain-buyer J. H. Ebeling, res. 1 w. 866 Dousman, Ft. H.

Bensel Martha L. Miss, clk. Jorgensen, Blesch Co., res. 1 w. 866 Dousman, Ft. H.
Benson Alexander, tailor Wm. Hoffman, res. 14 Parmentier blk.
Benson Emma (wid. Schuyler B.), res. 827 S. Monroe av.
Bentheimer Auguste (wid. John), dressmkr. res. 1403 Cedar.
Bentheimer George, butcher, res. 1249 Main.
Benthin Henry, porter 124 S. Washington, res. 1133 S. Monroe av.
Benthin John, lab., res. 1102 S. Jackson.
Benthin Joseph, section hand, res. 1133 S. Monroe av.
Benthin Lizzie Miss, res. 1133 S. Monroe av.
Benthin William, cigarmkr, res. 1133 S. Monroe av.
Benthin William, cigarmkr, res. 1102 S. Jackson.
Benthin William, switchman, res. Ferris Hotel, Ft. H.
Bently George W., carp., res. 708 2d, Ft. H.
Bently Pearl Miss, res. 708 2d, Ft. H.
Benton Perry T., supt. Business Practice Dept. Green Bay Business College, res. 709 S. Jefferson.
Berceau Felix, lab., res. 714 N. 12th.
Berceau Octave, lab., res. 629 N. 12th.
Berceau Simeon, res. 725 N. 12th.
Berceau Thimean, lab., res. 726 N. 12th.
Berendsen Alphons, ship clk., res. 416 S. Quincy.
Berendsen Barbara Miss, clk., res. 408 S. Quincy.
Berendsen Bernard M., res. 408 S. Quincy.
Berendsen Celin Miss, res. 408 S. Quincy.
Berendsen Charles, tailor, res. 408 S. Quincy.
Berendsen Henry T. E., res. 416 S. Quincy.
Berendsen Joseph J., boxmkr, res. 519 Chicago.
Berendsen Louis B., boxmkr, res. 519 Chicago.
Berendsen Mary Miss, res. 408 S. Quincy.
Berendsen Rosie Miss, res. 408 S. Quincy.
Berendsen William, printer, res. 416 S. Quincy.
Berendsen, see Beerntsen.
Berens Frederick, gen. mdse., 933-935 Walnut. res. 109 N. Webster av.
Berge Peter, conductor street car, res. 227 Cherry.
Berger Elizabeth Miss, dressmaker, res. 528 St. George.
Berger Margaret Miss, dressmaker, res. 528 St. George.
Berger Maria (wid. Desire), res. 528 St. George.
Bergin Peter J., engineer C., M. & St. P. R. R., res. 416 Walnut.
Bergmann Margaretha (wid. Julius F.), res. 410 2d, Ft. H.
Beriault Adolphus, cook, res. Columbia Hotel.
Beriault Fred., cook, res. Columbia Hotel.
Bernard Nancy (wid. John), res. s. w. cor. N. Madison and Pine.

Berner Charles, sec. and treas. Green Bay Dredging & Pile Driving Co., res. 218 N. Jefferson.
Berns Augusta, confectr., res. 1175 Stuart.
Berns Katie, confectr., res. 1175 Stuart.
Berns Mary (wid. James), res. 1175 Stuart.
Bero Joseph, barkpr., res. 216 N. Washington.
Bero Victoria, waitress Bodart House.
Bersie Arthur, teamster, res. 202 Cedar, Ft. H.
Bersie Bertie, barber, res. 202 Cedar, Ft. H.
Bersie Chas. H., brakeman C., M. & St. P. Ry., res. 825 Crooks.
Bersie Effie E. Miss, res. 116 Cedar, Ft. H.
Bersie Eliza (wid. Benjamin), res. 944 S. Quincy.
Bersie Elmer E., mngr. Star Trombone Band, res. 944 S. Quincy.
Bersie Florence Miss, res. 944 S. Quincy.
Bersie Gertrude M. Miss, res. 944 S. Quincy.
Bersie Philmea Mrs., res. 116 Cedar, Ft. H.
Bersie Samuel, res. 202 Cedar, Ft. H.
Bersie Samuel Jr., brakeman, res. 202 Cedar, Ft. H.
Bersie William, saw-filer, res. 114 Chestnut, Ft. H.
Bersie William A., brakeman, res. 944 S. Quincy.
Bertles Annie Miss, res. 926 S. Monroe av.
Bertles John F., sewing machines, 107 S. Washington, res. 926 S. Monroe av.
Bertles John F. Jr., clk. 107 S. Washington, res. 926 S. Monroe av.
Bertles Mary I. Miss, res. 926 S. Monroe av.
Bertram Alexander, res. The Beaumont.
Bertram Annie Miss, clk., res. 115 N. Adams.
Bertrand Joseph, barkpr. Cook's Hotel.
Bessanson Jerome, lab., res. s. s. Willow, 2 w. Pleasant.
Bessanson Peter, shepherd, res. 1411 Elm.
Best Louis, res. 732 Main.
Best T. Lyman, salesman The A. Spuhler Co., res. 732 Main.
Beth Anna M. Miss, res. 400 S. Monroe av.
Beth Conrad (John Beth & Son), res. 116 S. Monroe av.
Beth Frank J., clk. B. Fontaine Hardware Co., res. 1108 Walnut.
Beth Fred, delivery clk., res. 400 S. Monroe av.
Beth Henry, lab., res. 1173 Walnut.
Beth Jacob, plasterer, res. 700 N. 12th.
Beth John (John Beth & Son), res. 400 S. Monroe av.
Beth John Jr., plasterer, res. 529 N. 12th.
Beth John Valentine, clk. J. Beth & Son, res. 714 Doty.
**BETH JOHN & SON** (John and Conrad Beth), whol. and retail grocers, 315-319 N. Washington.
Beth Joseph, grocer, 1303 Walnut, res. same.

Beth Joseph, Jr., res. 1303 Walnut.
Beth Minnie, clk., res. 1303 Walnut.
Beth Rosie Miss, res. 1303 Walnut.
Beth Theodor J., plasterer, res. 1335 Cedar.
Bevers Bernhard, lab., res. 1249 Doty.
Bevers Cornelius, lab., res. 1245 Doty.
Bevers John, lab., res. 1245 Doty.
Bevier John W., tel. opr. Western Union, res. Huffman House, Ft. H.
Bey Charles G., teamster, res. 620 Cedar.
Bey George A., delivery clk. Hagemeister Brewing Co., res. 614 Cedar.
Beyer George, v.-pres. Fort Howard Lumber Co., res. Oconto.
Beyer Joseph, call-boy, res. 1121 S. Quincy.
Beyer Lizzie Miss, res. 1121 S. Quincy.
Beyer Michael, brewer, res. 1121 S. Quincy.
Beyer Michael Jr., bedmkr, res. 1121 S. Quincy.
Bhirdo Ida Miss, res. Columbia Hotel.
Bhirdo Peter, prop. Columbia Hotel, res. same.
Bibel Frank, saloon, n. w. cor. Manitowoc rd. and Charles, res. same.
Bibel John, lab., res. n. w. cor. Manitowoc rd. and Charles.
Bibel Katie Miss, res. n. w. cor. Manitowoc rd. and Charles.
Bibel Rosie (wid. Josef), res. 1634 Elm.
Bibo John B., lab., res. 803 Day.
Bidoul John, saloon, 705 Main, res. same.
Biehl Frank, res. 313 Cherry, Ft. H.
Biehl Lawrence, res. 313 Cherry, Ft. H.
Biemeret Alex., delivery clk. Brauns & Van, res. 1113 Cherry.
Biemeret Felix, timekpr., res. 610 St. George.
Biemeret Gabriel, janitor county court house, res. 610 St. George.
Biemeret Gregoir, lab., res. 618 St. George.
Biemeret Josephine (wid. John), res. 1113 Cherry.
Biemeret Josephine (wid. Peter), res. 1120 Cherry.
Biemeret Peter, lab., res. 618 St. George.
Biensen Martin, lab., res. 428 Pleasant.
Bierke Ferdinand (Mueller Bros. & Co.), res. 1200 Doty.
Bierke Gottfried, res. 1200 Doty.
Bierman Einor, clk., res. 203 Cherry, Ft. H.
Bigdall Emma Miss, teacher, res. w. s. Rich rd., 3 s. 9th, Ft. H.
Bigdall George, farmer, res. w. s. Rich rd., 3 s. 9th, Ft. H.
Billion John, lab., res. 318 N. Adams.
Bills Henry, compositor, res. 309 Pearl, Ft. H.
Binquart Charles, carpenter, res. 1306 Main.

**THE A. SPUHLER CO.**, GREEN BAY, WIS. **Fine Dress Goods**
Samples Furnished on Application.

BIN 69 BLE

Bins Frederick, teamster, res. 227 S. Quincy.
Bins Jacob, lab., res. 1374 Stuart.
Bins Lizzie, domestic 415 Crooks.
Birmeister Ida, domestic 129 S. Adams.
Birmingham Wm., saloon, 322 N. Washington, res. same.
Bitteau Mary, domestic 508 Walnut.
Bischinger John, brewer, res. town Preble.
Bishop Louis, lab., res. No. 5, n. end Monroe av., e. Murphy's Mill.
Bitter C. Henry, foreman car dept. C., M. & St. P. R. R., res. 811 3d av., Ft. H.
Bitter Christian H., carp., res. w. s. 2d av., 4 s. 8th, Ft. H.
Bitter Henry, patternmkr. res. 203 Baird, Ft. H.
Bitter Ida Miss, res. 203 Baird, Ft. H.
Bitter Mary, midwife, 203 Baird, res. same, Ft. H.
Bitter John H., res. w. s. 2d av., 4 s. 8th, Ft. H.
Bitting E. E., com. trav. Columbian Baking Co., res. Marquette, Mich.
Black Agnes, student, res. 306 2d, Ft. H.
Black Christian, section boss, res. 413 2d, Ft. H.
**BLACK JAMES J.**, livery, 3d av. nr. Broadway bridge, res. 410 2d, Ft. H.
Black Mary Miss, teacher, res. 306 2d, Ft. H.
Black Robert J., cattle-dlr., res. 306 2d, Ft. H.
Blackman Hattie M. Miss, dressmkr, res. 504 Moravian.
Blahnik Anton, lab., res. 1257 Crooks.
Blahnik Frank, watchman, res. 700 3d av., Ft. H.
Blahnik Mathias, lab., res. 700 3d av., Ft. H.
Blair Charles H., blksmith, res. w. s. 9th av., 2 n. 3d, Ft. H.
Blair Rebecca Miss, res. w. s. 9th av., 2 n. 3d, Ft. H.
Blanake Annie, domestic, 1130 Main.
Blandin Frank, restaurant, 222 Pine, res. same.
Blaney Catherine (wid. Peter), res. 608 Cherry, Ft. H.
Blaney Lucy, housekpr. The Beaumont.
Blaney Wm., barkpr. Broadway House, res. 608 Cherry, Ft. H.
Blank Emil, butcher, res. 821 Walnut.
Blase Frank, clk. Charles House, res. same.
Blazinski Nic, mason, res. Coopertown House.
Blesch Andrew, com. merchant, 717 Main, res. same.
Blesch Andrew C., fireman, res. 717 Main.
Blesch Antoinette (wid. Francis), res. 325 Willow, Ft. H.
Blesch Frank, engineer G. B. Hess Co., res. 717 Main.
Blesch Frank T., sec. and treas. Jorgensen Blesch Co., res. 325 Willow, Ft. H.

Blesch Louise A. Miss, music teacher, 325 Willow, Ft. H., res. same.
**BLIEDUNG CARL**, druggist, 215 Cherry, res. 217 S. Adams.
Bliedung Ella Miss, res. 217 S. Adams.
Blodgett Anna (wid. James), res. s. e. cor. 4th av. and 9th, Ft. H.
Blodgett Charles, lab., res. s. e. cor. 4th av. and 9th, Ft. H.
Blodgett Joseph, carp., res. s. e. cor. 4th av. and 9th, Ft. H.
Blodgett Marie, domestic 801 Cedar, Ft. H.
Blondin John, lab., res. 416 N. Madison.
Boaler Edwin, whol. fish, n. s. Willow, bet. Madison and Jefferson, res. 222 S. Jefferson.
Boaler Frank, student, res. 222 S. Jefferson.
Bockberger Joseph, lab., res. 303 N. Jefferson.
Bodart Adolph, lab., res. 517 Cedar.
**BODART AUGUST**, prop. Bodart House, 319 Main, res. same.
Bodart Eliza (wid. Jos.), res. 1114 Walnut.
Bodart Frank, fireman Hose No. 2, res. 1026 Main.
Bodart Henry, saloon, 702 Main, res. same.
**BODART HOUSE**, August Bodart, prop., 319 Main.
Bodart William, lab., res. 517 Cedar.
Bodoh Agnes Mrs., confectionery, 207 Chicago, res. same.
Bodoh Julius, teamster, res. 207 Chicago.
Bodoh Julius, Jr., lab., res. 207 Chicago.
Boen Charles W., fireman, res. Junction Hotel, Ft. H.
Boersch Sam., lab., res. 1424 Willow.
Boeth Fred., night porter, The Beaumont.
Bogan Wm., cook, The Beaumont.
Bogart Henrietta (wid. Richard), res. 427 S. Madison.
Bogewang Hans, painter, res. 105 4th av., Ft. H.
Boggs Samuel, saloon, s. w. cor. Manitowoc rd. and Finger rd.
Bohne Julia, domestic Bay City House.
Boileau Joseph, barber, S. Washington, n. e. cor. Stuart, res. 331 Chicago.
Boileau Moses, janitor St. John's school, res. 331 Chicago.
**BOLAND EDMUND P.**, real estate, P. O. blk., res. 505 Broadway, Ft. H.
Bolina Martin, lab., res. 1160 Crooks.
Bolton Bridget, domestic 702 S. Monroe av.
Bomber Joseph, grocer, 801 Harvey, res. same.
Bomber Samuel, clk. 801 Harvey, res. same.
Bon Lincoln L., conductor, res. 316 Mason.
Bonesho John, machine agt. res. Schauer Hotel.

**Headquarters for Boys' Clothing** THE A. SPUHLER CO. GREEN BAY.

Bong Annie, clk. Jorgensen Biesch Co., res. 301 S. Quincy.
Bong Gerhard, res. 301 S. Quincy.
Bong Gerhard J., clk. 312 N. Washington, res. 301 S. Quincy.
Bong John G., clk., res. 301 S. Quincy.
Bonne Frank, lab., res. 1180 Stuart.
Boonie Louis, carp., res. Willmar House.
Borman Joseph, flour packer, res. 312 S. 10th.
Bornheimer Fred, tel.-opr., res. 106 N. Monroe av.
Bornheimer Gertie Miss, tel.-opr., res. 106 N. Monroe av.
Borowich Adam, lab., res. 1180 Stuart.
Borofke Katie, domestic 316 Main.
Borremans Frank, lab., res. 5 w. 874 Dousman, Ft. H.
Borremans Fred, lab., res. s. s. Dousman, 3 e. C., M. & St. P. R'y track, Ft. H.
Borremans Joseph, clk. Peter Devroys, res. 702 Division, Ft. H.
Borremans Joseph, lab., res. 5 w. 874 Dousman, Ft. H.
Borremans Mary Miss, res. 5 w. 874 Dousman, Ft. H.
Borremans Peter, gardener, res. 5 w. 874 Dousman, Ft. H.
Boss Daniel, lab., res. 1200 Walnut.
Boss George W., train-dispatcher C., M. & St. P. Ry., res. 318 S. Jefferson.
Boss Tessie Miss, res. 1200 Walnut.
Bosschaerts Chas., lab., res. s. s. Duck Creek, 4 w. Mather, Ft. H.
Bosse Anatole, carp., res. n. s. Elm, nr. N. Jackson.
Bosse Arthur, res. 113 S. Monroe av.
Bosse August, cooper, res. 1112 Crooks.
Bosse Max, bridge-tender, res. 1112 Crooks.
Bosse Nestorine (wid. Constant), res. 113 S. Monroe av.
Bouchard Alfred H., prop. Empire House, res. 203 S. Washington.
Bouchard Anton, barn foreman McDonald's Lumber Yard, res. McQueen's Boarding House, Ft. H.
Bouchard Joseph, clk. Empire House, res. same.
Bouchard Louis, painter, res. 130 S. Webster av.
Boucher Charles, brakeman, res. Broadway House, Ft. H.
Boucher Felix, plasterer, res. 723 Harvey.
Boucher John, carp., res. 1227 Stuart.
Boucher Joseph A., plasterer, res. 1227 Stuart.
Boucher Mary Miss, res. 1227 Stuart.
Boucher Michael, lab., res. 520 S. Quincy.
Boucher Theodore, mason, res. 1264 Doty.
Boulanger Louie, lab., res. Bodart House.
Boulet Charles A., machinist, res. 1127 S. Quincy.
Boulet Charles Joseph, grocer, 431 Mason, res. same.

Boulet Maggie Miss, res. 431 Mason.
Bouman John, lab., res. 1101 S. Webster av.
Bouman Katie Miss, res. 1101 S. Webster av.
Bouman Peter, res. 1101 S. Webster av.
Bouman William, lab., res. 1101 S. Webster av.
Bourdeu Azre, student, res. 418 Cedar.
Bourdeu Exima Miss, res. 418 Cedar.
Bourdeu Georgiana Miss, dressmkr, 418 Cedar, res. same.
Bourdeu Jerry, res. 418 Cedar.
Bourguignon Joseph, lab., res. 1435 Smith.
Boushek Marie, domestic 415 Cherry, Ft. H.
Bowden William, res. 600 Pine.
Bowers Charles, lab., res. 527 S. Van Buren.
Bowers Leslie, loco.-fireman, res. 539 S. Jefferson.
Bowes Daniel W., lumber-scaler, res. 710 Main.
Bowes Theresa Miss, domestic 843 S. Monroe av.
Bows Robert, machinist, res. Bradley House.
Bowser Frederick A., livery, w. s. Broadway, 3 s. Hubbard, res. e. s. Broadway, 3 s. Hubbard, Ft. H.
Boyce Aug., blksmith, res. s. s. Christiania, 2 w. Willow, Ft. H.
Boyce George, clk. M. J. Corbett, res. 109 Broadway, Ft. H.
Boyce Josie Miss, res. 109 Broadway, Ft. H.
Boyce Marguerite (wid. Thomas), res. 109 Broadway, Ft. H.
Boyce Mary Miss, res. 109 Broadway, Ft. H.
Boyle Mary (wid. Michael), res. Bradley House.
Boynton Vincent E., cooper, res. 425 N. Monroe av.
Braasch Casper N., vet. surgeon, 608 S. Madison, res. same.
Braasch Eva Miss, res. 608 S. Madison.
Braasch Fred, painter, res. 608 S. Madison.
Braasch Olive Miss, teacher, res. 608 S. Madison.
Brantz Gustav, lab., res. 1201 Mason.
Brantz Henry, res. 1308 Cherry.
Brantz Herman, machinist, res. 1245 Mason.
Brantz Richard, lab., res. 1245 Mason.
Brantz William, lab., res. 1245 Mason.
**BRADLEY DANIEL P.,** prop. Bradley House, res. 409 S. Washington.
**BRADLEY HOUSE,** Daniel P. Bradley, prop., 409–411 S. Washington.
Bradley Samuel, conductor, res. Cook's Hotel.
Brady Alexis F., instructor Green Bay Athletic Assn., res. 310 Cedar, Ft. H.
Braeger Edward, machinist, res. Commercial Hotel, Ft. H.
Brainard Frank E., drug clk., res. 1012 Cherry.

**THE A. SPUHLER CO.** *LADIES', MISSES' and CHILDREN'S* **CLOAKS, CAPES, JACKETS**
**GREEN BAY**

Brainard Thomas, lab., res. 1012 Cherry.
Brandenstein Charlotte Miss, res. 710 Cherry.
**BRANDENSTEIN WILLIAM A.,** merchant tailor, 311 Cherry, res. 710 Cherry.
Brandt Christian, lab., res. 112 7th av., Ft. H.
Brans Joseph A., cigarmkr, res. 314 Pearl, Ft. H.
Brash Bertha (wid. Edwin), res. 108 S. Madison.
Brash Lizzie Miss, res. 108 S. Madison.
Brauer John, res. 1349 Walnut.
Braun Peter, res. 216 N. Jackson.
**BRAUNS AUGUST,** insurance agt. and county surveyor, 220 N. Washington, res. 401 S. Madison.
Brauns August E. (Brauns & Van) res. 331 S. Adams.
Brauns Lydia Miss, teacher, res. 331 S. Adams.
Brauns Mary M. Mrs., res. 331 S. Adams.
Brauns Otto F., dental student, res. 331 S. Adams.
Brauns & Van (August E. Brauns and Edward Van den Braak), grocers, 203 N. Washington.
Breecher James S., 'bus-driver, res. 215 N. Adams.
Brehme Anton, plumber, 217 Broadway, res. 208 Cherry, Ft. H.
Brehme August (Brehme & Kattner), res. 211 Broadway, Ft. H.
Brehme Caroline Miss, res. w. s. Broadway, 5 s. Main, Ft. H.
Brehme Charles, res. w. s. Pearl, 1st n. John, Ft. H.
Brehme Emma A., bookpr., res. w. s. Broadway, 5 s. Main, Ft. H.
**BREHME HERMAN E.,** grocer, 215 Main, res. 136 Chestnut., Ft. H.
Brehme & Kattner (August Brehme and Carl Kattner), wagonmkrs and blksmiths, 207-209 Broadway, Ft. H.
Brehmer Otto, mason, res. 1124 Cherry.
Brenner William, foreman J. P. Annen Candy Co., res. 900 S. Van Buren.
Bresnahan Catherine, clk. Jorgensen Blesch Co., res. 224 S. Adams.
Bresters Annie, domestic 324 S. Adams.
Brett Annie E. Miss, res. 231 S. Jefferson.
**BRETT BEN. C.,** physician and surgeon, 124 N. Adams, telephone 11-2 rings, res. 231 S. Jefferson, telephone 11-3 rings.
Brett Fred. N., medical student, res. 231 S. Jefferson.
Brett James, student, res. 231 S. Jefferson.
Brett Jennie M. Miss, res. 231 S. Jefferson.
Brett John, fireman, res. Arlington Hotel, Ft. H.
Brevig Peter E., shoemkr. 401 24, Ft. H., res. same.
Breyer Paul, res. 720 St. George.
Brezner Catherine (wid. John), res. s. w. cor. 9th and 4th av., Ft. H.

Brezner Catherine Miss, res. s. w. cor. 9th and 4th av., Ft. H.
Brezner Emma Miss, res. s. w. cor. 9th and 4th av., Ft. H.
Brezner Frank, farmer, res. s. w. cor. 9th and 4th av., Ft. H.
Brezner John, mill-hand, res. s. w. cor. 9th and 4th av., Ft. H.
Brezner Josephine Miss, res. s. w. cor. 9th and 4th av., Ft. H.
Brice Albert J., fireman Hose No. 2, res. 1122 Cedar.
Brice Cecil M. Miss, cashier I. B. Lineuthal, res. 1009 Walnut.
Brice Emil A., painter, res. 1009 Walnut.
Brice Frank W., police, res. 1253 Stuart.
Brice John, painter, res. 314 Cedar.
Brice Joseph, paper-hanger, res. 1502 Cedar.
Brice Louis C., painter, 1253 Stuart, res. same.
Brice Martha Miss, dressmkr, res. 1253 Stuart.
**BRICE OCTAVIEN J. B.,** Belgian Consul for Wisconsin, Minnesota and N. and S. Dakota, ocean steamship tickets, collection, real estate and insurance agt., 35 Parmentier blk., res. 443 S. Monroe av.
Brice Roland, painter, res. 1009 Walnut.
Brick Mary, domestic 309 N. Webster av.
Brighton John, lab., res. 315 S. Adams.
Brinneham Annie, waitress Columbia Hotel.
Brinneman Henry (Brinneman & La Chapelle), res. 520 Main.
Brinneman & La Chapelle (Henry Brinneman and Jos. La Chapelle), horseshoers, 509 Main.
Briquelet James, conductor, res. Charles House.
Briquelet John, res. American House.
Briquelet Joseph, farmer, res. e. s. De Pere rd., 1 n. Hochgreve Brewery.
Briquelet Virginia Miss, clk. Jorgensen Bleach Co., res. cor. N. Madison and Cedar.
Brisk Charles G., blksmith, res. 500 5th av., Ft. H.
Bristol John, clk., res. 814 Pine.
Britton Andrew J., farmer, res. n. s. 2d, S w. R. R. track, Ft. H.
**BRITTON DAVID W.,** mnfr. of cooperage, office, mill and shops n. end N. Monroe av., res. 614 Main.
Britton Elmer E. W., foreman D. W. Britton, res. 429 N. Monroe av.
**BROADWAY HOUSE,** Nicholas J. Terry prop., n. w. cor. Broadway and Dousman, Ft. H.
Brocki Frank, lab., res. Coopertown House.
Brodersen Katie, domestic 617 Chestnut, Ft. H.
Broeckl Franceska (wid. William), res. 1133 Walnut.
Brossig Herman, lab., res. 1119 Doty.
Brossig Max (Brossig & Klesse), res. Sturg. Bay rd., e. city limits

**THE A. SPUHLER CO., Green Bay** CARPETS, RUGS, OIL CLOTHS,
Draperies and Window Shades.

BROSSIG & KLESSE (Max Brossig and Bruno Klesse), potash mnfrs., Sturgeon Bay rd., e. city limits.
Brosteau Julia Mrs., res. 1209 Mason.
Brown County Fair and Park Assn., Henry Hagemeister, pres.; D. W. Flatley, sec.; H. B. Baker, treas., office 202 N. Adams.
Brown County Horticultural and Agricultural Society, J. D. McAllister, pres.; Miss H. Dickey, sec. and treas.; P. O. bldg.
Brown Edward, pres. Brown-Chapin Lumber Co., res. Chicago, Ill.
Brown Henry, farmer, res. n. s. Willow, 2 w. 12th.
Brown Henry Jr., painter, res. n. s. Willow, 2 w. 12th.
Brown John, com. trav., res. 724 Pine.
Brown Kate Mrs., cook Odd Fellows' Home.
Brown Peter, conductor, res. 303 3d, Ft. H.
Brown Robert, machinist, res. 411 S. Washington.
Brown Samuel A. (Brown & Tickler), res. 538 S. Jackson.
Brown Samuel C. Mrs., res. 427 S. Madison.
Brown Sanford, fisherman, res. s. e. cor. Cedar and Mather, Ft. H.
Brown Wallace, fisherman, res. s. e. cor. Cedar and Mather, Ft. H.
Brown William O., prin. High School, res. 309 S. Monroe av.
Brown & Tickler (Samuel A. Brown and Peter L. Tickler), hardware, 208 3d av., Ft. H.
Brown-Chapin Lumber Co., Edward Brown, pres.; R. L. Chapin, v.-pres. and treas.; s. w. cor. 2d av. and 10th, Ft. H.
Brown. See Braun and Brauns.
Browning Roy, brakeman, res. 636 S. Madison.
Broze Clara, domestic 1100 Main.
Brozzel Henry, engineer, res. Northwestern Hotel, Ft. H.
Bruce Arthur, clk. F. W. Basche, res. Huffman House, Ft. H.
Bruck Jacob, barn boss, res. Reis Hotel.
Brueckner Annie, laundress The Beaumont.
Brueckner Elizabeth (wid. Christian H.), res. w. s. 6th av., 1 s. 3d, Ft. H.
Brueckner Fredericka (wid. George), res. 232 S. Van Buren.
Brueckner Henry, butcher, res. 406 2d, Ft. H.
Brueckner Herman, painter, res. w. s. 6th av., 1 s. 3d, Ft. H.
Brueckner John, cabinetmkr, res. w. s. 6th av., 1 s. 3d, Ft. H.
Brueckner John, res. 817 N. 12th.
Brueggemann Eliza (wid. William), res. 1415 Mason.
Brueggemann John, lab., res. 1415 Mason.
Brueggemann Peter, painter, res. 1415 Mason.
Brunette Charlotte Miss, res. e. s. 5th av., 2 n. 10th, Ft. H.

Brunette David, res. e. s. 5th av., 2 n. 10th, Ft. H.
Brunette Elmer, lab., res. w. s. 2d av., 2 s. 10th, Ft. H.
Brunette Gustav, lab., res. w. s. 7th av., 1 s. 9th, Ft. H.
Brunette John, blksmith, res. 400 2d, Ft. H.
Brunette John, farmer, res. w. s. 2d av., 2 s. 10th, Ft. H.
Brunette John, lab., res. 616 St. George.
Brunette John, lab., res. e. s. 5th av., 2 n. 10th, Ft. H.
Brunette Joseph, lab., res. e. s. 5th av., 2 n. 10th, Ft. H.
Brunette Joseph, lab., res. w. s. 7th av., 1 s. 9th, Ft. H.
Brunette Martin, lab., res. e. s. 5th av., 2 n. 10th, Ft. H.
Brunette Walter, lab., res. w. s. 2d av., 2 s. 10th, Ft. H.
Brunette William, lab., res. w. s. 7th av., 1 s. 9th, Ft. H.
Brunner Barbara Miss, dressmkr, res. 409 S. Madison.
Brunner Joseph, clk. 312 N. Washington, res. 409 S. Madison.
Bruyere Alex. A., rec.-clk. 124 S. Washington, res. 908 Pine.
Bruyere August, lab., res. 711 N. 12th.
Bruyere Charles, clk., res. 1419 Main.
Bruyere Clara Miss, res. 700 St. George.
Bruyere Joseph, grocer, 1132 Cherry, res. same.
Bruyere Joseph G., lab., res. 1132 Cherry.
Bruyere Leopold, res. 700 St. George.
Buchanan Mary Mrs., res. Odd Fellows' Home.
Buchberger Joseph, deliveryman Green Bay Creamery Co., res. n. w. cor. N. Jefferson and Pine.
Buchenville Octavia, domestic 316 N. Van Buren.
Buchholz Gottfried, machinist, res. n. w. cor. Elmore and Cedar, Ft. H.
**BUCK CARLOS C.**, architect, Citizens' Nat. Bank blk., res. 714 Walnut.
Buckley Fred., baker, res. Adams House.
Buckman Horace H., cabinetmkr., res. 400 Cherry, Ft. H.
Budzis John, fisherman, res. w. s. McDonald, 3 s. lumber yard, Ft. H.
Buengener August (Buengener & Bur), res. 512 Cherry.
**BUENGENER & BUR** (August Buengener and Nicholas Bur, Jr.), whol. and retail grocers, 117-119 N. Washington.
**BUENGER HERMAN C.**, cigarmkr, 312 Cedar, Ft. H., res. same.
Buerschinger George, barber, res. 814 Pine.
Buerschinger John, clk. 312 N. Washington, res. 814 Pine.
Bullert Fred., lab., res. Junction House, Ft. H.
**BUNKER A. CYRILLE**, saloon, 224 Main, res. same.
Bunker George, bartender, res. 224 Main.
Buntin William H., conductor, res. 433 S. Quincy.

**THE A. SPUHLER CO., GREEN BAY, WIS.** **Fine Dress Goods**
Samples Furnished on Application.

Bur Nicholas, Sr., res. 123 S. Van Buren.
Bur Nicholas, Jr. (Buengener & Bur), res. 117 S. Van **Buren**.
Burdick Eugene, horse-trainer, res. 415 Main.
**BURDON ROWLAND T.**, real estate and insurance, 207 N. Washington, res. 204 S. Madison.
Buresh John, lab., res. 1284 Cedar.
Burghardt Frank (Burghardt & Duchateau), res. 322 N. Monroe av.
**BURGHARDT & DUCHATEAU** (Frank Burghardt and Theofil E. Duchateau), meatmkt, 505 Main.
Burkard Aggie Miss, res. 1342 Crooks.
Burkard Anna C. Miss, dressmkr, res. 927 Cherry.
Burkard Catherine (wid. Fred.) res. 927 Cherry.
**BURKARD JOHN E.** (Wuertz & Burkard), res. 927 Cherry
Burkard Joseph, lab., res. 1342 Crooks.
Burkard Joseph, wagonmkr, res. n. s. Elm, 2 e. Forest.
Burkard Rose, stenog., res. 927 Cherry.
Burkart Lizzie Miss, res. 802 Cherry.
Barkart Mary (wid. Anton), res. 802 Cherry.
Burkart Philip S., painter, res. 909 Pine.
Burke Andrew, beer-peddler Hochgreve Brewing **Co., res. w. s.** Monroe av. rd., 2¼ miles s. city limits.
Burke Charles, flagman, res. 505 Broadway Ft. H.
Burke Jerry, flagman, res. 505 Broadway, Ft. H.
Burke Martin, lab., res. Green Bay House.
Burke Peter, cooper, res. 418 N. Madison.
Burkley Charles H., hackdriver, res. 537 S. Monroe av.
Burkley George, hackdriver, res. 537 S. Monroe av.
Burlingame Charles, engineer, res. 445 S. Adams.
Burmann Dina (wid. Henry), res. 305 S. Van Buren.
Burmann Henry, lab., res. 305 S. Van Buren.
Burmeister Charles, brakeman, res. 209 Willow, Ft. H.
Burmeister Henry, tailor, res. s. s. Mather, 1 w. Willow, Ft. H.
Burnett John S., lab., res. n. w. cor. 4th av. and 2d, Ft. H.
Burnette Franklin E., carp., res. e. s. S. Monroe av. nr. city limits.
Burnham Emmons B., carp., res. 806 Cherry, Ft. H.
Burns Alex. B. (D. M. Burns & Son), res. s.w. cor. Chestnut and Hubbard, Ft. H.
Burns Annie, waitress Reis Hotel.
Burns Charles E., bkpr., res. 321 Chestnut, Ft. H.
Burns Daniel, carsmith, res. w s. 11th av., nr. G. **B., W. & St.** P. shops, Ft. H.
Burns D. M. & Son (David M. Burns and Alex. B. Burns), boiler works, e. s. Pearl, 1st and 3d s. Main, Ft. H.

Burns David M. (D. M. Burns & Son), res. s. w. cor. Chestnut and Hubbard, Ft. H.
Burns Emma, cook Reis Hotel.
Burns Frank, lab., res. w. s. 11th av., nr. Green Bay, W. & St. P. R. R. shops, Ft. H.
Burns James, fireman, res. Northwestern Hotel, Ft. H.
Burns John, lab., res. w. s. 11th av., nr. G. B., W. & St. P. R. R. shops, Ft. H.
Burns Joseph, lab., res. w. s. 11th av., nr. G. B., W. & St. P. R. R. shops, Ft. H.
Burns Maud Miss, res. 306 Cherry, Ft. H.
Burns May L. Miss, teacher, res. 306 Cherry, Ft. H.
Burns Patrick J., plumber, res. 316 Main.
Burns Rose Miss, res. 407 Broadway, Ft. H.
Burns Thomas, res. 407 Broadway, Ft. H.
Burns Thomas H., hardware, 111 N. Broadway, res. 306 Cherry, Ft. H.
Burns W. H., operator, res. Huffman House, Ft. H.
Burschinger Anton, machinist, res. 413 3d, Ft. H.
Burschinger Marie Miss, res. 413 3d, Ft. H.
Burschinger Peter, carp., res. 413 3d, Ft. H.
Burt William W., barber, res. 221 N. Adams.
Burton Amzi W., superintendent of schools, res. 415 Cherry, Ft. H.
Burton H. C., tallyman, res. Eldred's boarding house, Ft. H.
Burton William G., farmer, res. 102 Cedar, Ft. H.
Busch Emma Miss, res. 226 S. Madison.
Busch Jacob, clk. F. Coel & Son, res. 321 Webster av.
Busch Joseph, fireman, res. 638 S. Jefferson.
Busch Louis, meatmkt, 1249 Main, res. same.
Busche Joseph, lab., res. 715 S. Adams.
Buscher Clara, clk. Brauns & Van, res. 330 S. Washington.
Buscher Hannah Miss, clk. The A. Spuhler Co., res. 330 S. Washington.
Buscher Ida Miss, res. 330 S. Washington.
**BUSCHER JOSUA**, dyer, 330 S. Washington, res. same.
Bush Wilber, sawyer, res. s. w. cor. Dousman and Cherry, Ft. H.
Bushie Laura, cook Coopertown House.
Butler W. Seymour, salesman Jorgensen Blesch Co., res. 508 Walnut.
Butternovich Julia, domestic 415 S. Monroe av.
Bygdall George, farmer, res. w. s. Rich rd., 2 s. 9th, Ft. H.
Byram Charles, porter, res. 212 Doty.
Byram George, miller J. H. Ebeling, res. 212 Doty.

**Headquarters for Boys' Clothing** THE A. SPUHLER CO. GREEN BAY.

Byrne James, lab., res. w. s. Pearl, 2 s. Hubbard, Ft. H.
Bystrom Charles, blksmith, res. 315 7th av., Ft. H.

## C

CADIEUX George, cooper, res. 1221 Walnut.
Cady Fred. C. (Cady & Huntington), res. 702 S. Webster av.
Cady & Huntington (Fred. C. Cady and Solomon P. Huntington), lawyers, 205 N. Washington.
Caesar Simon, res. 1004 Dousman, Ft. H.
Caesar Stephan, lab., res. 1004 Dousman, Ft. H.
Caffery Peter C., fireman, res. 107 Broadway, Ft. H.
Cain Patrick, lab., res. w. s. 9th av., 2 n. 24, Ft. H.
Caine Daniel W., conductor, res. 115 6th av., Ft. H.
Cales Charles, res. Bodart House.
Calkins Lafayette A., lawyer, 218 Main, Ft. H., res. 321 Chestnut, Ft. H.
Call J. Bowman, clk. gen. pass. dept. G. B., W. & St. P. R. R., res. 726 Pine.
Call Jennie L. (wid. T. W.), res. 726 Pine.
Callaghan Bros. (Henry J. and Wm. Callaghan), grocers, 212 Main, Ft. H.
Callaghan Henry J. (Callaghan Bros.), res. 504 Chestnut, Ft. H.
Callaghan William (Callaghan Bros.), res. 504 Chestnut, Ft. H.
Callahan John, com. trav. 1155 Main, res. 1280 Walnut.
Callahan Joseph W., pres. Green Bay Plumbing & Heating Co., res. 19 Parmentier block.
Callahan William, del. clk. Hagemeister Brewing Co., res. 1254 Cherry.
Calowski Emma, domestic Junction Hotel, Ft. H.
Camm Edith M. Miss, music teacher, res. 318 Main, Ft. H.
Camm Herbert F. (Camm & Erbe), res. 318 Main, Ft. H.
Camm Thomas M., grocer, 221 Main, res. 318 Main, Ft. H.
Camm & Erbe (Herbert F. Camm and Henry C. Erbe), insurance and real estate, 312 Main, Ft. H.
Camp Claude, switchman, res. Northwestern Hotel, Ft. H.
Campbell Frank, tallyman, res. 131 S. Van Buren.
Campbell Harry L., res. 131 S. Van Buren.
Campbell H. Porter, city treas., res. 131 S. Van Buren.
Campbell Hiram P., salesman Jorgensen Blesch Co., res. 141 Broadway, Ft. H.
Campbell John, bartender, res. Columbia Hotel.
Campbell John H., res. 131 S. Van Buren.

Campbell Joseph, lumberman, res. n. s. Bond, 4 w. Cedar, Ft. H.
Campbell Louis, res. 913 3d av., Ft. H.
Campbell Maud V. Miss, artist, res. 131 S. Van Buren.
Campbell Samuel P., res. 131 S. Van Buren.
Campbell Thomas, baker, res. 318 N. Quincy.
Campbell William, lab., res. 709 Cherry, Ft. H.
Campschreuer Bernhard, lab., res. s. s. Elmore, 2 w. cross rds., Ft. H.
Campschreuer Edward, cabinetmkr, res. 408 3d, Ft. H.
Campschreuer Grace Miss, dressmkr., res. n. s. Elmore, 7 w. Cedar, Ft. H.
Campschreuer Gracie (wid. William), res. s. s. Elmore, 2 w. cross rds., Ft. H.
Campschreuer John, lumber-grader, res. 408 3d, Ft. H.
Campschreuer Robert, lab., res. n. s. Elmore, 7 w. Cedar, Ft. H.
Cannard John, lab., res. 1364 Elm.
Cannard Joseph, broommkr, res. 1364 Elm.
Cannard Mary (wid. Joseph), res. 1364 Elm.
Cannard Victoria Miss, dressmkr, 1364 Elm, res. same.
Cannon James, lab., res. s. s. 9th, 2 w. C. & N. W. R. R. track, Ft. H.
Capelle John, lab., res. s. s. Dousman, 1 w. 929, Ft. H.
Capelle Joseph, lab., res. s. s. Dousman, 1 w. 929, Ft. H.
Capelle Jules, cooper, res. s. s. Dousman, 1 w. 929, Ft. H.
Carabin Helen (wid. Louis), res. 306 S. Jefferson.
Cardinal Gilbert, teamster, res. Eldred's boarding house, Ft. H.
Carey Frank, teamster, res. Eldred's boarding house, Ft. H.
Carey Michael, teamster, res. Eldred's boarding house, Ft. H.
Carey William, teamster, res. Eldred's boarding house, Ft. H.
Cargill Samuel D. (W. W. Cargill Co.), res. Minneapolis.
**CARGILL W. W. CO.**, W. W. Cargill, pres.; Samuel D. Cargill, v.-pres.; whol. grain and salt, Fox River, n. Dousman, Ft. H.
Cargill William W. (W. W. Cargill Co.), res. La Crosse, Wis.
Carl Mary, domestic 216 S. Jefferson.
Carlin Owen, del.-clk. Jorgensen Blesch Co., res. Empire House.
**CARLIN PATRICK H.**, livery, boarding and sale stable, 103-105 S. Washington, res. 108 S. Quincy.
Carlisle James H., news depot, 315 Broadway, Ft. H. res. same.
Carney John, fireman, res. Broadway House, Ft. H.
Caron Ambrose, res. 103 Hubbard, Ft. H.
Caron Frank N., hair goods, 400 Broadway, Ft. H., res. same.
Carroll Edward J., chief clk. The Beaumont, res. 520 Doty.

**THE A. SPUHLER CO.** *LADIES', MISSES' and CHILDREN'S* **CLOAKS, CAPES, JACKETS**
GREEN BAY

| CAR | 81 | CAY |

Carson Darius, lab., res. e. s. 4th av., 4 s. 7th, Ft. H.
Carstensen Peter, mill hand, res. 312 7th av., Ft. H.
Carter Peter, carp., res. s. s. Dousman, 1 e. M. & N. R. R. track, Ft. H.
Cartier Joseph, brickmkr, res. n. w. cor. Shawano rd. and Fisk, Ft. H.
Cartier Phil., gardener, res. e. s. Oneida, 2 s. Shawano rd., Ft. H.
Carton Joseph, gardener, res. s. s. Elmore, 11 w. Cedar, Ft. H.
Cary Julius, lab., res. 1330 Chicago.
Case John H., mngr. Case & Co., res. 413 S. Madison.
Case & Co. (John H. Case, mngr.), plumbers, 217 N. Adams.
Casey William J., car accountant G. B., W. & St. P. R. R., res. 305 6th av., Ft. H.
Caskey Bertha, domestic 402 S. Adams.
Casper Alice, domestic s. e. cor. Elmore and Broadway, Ft. H.
Casper Lizzie Miss, dressmkr, 228 Pine, res. same.
Casperson Terrill, calker, res. 220 Walnut.
**CASTEELE EDWARD V. D.**, pres. and treas. Standard Printing Co. and editor Ooze Standaard, 315 Cherry, res. Depere, Wis.
Cathersal Frank, grocer, 513 Cedar, Ft. H., res. same.
Cathersal Susan Miss, res. 513 Cedar, Ft. H.
Cathersal Theresa Miss, clk. I. B. Linenthal, res. 513 Cedar, Ft. H.
Catlin Margaret (wid. Theodore), boarding, res. 204 S. Madison.
**CAUWENBERGH BROS.** (Gustav and Joseph Cauwenbergh), druggists, 213 N. Washington.
Cauwenbergh Edward D., teamster, res. 1035 Pine.
Cauwenbergh Eugene, lab., res. n. w. cor. Cherry and Elmore, Ft. H.
Cauwenbergh Fred., teamster, res. 312 N. Adams.
Cauwenbergh Gustav (Cauwenbergh Bros.), res. 405 S. Madison.
Cauwenbergh John, messenger Postal Tel. Cable Co., res. 213 N. Washington.
Cauwenbergh Joseph (Cauwenbergh Bros.). res. 213 N. Washington.
Cauwenbergh Jules, asst. mailing-clk. P. O., res. 413 N. Adams.
Cauwenbergh Louis C., mailing-clk. P. O., res. 413 N. Adams.
Cauwenbergh Sophie (wid. John B.), res. 413 N. Adams.
Cavanaugh Hugh P., train-dispatcher, res. 309 Stuart.
Cavanaugh Joseph P. teleg.-opr., res. 402 Willow, Ft. H.
Cavanaugh Philip H., conductor, res. Northwestern Hotel, Ft. H.
Cavanaugh Stella Miss, res. s. w. cor. Dousman and Cedar, Ft. H.
Cayer Felix, setter, res. 706 3d av., Ft. H.

Centen Helena Miss, res. 421 Mason.
Centen John, painter, res. 421 Mason.
Centen Peter, tailor, res. 421 Mason.
Centen Theodore, painter, res. 421 Mason.
Centen William, tailor, res. 421 Mason.
Cepp George, blksmith, res. 1344 St. Clair.
Chadwick Clarence, bill-clk. J. P. Annen Candy Co., res. 840 S. Madison.
Chadwick Isidora (wid. Edward), res. 840 S. Madison.
Chaflin Nettie, domestic 603 Main.
Challenger Drew Miss, res. 404 Hubbard, Ft. H.
Challenger Edgar J., mach., res. 107 Chestnut, Ft. H.
Challenger James, watchman, res. 404 Hubbard, Ft. H.
Champagne Blanche Miss, domestic 621 S. Monroe av.
Champagne Frank, lab., res. 703 S. Adams.
Champagne George, lab., res. No. 3, n. end Monroe av., e. Murphy's mill.
Champagne Joseph, saloon, 217 Main, res. same.
Champagne Jos., res. No. 3, n. end Monroe av., e. Murphy's mill.
Champagne Louis, teamster, res. No. 3, n. end Monroe av., e. Murphy's mill.
Champagne Mary Miss, res. No. 3, n. end Monroe av., e. Murphy's mill.
Champagne Theresa Miss, res. 703 S. Adams.
Champeau Joseph, lime and hair, 216 Cedar, res. Bay Settlement.
Champeau Patrick, mngr. Jos. Champeau, res. Bay Settlement.
Champion Coffee & Spice Mills, 118-124 S. Washington.
Champion Hal. A., clk. auditing dept. G. B., W. & St. P. R. R., res. 603 S. Quincy.
Champion Hotel, Wm. Engels, prop., 215 Main.
Champion Lalla M. Miss, res. 603 S. Quincy.
Champion Ora A. Miss, res. 603 S. Quincy.
Champion Seth W., gen. mngr. and purchasing agt. G. B., W. & St. P. R. R., res. 603 S. Quincy.
Chapin Fred W., supt. Brown-Chapin Lumber Co., res. Ferris Hotel, Ft. H.
Chapin R. L., v.-pres. Brown-Chapin Lumber Co., res. s. w. cor. 2d av. and 10th, Ft. H.
Chapman Block, n. w. cor. Pine and N. Adams.
Chapman Henley W., res. 333 S. Adams.
Charbonneau Francis X., cooper, res. 1108 Pine.
Charbonneau Frank Jr., cooper, res. 1108 Pine.
Charbonneau Joseph, cooper, res. 509 N. Jefferson.

**THE A. SPUHLER CO., Green Bay** CARPETS, RUGS, OIL CLOTHS, Draperies and Window Shades.

Charbonneau Philip, res. 1108 Pine.
Charbonneau Sarah Miss, res. 1108 Pine.
Charles Desire, carriage blksmith, res. 506 N. Jefferson.
Charles Fernande Miss, domestic 115 S. Madison.
Charles House, C. W. Redeman, prop., 108-110 S. Washington.
Charles Mary, domestic 425 Main.
Charlon Andrew, lab., res. 1 w. 758 Shawano rd, Ft. H.
Charlon Joseph, res. 1 w. 758 Shawano rd., Ft. H.
Charlon Louise, domestic 418 Walnut.
Charlon Pauline Miss, res. 1 w. 758 Shawano rd., Ft. H.
Charrier Victorine, cook Waterloo House.
Charwat Frank, lab., res. s. s. 9th, 2 w. C. & N. W. R'y tracks, Ft. H.
Chase Robert D., brakeman, res. St. James' Hotel.
Check Charles, car repairer, res. w. s. 4th av., 4 s. 8th, Ft. H.
Check Elizabeth (wid. Anton), res. w. s. 4th av., 4 s. 8th. Ft. H.
Check Frank, lab., res. w. s. 4th av., 4 s. 8th, Ft. H.
Check Louise Miss, res. w. s. 4th av., 4 s. 8th, Ft. H.
Chew O. H., laundryman, res. 113 N. Washington.
Chicago, Milwaukee & St. Paul R'y, James H. Flatley, agent, depot S. Washington foot of Crooks.
Chicago & Northwestern R'y, depot Dousman, cor. Pearl, Ft. H.
Chrisken Otto, lab., res. Junction Hotel, Ft. H.
Christ Elizabeth, laundress, res. 1301 Stuart.
Christ Simon, lab., res. 1301 Stuart.
Christens Andrea, lab., res. 4 w. 929 Dousman, Ft. H.
Christens Gustav, gardener, res. 4 w. 929 Dousman, Ft. H.
Christensen Christ, lab., res. 210 Willow, Ft. H.
Christensen Christ, blksmith, res. w. s. 4th av., 3 n. 10th, Ft. H.
Christensen Iver, lab. J. H. Ebeling, res. n. s. Elm, 2 e. 12th.
Christensen James A., lab., res. 105 5th av., Ft. H.
Christensen Jens C., mill-hand, res. w. s. 8th av., 3 n. 2d, Ft. H.
Christensen John, lab., res. n. s. Elmore, 3 w. Cedar, Ft. H.
Christensen Nels M., lab., res. n. s. Shawano rd., 3 w. Willow, Ft. H.
Christensen Nils, lab., res. e. s. Rich rd., 2 s. 9th, F. H.
Christensen Ole, res. n. s. Elmore, 3 w. Cedar, F. H.
Christensen Ole, porter The Beaumont, res. same.
Christensen Peter, teamster, res. 529 Cedar.
Christenson Adam, weighman W. W. Cargill Co., res. 308 7th av., Ft. H.
Christenson Christ, lab., res. 309 Cedar, Ft. H.
Christenson Hans, lab., res. s. s. 2d, 1 e. 5th av., Ft. H.
Christenson Ingeborg (wid. Peter), res. 309 Cedar, Ft. H.

Christenson John, painter, res. 309 Cedar, Ft. H.
Christiansen John, boilermkr, res. Ferris Hotel, Ft. H.
Christiansen Sophie (wid. Andrew), res. 402 4th, Ft. H.
Christman Anna Maria (wid. Anton), res. 1108 Cherry.
Christman Jacob, wood turner, res. 1108 Cherry.
Christman Peter (Christman & Du Bois), res. 1108 Cherry.
Christman & Du Bois (Peter Christman and Anton Du Bois), groceries, dry goods, flour, feed, etc., 932-934 Main.
Christofferson Hans, coachman, res. n. w. cor. S. Monroe av. and Eliza.
Christophersen Annie (wid. Martin), res. 729 Chicago.
Christophersen Dora, domestic 118 Cedar, Ft. H.
Christophersen Hilda, dressmaker, res. 212 3d av., Ft. H.
Christophersen Nels, teamster, res. 212 3d av., Ft. H.
Christophersen Ole, deliveryman Green Bay Creamery Co., res. 212 3d av., Ft. H.
Chrysler George, knot sawyer, res. Empire House.
Church Agnes Mrs, prop. St. James Hotel, res. same.
Church Allanson L., fireman Engine Co. No. 1, res. St. James Hotel.
Church James, captain hose cart No. 1, res. 223 S. Quincy.
Church Martin, student, res. St. James Hotel.
Church Maud Miss, res. St. James Hotel.
Church Wm., student, res. St. James Hotel.
Church of Christ, Scientist, n. e. cor. N. Adams and Walnut.
Cincick Mathias, confectioner, 204 N. Adams, res. same.
**CITIZENS' NATIONAL BANK**, H. S. Eldred, pres.; James H. Elmore, v.-pres.; W. P. Wagner, cashier, s. e. cor. N. Washington and Cherry.
City Hall, 113-115 S. Washington.
City Park, bet. 3d and 5th, 8th and 10th avs., Ft. H.
Clabots Emil, lab., res. 703 Elmore, Ft. H.
Clabots Fred C., bkpr. The State Gazette, res. 532 S. Jackson.
Claflin Amos A., cooper, res. 1363 Cherry.
Claflin Bert A., night clk. U. S. Ex. Co., res. 1267 Cherry.
Claflin Frederick C., mess. U. S. Ex. Co., res. 1208 Cherry.
Claflin Gianella D. Miss, dressmkr, res. 1363 Cherry.
Clancy James E., architect, 231 Pine.
Clarey Katherine Miss, res. 314 Stuart.
Clarey Maurice J., engineer, res. 314 Stuart.
Clark Dorr, cattle-dlr., res. n. w. cor. S. Monroe av. and Eliza.
Clark Esther, domestic 905 S. Monroe av.
Clark Frank J. (Clark & Fiedler), res. 23 Parmentier block.
Clark Hannah Miss, res. 307 8th av., Ft. H.

# Clark & Fiedler,
## ...Printers

DO ALL KINDS OF

WE PRINT
Letter Heads,
Note Heads,
Bill Heads,
Statements,
Circulars,
Envelopes,
Shipping Tags,
Law Briefs,
Programmes,
Invitations,
Etc., Etc.

FIRST-CLASS

## BOOK AND JOB PRINTING

OF EVERY DESCRIPTION.

Estimates Furnished. All Work Executed as Cheap as is Consistent with First-Class Work. . . . .

. . . 214 N. WASHINGTON STREET. . . .

GREEN BAY, WIS.

FINE CATALOGUE WORK A SPECIALTY.

Clark Joseph, res. Odd Fellows' Home
Clark Joseph B., bkpr. Jorgensen Blesch Co., res. n. w. cor. Broadway and Mather, Ft. H.
Clark Penal R. (Clark & Miller), res. s. w. cor. Elmore and Broadway, Ft. H.
Clark Wm., clk., res. 106 S. Adams.
Clark William, teamster, res. e. s. 8th av. 3 n. 5th, Ft. H.
**CLARK & FIEDLER** (Frank J. Clark and Otto L. Fiedler), printers and binders, 214 N. Washington.
Clark & Miller (Penal R. Clark and Emanuel F. Miller), dry goods, Broadway, n. e. cor. Main, Ft. H.
Clausen Chris., teamster J. H. Ebeling, res. 211 S. Monroe av.
Clausen Louis, tie inspector, res. 501 Cedar, Ft. H.
Cleary Annie Miss, res. 673 Elmore, Ft. H.
Cleary James, fireman, res. n. e. cor. Chestnut and Bond, Ft. H.
Cleary Martin, lab., res. 1 w. 663 Elmore, Ft. H.
Cleary Martin, mail driver, res. n. e. cor. Chestnut and Bond, Ft. H.
Cleary Patrick, lab., res. 711 Cherry, Ft. H
Cleary Patrick J., gardener, res. 673 Elmore, Ft. H.
Cleary Sarah Miss, res. 711 Cherry, Ft. H.
Cleary Timothy, compositor, res. 711 Cherry, Ft. H.
Cleeremans Alexander, janitor, res. 847 Dousman, Ft. H.
Cleeremans Caecilia Miss, res. 847 Dousman, Ft. H.
Cleeremans Jennie, domestic 606 Hubbard, Ft. H.
Cleeremans John, gardener, res. n. s. south city line, 1 w. Rich rd., Ft. H.
Cleeremans John, farmer, res. s. s. Shawano rd., 3 w. Hazel, Ft. H.
Cleeremans John Jr., res. n. s. south city line, 1 w. Rich rd., Ft. H.
Cleeremans Joseph, res. n. s. south city line, 1 w. Rich rd., Ft. H.
Cleeremans Mary Miss, res. n. s. south city line, 1 w. Rich rd., Ft. H.
Clements Mabel Miss, clk. The A. Spuhler Co., res. 501 Main, Ft. H.
Clements Oliver, clk. res. 501 Main, Ft. H.
Clemetsen Mads, ship-carp., res. 406 4th av., Ft. H.
Clemons Grace, stenog., res. 601 S. Jackson.
Clerin Xavier, gardener, res. 851 Dousman, Ft. H.
Cleveland Addison, lab., res. w. s. Willow, nr. the slough, Ft. H.
Clifford John, fireman, res. Northwestern Hotel, Ft. H.
Clifton James H., brakeman, res. 300 7th av., Ft. H.

Clinton John W., cooper, res. 433 Cedar.
Clorn Thomas, lab., res. 900 3d av., Ft. H.
Closuit Fred., brakeman, res. 130 Broadway, Ft. H.
Clough Albert, fireman, res. 521 S. Adams.
Clough Cornelius, res. 521 S. Adams.
Clough Frederick, fireman, res. 521 S. Adams.
Clough Louis, tailor, res. 521 S. Adams.
Clough Wm. O., express messenger, res. 412 Howard.
Clowry John, car-repairer, res. 801 Cherry, Ft. H.
Clowry Lizzie Miss, teacher, res. 801 Cherry, Ft. H.
Clowry Maggie Miss, teacher, res. 801 Cherry, Ft. H.
Clowry Mamie Miss, res. 801 Cherry, Ft. H.
Clusman Louis, lab., res. 1411 Day.
Coates Ralph, res. 317 Cass.
Cobb William, car-repairer, res. 797 Shawano rd., Ft. H.
Cobusson Frank, res. n. e. cor. Cedar and Elmore, Ft. H.
Cochlin John, conductor, res. N. W. Hotel, Ft. H.
Coco Delphine Miss, domestic 413 N. Adams.
Cody Cora Miss, res. 121 3d av., Ft. H.
Cody Delia Miss, ice cream parlor, 201 3d av., res. cor. 3d av. and 1st, Ft. H.
Cody John, city assessor, res. 121 3d av., Ft. H.
Cody William A., shingle mnfr., res. 514 Chestnut, Ft. H.
Coel Celina Miss, res. 228 N. Madison.
Coel Emma Miss, res. 228 N. Madison.
**COEL F. & SON** (Fabian and Joseph Coel), clothing, men's furnishing, 310 N. Washington.
Coel Fabian (F. Coel & Son) prop. Waterloo House, res. 228 N. Madison.
Coel Joseph S. (F. Coel & Son), res. 228 N. Madison.
Coel Tell, clk. Waterloo House, res. same.
**COFFEEN WELLINGTON B.**, physician, 313 Cherry, res. same.
Cohen Charles, clk. L. Cohen, res. 106 S. Monroe av.
Cohen Esther C. Miss, clk. I. B. Linenthal, res. 312 Stuart.
Cohen Fanny Miss, res. 106 S. Monroe av.
Cohen Harry, clk. L. Cohen, res. 106 S. Monroe av.
Cohen Isaac, dry goods and clothing, 124 N. Washington, res. same.
Cohen Louis, clothing, 207 N. Washington, res. 106 S. Monroe av.
Cohen Sarah Miss, res. 106 S. Monroe av.
Cohen William, bkpr., res. 124 N. Washington.
Cohler Joseph C., lab., res. 602 Cedar, Ft. H.
Cohn Edward A. (Cohn & Gotto), res. 316 S. Adams.

**Headquarters for Boys' Clothing** THE A. SPUHLER CO. GREEN BAY.

Cohn & Gotto (Edward A. Cohn and Eli Gotto), clothing, 300 N. Washington.
Cointe Aristide J., mnfr. mineral paints, e. s. 5th av., nr. G. B., W. & St. P. Ry. tracks, res. w. s. 6th av., 3 s. bridge, Ft. H.
Colburn Naomi (wid. William D.), res. 319 S. Adams.
Cole Daniel, res. 620 Walnut.
Coleman Marie, domestic Hall House, Ft. H.
Collard Barbara (wid. August), res. 1283 Elm.
Collard Desire Sr., res. 1529 Willow.
Collard Desire, carp., res. 1449 Day.
Collard Desire, watchman, res. 1379 Day.
Collard Edward, lab., res. 1436 Smith.
Collard John, gardener, res. 1283 Elm.
Collard Joseph, lab., res. 1283 Elm.
Collard Theophile, lab., res. 623 N. 12th.
Collard Victor, clk. 503 Main, res. 1321 Day.
Collette Wm. E., com. trav. 124 S. Washington, res. Menominee, Mich.
Collins Carroll, mngr. Green Bay & Ft. Howard Gas & Electric Light Co., res. 213 N. Monroe.
Collins Frank, teamster, res. Eldred's boarding house, Ft. H.
Collins Thomas, engineer, res. Northwestern Hotel, Ft. H.
Collins William D., driver, res. w. s. Pearl, 5 s. Hubbard, Ft. H.
Collier Ed., stenog., res. 319 Pine.
Collovard Frank, lab., res. 1433 Harvey.
Collovard Mary Mrs., res. 1433 Harvey.
Collopy Michael, res. 307 Cedar, Ft. H.
**COLUMBIAN BAKING CO.**, John H. Ebeling, pres.; Mitchell Joannes, v.-pres.; Llewellyn C. Reber, sec. and treas.; mnfrs. crackers and candy, 401-411 Walnut.
Columbia Hotel, P. Bhirdo, prop., 1106 Main.
Colver Harry W., conductor, res. 514 Crooks.
Colwell Annie Miss, res. 610 Cedar.
Colwell Elsie Miss, res. 610 Cedar.
Colwell John, engineer, res. 610 Cedar.
**COMMERCIAL HOTEL**, D. J. Smith, prop., 105 Broadway, Ft. H.
Como Isidore, R. R. hand, res. w. s. 10th av., cor. 2d, Ft. H.
Company John, teamster, res. 620 Cedar.
Comstock Mary Miss, res. 504 Moravian.
Condon Edward, lab., res. 309 2d, Ft. H.
Condon Maggie, dressmkr, res. 309 2d, Ft. H.
Conklin Chas., blksmith, res. s. s. Shawano rd., 2 w. Oak, Ft. H.
Conley Ethel Miss, res. w. s. McDonald, 5 s. lumber yd., Ft. H.

Conley Horace J., boat-builder, sail, tent and awningmkr, ft. Stuart, res. 300 S. Washington.
Conley Louis, clk., res. w. s. McDonald, 5 s. lumber yd., Ft. H.
Conley Vincent, res. w. s. McDonald, 5 s. lumber yd., Ft. H.
Conley William, ship-carp., res. w. s. McDonald, 4 s. lumber yd. Ft. H.
Connell Sarah A., teacher, res. 527 School.
Conrad Frederick W., observer U. S. Weath. Bureau, res. 600 Pine.
Conrad Gustav, carp., res. 1257 Doty.
Conradsen Nels. P., laundry, 303 3d, Ft. H., res. same.
Constance George, engineer, res. 729 S. Jefferson.
**CONVENT OF NOTRE DAME,** Sister M. Leopoldine, superioress, 139 S. Monroe av.
Conway Thomas, agt., res. 229 S. Washington.
Coogan Peter, agent, res. 629 Main.
Cook Charles, engineer, res. 520 Cedar, Ft. H.
Cook Ernest M., clk. I. B. Linenthal, res. 544 S. Jefferson.
Cook James McG., saloon, 323 N. Washington, res. 406 N. Adams.
Cook Rose (wid. Robert), res. 406 N. Adams.
**COOK'S HOTEL,** Jos. LeRoy and Melchior Theisen, props., s. w. cor. N. Washington and Cherry.
Cooke Catherine (wid. Constantine), res. 221 S. Adams.
Cooke Enos, lab., res. Columbia Hotel.
Cooke Mary E., stenog. 124 N. Washington, res. 221 S. Adams.
**COOKE WILLIAM D.,** hardware, sash, doors and blinds, 201 N. Washington, res. 431 S. Adams.
Coolahan Edward E., conductor, res. 307 Cedar, Ft. H.
Coonen John, lab., res. 208 Cedar, Ft. H.
Coonen Theodor, carp., res. 208 Cedar, Ft. H.
Cooper Addie, waitress Empire House.
Cooper Jacob, lab., res. 625 S. Jefferson.
Coopertown House, Thomas Kolocheske, prop., 617 Main.
Coopmans Frank, lab., res. s. s. Elmore, 3 w. Cross rd., Ft. H.
Coopmans Henry, lab., res. 509 Broadway, Ft. H.
Copp Howard, res. 532 S. Van Buren.
Copp Minnie (wid. William), res. 532 S. Van Buren.
Coppersmith Marshall, stone-ctr., res. s. s. St. Clair, 2 e. N. 12th.
Coppersmith Mary Miss, res. s. s. St. Clair, 2 e. N. 12th.
**COPPERSMITH THEODORE,** grocer, 820 Crooks, res. same.
Copt Adele Miss, res. e. s. 4th av., 4 s. 8th, Ft. H.
Copt Nicholas, lab., res. e. s. 4th av., 4 s. 8th, Ft. H.
**CORBETT MICHAEL J.,** whol. and retail grocer, 214-216 Main, Ft. H., res. 302 Cherry, Ft. H.

**THE A. SPUHLER CO.** *LADIES', MISSES' and CHILDREN'S*
**GREEN BAY** — **CLOAKS, CAPES, JACKETS**

| COR | 89 | CRA |
|---|---|---|

Corby John, carp., res. w. s. Pearl, 4 s. Hubbard, Ft. H.
Cormier Fabian, carp., res. 505 S. Adams.
Cormier Fabian, lab., res. w. s. 4th av., 1 s. 7th, Ft. H.
Corp Thomas, clothes cleaner, res. Empire House.
Cotton Charles A., engineer, res. 603 Main.
Cotton Mary B. (wid. Winslow), res. 216 S. Jefferson.
Cottrell Hattie L. (wid. Peter), res. 509 S. Monroe av.
Couch Thomas, agt. Beaumont House baggage and 'bus line, res. 912 Main.
Coughlin Edward, conductor, res. Bradley House.
Coughlin John, conductor, res. Northwestern Hotel, Ft. H.
Coulter George, engineer, res. 909 Pine.
Coulter Willard, lab., res. 529 S. Monroe av.
Counard Annie Miss, res. 510 Elm.
Counard Celia Miss, res. 510 Elm.
Counard Christine Miss, res. 409 S. Quincy.
Counard Desire, lab., res. 615 N. 12th.
Counard Frank, clk. Findeisen Bros., res. 510 Elm.
Counard Gustav, cooper, res. 510 Elm.
Counard Gustav, mason, res. 409 S. Quincy.
Counard John, mason, res. 409 S. Quincy.
Counard Joseph, clk., res. 510 Elm.
Counard Joseph, mason, res. 409 S. Quincy.
Counard Joseph, lab., res. 302 Stuart.
Counard Jules, clk. J. Delaporte & Son, res. **319 Main.**
Counard Michael, cooper, res. 519 Elm.
Counard Michael, lab., res. n. 701 N. Madison.
Counard Paul, lab., res. 510 Elm.
Counard Theophile, lab., res. 510 Elm.
Counard Virginia Miss, res. 510 Elm.
County Court House, Cherry, s. w. cor. N. Jefferson.
Courbet Joseph, carp., res. Waterloo House.
Cowles George W., mngr. Rouss' Savings Bank, res. 800 Pine.
Cowles Mary (wid. H. K.), res. 214 S. Webster av.
Cox Anton, policeman, res. 327 S. Jackson.
Cox Anton Jr., tailor, res. 327 S. Jackson.
Cox Joseph, res. 327 S. Jackson.
Cox Josephine Miss, dressmkr, res. 327 S. Jackson.
Cox Mary Miss, res. 327 S. Jackson.
Crab Henry, mill-hand, res. s. s. Duck **Creek rd.**, 10 w. Mather, Ft. H.
Crab Joseph, lab., res. 1411 Day.
Craig Wm., fireman, res. Northwestern Hotel, Ft. H.
Cramer Albert, lab., res. 1115 Pine.

Cramer Bertha Miss, res. 1106 Stuart.
Cramer Edward E., carp., res. 1115 Pine.
Cramer Fred. W., butcher, res. 1115 Pine.
Cramer Gustav, painter, res. 1115 Pine.
Cramer. See Kraemer.
Crandall John, engineer Eldred's saw-mill, res. Eldred's boarding house, Ft. H.
Crane Charles E., physician, 207 N. Washington, res. 605 Cherry.
Crane Fredericka A. Miss, res. 336 S. Jefferson.
Crane James, lab., res. Eldred's boarding house, Ft. H.
Crane Mary O. (wid. Dr. H. O.) res. 336 S. Jefferson.
Crane Robert C., fireman, res. 321 S. Washington.
Crary Marie Mrs., carpet-weaver, 514 Cedar, Ft. H., res. same.
Crikelair Frank, painter and paper-hanger, 120 N. Adams, res. same.
Crikelair Gustav, res. 406 Broadway, Ft. H.
Crikelair Mary Miss, bkpr. F. DeCremer, res. 406 Broadway, Ft. H.
Crim Dayton W., lab., res. 1701 Cedar.
Crim Ella Miss, res. 1701 Cedar.
Crim Joseph, res. 1701 Cedar.
Crimmins Jim, groceries and notions, 1138 Main, res. 1130 Main.
Crocker Ephraim (R. Henderson & Co.), livery, 208 Broadway, res. 323 Broadway, Ft. H.
Crone Joshua (Crone & Van der Steen), res. 1707 Cedar.
Crone Mary (wid. John), res. 1545 Morrow.
**CRONE & VAN DER STEEN** (Joshua Crone and Henry Van der Steen) carpenter-contractors, 1707 Cedar.
Cropsey William, hostler, res. Adams House.
Cross Fred, clk. 932 Main, res. 1101 Cherry.
Cross Lena (wid. Fred), res. 1101 Cherry.
Crowley Hilbert, clk. 1155 Main, res. 803 Cherry.
Cublit James, machinist, res. Columbia Hotel.
Cull John, drayman, res. 326 S. Jackson.
Cull May Miss, res. 326 S. Jackson.
Cull. See also Kull and Koll.
Cummings Jennie, domestic 100 N. Madison.
Cunningham Edward P., lab., res. 912 Dousman, Ft. H.
Cunningham William, engineer, res. 912 Dousman, Ft. H.
Cunningham William Jr., brakeman, res. 912 Dousman, Ft. H.
Curran Anna, dressmkr, res. 231 S. Adams.
Curran James, fireman, res. 231 S. Adams.
Curran Kittie, stenog., res. 231 S. Adams.
Curran Minnie, dressmkr, res. 231 S. Adams.

**THE A. SPUHLER CO., Green Bay** CARPETS, RUGS, OIL CLOTHS, Draperies and Window Shades.

Curran Theresa, milliner, res. 231 S. Adams.
Curtice Frank, brakeman, res. 213 S. Quincy.
Curtice Lucia (wid. Solon), res. 213 S. Quincy.
Curtis John E., barkpr. Henry Lachance, res. 225 Cherry.
Cusack Frank, engineer, res. 202 S. Jefferson.
Cusick Ella, teacher 2d Ward School, res. s. s. Dousman, 2 w. Willow, Ft. H.
Cusick James D., sailor, res. s. s. Dousman, 2 w. **Willow, Ft. H.**
Cusick John A., captain, res. 333 S. Washington.
Cusick Marie (wid. John), res. s. s. Dousman, **2 w. Willow,** F. H.
Cusick Marie Miss, dressmkr, res. s. s. Dousman, 2 w. Willow, Ft. H.
Cusick Sarah Miss, res. s. s. **Dousman, 2 w. Willow, Ft. H.**
Custer Charles R., clk. car **accountant G. B., W. & St. P. R. R.,** res. 603 S. Quincy.
Custer Louis, conductor, res. Northwestern **Hotel, Ft. H.**
Custom House, 321 N. Washington.
Cutting Octavius B., miller, res. 917 Walnut.
Czahansky Andrew, lab., res. 1320 Doty.
Czahansky Constancia Miss, clk. 1220 Walnut.
Czahansky George A., res. 1220 Walnut.

# D

DACHELET Henry, res. 1130 Mason.
**DAEMS AUGUST,** baker, 212 N. Adams, res. same.
Daems Celina Miss, res. 212 N. Adams.
Daems Emma Miss, res. 212 N. Adams.
Daems Irma Miss, res. 212 N. Adams.
Daems Theodore, clk., res. 212 N. Adams.
Dagen Charles, stock-dealer, res. 206 Main, Ft. H.
Daggett Charles M., carp.-contr., 118 6th av., Ft. H., res. same.
Daggett Clarence M., machinist, res. 118 6th av., Ft. H.
Daggett Louis G., clk. Goodrich Trans. Co., res. 118 th av. Ft. H.
Daggett Susan M. Miss, bkpr., res. 118 6th av., Ft. H.
Dagneau Joseph J., lab., res. w. s. 2d av., 2 s. 9th, Ft. H.
Dagneau Lizzie Miss, res. w. s. 2d av., 1 s. 9th, Ft. H.
Dagneau Peter, lab., res. Bodart House.
Dagneau William, mill-hand, res. w. s. 2d av., 2 s. 9th, Ft. H.
Dahin Frank, carp., res. 1149 Doty.
Dahin John, cigarmkr, res. 1149 Doty.
Dahin Mary Miss, res. 1149 Doty.

Daily State Gazette, 116 N. Washington.
Daix Constant, res. 1120 Main.
Daix Frank, res. 214 S. 10th.
Daix Mary Miss, res. 1120 Main.
Daix Victor, plasterer, res. 214 S. 10th.
Dakota Levy, sailor, res. n. s. Willow, 1 w. 12th.
Dalveau Mary (wid. Max.) res. 1141 Stuart.
Dambach Andrew, res. 1259 Cherry.
Dambach Maggie, clk. Jorgensen Blesch Co., res. 1259 Cherry.
Dandouaye Etienne, res. rear 1118 Cedar.
Dandoy Ferdinand, carp.-contractor, 701 S. Jefferson, res. same.
Dandoy Flora Miss, res. 701 S. Jefferson.
Dandoy Frank, carpenter, res. 701 S. Jefferson.
Dandoy Hattie Miss, res. 1120 Doty.
Dandoy Thanis, res. 1120 Doty.
Daniel Catherine, dressmaker, res. 1151 Crooks.
Daniel Edward, lab., res. 1362 Willow.
Daniel Elizabeth, res. 1151 Crooks.
Daniel Frances Miss, dressmaker, res. 1151 Crooks.
Daniel Frank, lab., res. 1435 Cedar.
Daniel Gertie, candy-packer, res. 1134 Doty.
Daniel John, res. 1134 Doty.
Daniel Joseph, lab., res. 1435 Cedar.
Daniel Katie M., candy-packer, res. 1134 Doty.
Daniel Katie Miss, dressmkr, 120 N. Adams, res. 1151 Crooks.
Daniel Lizzie Miss, res. 1151 Crooks.
Daniel Mary Miss, res. 1151 Crooks.
Daniel Mathins, mason, res. 1151 Crooks.
Daniels Christopher, scaler, res. Eldred's boarding house, Ft. H.
Daniels John, candymkr, res. 900 Van Buren.
Daniels Leander, lab., res. 1141 Stuart.
Danielson Andrew, lab., res. s. s. 5th, 2 w. 3d av., Ft. H.
Danielson William, machinist, res. 400 6th av., Ft. H.
Dano Charles, lab., res. 610 Cedar.
Danz Adolph, jeweler, res. 718 Cherry.
Danz Hillmar, stoves and tinware, 318 Main, res. 718 Cherry.
Danz Hillmar Jr., clk. Theodore Mueller & Co., res. 718 Cherry.
Danz Ida Miss, res. 718 Cherry.
Danz John P., res. 700 Pine.
Danz Liebert, carsmith, res. n. e. cor. 4th av. and 4th, Ft. H.
Dargan Thomas, res. 1133 Cass.
Darte Xavier, wood-carver, res. 512 Cherry, Ft. H.
Dashnier Edward, lab., res. 516 Cherry, Ft. H.
Daul Charles, res. 1016 Doty.

Dave Euphrosine Miss, res. 1227 Day.
Dave Isidore, lab., res. 1227 Day.
Dave Isidore Jr., tailor, res. 1430 Harvey.
Dave Joseph, conductor, res. 1177 Walnut.
Dave Mary Miss, res. 1227 Day.
Davern Thomas, blksmith, res. 305 Cedar, Ft. H.
Davidson David J., pres. J. M. Voigt Mnfg. Co., res. 120 6th av., Ft. H.
Davidson Mary Miss, res. 404 5th, Ft. H.
Davidson Thomas, res. 404 5th, Ft. H.
Davis Frank J., lineman, res. American House.
Davis Hosiah A., fish-dealer, res. 514 Cedar, Ft. H.
Davis J. Oliver, lab., res. 1462 Mason.
Davis James, cook The Beaumont.
Davis Martha (wid. Eaton), res. 501 Main, Ft. H.
Davis Samuel, saloonkpr. res. 229 Main.
Davreux Emma, clk. Theo. Mueller & Co., res. 1100 Pine.
Davreux Leon, cooper, res. 1100 Pine.
Davreux Mary (wid. Albert), res. 1100 Pine.
Dawson Herbert E., broommkr, res. 1711 Morrow.
Dawson William H., teamster, res. 1711 Morrow.
Dean Emma (wid. James), res. 746 S. Jefferson.
Dean Joseph, bridge-tender, res. 527 S. Jefferson.
Dean Louise Miss, teacher, res. 746 S. Jefferson.
Dean Maud Miss, res. 746 S. Jefferson.
Dean Olive Miss, dressmkr, res. 527 S. Jefferson.
Deaisch Emil J., bartender, res. 1131 Main.
Deaisch Joseph, saloon, 1129 Main, res. 1131 Main.
Deboth Jacob, lab., res. s. s. Mather, 4 w. Willow, Ft. H.
Deboth John, ry.-hand, res. n. s. Dousman, w. Guesnier, Ft. H.
Deboth Martin, res. 311 N. Adams.
Deboth Marie Miss, res. n. s. Dousman, w. Guesnier, Ft. H.
Deboth Mary V. Mrs., milliner, 311 N. Adams, res. same.
Deboth Nettie Miss, res. 311 N. Adams.
Deboth Peter, lab., res. n. s. Dousman, w. Guesnier, Ft. H.
De Broux Alfred, lab., res. Waterloo House.
De Broux Frank, clk. F. De Cremer, res. n. s. Elm, 1 w. Van Buren.
De Broux Fred., lab., res. Waterloo House.
De Brue John, gardener, res. 716 Baird.
De Brue Joseph, lab., res. 716 Baird.
De Brue Mary Miss, res. 716 Baird.
Debrule Flora Miss, tailoress, res. 627 Walnut.
Debrule Josie, hair-dresser, res. 627 Walnut.

Debrule Louis, res. 627 Walnut.
Debrule Peter, tailor, res. 627 Walnut.
Debush Oliver, lab., res. 12th, cor. Smith.
De Byl Henry, ice-peddler, res. 421 S. Quincy.
Decker Alexander, lab., res. 1 w. 874 Dousman, Ft. **H.**
Decker David, v.-pres. The Green Bay Advocate Co., **res. Ahn**-spee, Wis.
Decker Charles, R. R.-hand, res. n. s. Bond, 8 w. Cedar, Ft. H.
Decker Henry, blksmith, res. n. s. Bond, 3 w. Cedar, Ft. H.
Deckers Martin, carp., res. 1245 Doty.
Decock Felix, plasterer, res. 1256 Day.
De Coster Joseph, lab., res. Wisconsin House.
De Coster Peter, lab., res. Wisconsin House.
De Cremer Alvina M. Miss, dressmkr, res. 1009 Pine.
De Cremer Charles, res. 1009 Pine.
De Cremer Emil, cooper, res. 1009 Pine.
De Cremer Florian, grocer, 316 N. Washington, res. same.
De Cremer Israel, res. 1009 Pine.
De Cremer Jules V., mngr. 316 N. Washington, res. same.
De Cremer Louis H., clk. F. De Cremer, res. 1009 Pine.
Dedrickson Kate, dressmkr, res. 639 Pine.
De Forest L. Beekman, boots and shoes, 210 Main, **Ft. H.**, **res.** 116 Cedar, Ft. H.
De Forest Lansing, foreman, res. 116 Cedar, Ft. H.
De Foy John, lab., res. 511 S. Adams.
De Foy Thomas, lab., res. 511 S. Adams.
De Godt Timothy, cooper, res. 430 N. Madison.
De Graaf Carrie Miss, res. 115 Chestnut, Ft. H.
De Graaf Joseph, janitor, res. 115 Chestnut, Ft. **H.**
De Graaf Maggie Miss, res. 115 Chestnut, Ft. H.
De Graaf William, brakeman, res. 115 Chestnut, Ft. H.
De Grandgagnage Felician, hostler, res. Waterloo House.
De Grandgagnage Louie, lab., res. Bodart House.
De Greef Joseph, lab., res. n. s. Bellevue, 2 e. Manitowoc **rd.**
De Groot Adrian, carp., res. 320 S. 10th.
De Groot Henry, lather, res. 1419 Smith.
De Groot John, lab., res. 1230 Walnut.
De Groot John, blksmith and wagonmkr, **1357 Main, res. 1356 Main.**
De Groot Martin, lather, res. 1106 Chicago.
De Groot Martin A., lab., res. s. w. cor. Cass and 14th.
De Groot Peter, carp.-contr., 1020 Stuart, res. same.
De Guire Philip H., engineer C., M. & St. P. R. R., res. 819 Crooks.

**Headquarters for Boys' Clothing** THE A. SPUHLER CO.
GREEN BAY.

DEK 95 DEL

De Kelver Kate, domestic 644 S. Monroe av.
De Keuster Joseph, res. 1029 Main.
De Keyser George, lab., res. 1124 Crooks.
De Keyser Henry, lab., res. 1431 Smith.
De Keyser John, lab., res. 716 Pleasant.
De Keyser John, lab., res. 1408 Porlier.
De Keyser Joseph, lab., res. 1124 Crooks.
De Keyser Mary Miss, res. 716 Pleasant.
De Keyser Minnie, domestic Charles House.
De Keyser Nettie Miss, res. 1124 Crooks.
De Keyser William, lab., res. 716 Pleasant.
De Kindere Peter, painter, res. Waterloo House.
De Kyser Edmund, bridge tender, res. 807 Day.
De Kyser Frank, lab., res. 807 Day.
De Kyser Gabriel, carpenter, res. 820 Day.
De Kyser Joseph, lab., res. 807 Day.
De Kyser Walter, bridge tender, res. 807 Day.
De la Censerie Aime L., fireman, res. 716 Pine.
De la Censerie Annie Miss, bkpr., res. 716 Pine.
De la Censerie Celestine E., cashier, res. 716 Pine.
De la Censerie Emil, bkpr. W. W. Cargill Co., res. 716 Pine.
De la Censerie Helen Miss, res. 716 Pine.
Delahout Jerome, gardener, res. w. s. Hazel, 2 s. Shawano rd., Ft. H.
Delahout Leon, gardener, res. w. s. Hazel, 2 s. Shawano rd., Ft.H.
Delahout Lucien, carp., res. w. s. Hazel, 2 s. Shawano rd., Ft. H.
De Lair Catherine (wid. Frank), res. 135 N. Adams.
De Lair Joseph, hack-driver, res. 135 N. Adams.
Delaney Alice E. (wid. Michael), res. 507 Baird, Ft. H.
Delaney Anna M. (wid. James), res. 501 Cherry, Ft. H.
Delaney Edmund J., time-keeper, res. 507 Baird, Ft. H.
Delaney Ethel Miss, res. 625 Pine.
Delaney J. Henry, merchant tailor, 122 N. Washington, res. 625 Pine.
Delaney James K. (J. H. Elmore & Co.), grading contr., 531 Main, Ft. H., res. same.
Delaney John M., postal clk., res. 501 Cherry, Ft. H.
Delaney Joseph, res. 1002 Cherry.
Delaney Marie A. Miss, res. 501 Cherry, Ft. H.
Delaporte Albert H. E. (J. Delaporte & Son), res. 802 Doty.
Delaporte Charles, mngr. J. Delaporte & Son, res. 802 Doty.
Delaporte Edward, clk., res. 802 Doty.
Delaporte J. & Son (Jennie and Albert Delaporte), clothing, 218 N. Washington.

Delaporte Jennie Mrs. (J. Delaporte & Son), res. 802 Doty.
Delaporte William, clk., res. 802 Doty.
De Laruelle Arthur, student, res. 710 2d, Ft. H.
De Laruelle H. Joseph, carp., res. 710 2d, Ft. H.
De Laruelle Mitchell, mason, res. 1405 Mason.
Deleers Katie, domestic 308 S. Adams.
Delforge Adolphine (wid. August), res. 1034 Main.
Delforge Albert, plumber res. 1034 Main.
Delforge Gertie (wid. Frank), res. s. s. Bellevue, Town Preble.
Delforge Hattie Miss, res. 1034 Main.
Delimont Charles, carp., res. n. s. Willow, 2 w. 12th.
Delloye Anton, carp.-contr., 1111 Walnut, res. same.
Delitre August, cigarmkr, res. 1330 Walnut.
Delitre Christoph, cigarmkr, res. 1330 Walnut.
Delmarcelle Bros. (Joseph and Donne Delmarcelle), mer. tailors, 1117 Walnut.
Delmarcelle Camille, cook, res. 908 Dousman, Ft. H.
Delmarcelle Constant, res. 1117 Walnut.
Delmarcelle Donne (Delmarcelle Bros.), res. 1117 Walnut.
Delmarcelle Joseph (Delmarcelle Bros.), res. 1117 Walnut.
Del Marcels Joseph, lab., res. 1209 Day.
Deloria Joseph, conductor, res. Northwestern Hotel, Ft. H.
Deloria Napoleon, baggageman, res. n. e. cor. Chestnut and Elmore, Ft. H.
Delvaux Charles, res. 616 St. George.
Delwiche Frank W., clk. A. Duchateau, res. 414 N. Monroe.
Delwiche Gustave, fireman, Truck No. 1, res. 426 N. Adams.
Delwiche Julius J., harnessmaker, res. 918 Cherry.
Delwiche Laura, tailoress, res. 918 Cherry.
Delwiche Lizzie Miss, res. 601 Pine.
Delwiche Mary, domestic, res. 532 Cherry.
Delwiche Virginia (wid. Wm.), res. 918 Cherry.
Delwiche William, porter 124 S. Washington, res. 918 Cherry.
Demain Manuel, gardener, res. e. s. Oak, 2 s. Shawano rd., Ft. H.
Deman Joseph, joiner, res. Broadway House, Ft. H.
De Moore John B., painter, 327 Main, res. same.
Demuth Lizzie Miss, domestic 503 S. Monroe av.
Dendooven Fabian, clk. J. P. C. Schmit, res. 514 S. Quincy.
Dendooven Mary Miss, res. 514 S. Quincy.
Dendooven Virginia Miss, clk. Jorgensen Blesch Co., res. 514 S. Quincy.
Denessen Cornelius, beer-pdlr., res. w. s. Monroe av. rd., 2½ miles s. city limits.
Denessen Henry, fireman, res. 615 Cherry, Ft. H.

**THE A. SPUHLER CO.** LADIES', MISSES' and CHILDREN'S
**GREEN BAY** — **CLOAKS, CAPES, JACKETS**

| DEN | 97 | DER |

Denessen John, capt. lake steamer, res. 615 Cherry, **Ft. H.**
Denessen Joseph, captain, res. 802 Cherry, Ft. H.
Denessen Josephine Miss, res. 615 Cherry, Ft. H.
Denessen Marie Miss, clk., res. 609 Cherry, Ft. H.
Denessen Theodor, captain, res. 609 Cherry, Ft. H.
Denessen Wm., lake capt., res. s. e. cor. Bond and Cedar, **Ft. H.**
De Neveu Delia (wid. Gustav), res. 910 Cherry.
Denimore Solomon, lab., res. 807 Day.
Denis David, bridge tender, res. 513 N. Madison.
Denis Emil, clk. Hoeffel Bros. Shoe Co., res. 513 N. Madison.
Denis Frank, sailor, res. 1300 Chicago.
Denis Honorine (wid. Leopold), res. 1300 Chicago.
Denis James, fireman, res. 1300 Chicago.
Denis Johanna (wid. Louis), res. 433 Cedar.
Denis James P., salesman 124 S. Washington, res. 325 **S. Van** Buren.
Denis Joseph, tug capt., res. 325 S. Van Buren.
Denis Jos. Jr., porter 124 S. Washington, res. 325 S. Van **Buren.**
Denis Lucy R. Miss, res. 325 S. Van Buren.
Denis Joseph, lab., res. Waterloo **House.**
Denis Joseph, res. 709 Pine.
Denis Paul, engineer, res. 429 N. Jefferson.
Denis Victor, fireman, res. 1300 Chicago.
Denistey Emil, lab., res. 1327 Day.
Denney Abram, carp., res. 729 N. 11th.
Dennis Frank J., lab., res. 515 N. Madison.
Dennis Josephine (wid. John), res. 406 Broadway, Ft. H.
Dennisen Cornelius, lake captain, res. n. s. Mather, 1 w. Cedar, Ft. H.
Denruyter Frank, gardener, res. 857 Dousman, Ft. H.
Densback Mary, domestic 333 S. Jefferson.
Dentun Max., painter, res. 907 Broadway, Ft. H.
Depas Clement, lab., res. Bodart House.
Deprez Hattie, domestic Wilmar House.
De Quindre Benjamin, res. 530 S. Jefferson.
De Ranitz Sigismund J., clk. Robinson's drug store, res. 520 Chestnut, Ft. H.
De Ranitz Sigismund T., trav. agt., res. 520 Chestnut, Ft. H.
De Ranitz William, res. 520 Chestnut, Ft. H.
Derieze Alexander, res. 1136 Cedar.
Derler Magdalene, housekpr. 128 S. Monroe av.
De Rop Joseph, lab., res. 1 w. 773 Elmore, Ft. H.
De Roost Frank, gardener, **res. n.** s. Shawano rd., 1 w. 854, Ft. H.

13

| DER | 98 | DET |

De Roost Fred., lab., res. s. s. Duck Creek rd., 9 w. Mather, Ft. H.
De Roost John, gardener, res. n. s. Shawano rd., 1 w. 851, Ft. H.
Derpinghaus Aug., ice-peddler, res. e. s. 11th av., 2 n. 2d, Ft. H.
Derrick Eva Miss, res. 733 Cherry.
Derrick Leslie, bookkpr., res. 733 Cherry.
Derrick Lyman H., com. trav. J. P. Annen Candy Co., res. 733 Cherry.
Derwae Arnold C., grocer, 1300 Cherry, res. same.
Derwae Cecelia Miss, res. 1300 Cherry.
Desallier Peter, brakeman, res. Ferris Hotel, Ft. H.
Desnoyers Elizabeth C. Miss, res. 605 Cherry.
Desnoyers Frank B. (Desnoyers & Duchateau) res. 605 Cherry.
Desnoyers Joseph, plasterer, res. Waterloo House.
Desnoyers Marie L. Miss, res. 605 Cherry.
Desnoyers Minnie, waitress The Beaumont.
Desnoyers & Duchateau (Frank B. Desnoyers and Frank J. B. Duchateau), horse breeders, 329 N. Washington.
Despins Agnes Miss, clk. A. L. Gray, res. 510 Chestnut, Ft. H.
Despins Albert, res. 510 Chestnut, Ft. H.
Dessain Louis, painter, n. s. cor. Guesnier and Dousman, Ft. H., res. same.
Dessart Joseph, lab., res. 707 Chestnut, Ft. H.
Destiche Lizzie, domestic s. w. cor. Willow and Baird, Ft. H.
Destree Frank, mason contractor, 729 Harvey, res. same.
Destree John, lab., res. 1266 Elm.
Destree Leon, lab., res. 1266 Elm.
Destree Leontine Miss, res. 1266 Elm.
De Tennis Harry, teamster, res. 720 S. Webster av.
Detervinne August, butcher, res. Duck Creek rd., 17 w. Mather, Ft. H.
Detervinne Josie Miss, res. s. s. Duck Creek rd., 17 w. Mather, Ft. H.
Detervinne Zilda Miss, res. s. s. Duck Creek rd., 17 w. Mather, Ft. H.
Detienne Bros. (Dave E. and Sam. B. Detienne), merchant tailors, 126 N. Washington.
Detienne Dave E. (Detienne Bros.), res. 619 Walnut.
Detienne John, lab., res. 221 S. Jackson.
Detienne John B., res. 826 Walnut.
Detienne Sam. B. (Detienne Bros.), res. 826 Walnut.
Detienne Thamar Miss, res. 826 Walnut.
Detienne Victor, painter, res. 336 S. Jackson.
Detry Alexander, painter, res. s. s. Elmore, 8 w. Cedar, Ft. H.

**THE A. SPUHLER CO., Green Bay** CARPETS, RUGS, OIL CLOTHS, Draperies and Window Shades.

DET 99 DIC

Detry Augusta (wid. Emil), tailoress, res. 222 Main.
Detry Emilie, tailoress, res. 222 Main.
d'Eustage Leonard, res. n. s. Willow, 1 w. 12th.
Deuster Barbara (wid. Frank), res. 1251 Day.
Deuster Henry, miller J. H. Ebeling, res. 724 Walnut.
Deuster James L., bkpr. J. P. C. Schmit, res. 308 S. Jackson.
Deuster John J., miller J. H. Ebeling, res. 113 S. Monroe av.
Deuster Lizzie Miss, dressmkr, 1251 Day, res. same.
Deuster Mary Miss, res. 1020 Stuart.
Deuster Tillie, domestic n. e. cor. S. Madison and Porlier.
Devillers Mary Miss, dressmkr, res. 1118 Cedar.
Devroey D. Mrs., boarding house, res. 303 N. Jefferson.
Devroey Daniel, whitewasher, 303 N. Jefferson, res. same.
Devroey Daniel, clk. 124 S. Washington, res. 303 N. Jefferson.
Devroey Lillie Miss, res. 303 N. Jefferson.
Devroy Anton, lab., res. n. e. cor. Dousman and George, Ft. H.
Devroy August, lab., res. n. s. Elmore, 9 w. Willow, Ft. H.
Devroy Ida Miss, res. 516 N. Jefferson.
Devroy John, clk. Wm. Larsen, res. Division, 2 n. George, Ft. H.
Devroy Peter, grocer, 308 Dousman, res. 702 Division, Ft. H.
Devroy Theresa (wid. Frank), res. 516 N. Jefferson.
Devan Johanna, domestic s. s. Elmore, 11 w. Cedar, Ft. H.
De Walens Jacob, lab., res. 318 N. Adams.
Dewan Eugene J., furniture, 226 Main, res. 415 N. Monroe av.
Dewan Frank, res. 415 N. Monroe av.
Dewan Henry, furniture-dlr., res. 415 N. **Monroe av.**
Dewan Joseph, clk., res. 415 N. Monroe av.
Dewan Mary J. Miss, res. 415 N. Monroe av.
Dewane Denis, carp., res. s. s. Shawano rd., 9 w. Willow, Ft. **H.**
De Wane Polly, waitress Green Bay House.
De Witt Albert, lab., res. 1212 Cass.
Dewitt Alex., bartender, res. 1209 Day.
De Witt Annie Miss, res. 1175 Crooks.
De Witt George, lab., res. 1212 Cass.
De Witt Henry M., blksmith, res. 1212 Cass.
De Witt Herman, lab., res. 1212 Cass.
De Witt Martin, gardener, 1161 Cherry, res. same.
De Witt Regina (wid. Henry), res. 1147 Pine.
Dewitt William, ice-dlr., res. 132 Broadway, Ft. H.
De Wolder Frederick, night police, res. 874 Dousman, Ft. H.
Dickason Frank, lab., res. 316 Main.
Dickey Horace N., fireman, res. 445 S. Adams.
Dickey Jasper Hanford, bkpr. and ship.-clk. Weise **Furniture**
    Co., res. 1145 Cherry.

Dickinson Albert N., student, res. 532 S. Monroe av.
Dickinson Charles F., clk., res. 532 S. Monroe av.
Dickinson Charles M., mngr. Dickinson Music Co., res. 532 S. Monroe av.
Dickinson Edwin M., news depot, 206 N. Adams, res. 532 S. Monroe av.
Dickinson Helen R. Miss, res. 532 S. Monroe av.
Dickinson Music Co., Chas. M. Dickinson, mngr., 206 N. Adams.
Didama Simon, res. Odd Fellows' Home.
Dieckmann Fred A., sec.-treas. J. M. Voigt Mnfg. Co., res. 128 Chestnut, Ft. H.
Dielen Jacob, milkman, 1400 Baird, res. same.
Dietz George, barber and hair tonic mnfr., 111 N. Washington, res. 333 S. Webster av.
Dietz Harry, loco.-engr., res. n.w. cor. Dousman and Cedar, Ft.H.
Dietz Isadora (wid. John), res. n. w. cor. Dousman and Cedar, Ft. H.
Dietz Jesse C., clk. James Tiernan, res. n. e. cor. Cedar and Dousman, Ft. H.
Dietz Michael, res. 610 N. 12th.
Dievienes Katie, domestic The Beaumont.
Dilkens Jacob, lab., res. 738 Elmore, Ft. H.
Dillon John, cooper, res. 900 Cherry.
Dillon Joseph, cooper, res. 900 Cherry.
Dillon Julia Miss, compositor, res. 900 Cherry.
Dillon Lizzie Miss, res. 900 Cherry.
Dillon Nettie Miss, res. 900 Cherry.
Dillon William, conductor, res. Northwestern Hotel, Ft. H.
Dillon Wm. J., asst. postmaster Ft. Howard P. O., res. e. s. Willow, 2 n. Baird, Ft. H.
Dineau Henry, lab., res. Waterloo House.
Dingman L., lab., res. 117 Broadway, Ft. H.
**DIOCESE OF GREEN BAY,** Right Rev. S. G. Messmer, bishop ; Very Rev. J. J. Fox, vicar-general ; office, 139 S. Madison.
Discher Oscar, harnessmkr., res. 316 Pine.
Dischno Joseph, lab., res. 511 Chestnut, Ft. H.
Dittmer Frank, barkpr., res. 1014 Main.
Dittmer Ludwig, saloon, 319 N. Adams, res. same.
Dittmer Robert, shoemkr., res. 1008 Main.
Dittmer William, boots and shoes, 1008 Main, res. same.
Dixon John, brakeman, res. n. w. cor. Elmore & Chestnut, Ft. H.
Dixon Marie (wid. Patrick), res. n. w. cor. Elmore and Chestnut, Ft. H.

**THE A. SPUHLER CO., GREEN BAY, WIS.** **Fine Dress Goods**
Samples Furnished on Application.

Dixon Patrick, painter, res. n. w. cor. Elmore and Chestnut, Ft. H.
Doak Alexander M., captain, res. 510 Cherry, Ft. H.
Dobry Adam, mngr. Josephine Dobry, res. 404 N. Van Buren.
Dobry Anna Miss, res. s. s. Willow, 3 w. Pleasant.
Dobry Charles, clk., res. s. s. Willow, 3 w. Pleasant.
Dobry Emil, bkpr., res. 404 N. Van Buren.
Dobry Emma Miss, res. 404 N. Van Buren.
Dobry John, horsetrader, res. s. s. Willow, 3 w. Pleasant.
Dobry Joseph, res. 404 N. Van Buren.
Dobry Josephine, mnfr. lumber, lath and shingles, cor. **Van** Buren and Cedar, res. 404 N. Van Buren.
Dobry Josie Miss, res. 404 N. Van Buren.
Dobry Nettie Miss, res. 404 N. Van Buren.
Dockery Michael, res. Howard House, Ft. H.
Dockry John F., journalist, res. 715 Pine.
Dodge John, carp., res. 304 6th av., Ft. H.
Doeren Anton, lab., res. 1209 S. Quincy.
Doerfler Joseph, baker, res. 115 N. Adams.
Dogot Lizzie Mrs., res. 1130 Mason.
Doherty George F., engineer, res. 431 S. Washington.
Dolan George, lab., res. s. w. cor. 3d and 10th av., Ft. H.
Dolan John, conductor, res. Northwestern Hotel, Ft. H.
Dolan Theresa E. Miss, teacher, res. 344 S. Monroe av.
Domni Amelia, domestic 111 N. Van Buren.
Domni Emil, brickmkr, res. 1376 Porlier.
Domni Hilda, domestic 110 S. Madison.
Domni Rudolph, carp., res. 1376 Porlier.
Donaldson Lizzie, cook Columbia Hotel.
Donavan Matt., switchman, res. St. James Hotel.
Doney Albert, cooper, res. 519 N. Madison.
Doney George A., cooper, res. 1026 Pine.
Doney W. Thomas, fisherman, res. 1115 Cedar.
Donkers Rudolph, res. 201 S. Quincy.
Donnovan Daniel, engineer, res. Northwestern Hotel, Ft. H.
Dopkins Earle, lab., res. e. s. Broadway, 3 s. Hubbard, Ft. H.
Doran Harry, fireman, res. 202 S. Jefferson.
Doran John, farmer, res. s. s. Shawano rd., 7 w. R. **R. track,** Ft. H.
Doran Lizzie Miss, domestic 115 6th av., Ft. H.
Doran William, night foreman C., M. & St. P. R. R., res. **402** 4th av., Ft. H.
Dorn Alonzo L., agent Standard Oil Co., res. 1015 Pine.
Dorschel Gregor (L. D. Dorschel & Bro.), res. Chilton, Wis.

Dorschel Joseph, clk. 116 S. Washington, res. Bay City House.
Dorschel L. D. & Bro. (Lucas D. and Gregor Dorschel), whol. produce, 114-116 S. Washington.
Dorschel Lucas D. (L. D. Dorschel & Bro.), res. Chilton, Wis.
Dorschel Peter F., mngr. L. D. Dorschel & Bro., res. American House.
Doty Charles W., res. 601 Cherry, Ft. H.
Dougherty Helen M., domestic 417 S. Adams.
Dougherty John, milk peddler, res. n. w. cor. Chestnut and Kellogg, Ft. H.
Dougherty William H., salesman. res. n. w. cor. Kellogg and Chestnut, Ft. H.
Dousman William, lab., res. w. s. Willow, nr. the slough, Ft. H.
Downey Thomas, cattledlr., res. 341 S. Jackson.
Doyle James, brakeman, res. 344 S. Adams.
Doyle James, lab., res. w. s. 9th av., 3 n. 2d, Ft. H.
Doyle Joseph, fireman, res. w. s. 9th av., 3 n. 2d, Ft. H.
Drake David M., night watchman, res. s. e. cor. Chestnut and Bond, Ft. H.
Drake James, nurseryman, res. 912 S. Jackson.
**DRAKE JENNIE E. MRS.**, matron Foundlings' Home, res. 912 S. Jackson.
Draper William A., com. trav., res. 902 Pine.
Draye Anton, lab., res. 1363 Cedar.
Draye Joseph, plasterer, res. 1359 Cedar.
Dreher Jacob, supt. Green Bay Gazette, res. Cook's Hotel.
Drion Flora Miss, res. 1231 Doty.
Drion Gustav J., res. 1231 Doty.
Drion Julius, lab., res. 1231 Doty.
Driscoll Catherine (wid. Marty), res. 319 Cedar.
Driscoll John, lumber and cigar mnfr., res. 103 S. Jefferson.
Driscoll Margaret Miss, res. 319 Cedar.
Driscoll Maud Miss, res. 103 S. Jefferson.
Driscoll Patrick, res. 319 Cedar.
Driscoll William, city marshal, res. 511 Cherry, Ft. H.
Drissen Catherine (wid. Peter), res. 420 N. Madison.
Drissen Jos. V., clk. Murphy Lumber Co., res. 420 N. Madison.
Du Bois Anton (Christman & Du Bois), res. 326 N. Webster av.
Du Bois Cornelius E., res. 734 S. Jackson.
Du Bois Frank E., conductor, res. 734 S. Jackson.
Du Bois John B., bookkpr. 1155 Main, res. 1124 Main.
Du Bois John W., engineer, res. 514 S. Monroe av.
Ducat Eliza, domestic 336 S. Jefferson.
Duchaine Jerome, lab., res. 502 N. Jefferson.

**Headquarters for Boys' Clothing** THE A. SPUHLER CO.
GREEN BAY.

Ducharme Charles, fisherman, res. w. s. De Pere rd., 3 s. Hochgreve brewery.
Ducharme Fred., musician, res. e. s. De Pere rd., 1 s. Hochgreve brewery.
Ducharme Joseph, musician, res. w. s. De Pere rd., 4 s. Hochgreve brewery.
Duchateau A. (Felicite and Frank J. B. Duchateau), wholesale liquors, 329 N. Washington.
Duchateau Alice Miss, dressmkr, res. 401 S. Madison.
Duchateau Arthur H., bookpr. A. Duchateau, res. 332 S. Webster av.
Duchateau Ceil Miss, res. 401 S. Madison.
Duchateau Felicite (A. Duchateau), res. 601 Pine,
Duchateau Felix, carp., res. e. s. Cedar, 2 n. Dousman. Ft. H.
Du Chateau Frances, res. 3 w. 854 Shawano rd., Ft. H.
Du Chateau Frank, butcher, res. 928 Main.
Duchateau Frank, R. R.-hand, res. s. s. Duck Creek rd., 13 w. Mather, Ft. H.
Duchateau Frank J. B. (A. Duchateau), res. 532 Main.
**DUCHATEAU FRED.**, ice-dlr., res. s. s. Mather, 3 w. Willow, Ft. H.
Duchateau Fred., lab., res. s. s. Elmore, 10 w. Cedar, Ft. H.
Du Chateau Joseph, lab., res. 319 N. Jefferson.
Du Chateau Laura Miss, res. 401 S. Madison.
Duchateau Rose Miss. res. 601 Pine.
Duchateau Theofile E. (Burghardt & Duchateau), res. 401 S. Madison.
Ducker Frank, carp., res. 1271 Mason.
Duering Dora, domestic 116 S. Monroe av.
Duescher Oscar, harnessmkr, res. 316 Pine.
Duffy Eliza, laundress Cook's Hotel.
Duggan Johanna (wid. Wenzel), res. 1409 Cedar.
Dolan Michael, brakeman, res. Northwestern Hotel, Ft. H.
Dulan Peter, conductor, res. Northwestern Hotel, Ft. H.
Dulan William, brakeman, res. Northwestern Hotel, Ft. H.
**DUNCAN ARCHIBALD M.**, prop. Howard Foundry and Machine Works, res. 410 Main, Ft. H.
Dunk Joseph, gardener, e. s. Goodell, cor. Eliza, res. same.
Dunlap Daisy H. Miss, res. 764 Shawano rd., Ft. H.
Dunlap Elsie S. Miss, teacher, res. 764 Shawano rd., Ft. H.
Dunlap Gilbert L., carp., res. 764 Shawano rd., Ft. H.
Dunlap George L., res. n. s. Cedar, 1 e. N. Quincy.
Dunlap Penelope D. (wid. John W.), res. 319 Chestnut, Ft. H.
Dunleavey Peter, foreman D. Flatley, res. 220 N. Adams.

Dunlevy Peter, yard foreman, res. Eldred's boarding house, Ft. H.
Dunlevy William, teamster, res. Eldred's boarding house, Ft. H.
Dunn James A., wiper, res. 109 Broadway, Ft. H.
Dunn Jennie Miss, prin. 5th Ward School, res. 310 6th av., Ft. H
Dunn Marie Etta Miss, stenog., res. 310 6th av., Ft. H.
Dunn Robert, boilermkr, res. 310 6th av., Ft. H.
Dunn Robert Jr., loco.-engineer, res. s. w. cor. Main and Willow, Ft. H.
Dunnett Mary (wid. James H.), res. 818 Walnut.
Dupont John, police, res. 212 S. Van Buren.
Dupont Manuel, mason, res. 617 N. Madison.
Dupont William, clk. Brauns & Van, res. 212 S. Van Buren.
Dupont Xavier, res. 1315 Day.
Du Pre Louis, maltster Henry Rahr's Sons, res. 1324 Cedar.
Dupry Frank, lab., res. 435 N. 11th.
Duquaine Desire, com.-trav. A. Duchateau, res. 906 Walnut.
Duquaine Theodore, lab., res. 1284 Elm.
Duree Gaspard, lab., res. 931 Day.
Du Rocher Aloisius, watchman, res. 944 S. Jackson.
Du Rocher Mathilda (wid. Alexander), res. 944 S. Jackson.
Dusenbery Charles E , grain buyer W. W. Cargill Co., res. e. s. Jackson, 2 s. Mason.
Dusenbery William, conductor, res. 729 Chicago.
Dutton Harley E., sec. to gen. mngr. G. B., W. & St. P. R. R., res. 711 S. Madison.
Dvorak John, lab., res. e. s. 5th av., 2 s. 9th, Ft. H.
Dvorak Mary (wid. Frank), res. e. s. 5th av., 2 s. 9th, Ft. H.
Dwyer Michael, engineer, res. e. s. 7th av., 2 s. 5th, Ft. H.
Dyke T. A., well digger, res. Bradley House.
Dysland Andrew, carpenter, res. 402 4th, Ft. H.
Dysland Julius, lab., res. 407 4th, Ft. H.
Dysland William, lab., res. e. s. 4th av., 4 n. 10th, Ft. H.

E

EAGLE Foundry, James Hughes, prop., n. w. cor. Pearl and Baird, Ft. H.
Earl Eli, res. Odd Fellows' Home.
Earley Peter, res. 427 S. Monroe av.
**EAST RIVER BREWERY,** Henry Rahr's Sons, props., 1323 Main.
East River Foundry & Machine Shop, C. Schwartze & Son, props., 1207 Main.

**THE A. SPUHLER CO.** *LADIES', MISSES' and CHILDREN'S*
**GREEN BAY** — **CLOAKS, CAPES, JACKETS**

East River Hotel, Frederick Gronnert, prop., 1273 Main.
East River Public School, n. e. cor. Elm and N. 12th.
Ebeling Fred. C., com. trav. J. H. Ebeling, res. 234 S. Adams.
**EBELING JOHN H.**, flour mills and grain elevator, n. w. cor. S. Washington and Doty, res. 234 S. Adams.
Ebeling John H. Jr., engineer, res. 234 S. Adams.
Ebeling Marie C. Miss, res. 234 S. Adams.
Ebeling William T., asst. bookkpr. John H. Ebeling, res. 234 S. Adams.
Echtner Jacob L., bookkpr. Hoeffel Bros. Shoe Co., res. 319 Pine.
Eckhardt Oswald, cigar mnfr., 200 S. Quincy, res. same.
Eckhardt Reinhold, cigarmkr, res. 200 S. Quincy.
Eckhardt Theodore, tailor, res. 200 S. Quincy.
Edges George, lab., res. 1423 Cedar.
Edges John, lab., res. 1423 Cedar.
Edges Joseph, lab., res. 1403 Cedar.
Edwards Alla Mrs., res. s. s. Mason, 1 e. Mason-st. bridge.
Edwards Charles, loco.- engineer, res. 308 Dousman, Ft. H.
Edwards Henry, lab., res. w. s. 9th av., 1 n. 1st, Ft. H.
Edwards Isaac L. (Joannes & Edwards) res. 539 S. Quincy.
Edwards May Miss, res. w. s. 9th av., 1 n. 1st, Ft. H.
Edwards Rose Miss, res. w. s. 9th av., 1 n. 1st, Ft. H.
Eggner Peter (Jones & Eggner), res. 213 Broadway, Ft. H.
Egl Joseph, blksmith, res. 310 N. Quincy.
Ehle Herman, carp., res. 302 3d av., Ft. H.
Ehrhardt Christine (wid. Christian), res. 1244 Walnut.
Ehrhardt Louis, lab., res. 1244 Walnut.
Eichwald August, teamster, res. 1115 Stuart.
Eisman John H., tel. opr. G. B., W. & St. P., res. 501 Main, Ft. H.
Elain Hattie Mrs., res. 614 N. Jefferson.
Eldred Anson (Anson Eldred & Son), res. Milwaukee.
Eldred Anson & Son (Anson and H. S. Eldred), saw-mill, o. s. 2d av., s. 10th, Ft. H.
Eldred George, lab., res. 101 Cherry, Ft. H.
Eldred Henry W., lab., res. 612 St. George.
**ELDRED HOWARD S.** (Anson Eldred & Son), pres. Citizens' National Bank, res. Milwaukee, Wis.
Eldred Sarah (wid. George W.), res. 612 St. George.
Eldredge Percy C., train master C., M. & St. P. R. R., res. 310 S. Jefferson.
Eliason Anna (wid. Ellis) res. 709 Harvey.
Eliason Charles, mason, res. 709 Harvey.
Eliasson John, carp., res. Junction Hotel, Ft. H.

Ellefson Nels, fisherman, res. 505 Broadway, Ft. H.
Ellingson Gunder, carp., res. 704 3d av., Ft. H.
Elliott Bert, engineer, res. 631 S. Jefferson.
Elliott Charles E., fireman, res. 106 S. Adams.
Ellis E. Holmes (Ellis & Merrill), res. 336 S. Jefferson.
**ELLIS & MERRILL** (E. Holmes Ellis and Carlton Merrill), lawyers, 4–7 Parmentier blk.
**ELLSWORTH ALBERT H. SR.**, dentist, 206 N. Washington, res. 515 Cherry.
Ellsworth Albert H. Jr., res. 515 Cherry.
Ellsworth Frank H., mngr. Knox & Wilner, res. 529 Cherry.
Ellsworth Lillie H. Miss, res. 515 Cherry.
Ellsworth Mary E. Mrs., res. 115 S. Adams.
Elmore Andrew E., postmaster Ft. Howard, res. n. w. cor. James and McDonald, Ft. H.
Elmore Augusta P. Miss, res. n. w. cor. James and McDonald, Ft. H.
**ELMORE J. H. & CO.** (James H. Elmore and James Delaney), cedar ties, 227 Pine.
**ELMORE JAMES H.** (J. H. Elmore & Co.), mayor Green Bay, res. 644 S. Monroe av.
Elmore Mary J. Miss, res. n. w. cor. James and McDonald, Ft. H.
Elmore Phoebe D. Miss, res. n. w. cor. James and McDonald, Ft. H.
Emig Louis, trav.-agent Gotfredson Bros., res. 222 N. 11th.
Emmerson Hans, lab., res. 800 3d av., Ft. H.
Empire House, Alfred H. Bouchard, prop., 203 S. Washington.
Emty ———, fireman, res. Junction Hotel, Ft. H.
Enderby George, hostler, res. Reis Hotel.
Enderby William, blksmith, res. 1310 Cedar.
Endrup Andrew, mill-hand, res. 306 3d, Ft. H.
Engels Edward (Engels & Mohr), res. 324 S. Van Buren.
Engels Frank, conductor, res. Empire House.
Engels Henry E., blksmith, res. 335 S. Van Buren.
Engels John, fireman, res. 324 S. Van Buren.
Engels Jos., gardener, res. n. s. Elmore, 4 w. Gnesnier, Ft. H.
Engels Louis J., clk. Engels & Mohr, res. 324 S. Van Buren.
Engels Nicholas, lab., res. s. s. 2d, 7 w. R. R. track, Ft. H.
Engels William, prop. Champion Hotel, res. same.
**ENGELS & MOHR** (Edward Engels and John Mohr), boots and shoes, 206 N. Washington.
Engelson Axel, lab., res. 316 Pearl, Ft. H.
English Lester A., res. 518 Walnut.

**THE A. SPUHLER CO., Green Bay** CARPETS, RUGS, OIL CLOTHS, Draperies and Window Shades.

ENG 107 EVE

English Mark, stone contr. res. 518 Walnut.
English Nottie C. Miss, res. 518 Walnut.
Engstrom Sophia (wid. Jonas P.), res. e. s. 4th av., 2 n. 4th, Ft. H.
Enoch Charles, broommkr, res. 533 S. Jackson.
Enos John, section-hand, res. 111 Broadway, Ft. H.
Enoch George, machinist, res. 533 S. Jackson.
Erbe Henry C. (Camm & Erbe), res. n. e. cor. Willow and Main, Ft. H.
Erdmann Albert N. (Erdmann & Lippert), res. 315 S. Madison.
Erdmann Annie Miss, res. 345 S. Madison.
Erdmann August (First & Erdmann), res. 805 Walnut.
Erdmann Charles, lab., res. 207 S. Van Buren.
Erdmann Christian, carp., res. 801 Walnut.
Erdmann Christian Jr., carp., res. 809 Walnut.
Erdmann Edward, plumber, res. w. s. S. Webster av., 2 s. Mason.
Erdmann Fred., carp., res. w. s. S. Webster av., 2 s. Mason.
Erdmann Gustav, carp., res. 802 S. Van Buren.
Erdmann Mary (wid. Edward), res. 207 S. Van Buren.
Erdmann & Lippert (Albert Erdmann and John Lippert), barbers, 210 Main.
Ericksen Elizabeth Miss, res. 409 S. Monroe av.
Ericksen Lyda Miss, res. 409 S. Monroe av.
**ERICKSEN MARTIN**, fresco artist, 335 Broadway, Ft. H., res. 409 S. Monroe av.
Erickson Andrew, car-smith, res. 705 3d av., Ft. H.
Erickson Christian, carp., res. 304 4th, Ft. H.
Erickson Hans, lab., res. 912 3d av., Ft. H.
Erickson Louis, fisherman, res. 623 Mather, Ft. H.
Ernest Charles, section-hand, res. 1508 Elm.
Ernst Minnie, domestic Champion Hotel.
Erpling Frederick Rev., res. 1026 Cherry.
Esselstyn Henry W., res. 712 S. Madison.
Eugene Elie, lab., res. 1116 Cedar.
Eugene Florent, lab., res. 1116 Cedar.
Eugene Jerome, edger, res. 1143 Walnut.
Eugene Mary Miss, dressmkr, res. 1116 Cedar.
Evans Michael, sawyer, res. n. s. Bond, 3 w. Cedar, Ft. H.
Evans Patrick, night watchman Broadway House, Ft. H.
Evans Thomas O., upholsterer, w. s. Cedar, 2 s. Dousman, Ft. H., res. same.
Everts Adeline Miss, res. 435 Elm.
Everts John, cooper, res. 435 Elm.
Everts Jules, lab., res. 435 Elm.

Everts Jules Jr., lab., res. 435 Elm.
Evraets John B., spiritualist medium, 817 Main, res. same.
Evraets Victor, carp., res. 1330 Cherry.
Evrard Joseph, gardener, res. n. s. Shawano av., 2 w. Fisk.
Evrard Josephine Miss, res. n. s. Shawano av., 2 w. Fisk.
Ewig John, fireman, res. 618 S. Jefferson.
Eycleshimer John L. D., grain-buyer, res. 620 Walnut.

## F

**FABRY Ferdinand**, cooper, res. 314 Cedar.
Fabry Joseph, tailor, res. 314 Cedar.
Fabry Louis (Fabry & Henkelmann), res. 330 S. Jackson.
Fabry Tillie Miss, tailoress, res. 314 Cedar.
**FABRY & HENKELMANN** (Louis Fabry and Edward Henkelmann), mason-contractors, 330 S. Jackson.
**FAIRFIELD WILLIAM E.**, physician and surgeon, Citizens' National Bank building, res. 733 Cherry.
Falanon Anton, shoemkr, res. 1441 Cedar.
Fancey Uriah, lab., res. 118 N. Monroe av.
Fannan John, res. 1227 Walnut.
Farnsworth Joseph, mill-hand, res. 309 3d, Ft. H.
Farr Albert, lab., res. s. w. cor. 2d av. and 10th, Ft. H.
Farrell Julia Miss, res. n. s. Duck Creek rd., 1 w. Mather, Ft. H.
Farrell Maggie Miss, res. n. s. Duck Creek rd., 1 w. Mather, Ft. H.
Farrell Marie Miss, teacher 5th Ward School, res. n. s. Duck Creek rd., 1 w. Mather, Ft. H.
Farrell Richard, carp., res. n. s. Duck Creek rd., 1. w. Mather, Ft. H.
Farrell Thomas, blksmith, res. 200 Cherry, Ft. H.
Farron Victor, butcher, res. 1329 Harvey.
Fasel Antoinette Miss, res. 1344 Stuart.
Fasel Frank, tailor, res. 1344 Stuart.
Fasel John, lab., res. 1344 Stuart.
Fastnacht Katherine (wid. Jacob), res. 832 Pine.
Fastry William, saloon, 329 N. Washington, res. 1014 Walnut.
Faulkner Henry, lab., res. 150 Broadway, Ft. H.
Faulkner Kate (wid. Edward), res. 150 Broadway, Ft. H.
Faulkner Libbie (wid. Frank), res. 101 S. Adams.
Fay Frank, upholsterer, res. 530 S. Jefferson.
Feely Dennis, conductor, res. 230 S. Quincy.
Feldhausen Charles, lab., res. 1634 Elm.
Feldhausen John, lab., res. 1634 Elm.

**THE A. SPUHLER CO., GREEN BAY, WIS. Fine Dress Goods**
Samples Furnished on Application.

Feldhausen Joseph, lab., res. 1605 Elm.
Feldhausen Matheus, lab., res. 1634 Elm.
Feldhausen Nicholas, carp., res. 1223 Cherry.
Feldhausen Paul, teamster, res. 1158 Pine.
Feley James, saw-filer, res. w. s. 8th, 1 n. 2d av., Ft. H.
Fellow Baptist, lab., res. 758 Shawano rd., Ft. H.
Felt John, lab., res. 1163 Stuart.
Fenctuman Charles, glazier, res. Adams House.
Fenlason Freeman, lab., res. w. s. Pearl, 3 s. Hubbard, Ft. H.
Fennondale Selina, domestic Waterloo House.
Fenske Florentine (wid. Julius), res. 1181 Mason.
Fenwick Andrew, master mechanic G. B., W. & St. P. Ry, res. 418 Walnut.
Fenwick Ina H. Miss, res. 418 Walnut.
Ferguson Samuel, lab., res. 617 Cedar.
Ferguson W. D., plumber, res. Adams House.
**FERRIS HOTEL**, James P. Ferris, prop., 216-218 3d av., Ft. H.
Ferris James P., prop. Ferris Hotel, res. 216-218 3d av., Ft. H.
Ferris Napoleon, engineer, res. 316 Main.
Ferriter Theresa Mrs., res. 426 N. 11th.
Ferron Josephine Mrs., res. n. e. cor. Pine and N. Quincy.
Ferslev Marie, domestic 404 Chestnut, Ft. H.
Ferslev Mark, teamster, res. s. s. Shawano rd., 5 w. Hazel, Ft. H.
Ferslev Mary (wid. Nels), res. s. s. Shawano rd., 5 w. Hazel, Ft. H.
Ferslev Peter, lab., res. s. s. Shawano rd., 5 w. Hazel, Ft. H.
Feurig Gustav, photographer, res. 212 Cherry.
Fiedler H. Ludolf, blksmith, res. 347 S. 10th.
Fiedler Ludolf, wagonmkr, res. 347 S. 10th.
Fiedler Otto L. (Clark & Fiedler), res. w. s. Cherry, 7 n. Donsman, Ft. H.
Field George, res. 712 S. Madison.
Field Gustav, res. 512 Cherry, Ft. H.
Field William H., bookkpr. McGrath & Anderson, res. 712 S. Madison.
Fields Victor, lab., res. East River rd., e. Rahr's Brewery.
Fignier Carmel, res. 123 S. 10th.
Fignier Catherine (wid. Charles), res. 123 S. 10th.
Fignier Charles Jr., cooper, res. 123 S. 10th.
Fignier Clement, clk. The Green Bay Advocate Co., res. 123 S. 10th.
Fignier Eli, lab., res. 123 S. 10th.
Fignier Henrietta, res. 123 S. 10th.
Fignier Joseph C., clk., res. 123 S. 10th.

**FINDEISEN BROS.** (Louis W. and Leonard Findeisen), hardware, stoves and tinware, 309 N. Washington.
Findeisen Leonard (Findeisen Bros.), res. 517 Walnut.
Findeisen Louis W. (Findeisen Bros.), res. 114 N. Madison.
Finnegan A. H., mngr. Finnegan's Brickyard, res. w. s. 2d av., 3 s. 10th, Ft. H.
Finnegan Annie Miss, res. 432 S. Quincy.
Finnegan Jane (wid. Martin), res. 701 Pine.
Finnegan John, lab., res. 701 Pine.
Finnegan Mary Miss, res. 432 S. Quincy.
Finnegan Peter, lab., res. 701 Pine.
Finnegan William, prop. Finnegan's Brick Yards, res. Duck Creek.
Finnegan William, fireman, res. Northwestern Hotel, Ft. H.
Finnertz A. G., lab., res. Junction Hotel, Ft. H.
First C. Edward (First & Erdmann), res. 1174 Walnut.
First Henry, res. 120 S. 11th.
**FIRST & ERDMANN** (Charles Ed. First and August Erdmann), barbers, 213 Cherry.
Fischer August, filer, res. Eldred's boarding house, Ft. H.
Fischer John A., engineer, res. Northwestern Hotel, Ft. H.
Fischer Stella Miss, res. 1163 Stuart.
Fisher G. William, cooper, res. 1222 St. Clair.
Fisher Louis A., musician, res. 221 N. Madison.
Fisher Oscar, filer, res. Eldred's boarding house.
Fisk G. Wallace, bkpr. Kellogg National Bank, res. n. s. Shawano rd., 1 w. Willow, Ft. H.
Fisk Harry W., pres. The Fisk Land and Lumber Co., res. 113 Willow, Ft. H.
**FISK LAND & LUMBER CO.,** H. W. Fisk, pres.; W. J. Fisk, sec. and treas., C. & N. W. Ry. depot, Ft. H.
Fisk W. D. & Co. (W. D. and H. W. Fisk), dealers in ties and posts, C. & N. W. Ry. depot, Ft. H.
Fisk Wilbur D., v.-pres The Fisk Land & Lumber Co., res. 303 Chestnut, Ft. H.
Fisk William, sawyer, res. Eldred's boarding house, Ft. H.
**FISK WILLIAM J.,** pres. The Kellogg National Bank, res. n. w. cor. Willow and Shawano av., Ft. H.
Fitzgerald Garrett, car insp., res. n. s. Baird, cor. Willow, Ft. H.
Fitzgerald William M., cooper, res. 315 S. Jackson.
Fitzmorris James H., res. e. s. Chestnut, 3 s. Elmore, Ft. H.
Flanders Edward D., conductor, res. 521 Cedar, Ft. H.
Flatley Alice Miss, bkpr. 212 Main, res. 504 Chestnut, Ft. H.
Flatley Annie Miss, res. 626 Pine.

**Headquarters for Boys' Clothing** THE A. SPUHLER CO. GREEN BAY.

Flatley Bridget (wid Patrick), res. 412 S. Adams.
**FLATLEY DOMINICK**, livery and sale stable, 220 **N**. Adams, res. 632 Main.
Flatley Dominick W. (McCormick & Flatley), res. 412 S. Adams.
Flatley Ellen Miss, res. 626 Pine.
Flatley Ellen A. (wid. Hugh), res. 504 Chestnut, Ft. H.
Flatley George H., ship.-clk., res. 632 Main.
Flatley James, res. 632 Pine.
Flatley James H., station agt. C., M. & St. P. R. R., res. 412 S. Adams.
Flatley James P., clk. 212 Main, Ft. H., res. 504 Chestnut, Ft. H.
Flatley John E., ticket agt. C., M. & St. P. R. R., res. 412 S. Adams.
Flatley Kate L. Miss, res. 632 Main.
Flatley Margaret Miss, res. 412 S. Adams.
Flatley Michael, cattle dlr., res. 621 Walnut.
Flatley Thomas, res. 412 S. Adams.
Flatley William, prescription clk. J. Robinson, res. 632 Main.
Fleming Ella Miss, res. 1126 Main.
Fleming John, police, res. 518 Main.
Fleming Lawrence, fireman Hose Cart **No. 1, res**. 1101 Doty.
Fleming Patrick, res. 1126 Main.
Flemming Charles S., barber, res. American House.
Flemming Susanna (wid. Frank), res. 922 N. 12th.
Florentine Joseph, machinist, res. 1136 Crooks.
Foerster Herman, carriagemkr, res. 1520 Elm.
Foerster Otto, tailor, res. 1348 St. Clair.
Foerster William, carp., res. 1348 St. Clair.
Fogarty Nora, domestic, res. cor. Dousman and Chestnut, Ft. H.
Foggatt Archibald R., clk. Cook's Hotel.
Fohrmann Joseph, res. 225 S. Adams.
Foley Annie Miss, clk. Jorgensen Blesch Co., res. 604 Chestnut, Ft. H.
Foley Dennis, barkpr., res. 502 N. Jefferson.
Foley Matt., engineer C., M. & St. P., res. Bradley House.
Follett Alice R. Miss, res. 926 Cherry.
Follett Catherine (wid. Emmons W.), res. 100 S. Monroe av.
Follett Charles E., butcher, res. 926 Cherry.
Follett George B., hardware, tinware, etc., 1234 **Main, res**. 113 S. Van Buren.
Follett John C., res. 100 S. Monroe av.
Follett Linda Miss, res. 926 Cherry.
Follett William D., meat cutter G. D. Nau, res. 926 Cherry.
Follett William W., tinsmith, res. 926 Cherry.

Fonder Annie Miss, res. 600 St. George.
Fonder David, butcher, res. 502 S. Quincy.
Fonder John, lab., res. 600 St. George.
Fonder Joseph, lab., res. 600 St. George.
Fonder Lambert (E. Humpfner & Co.), res. 502 S. Quincy.
Fonder Nestor, lab., res. 600 St. George.
Fontaine Albert J., with B. Fontaine Hardware Co., res. 428 N. Jefferson.
Fontaine Arthur, student, res. 428 N. Jefferson.
Fontaine B. Hardware Co., Benjamin F. Fontaine, pres.; Raphael Fontaine, sec. and treas., 218 Main.
Fontaine Benjamin F., pres. B. Fontaine Hardware Co., res. 428 N. Jefferson.
Fontaine Raphael, sec. and treas. B. Fontaine Hardware Co., res. 621 St. George.
Ford Edward A., helper, res. 809 Cherry, Ft. H.
Ford James K., machinist, res. 809 Cherry, Ft. H.
Formes Annie, domestic 1142 Main.
Formes William, bartender, res. Reis Hotel.
**FORRER EDWARD W.**, ins. and manager Arnold Yeast Co., 229 S. Washington, res. same.
Forst Christian, res. 322 N. Webster av.
Forst Herman, porter 124 S. Washington, res. 322 N. Webster av.
**FORT HOWARD CORNET BAND**, H. C. Buenger, leader, e. s. Cedar, bet. Main and Hubbard, Ft. H.
Fort Howard Elevator, n. e. cor. Hubbard and Pearl, Ft. H.
Fort Howard Lumber Co., Fred Hurlbut, pres.; George Beyer, v.-pres.; F. R. Weeks, sec. and treas., w. s. 2d av., nr. 10th, Ft. H.
**FORT HOWARD REVIEW**, James Kerr & Son, props.; 309 Pearl, Ft. H.
Foster Charles S., brakeman, res. 742 S. Jefferson.
Foster Dell N., fireman, res. 206 3d av., Ft. H.
Foster Hattie Miss, dental asst. C. O. Gage, res. 1014 Walnut.
Foster Wm. (Peterman & Foster), res. town Allouez.
Foster. See Foerster.
Fournier Albert, carp., res. s. s. Shawano rd., 3 w. R. R. track, Ft. H.
Fournier Charles, res. s. s. Shawano rd., 3 w. R. R. track, Ft. H.
Fournier Manuel, sawyer, res. 619 Main.
Fowles Carlton C., prop. Fowles' ship-yards on Fox River, e. s. McDonald n. James, Ft. H., res. same.
Fowles Foster W., sew. mach. agt., res. w. s. McDonald, 7 s. lumber yard, Ft. H.

**THE A. SPUHLER CO.** LADIES', MISSES' and CHILDREN'S
GREEN BAY — **CLOAKS, CAPES, JACKETS**

Fowles John M., cook, res. w. s. McDonald, 7 s. lumber yard, Ft. H.
Fowles Samuel, ship-carp., res. w. s. McDonald, 7 s. lumber yard, Ft. H.
Fowles William C., lab., res. w. s. McDonald, 6 s. lumber yard, Ft. H.
Fowles William E., ship-carp., res. w. s. McDonald, 6 s. lumber yard, Ft. H.
Fox Fannie Miss, res. 306 Dousman, Ft. H.
Fox Fern Ivy Miss, res. 306 Dousman, Ft. H.
Fox John W., fisherman, res. 507 Cedar.
Fox Joseph J. Very Rev., Vicar General Diocese of Green Bay, res. 139 S. Madison.
Fox J. T. (wid. John), res. 308 Dousman, Ft. H.
Fox Lizzie D. Miss, teacher, res. 421 S. Webster av.
Fox Matthew, brakeman, res. 414 N. Quincy.
**FOX RIVER ELECTRIC RAILWAY CO.**, Wm. P. Harvey, mngr., 312–320 S. Washington.
Foy William, lab., res. 202 S. Jefferson.
Franc Alex C., res. 439 S. Quincy.
Francar Anton, lab., res. 1108 Cedar.
Francar Emil, drug clk. 225 Main, res. 1108 Cedar.
Francart Frank, watchman, res. 1219 Cass.
Francart Milka Miss, res. 1219 Cass.
Francis Elie, lab., res. 1112 Cedar.
Francis Joseph, tinsmith, res. 1112 Cedar.
Francois Frank, painter, res. 1375 Mason.
Francois Henry, painter, res. 1375 Mason.
Francois John B., carp., res. 1375 Mason.
Francois Joseph, carver, res. 1375 Mason.
Francois Lambert, lab., res. 1021 Doty.
Francois Peter, res. 1501 Mason.
Franey Honora (wid. Thomas), res. 632 Cherry.
Frank Emma, teacher, res. s. s. Dousman, 3 w. Willow, Ft. H.
Frank George, jeweler, e. s. Broadway, 2 n. Main, res. s. s. Dousman, 2 w. the slough, Ft. H.
Frank Geo. P., clk. n. w. cor. 3d av. and 4th, res. same, Ft. H.
Frank Ida Miss, res. s. s. Dousman, 3 w. Willow, Ft. H.
Franks Charles E., carsmith, res. 902 S. Quincy.
Franssens Adele Miss, res. 434 S. Jackson.
Franssens Alphons J., student, res. 434 S. Jackson.
Franssens Charles L., student, res. 434 S. Jackson.
Franssens John M., harnessmkr, 223 Main, res. 434 S. Jackson.
Frare Gustav, lab., res. 201 S. Webster av.

Frawley Mary, cook Green Bay House.
Frederickson William, barkpr. Robert N. Wilson, res. Union House, Ft. H.
Freeman Adelbert E., engineer Green Bay and Ft. Howard Water Works Co., res. 607 S. Adams.
Freeman Chauncey A., lake capt., res. 114 6th av., Ft. H.
Freeman G. Edmund, conductor C., M. & St. P. R. R., res. 419 S. Madison.
Freeman Mary A. (wid. Wm.), res. 419 S. Madison.
Freiheit Samuel, captain Salvation Army, res. 217 S. Washington.
Freimann Celia Miss, res. 513 N. Jefferson.
Freimann Michael, saloon, 347 S. Washington, res. 513 N. Jefferson.
Freimann Rose Miss, res. 513 N. Jefferson.
Fremale Frank, res. s. e. cor. Forest and Elm.
French Presbyterian Church, Rev. George C. Mousseau, pastor; Doty, bet. S. Adams and S. Jefferson.
Freriks Celia Miss, res. 1257 Day.
Freriks Lambert, carp., res. 1257 Day.
Freriks Lizzie Miss, res. 1257 Day.
Freriks Louis, carp., res. 1245 Day.
Freriks Philipine Miss, res. 1257 Day.
Frewerd Charles, printer, res. 712 Cedar.
Frewerd Peter Sr., plasterer, res. 712 Cedar.
Frewerd Peter Jr., lab., res. 702 Cedar.
Friderici Christian, farmer, res. e. s. Oneida rd., 1 s. 2d, Ft. H.
Friderici Christian A., farmer, res. e. s. Oneida rd., 1 s. 2d, Ft. H.
Friedel Annie, domestic 218 S. Adams.
Friedel John Jr., train dispatcher, res. 1234 Chicago.
Friedel Rose (wid. John), res. 1234 Chicago.
Friedel Rose Miss, dressmkr, res. 1234 Chicago.
Friese Gottfried, res. 125 6th av., Ft. H.
Frisk John V., engineer, res. s. e. cor. Cherry and Mather, Ft. H.
Frisque Antoinette Mrs., res. 331 S. Jackson.
Frisque Edward, tailor, res. 121 S. Webster av.
Frisque Eugene, tailor, res. 331 S. Jackson.
**FRISQUE FLORENTIN,** merchant tailor, 232 Main, res. 119 S. Jackson.
Frisque George, tel. opr., res. 331 S. Jackson.
Frisque George, lab., res. 119 S. Jackson.
Frisque John, clk. 932 Main, res. 610 Cedar.
Frisque John, tailor, res. 119 S. Jackson.
Frisque Joseph, tailor, res. 331 S. Jackson.

**THE A. SPUHLER CO., Green Bay** CARPETS, RUGS, OIL CLOTHS, Draperies and Window Shades.

Fritscher Theresa Mrs., res. 117 S. Jefferson.
Froemke Emeline Miss, res. 821 Cherry.
Froemke Frederick W., auditor and cashier G. B., W. & St. P. R. R., res. 821 Cherry.
Froemke Hattie Miss, res. 821 Cherry.
Froemke Wm. C., clk. auditor G. B., W. & St. P. R. R., res. 218 N. Van Buren.
Froncee Francis, res. 1432 Elm.
Fuller Frank H., agt. U. S. Ex. Co., res. 1139 Walnut.
Fuller George B., clk. U. S. Ex. Co., res. 1139 Walnut.
Fuller Mary J. (wid. Daniel), res. 1031 Mason.
Fulton John E., painter, res. Ferris Hotel, Ft. H.
Furo Rena Miss, dressmkr, res. 308 Cherry, Ft. H.

## G

GABRISZAK Julius, lab., res. 1332 Doty.
Gabriszak Louis, lab., res. 1332 Doty.
Gabriszak Stanislaus, lab., res. 1332 Doty.
Gaddes Atta B., teacher, res. 142 Pearl, Ft. H.
Gaddes George, engineer, res. 142 Pearl, Ft. H.
Gaddes Gertie Miss, res. 142 Pearl, Ft. H.
Gaffney Daniel, res. 317 Cherry.
Gaffney Edwin, undersheriff, res. 317 Cherry.
Gaffney Louis H., mnfr. of boxes, cisterns, etc., 224 S. Van Buren, res. same.
Gaffney Marcella Miss, res. 317 Cherry.
Gaffney Martin, conductor, res. Northwestern House, Ft. H.
Gaffney Thos., prop. Arlington Hotel, res. 419 Broadway, Ft. H.
Gaffron E. Max, bkpr. Brown-Chapin Lumber Co., res. 235 S. Adams.
Gage Colonel O., dentist, 221 N. Washington. res. 414 S. Webster av.
Gage Stephen, brakeman, res. 109 Broadway, Ft. H.
Gagnon Albert, baker, res. 1021 Main.
Gagnon Frank, lab., res. 1021 Main.
Gagnon Herbert, lab., res. 1021 Main.
Gagnon Maxon, barber, 120 N. Washington, res. American House.
Gajewski Frank, res. 1101 Stuart.
Gajewski Verna Miss, res. 407 N. Madison.
Galentine Samuel, res. Odd Fellows' Home.
Galineau Emory D., barber, res. 333 Webster av.
Gallagher Bridget Mrs., res. 1113 Mason.

Gallagher Marguerite (wid. Neil), res. 405 Hubbard, Ft. H.
Gallagher Patrick, carp., res. e. s. 10th av., 4 n. 2d, Ft. H.
Gamalski August, res. e. s. Hazel, 3 s. Shawano rd., Ft. H.
Gamble John J., baggageman, res. 601 S. Jackson.
Gant Frederick, cook Cook's Hotel.
Gantz Charles, cooper, res. 615 Cedar.
Gantz Henry, cooper, res. 615 Cedar.
Gantz Julia Miss, res. 615 Cedar.
Gantz Minnie (wid. Henry), res. 615 Cedar.
Gantz Minnie Miss, res. 615 Cedar.
Gantz William, cooper, res. 312 N. 11th.
Gardiner Addie, bookkpr. 124 S. Washington, res. 421 S. Webster av.
Gardiner Ethel L. Miss, bookkpr. Buengener & Bur, res. 421 S. Webster av.
Gardiner Howard C., res. 421 S. Webster av.
Gardner Emma M. Miss, stenog., res. 433 S. Monroe av.
Gardner Mary E. (wid. B. C.), res. 433 S. Monroe av.
**GARDNER WALTER E.**, prop. and editor The State Gazette, res. 108 N. Adams.
Garland Thomas, engineer, res. Northwestern Hotel, Ft. H.
Garlock Benj. F., carp., res. s. w. cor. Guesnier and Division, Ft. H.
**GARNER WILLIAM**, saloon, 222 N. Washington, res. sa me
Garot Adolph, plumber, res. 531 S. Madison.
Garot Edward, plumber, res. 531 S. Madison.
Garot Frank, engineer, res. 531 S. Madison.
Garot Joseph, engineer, res. 531 S. Madison.
Garot Louis, lab., res. 531 S. Madison.
Gass Clara Miss, clk., res. 416 Stuart.
Gass Elsie Miss, clk., res. 416 Stuart.
Gass Frank, cook, res. 416 Stuart.
Gass Louis, restaurant and bakery, 219 Cherry, res. 416 Stuart.
Gates Christian, lab., res. 407 3d av., Ft. H.
Gauthier Emil, student, res. 1374 Chicago.
Gauthier Emma Miss, dressmkr, res. 1374 Chicago.
Gauthier John, res. 618 S. 12th.
Gauthier John, fireman, res. 1374 Chicago.
Gauthier Peter, lab., res. 1374 Chicago.
Gauthier Therese (wid. John), res. 1374 Chicago.
Gavin Philip M., fireman, res. Ferris Hotel, Ft. H.
Gay Thomas, captain, res. n. e. cor. Cedar and Kellogg, Ft. H.
Gaylord Catherine Miss, teacher South Ward School, res. 547 S. Quincy.

**THE A. SPUHLER CO., GREEN BAY, WIS.** Fine Dress Goods
Samples Furnished on Application.

Gaylord George A., captain, kpr. lighthouse, res. 547 S. Quincy.
Gayton Dalanson C., civil engineer 216 N. Washington, res. 330 Willow, Ft. H.
Gazette George, confectr., res. Bay City House.
Geall Desire, gardener, res. 1301 Day.
Geall George, cigarmkr, res. 1350 Day.
Geall John, lab., res. 1301 Day.
Geall Joseph, lab., res. 1602 Elm.
Geall Nicol, lab., res. 1350 Day.
Gearapan William, foreman, res. s. s. 7th, 1 w. 3d av., Ft. H.
Geer Alice L. Miss, res. 521 S. Jackson.
Geer Edwin L., express messenger, res. 521 S. Jackson.
Geer Joseph L., conductor, res. 521 S. Jackson.
Geer Mary E. Miss, res. 521 S. Jackson.
Geerts August, lab., res. 509 Broadway, Ft. H.
Gehler Wm., lab., res. 1325 Cherry.
**GEHR FREDERICK**, saloon, 318 N. Washington, res. 217 N. Jefferson.
Gehr Jacob, barkpr., res. 734 Walnut.
Gehrke August F., lab., res. 218 S. Jackson.
Gehrke Elizabeth Miss, res. 218 S. Jackson.
Gehrke Rosie Miss, res. 218 S. Jackson.
Gehrke William, lab., res. 218 S. Jackson.
Gehrke Wm., machinist, res. Bodart House.
Geiger Joseph, lab., res. 306 Cass.
Geisenberg Isidor J., com. trav. 124 S. Washington, res. 305 3d, Ft. H.
Geisenberg Marie, milliner, 313 Broadway, Ft. H., res. same.
Genoau Jacob, mill-hand, res. s. w. cor. 2d av. and 9th, Ft. H.
Geniesse Charles, lab., res. 411 Elm.
Geniesse Eugene, knot sawyer, res. Bodart House.
Geniesse Frances (wid. Clement), res. 411 Elm.
Geniesse Flora, dressmkr, res. 1244 Stuart.
Geniesse John B., watchman, res. 806 S. Quincy.
Geniesse Jules H., carp.-contr., 322 S. Van Buren, res. same.
Gennieux Anna (wid. Andree), res. 435 N. 11th.
Gentchens William C., foreman, res. Eldred's boarding house, Ft. H.
George Samuel, lather, res. 320 Willow, Ft. H.
Gerhard Nels, lab., res. 1351 Cherry.
German M. E. Church, Rev. A. M. Wieting, pastor, s. w. cor. Doty and S. 10th.
Germiat Desire, carp., res. 1374 Day.
Germiat Joseph, lab., res. 1374 Day.

Germiat Joseph, sailor, res. 428 Pleasant.
Germiat Natalie (wid. Frank), res. 1374 Day.
Germiat Theodore, res. 1374 Day.
Gerondale Alexander, lab., res. 1235 Day.
Gerondale Joseph, beer peddler, res. 824 Crooks.
Gerpin Barbara (wid. Hugo), res. 708 3d av., Ft. H.
Gerpin Clara Miss, res. 708 3d av., Ft. H.
Gerpin John, lab., res. 708 3d av., Ft. H.
Gerpin Lillie Miss, res. 708 3d av., Ft. H.
Gerpin Lizzie Miss, dressmkr, res. 708 3d av., Ft. H.
Gerpin Winnis, engineer, res. 708 3d av., Ft. H.
Getts Frank, res. 101 S. Adams.
Getts John A., harnessmkr, res. 101 S. Adams.
Getts Pearl Miss, res. 101 S. Adams.
Getzlaff Herman, yardmaster C., M. & St. P. Ry., res. Bradley House.
Geyer Anton A., cooper, res. 627 St. George.
Geyer Damian, fireman, res. w. s. St. George, 1 n. Willow.
Geyer Elizabeth (wid. Damian), res. 731 St. George.
Geyer George, res. 731 St. George.
Geyer Henry, res. 1356 Walnut.
Geyer John, res. 731 St. George.
Geyer Joseph, lab., res. 1284 Elm.
Gibbons Patrick, lab., res. Wisconsin House.
Gibbs Melvin E., com.-trav., res. 504 Doty.
Gibson Andrew, lab., res. Main-st. Hotel.
Gibson Wm. H., grocer, 503 Main, res. same.
Giersbach William, lab., res. 1005 Cedar.
Giese A. August, lab., res. 1322 Lawe.
Giese Albert R., carriagemkr, res. 545 S. Jackson.
Giese August, lab., res. 1210 Chicago.
Giese Conrad, lab., res. 401 6th av., Ft. H.
Giese Emma Miss, res. 1143 Mason.
Giese Frederick W., carp., res. 1143 Mason.
Giese Gottfried, lab., res. 1116 Cass.
Giese Hulda Miss, res. 1143 Mason.
Giese John, lab., res. 1239 Crooks.
Giese Lena, domestic 521 Cherry.
Giese Marie, domestic, res. 107 6th av., Ft. H.
Giese Mary, domestic 310 S. Jefferson.
Giese Michael, lab., res. 1215 S. Quincy.
Giese Otto, lab., res. 1322 Lawe.
Giesler Edward, teamster, res. 1142 Walnut.
Giesler Ernestine (wid. Charles), res. 1221 Mason.

**Headquarters for Boys' Clothing** THE A. SPUHLER CO. GREEN BAY.

Giesler Frederic, R. R.-hand, res. e. s. 4th av., 2 n. 8th, Ft. H.
Giesler Louis H., clk. Mohr & Lenz, res. 1142 Walnut.
Gieszler Christiana (wid. Christian), res. 1234 Chicago.
Gigler Jacob, cigar mnfr., 517 Main, res. 1136 Cherry.
Gilger Alvin, cooper, res. 1367 Walnut.
Gilger Eleanor (wid. Charles), res. 312 N. 11th.
Gilger Frederick C., cooper, res. 1220 Doty.
Gilger Minnie L. Miss, res. 312 N. 11th.
Gilger Morris, cooper, res. 1314 Cherry.
Gill Christ, fireman, res. Bradley House.
Gille Desire, teamster, res. 819 N. 12th.
Gille George, cigarmkr, res. 1352 Day.
Gille Nicholas, mason, res. 1352 Day.
Gillespie Andrew W., canvasser, res. Broadway Hotel, Ft. H.
**GILLESPIE WILLIAM G.**, mngr. Singer Sewing Machine Co., res. 421 S. Jefferson.
Gilling Jeremiah, lab., res. n. s. Elmore, 6 w. Cedar, Ft. H.
Gilling Mary (wid. Frank), res. 2 w. 723 Bond, Ft. H.
Gillis Alvina, domestic 714 Doty.
Gillis Delia Miss, clk. Jorgensen-Blesch Co., **res. 310 Chestnut**, Ft. H.
Gilman Martha (wid. Charles), res. 403 Mather, Ft. H.
Gilson Gustave, lab., res. No. 7, n. end Monroe av., e. Murphy's mill.
Gilson Jule, lab., res. 445 S. Madison.
Gilsoul Gustav, lab., res. 1118 Day.
Glaser Annie Miss, res. 413 S. Quincy.
Glaser Gustav, lab., res. 413 S. Quincy.
Glaser Louis, res. 413 S. Quincy.
Glaser Otto, bottler, res. 413 S. Quincy.
Glass Eva Miss, res. 324 Willow, Ft. H.
**GLASS JOHN**, ice dealer, ft. N. Jefferson, res. 324 Willow, Ft. H.
Glassel Mary, head waiter Cook's Hotel.
Glasser George, lab., res. 1236 Day.
Glasser Lena Miss, res. 1236 Day.
Glasser Mathilda Miss, res. 1236 Day.
Gleason Bartholomew, farmer, res. 907 Main.
Gleason James, motorman, res. 1020 Walnut.
Gleason John, farmer, res. 907 Main.
Gleason Michael, well-driller, 1233 Stuart, res. same.
Gobler William, harnessmkr, res. 212 S. Quincy.
Godfirnon Gerard, stone-cutter, res. n. s. Dousman, 20 w. Guesnier, Ft. H.

Godfirnon Geraldine Miss, clk., res. 115 S. Madison.
Godfirnon Selina Miss, clk., res. n. s. Dousman, 20 w. Gnesnier, Ft. H.
Godfrey Clementine Miss, res. 215 S. Jackson.
Godfrey George, lab., res. Adams House.
Goebel George, lab., res. 1260 Cedar.
Goeben. See Von Goeben.
Goetsch Albert G., com. trav. The Weise-Hollman Co., h. 1125 Walnut.
Goetz Annie Miss, res. 601 S. Monroe av.
Goffard Henry, lab., res. s. w. cor. Shawano rd. and Oak, Ft. H.
Golden Mercer, peddler, res. 118 S. Quincy.
Goldse Henry, painter, res. Junction Hotel, Ft. H.
Gollo Frank, carp., res. 204 7th av., Ft. H.
**GOLUCKE CHARLES**, mason-contr., 921 Cherry, res. same.
Golz Emma, domestic, res. 123 Broadway, Ft. H.
Gonion Napoleon H., agricultural implts., 413 Main, res. Schauer Hotel.
Gonion Paul, machinist, res. 506 N. Jefferson.
Gonse Edward, gardener, res. 836 Dousman, Ft. H.
Gonse Fred., lab., res. 513 S. Adams.
Gonse Henry, gardener, res. 836 Dousman, Ft. H.
Gonse William, barber, res. 836 Dousman, Ft. H.
Goodchild Louis, buttermkr, res. 410 Cherry, Ft. H.
Goodell Hattie Miss, teacher, res. 111 N. Van Buren.
Goodhue Delia (wid. Charles F.), res. 344 S. Quincy.
Goodrich Transportation Co., M. J. McCormick, agent, ft. Pine.
Goopmans Frank, lab., res. s. s. Elmore, 3 w. Cross rds., Ft. H.
Gooeney Peter, mill-hand, res. Eldred's boarding house, Ft. H.
Gore Anton, mason, res. 1461 Mason.
Gorgensen Martin, carp., res. Junction Hotel, Ft. H.
Gotfredson Benjamin (Gotfredson Bros.), res. 803 Cherry.
Gotfredson Bros. (Lawrence and Benjamin Gotfredson), hardware, 1155-1157 Main, and horses, Main, next to East River bridge.
Gotfredson Lawrence (Gotfredson Bros.), res. 630 Walnut.
**GOTHE FREDERICK**, grocer, saloon and blksmith shop, s. s. Shawano rd., nr. city limits, Ft. H.
Gotto Eli (Cohn & Gotto), res. 817 Walnut.
Gotto Eli Jr., clk., res. 817 Walnut.
Gotto Joseph, house-furnishing goods, 231 Pine, res. 411 N. Monroe av.
Gotto Nora Miss, res. 817 Walnut.

**THE A. SPUHLER CO.** *LADIES', MISSES' and CHILDREN'S*
**GREEN BAY** **CLOAKS, CAPES, JACKETS**

Gougnard Eugene, mason, res. 117 S. Jackson.
Gould Charles, engineer, res. 126 S. Webster av.
Gould M. C., clothes cleaner, res. Howard House, Ft. H.
Gourlay Frank, boilermkr, res. w. s. 8th av., 2 n. 2d, Ft. H.
Grace James, tallyman, res. Eldred's boarding house, Ft. H.
Graetens Michael, beer peddler Henry Rahr's Sons, res. 1171 Harvey.
Grainer Martin, brakeman, res. 208 6th av., Ft. H.
Graner Edward, cattle-dlr., 1015 Main, res. same.
Graner Emma Miss, res. 1015 Main.
Graner Robert, cattle-dlr., 1015 Main, res. same.
Grassens John, lab., res. 1315 Harvey.
Graves Abbie (wid. Orlo), res. 2 w. 792 Shawano rd., Ft. H.
Graves Bradley, clk., res. 2 w. 792 Shawano rd., Ft. H.
Graves Charles, captain, res. 1521 Morrow.
Graves Elizabeth (wid. O. B.), res. 1521 Morrow.
Graves Ellen (wid. Chester), res. 1515 Cedar.
Graves Louise Miss, res. 2 w. 792 Shawano rd., Ft. H.
Graves Lucie, res. 1515 Cedar.
Graves Ralph, lab., res. 2 w. 792 Shawano rd., Ft. H.
Graves Walter, lab., res. 1515 Cedar.
Gravy John, housemover, res. n. e. cor. Division and Fink, Ft. H.
Gravy Josephine Mrs., res. 513 Cherry, Ft. H.
Gray Albert L., dry goods, 217 Main, res. 312 Chestnut, Ft. H.
Gray Ethel Miss, res. 312 Chestnut, Ft. H.
Gray Leona Miss, clk. Jorgensen Blesch Co., res. 312 Chestnut, Ft. H.
Greatens Michael, peddler, res. 1171 Harvey.
**GREEN ADOLPH**, general building contractor, 1019 Pine, res. same.
Green Albert, well-driller, res. 339 S. Madison.
Green Alvin, teamster, res. 339 S. Madison.
Green Anne M. Miss, res. 620 Walnut.
**GREEN BROS. & CO.** (Gustav K. and Charles Green and Robert Armstrong), artesian well contrs., 1215 Stuart.
**GREEN CHARLES L.** (Green Bros. & Co.), res. 1203 Stuart.
Green George, jeweler, res. 1019 Pine.
Green George W., clk. G. B., W. & St. P. R. R., res. 118 Walnut.
**GREEN GUSTAVE K.** (Green Bros. & Co.), res. 1215 Stuart.
Green Jacob, well-driller, res. 1203 Stuart.
Green Mary J. (wid. George), res. 620 Walnut.

Green Otto, clk. Buengener & Bur. res. 1019 Pine.
**GREEN BAY ADVOCATE,** The Green Bay Advocate Co., props., Frank Tilton, editor, 216 Pine.
**GREEN BAY ADVOCATE CO. THE,** Edward Decker, pres.; David Decker, v.-pres.; W. C. Jenkins, sec.; props. and pubs. Green Bay Advocate and blank book mnfrs., dealers in stationery, and book and job printers, 216 Pine.
Green Bay Athletic Assn., n. w. cor. Doty and Adams.
Green Bay Business Men's Assn., Fred. Hollman, pres.; M. J. McCormick, sec.; n. e. cor. N. Adams and Walnut.
**GREEN BAY BUSINESS COLLEGE,** J. M. McCunn, prop., n. e. cor. N. Adams and Walnut.
**GREEN BAY CARRIAGE CO. THE,** A. Weise, pres.; Joseph Hebert, v.-pres. and mngr.; H. B. Baker, sec. and treas.; 419 N. Adams.
**GREEN BAY CREAMERY CO.,** W. H. Woodruff, mngr., n. e. cor. S. Adams and Doty.
**GREEN BAY DAILY & WEEKLY GAZETTE,** W. E. Gardner, prop., 114 N. Washington.
Green Bay Dairymen's Board of Trade, H. F. Meyers, pres.; J. R. Meyers, v.-pres.; Worden Reynolds, sec.; American House.
Green Bay Dredging and Pile Driving Co., Christ. Schwarz, pres.; Charles Berner, sec. and treas.; 218 N. Jefferson.
**GREEN BAY ELEVATOR,** W. W. Cargill Co., props., w. s. Fox River, n. Dousman, Ft. H.
Green Bay House, Patrick Penney, prop., 328 N. Adams, cor. Main
**GREEN BAY IRON & BRASS FOUNDRY,** Jos. F. Rothe, prop., 318 N. 11th.
Green Bay Mineral Spring Co. (Theodore Van Hoven and Albert Hunter), bottlers, 300 S. Jackson.
**GREEN BAY PLANING MILL CO.,** C. Schwarz, pres.; Fred. Hurlbut, v.-pres.; James Robb, sec. and treas.; N. Adams, n. e. cor. Cedar.
**GREEN BAY PLUMBING & HEATING CO.,** Joseph W. Callahan, pres.; John Anderson, sec. and treas.; 224 Pine.
**GREEN BAY PUBLIC LIBRARY,** Samuel D. Hastings Jr., pres.; Mrs. Ella H. Neville, v.-pres.; A. H. Reynolds, sec. and treas.; Anna H. McDonnell, librarian; P. O. blk.
Green Bay Roller Mills, J. Noffz, prop., S. Washington, s. w. cor. Doty.
**GREEN BAY STEAM LAUNDRY, NO. 1,** Wm. H. Hiller, prop., 408-410 N. Adams.

E. Decker, Pres.    David Decker, Vice-Pres.    W. C. Jenkins, Sec.

# Green Bay Advocate Co.

## Book Binders,
### BLANK BOOK MANUFACTURERS AND STATIONERS

## Book
### —AND—
## Job Printers.

PROPRIETORS OF THE

## Green Bay Advocate.

ESTABLISHED 1846.

TERMS, $2.00 Per Year in Advance.

# Green Bay Advocate Co.,

## Book and Job Printing.

Blank Books of all descriptions kept in stock and special ruled books made to order.

## LUMBERMEN'S BOOKS A SPECIALTY.

*A Complete Assortment of Legal Blanks Kept in Stock.*

**ORDERS RECEIVE PROMPT ATTENTION.**

**THE A. SPUHLER CO., Green Bay** CARPETS, RUGS, OIL CLOTHS, Draperies and Window Shades.

Green Bay Trunk Factory, W. H. Marvin, prop., 325½ N. Washington.
**GREEN BAY TURN VEREIN,** n. w. cor. Walnut and N. Monroe.
**GREEN BAY, WINONA & ST. PAUL R. R.,** S. W. Champion, gen. mngr.; John B. Last, gen. freight and pass. agt, s. e. cor. Adams and Pine, depot cor. Pearl and 3d, Ft.H.
Green Bay and Fort Howard Gas and Electric Light Co., Carroll Collins, pres. and mngr.; H. B. Baker, sec. and treas., n. e. cor. Elm and Jefferson.
**GREEN BAY AND FORT HOWARD WATER WORKS CO.,** John F. Bertles, pres.; Mitchell **Joannes,** treas.; **A.** C. Neville, sec.; A. B. Palmer, supt., offices Weise's block.
Greene George G. (Greene & Vroman), res. 904 S. Monroe av.
**GREENE & VROMAN** (George G. Greene and Charles E. Vroman), lawyers, 301 N. Washington.
Gregare Frank, lab., res. 8 w. 874 Dousman, **Ft.** H.
Gregor Frank, saloon, 718 Main, res. same.
Gregor Robert, res. 718 Main.
**GREILING BROS.** (Charles H. and **Herman H. Greiling),** general contractors, P. O. box 1556.
Greiling Charles H. (Greiling Bros.), res. 303 N. **Jefferson.**
Greiling Herman H. (Greiling Bros.), res. 303 N. Jefferson.
Greiser Anna Miss, res. n. s. Division, 2 w. Guesnier, Ft. H.
Greiser Charles, lab., res. s. s. Elmore, 4. w. Cedar, Ft. H.
Greiser Gottlieb, res. s. s. Elmore, 4 w. Cedar, Ft. H.
Greiser John, lab., res. n. s. Division, 2 w. Guesnier, Ft. H.
Greiser Louis, painter, res. n. s. Division, 2 w. Guesnier, **Ft.** H.
Greiser Martha Miss, res. n. s. Division, 2 **w.** Guesnier, Ft. **H.**
Grible John, mason, res. American House.
Griebling William, foreman A. Kimball, res. 316 S. **Adams.**
Griffiths William T., ship.-clk., res. 803 2d, Ft. H.
Grignon Arthur A., machine-hd., res. 1227 S. Monroe av.
Grignon Charles, bottler, res. 1227 S. Monroe av.
Grignon Charles D., lumber grader, res. 1227 S. **Monroe av.**
Grignon David H., justice of the peace and lawyer, 112 N. Washington, res. 827 S. Adams.
Grignon Kittie Miss, res. 827 S. Adams.
Grignon Rachael Miss, res. 827 S. Adams.
Grimes Daniel, conductor, res. Northwestern Hotel, Ft. H.
Griswold James D., claim agt. C., M. & St. P. R. R., **res.** 327 S. Madison.
Griswold Myron B., **res.** 327 S. **Madison.**

Griswold William E., law student Greene & Vroman, res. 904 S. Monroe av.
Grizelle Julia Miss, domestic 114 N. Monroe av.
Groat Frederick, loco.-fireman, res. 508 Chestnut, Ft. H.
Groenfeld John J. Rev., pastor Moravian Church, res. 409 4th, Ft. H.
Groening. See Kroening.
Groessl Frank, brewer, res. 515 S. Quincy.
Groessl George, foreman, res. 515 S. Quincy.
Groessl George Jr., student, res. 515 S. Quincy.
Grognet Jules (Grognet & Monnabach), res. 120 10th.
Grognet & Monnabach (Jules Grognet and Theodore Monnabach), saloon, 231 Cherry.
Grognet Nettie (wid. Julian), res. 1012 Doty.
Gronnert Fred., prop. East River Hotel and saloon, res. 1273 Main.
Gronnert John, del.-clk. 1149 Main, res. 1273 Main.
**GROSS FREDERICK P.**, saloon, 215 Broadway, res. 302 Willow, Ft. H.
Gross George, lab., res. s. w. cor. 9th av. and 5th, Ft. H.
Gross Gottfried, barkpr, res. s. w. cor. Pearl and Main, Ft. H.
Gross John, lab., res. 1281 Cedar.
**GROSS JOHN G.**, saloon, s. w. cor. Main and Pearl, Ft. H., res. same.
Gross Joseph, lab., res. 1161 Doty.
Gross Marie, dressmkr, s.w. cor. 9th av. and 5th, res. same, Ft. H.
Grossen John, res. 1433 Harvey.
Grossen Lizzie Miss, res. Wisconsin House.
Grossen Louie, prop. Wisconsin House, res. 315 Main.
Grossmann Charles, lab., res. 227 S. Webster av.
Grosswinkel Lena Miss, res. 102 S. Van Buren.
Grosswinkel Peter, lab., res. 102 S. Van Buren.
Grundmann Elias, lab., res. e. s. Bellevue, 1 s. Charles.
Grusselle George, lab., res. 621 N. Madison.
Grusselle Louis, lab., res. 621 N. Madison.
Gueinzius Walter B., mngr. W. W. Cargill Co., res. 216 S. Jefferson.
Guerning Frank, lab., res. Bodart House.
Guiley Daisy Miss, res. 419 N. Monroe av.
Guiley Henry F., foreman Murphy Lumber Co., res. 419 N. Monroe av.
Guillaume Emil, farmer, res. n. s. 9th, 1 w. C. & N. W. R. R. track, Ft. H.
Gula Joseph, tailor, res. 1409 Cedar.
Gundersen Anton B., cooper, res. 839 S. Jackson.

**THE A. SPUHLER CO., GREEN BAY, WIS.** **Fine Dress Goods**
Samples Furnished on Application.

Gundersen Mary (wid. Sam), res. 839 S. Jackson.
Gundersen William, clk., res. 839 S. Jackson.
Gunderson Ingelberg (wid. Salve), res. 144 Pearl, Ft. H.
Gunn Edward E., clk., res. 533 S. Jefferson.
Gunn Eleanor Miss, teacher, res. 619 Cherry.
Guns William, carp., res. 508 Cedar, Ft. H.
Gurta Gertrude (wid. Anton), res. 1280 Cherry.
Gustaffs Nels, clk., res. Ferris Hotel, Ft. H.
Gutzske William, lab., res. 1368 Walnut.
Gutzlaff John, res. 300 5th av., Ft. H.
Gyron Henry, lab., res. w. s. 2d av., 1 s. 9th, Ft. H.
Gyron May Miss, res. w. s. 2d av., 1 s. 9th, Ft. H.

# H

HAAS Jacob, cooper, res. s. s. Cedar, 1 w. Monroe av.
Hacker Joseph, teamster, res. 1333 Cedar.
Hacker Theresa (wid. Joseph), res. 1333 Cedar.
Haevers Philibert, clk., res. 1430 Harvey.
Haff Emily C. Miss, res. 419 Cherry.
Haff Franklin R. Rev., pastor Christ Church, res. 419 Cherry.
Hafner John, engineer, res. Northwestern Hotel, Ft. H.
Hagemeister Albert, sec. and treas. Hagemeister Brewing Co., res. 615 Cherry.
Hagemeister Bessie R. Miss, res. 304 N. Adams.
**HAGEMEISTER BREWING CO.,** Henry F. Hagemeister, pres.; George Schober, v.-pres. and supt.; A. Hagemeister, sec. and treas., 310 N. Adams; brewery Manitowoc rd., town of Preble.
Hagemeister Henry F., pres. Hagemeister Brewing Co., res. 310 N. Adams.
**HAGEMEISTER LOUIS W.,** boots and shoes, 312 N. Washington. res. 304 N. Adams.
Hagemeister Minnie Miss, res. 304 N. Adams.
Hagen Frank A., stone quarry and steamboat line, 217 N. Adams, res. 403 S. Jefferson.
Hagen Mary Miss, res. 403 S. Jefferson.
Hagen Walter T., oculist and aurist, 217 N. Washington, res. 403 S. Jefferson.
Hagerty Dominick M., oil inspector, res. 118 N. Jackson.
Hagerty Ellen (wid. John), res. 426 S. Webster av.
Hagerty John, res. American House.
Hagerty John W. Jr., com. trav., res. 509 Pine.
Hagerty Thomas R., com. trav., res. 426 S. Webster av.

Hahn Emil, tinsmith, res. 316 Main.
Halbach Albert, iron works, w. s. Pearl, 2 s. Main, res. 123 Cherry, Ft. H.
Halbach Valeska Miss, res. 123 Cherry, Ft. H.
Halfpap August, machinist, res. 120 Broadway, Ft. H.
Halgersen. See Helgerson.
Hall Edward, engineer, res. Northwestern Hotel, Ft. H.
Hall Elmer S., bill-clk. C. & N. W. R. R., res. e. s. Willow, 2 n. the slough, Ft. H.
Hall House, E. Terry, prop., Broadway, n. w. cor. Baird, Ft. H.
Hall James R., lab., res. 114 5th av., Ft. H.
Hall Sofus, lab., res. s. s. 9th, 2 w. C. & N. W. R. R. track, Ft. H.
Hall William C., blksmith, res. 210 Cherry, Ft. H.
Hallock Sadie (wid. Eli), res. 620 Cherry.
Hallet Virginia Miss, res. 516 N. Jefferson.
Hallvin Emil, lab., res. 628 Pleasant.
Hambitzer Fred. W., tinsmith, res. 218 Cherry.
**HAMBITZER JOSEPH,** tinsmith, 218 Cherry, res. same.
Hamernik Frank, lab., res. 717 3d av., Ft. H.
Hamm Kate Miss, res. 619 S. Jefferson.
Hamm Lizzie Miss, res. 619 S. Jefferson.
Hamm Louis C., porter Joannes Bros., res. 619 S. Jefferson.
Hammer Minnie M., dressmkr, res. 301 Main.
Hammett Frank, engineer, res. 321 S. Washington.
Hancock Henry, engineer, res. 321 S. Washington.
**HANDLEN JOHN J.,** prop. Lebens-Wasser Mineral Spring, 529 S. Monroe av., res. same.
Hanes Ida (wid. Frank), res. 505 Willow, Ft. H.
Hannan Jane (wid. J. J.), res. 1026 Walnut.
Hannan Josie, domestic 421 S. Webster av.
Hannan Mathilda, domestic 421 S. Webster av.
Hannon Catherine (wid. Frank), res. 1101 Main.
Hannon David, clk. 305 Main, res. 1117 Harvey.
Hannon Edward, lab., res. No. 2, n. end Monroe av., e. Murphy's mill.
Hannon Emily (wid Alex.), res. No. 2, n. end Monroe av., e. Murphy's mill.
**HANNON FELIX J.,** druggist, n. w. cor. Broadway and Main, res. w. s. Chestnut, 5 s. Baird, Ft. H.
Hannon Gustav, lab., res. No. 2, n. end Monroe av., e. Murphy's mill.
Hannon Henry, lab., res. No. 2, n. end Monroe av., e. Murphy's mill.

**Headquarters for Boys' Clothing** THE A. SPUHLER CO.
GREEN BAY.

Hannon John B., carp., res. Bodart House.
Hannon Joseph A., lab., res. 703 N. 12th.
Hannon Mary, cook Bodart House.
Hannon Moses, lab., res. No. 2, n. end Monroe av., e. Murphy's mill.
Hanrahan Annie, domestic 505 Broadway, Ft. H.
Hanrahan Michael, boarding house, 505 Broadway, Ft. H., res. same.
Hanrahan Thomas, blksmith, res. 115 Cherry, Ft. H.
Hansen A. Izora, bkpr 124 S. Washington, res. 100 N. Madison.
Hansen Andrew, lab., res. 908 3d av., Ft. H.
Hansen Anton, lab., res. w. s. 2d av., 4 s. 7th, Ft. H.
Hansen Arthur B., clk. C. P. Miller & Co., res. 803 Main.
Hansen Bernard Nels P., shoemkr, w. s. 3d av., 4 s. 2d, Ft. H., res. same.
Hansen Bertha Miss, res. 105 Chestnut, Ft. H.
Hansen Carrie Miss, res. 313 4th, Ft. H.
Hansen Carrie Miss, dressmkr, res. 127 Chestnut, Ft. H.
Hansen Catherine (wid. Jacob), res. 706 2d, Ft. H.
Hansen Catherine (wid. Nels), res. 706 2d, Ft. H.
Hansen Catherine, domestic 305 Cedar, Ft. H.
Hansen Charles, lab., res. w. s. 2d av., 4 s. 7th, Ft. H.
Hansen Charles, tinsmith, res. 223 N. Quincy.
Hansen Charlotte A. Miss, dressmkr., res. 1303 Cherry.
Hansen Christian, lab., res. 1336 Cherry.
Hansen Christine, domestic s. e. cor. Dousman and Cedar, Ft. H.
Hansen Christopher, mill-hand, res. s. w. cor. 8th and 4th av., Ft. H.
Hansen Hannah Miss, dressmkr, res. 733 Pine.
Hansen Hans, fisherman, res. 1314 Cherry.
Hansen Hans, mill-hand, res. w. s. 2d av., 4 s. 7th, Ft. H.
Hansen Hans M., lab., res. 904 3d av., Ft. H.
Hansen Ingeborg Miss, teacher 5th Ward School, res. 313 4th, Ft. H.
Hansen Jacob, mason, res. n. e. cor. 3d and 10th av., Ft. H.
Hansen James, canvasser, res. Adams House.
Hansen John, lab., res. n. s. 5th, 3 w. 3d av., Ft. H.
Hansen John J., blksmith, res. 200 Chestnut, Ft. H.
Hansen John W., messenger McCartney Bank, res. 200 Chestnut, Ft. H.
Hansen Jorgen, wagonmkr and blksmith, 128 Broadway, res. 200 Chestnut, Ft. H.
Hansen Louis, ship-carp., res. s. s. 4th, 2 e. 4th av., Ft. H.
Hansen Martha Miss, dressmkr, res. 733 Pine.

Hansen Mary Miss, res. n. w. cor. 4th av. and 9th, Ft. H.
Hansen Neils, mill-hand, res. n. w. cor. 4th av. and 9th, Ft. H.
Hansen Nells, carp.-contr., 105 Chestnut, Ft. H., res. same.
Hansen Nels, lab., res. 109 5th av., Ft. H.
Hansen Niels M., carriage trimmer, res. 200 Chestnut, Ft. H.
Hansen Ole Sr., res. 1320 Cherry.
Hansen Ole, lake captain, res. 1320 Cherry.
Hansen Peter, carp., res. s. w. cor. 8th and 4th av , Ft. H.
Hansen Peter, fisherman, res. w. s. Pearl, 4 s. Hubbard, Ft. H.
Hansen Peter, lab., res. 111 5th av., Ft. H.
Hansen Peter L., carp., res. 309 4th, Ft. H.
Hansen Robert, clk., res. w. s. 6th av., 1 s. bridge, Ft. H.
Hansen Rasmus, tailor, res. 313 4th, Ft. H.
Hansen Samuel, clk. Jos. Spitz, res. 316 S. Adams.
Hansford Christina Miss, res. e. s. 4th av., 2 s. 8th, Ft. H.
Hansford George, lab., res. e. s. 4th av., 2 s. 8th, Ft. H.
Hansford John, horse trader, res. e. s. 4th av., 2 s. 8th, Ft. H.
Hanson Betsey (wid. Andrew), res. 320 S. Jackson.
Hanson Carrie, domestic s. e. cor. Dousman and Cedar, Ft. H.
Hanson Charles, lab., res. 116 7th av., Ft. H.
Hanson Charles, lab., res. 914 Walnut.
Hanson Christian, lab., res. 307 3d av., Ft. H.
Hanson Gunder, res. 914 Walnut.
Hanson Hanna, dressmkr. res. 320 S. Jackson.
Hanson Hans, carp., res. s. w. cor. 9th av. and 2d, Ft. H.
Hanson Hans N., fisherman, res. 150 Broadway, Ft. H.
Hanson Hans P., mason, res. 116 7th av., Ft. H.
Hanson Kittie, dressmkr., res. 320 S. Jackson.
Hanson Lawrence M., carp., res. 114 7th av., Ft. H.
Hanson Mary, dressmkr. res. 320 S. Jackson.
Hanson Robert B., clk. W. D. Cooke.
Hanson Theodore, lab., res. 914 Walnut.
Haran Maggie Miss, clk., res. 618 Pine.
Haran Sarah (wid. John), res. 618 Pine.
Haran Sarah Miss, dressmkr, res. 621 S. Monroe av.
Harasta Frank, lab., res. 1154 Doty.
Harasta Mary Miss, res. 1154 Doty.
Harden Nathan D., farmer, res. 401 Willow.
Harder Frank F., gunsmith, res. 820 S. Jefferson.
Harder John, brakeman, res. 215 S. Jackson.
Harder Mamie Miss, clk., res. 820 S. Jefferson.
Harder Omar L., saw repairing and furnishing, 227 Cherry, res. 508 Cherry.
Harder Rebecca Miss, res. 820 S. Jefferson.

**THE A. SPUHLER CO.** LADIES', MISSES' and CHILDREN'S
/GREEN BAY **CLOAKS, CAPES, JACKETS**

Harding Katie Miss, res. 200 Cherry, Ft. H.
Hardwick Anastasia Mrs., teacher, res. 914 S. Van Buren.
Hare Susan Miss, res. 866 Dousman, Ft. H.
Harkness Minor, driver, res. 300 3d av., Ft. H.
Harman William (Porth & Harman), res. 428 N. Madison.
Harney R. L. carriage trimmer, res. Adams House.
Harris Henry, lumber scaler, res. 1329 Harvey.
Harris Theodore E., tin and sheet iron roofer, 125 S. Washington, res. 918 S. Madison.
Harrison Henriette Mrs., res. 145 Broadway, Ft. H.
Hart Adelaide Miss, teacher, res. 1124 Cedar.
Hart Albert, res. 1124 Cedar.
Hart Clarissa (wid. Azel), res. 102 N. Monroe av.
Hart Clifford B. (H. W. & C. B. Hart), res. 308 S. Adams.
Hart Edwin W., clk., res. 402 S. Adams.
Hart Elsie Mrs., housekpr., res. 431 Walnut.
Hart H. W. & C. B. (Henry W. and Clifford B. Hart), props. Hart's Steamboat Line, foot Cherry.
Hart Harvey, teacher, res. 1124 Cedar.
Hart Henry W. (H. W. & C. B. Hart), res. 402 S. Adams.
Hart Lee W., clk. Welcome, res. 621 Pine.
Hart Peter C., chief clk. C., M. & St. P. R. R., res. s. e. cor. Cedar and Hubbard, Ft. H.
Hart Sarah M. (wid. Albert), res. 1124 Cedar.
Hart William H., R. R. engineer, res. 204 6th av., Ft. H.
Hart William N., com. trav., res. 102 N. Monroe av.
Hart's Steamboat Line, H. W. & C. B. Hart, props., ft. Cherry.
Harteau David M., architect, 505 Main, res. 1003 Cedar.
Harteau Samuel W., com. trav. 124 S. Washington, res. 432 Howard.
Hartley Clarence G., brakeman, res. 405 1st, Ft. H.
Hartley Marshall P., res. 405 1st, Ft. H.
Hartley Stella M. Miss, res. 405 1st, Ft. H.
Hartmann Carl, machinist, res. 213 Willow, Ft. H.
Hartmann Ernst, clk. Bay City House, res. same.
Hartmann Ida, clk., res. 213 Willow, Ft. H.
Hartmann Louis, brewer Hochgreve Brewing Co., res. w. s. Monroe av. rd., 2¼ miles s. city limits.
Hartmann Marie Miss, res. 213 Willow, Ft. H.
Hartmann Otto, candymkr, res. 213 Willow, Ft. H.
**HARTMANN SYLVESTER**, grocer, 301 Willow, res. 213 Willow, Ft. H.
Hartmann William, clk., res. 213 Willow, Ft. H.
Hartske Charles, lab., res. n. s. Duck Creek, 2 w. Mather, Ft. H.

Hartung Charles, hardware, 105 N. Washington, res. 203 S. Monroe av.
Hartung Clara Miss, res. 203 S. Monroe av.
Hartung Emma Miss, res. 203 S. Monroe av.
Hartwig Martin, res. 126 N. Washington.
Harvey William P., mngr. Fox River Electric Railway Co., res. 320 S. Washington.
Harwin Jonathan H., loco.-engineer, res. 416 Crooks.
Haselbauer Frank J., lab., res. 721 S. Adams.
Haselbauer John C., painter, res. 721 S. Adams.
Haselbauer Matt., lab., res. 721 S. Adams.
Haselbauer Matt. Jr., lab., res. 721 S. Adams.
Hashek John, cabinetmkr, res. s. s. Shawano rd., 2 w. Willow, Ft. H.
Haslam Wm., drayman, res. s. e. cor. Willow and Baird, Ft. H.
Hastings Samuel D. Jr., circuit judge, res. 827 S. Monroe av.
Hathaway Harry M., clk., res. 338 S. Quincy.
Hathaway Oscar C. (Barkhausen & Hathaway), res. 338 S. Quincy.
Haugh Anna M. (wid. John), res. 308 S. Jackson.
Haugh Katie Miss, clk., res. 308 S. Jackson.
Haupt August, lab., res. n. e. cor. 11th av. and 2d, Ft. H.
Haupt Clara Miss, res. 211 Broadway, Ft. H.
Haupt George (Geo. Haupt & Co.), res. 211 Broadway, Ft. H.
Haupt George Jr., clk. 109 S. Washington, res. 211 Broadway, Ft. H.
**HAUPT GEORGE & CO.** (George Haupt and Charles W. Redeman), furniture and undertakers, 109 S. Washington.
Haupt John, res. 402 5th av., Ft. H.
Haupt Rudolph, machinist, res. 402 5th av., Ft. H.
Havens Edgar N., marble-cutter, res. s. w. cor. Chestnut and Shawano, Ft. H.
Havey Edward, engineer, res. Ferris Hotel, Ft. H.
Havey John, conductor, res. Cook's Hotel.
Hawley Alice M., stenog. Greene & Vroman, res. 108 Kellogg, Ft. H.
Hawley George, brakeman, res. 408 Kellogg, Ft. H.
Hawley Katie Miss, res. 408 Kellogg, Ft. H.
Hawley Thomas, lake captain, res. 408 Kellogg, Ft. H.
Hawley Thomas Jr., policeman, res. 408 Kellogg, Ft. H.
Haworth John, painter, res. 508 S. Quincy.
Haworth William, painter, res. 508 S. Quincy.
Hay John, lab., res. 624 N. Jefferson.
Hayden Elizabeth (wid. Fred.), res. 442 S. Quincy.

**THE A. SPUHLER CO., Green Bay** CARPETS, RUGS, OIL CLOTHS, Draperies and Window Shades.

Hayden John, hostler, res. 803 Chestnut, Ft. H.
Hayden Peter, boilermkr, res. 109 Broadway, Ft. H.
Hayes Annie Miss, res. 405 2d, Ft. H.
Hayes John, farmer, res. 304 Cedar, Ft. H.
Hayes Joseph, baggageman, res. 405 2d, Ft. H.
Hayes Nellie, dressmkr, res. 230 S. Quincy.
Hayes Oldin, lab., res. 304 Cedar, Ft. H.
Hayes Thomas, fireman, res. 230 S. Quincy.
Hayes William, foreman, res. 405 2d, Ft. H.
Hazackers Lena, domestic American House.
Healy Marie Miss, res. 514 Chestnut, Ft. H.
Heath Mortimer J., com. trav. 124 S. Washington, res. w. s. S. Quincy, 2 s. Cass.
Heaver Philip, clk., res. 1430 Harvey.
Hebert Andrew, lab., res. 316 Main.
Hebert Joseph, v.-pres. and gen. mngr. Green **Bay Carriage** Co., res. 336 S. Monroe av.
Hedberg Andrew, boilermkr, res. 107 4th av., Ft. H.
Hedberg Nickolene Miss, res. 107 4th av., Ft. H.
Hedberg Sievert, switchman, res. 401 2d, Ft. H.
Heesakers Martin, brewer, res. 428 Pleasant.
Heesen Henry, clk. Buengener & Bur, res. 114 N. Quincy.
Heffernan Agnes, domestic 504 Main, Ft. H.
Heffernan James, lab., res. s. s. Dousman, 3 w. **Willow, Ft. H.**
Heft Charles G., insurance agent, res. 316 Main.
Heideman Lavina (wid. Joseph), res. 721 S. Webster av.
Heidgen John, blksmith, res. 207 Cherry, Ft. H.
Heidgen Marie Miss, res. 207 Cherry, Ft. H.
Heidgen Martin, machinist, res. 207 Cherry, Ft. H.
Heidgen Mathias, blksmith and wagonmkr, 212-214 Broadway, res. 207 Cherry, Ft. H.
Helgersen Christian, carp., res. e. s. 7th av., 2 s. 2d, Ft. H.
Helgerson Anton, lab., res. n. s. 2d, 2 w. R. R. track, Ft. H.
Helgerson Harry, farmer, res. n. s. 2d, 2 w. R. R. track, Ft. H.
Helgerson Mary Miss, res. n. s. 2d, 2 w. R. R. track, Ft. H.
Heller William, shingle mnfr., res. rear 1139 Walnut.
Helmer Walter, ry.-man, res. 145 Broadway, Ft. H.
Helms Theodore, mason, res. 901 Walnut.
Helnore Charles, mill-hand, **res. n. e. cor. 4th av. and 9th,** Ft. H.
Helnore Tore, lab., res. 769 4th av., Ft. H.
Hemmen Anna, domestic 629 Main.
Hemming Barbara, domestic Green Bay House.
Henderson Frank, res. n. e. cor. Hubbard and Cedar, Ft. H.

Henderson Fred., clk. Robert Henderson & Co., res. 200 Broadway, Ft. H.
Henderson James L., painter, res. 411 Cherry, Ft. H.
Henderson Robert (Robert Henderson & Co), res. 200 Broadway, Ft. H.
Henderson Robert & Co. (Robert Henderson and Ephraim Crocker), paint mnfrs., 202 Broadway, Ft. H.
Henderson William, painter, res. s. s. Mather, 3 w. Cedar, Ft. H.
Hendricks Angeline Miss, res. 1358 Crooks.
Hendricks Desire, lab., res. 1358 Crooks.
Hendricks Katie, domestic 221 S. Webster av.
Hendricks William, lab., res. 125 S. Madison.
Hendricks Wm. P., clk. A. Kimball, res. 624 S. Jefferson.
Hendrickson Peter, clk. H. E. Brehma, res. s. s. Shawano av., 2 w. Willow, Ft. H.
Heney Mary Ann (wid. Thomas), res. 520 N. Madison.
Heney Thomas, res. 520 N. Madison.
Henkel Michael, tailor, res. 305 Cherry, Ft. H.
Henkel Otto, lab., res. 305 Cherry, Ft. H.
Henkelmann Albert, fireman, 628 S. 11th.
Henkelmann Antonia Miss, res. 628 S. 11th.
Henkelmann Edward (Fabry & Henkelman), res. 1124 Cass.
Henkelmann Ernestine (wid. Christain), res. 628 S. 11th.
Henkelmann William, res. 1144 S. Quincy.
Henry Jacob, res. 515 Elm.
Henry James C., farmer, res. s. s. 2d, 8 w. R. R. track, Ft. H.
Henshall Calista (wid. James G.), res. 504 Moravian.
Herbigneaux Joseph, planer, res. s. w. cor. Pearl and Hubbard, Ft. H.
Herman Jacob, scaler, res. 1000 Dousman, Ft. H.
Hermann Edward, lab., res. 1 w. 773 Elmore, Ft. H.
Hermann. See Heyrman.
**HERMES ARNOLD,** fisherman, res. e. s. McDonald, 2 s. lumber yard, Ft. H.
**HERMES HENRY,** fisherman, res. w. s. McDonald, 2 s. lumber yard, Ft. H.
Hermes John, fireman, res. Ferris Hotel, Ft. H.
Hermes Joseph, fisherman, res. e. s. McDonald, 2 s. lumber yard, Ft. H.
Hermsen Dora Miss, compositor Onze Standaard, res. Depere, Wis.
Hermsen Henry, lab., res. 302 N. Quincy.
Herrmann Carl (John Herrmann & Son), res. 301 S. Monroe av.
Herrmann John (John Herrmann & Son), res. 718 Walnut.

THE A. SPUHLER CO., GREEN BAY, WIS. **Fine Dress Goods**
Samples Furnished on Application.

Herrmann John & Son (John and Carl Herrmann), bookbndrs, 229 Pine.
Herrmann. See Harman, Hermann and Heyrman.
Hess Charles H., asst. supt. Metropolitan Life Ins. Co., 9 Parmentier blk., res. cor. Chestnut and Dousman, Ft. H.
Hess George B., sec. and treas. George B. Hess Co., res. Cedar, n. w. cor. N. Quincy.
**HESS GEORGE B. CO.**, H. A. Walter, pres.; Clement Massey, v.-pres.; George B. Hess, sec. and treas.; flour mills, n. w. cor. Cedar and N. Quincy.
Hess John, student, res. 416 N. Monroe av.
Hess Wm. F., bkpr., res. Adams House.
Hessel Anton, barkpr., res. 312 Willow, Ft. H.
Hessell John, fireman, res. 445 S. Adams.
Hewitt George P., student, res. 417 S. Adams.
Hewitt John L. Rev., pastor First Presbyterian Church, res. 417 S. Adams.
Hewitt May Belle Miss, stenog., res. 417 S. Adams.
Heyde Robert, helper, res. 317 6th av., Ft. H.
Heydemann Maria Mrs., res. 414 N. Quincy.
Heyrman Addie, domestic 805 Walnut.
Heyrman Carrie Miss, res. 323 N. Adams.
**HEYRMAN CHARLES**, foreman St. John Mineral Spring Co., res. 600 Chestnut, Ft. H.
Heyrman Elizabeth (wid. Joseph), res. 323 N. Adams.
Heyrman Frank, drug-clk. J. Robinson, res. 323 N. Adams.
Heyrman Hattie Miss, res. 323 N. Adams.
Heyrman William J., clk. 503 Main, res. 323 N. Adams.
Heyrman. See Hermann.
Hickey John, engineer, res. 301 Cedar, Ft. H.
Hickey John T., brakeman, res. Commercial Hotel, Ft. H.
Hickey Martin, section-boss, res. 308 Cedar, Ft. H.
Hickey Michael, ry.-hand, res. 308 Cedar, Ft. H.
Hickey Patrick, res. s. s. Baird, e. Willow, Ft. H.
Hickok Thomas A., gunsmith and general repair shop, 401 Willow, res. same.
Hickox James A., cooper, res. s. s. Smith, 2 e. Jackson.
Hickox James Jr., cooper D. W. Britton, res. s. s. Smith, 2 e. Jackson.
Hickox Milton P., lab., res. s. s. Smith, 2 e. Jackson.
Hicks Joseph, fireman, res. 116 S. Jackson.
High School, s. e. cor. S. Webster av. and Chicago.
Hilderbrand Fred, res. 1125 Doty.
Hilderbrand Minnie Miss, res. 1125 Doty.

Hilderbrand Peter, res. 1125 Doty.
Hill Thomas, lab., res. 728 S. Jefferson.
Hiller John, cook, res. 816 Crooks.
Hiller Marsh, lab., res. 418 N. Adams.
Hiller Sylvester, carp., res. w. s. Pearl, 5 s. Hubbard, Ft. H.
**HILLER WILLIAM H.**, prop. Green Bay Steam Laundry No. 1, res. 408 N. Adams.
Hills John P., mngr. L. Hills, res. 316 Pine.
Hills L. (John P. Hills, mngr.), harness and saddlery, 210 Cherry.
Hills Lizzie Miss, dressmkr, 316 Pine, res. same.
Hills Theodore, confectr., res. 316 Pine.
Hills William T., harnessmkr, res. 316 Pine.
Hilts Margaret (wid. Christian), res. 1419 Crooks.
Hines John, switchman, res. Broadway House, Ft. H.
Hinkley Eliza, stewardess The Beaumont.
Hinks Katie Mrs., dressmkr, 328 Pine, res. same.
Hinks Thomas, fisherman, res. 328 Pine.
**HINSDALE WM. C.**, agt. American Express Co., 224 N. Adams, res. 433 S. Monroe av.
Hinsey John, clk., res. 114 S. Jackson.
Hintz Anna, dressmkr, res. 1182 Day.
Hintz August, lab., res. 1182 Day.
Hintz Fred., lab., res. 1182 Day.
Hintz Otto, res. 1182 Day.
Hinz Fred., res. 1314 Walnut.
Hinz Lizzie Miss, res. 1314 Walnut.
Hinz Otto, printer, res. 1314 Walnut.
Hitchings Clifford T., barn boss P. H. Carlin, res. Charles House.
Hittner Henry M., physician, 10 Parmentier blk., res. 209 S. Adams.
**HOCHGREVE ADOLPH**, mngr. Hochgreve Brewing Co., res. w. s. Monroe av. rd., 2½ miles s. city limits.
Hochgreve August, saloon, 320 Main, res. same.
Hochgreve Augusta Miss, res. w. s. Monroe av. rd., 2½ miles s. city limits.
**HOCHGREVE BREWING CO.**, Mrs. Caroline Hochgreve, pres.; Adolph Hochgreve, mngr.; Depere rd., 2½ miles s. city.
Hochgreve Caroline Mrs., pres. Hochgreve Brewing Co., res. Depere rd., 2½ miles s. city.
Hochgreve Christian, bookkpr. Hochgreve Brewing Co., res. w. s. Monroe av. rd., 2½ miles s. city limits.

**Headquarters for Boys' Clothing** THE A. SPUHLER CO. GREEN BAY.

Hochgreve Etta Miss, res. w. s. Monroe av. rd., 2½ miles s. city limits.
Hochgreve Louisa Miss, res. w. s. Monroe av. rd., 2½ miles s. city limits.
Hochgreve Mamie Miss, res. w. s. Monroe av. rd., 2½ miles s. city limits.
Hock Joseph, brakeman, res. 723 S. Jefferson.
Hocking Steve, hostler, res. w. s. 5th av., 2 n. 10th, Ft. H.
Hocking William T., lab., res. w. s. 5th av., 2 n. 10th, Ft. H.
Hodges Homer R., lumber insp., res. end of Broadway, nr. R. R. track, Ft. H.
Hodges J., fireman, res. Northwestern Hotel, Ft. H.
Hoeffel Angeline Miss, res. 306 S. Jefferson.
Hoeffel Anna M. Miss, res. 306 S. Jefferson.
Hoeffel Bros. Shoe Co. (Joseph P. and James I. Hoeffel), boots and shoes, 302 N. Washington.
Hoeffel Cornelia A. Miss, res. 306 S. Jefferson.
Hoeffel James I. (Hoeffel Bros. Shoe Co.), sec. Allouez Mineral Spring Co., res. 515 S. Jackson.
Hoeffel Joseph, pres. Allouez Mineral Spring Co., res. 537 S. Van Buren.
Hoeffel Joseph P. (Hoeffel Bros. Shoe Co.), mngr. Allouez Mineral Spring Co., res. 515 S. Jackson.
Hoeffel Kate, clk. 121 S. Washington, res. 306 S. Jefferson.
Hoeffel Louis, res. 306 S. Jefferson.
Hoefs Frank A., station agent G. B., W. & St. P. R. R., res. 104 3d av., Ft. H.
Hoell Anna Miss, typesetter, res. 1119 Walnut.
Hoell Anton, tailor, res. 1219 Doty.
Hoell John, bottler, res. 1119 Walnut.
Hoell Joseph, tailor, res. 1119 Walnut.
Hoell Lizzie Miss, res. 1119 Walnut.
Hoeren John, peddler, res. w. s. Oneida, 4 s. Shawano rd., Ft. H.
Hoeren John Jr., peddler, res. w. s. Oneida, 4 s. Shawano rd., Ft. H.
Hoeren Peter, gardener, res. w. s. Oneida, 4 s. Shawano rd., Ft. H.
Hoffman Robert, dry goods, etc., 125–127 N. Washington, res. 231 Walnut.
Hoffmann Annie, domestic 309 Willow, Ft. H.
Hoffmann August, lab., res. n. s. Main, on Ellis Creek, town Preble.
Hoffmann Ernest, butcher, res. 314 S. Adams.
Hoffmann George P., clk., res. 505 S. Van Buren.

Hoffmann Harold W., res. 505 S. Van Buren.
Hoffmann Louis W., com. trav., res. 505 S. Van Buren.
Hoffmann Minnie, domestic 514 S. Monroe av.
**HOFFMANN WILLIAM,** clothing and merchant tailor, 224 N. Washington, res. 505 S. Van Buren.
Hogan Daniel, fireman, res. n. s. Elmore, 7 w. Cedar, Ft. H.
Hogan Dennis, blksmith, res. 403 2d, Ft. H.
Hogan Dennis E., engineer, res. n. s. Elmore, 4 w. Cedar, Ft. H.
Hogan James, res. 663 Elmore, Ft. H.
Hogan Jennie Miss, teacher 2d Ward school, res. 663 Elmore, Ft. H.
Hogan John, check clk. N. W. Ry., res. 608 Elmore, Ft. H.
Hogan Katie Miss, teacher, res. 663 Elmore, Ft. H.
Hogan Maggie Miss, res. n. s. Elmore, 2 w. Cedar, Ft. H.
Hogan Matthew, lab., res. n. s. Elmore, 4 w. Cedar, Ft. H.
Hogan Nora Miss, res. n. s. Elmore, 4 w. Cedar, Ft. H.
Hogan Patrick, watchman, res. n. s. Elmore, 2 w. Cedar, Ft. H.
Hogan Sarah Miss, res. n. s. Elmore, 4 w. Cedar, Ft. H.
Hogan Spencer, barber The Beaumont, res. same.
Hogan Timothy E., loco.-engineer, res. 615 Chestnut, Ft. H.
Hogan Walter J., blksmith foreman C., M. & St. P. R. R., res. 413 5th, Ft. H.
Hogon Frank, lab., res. Lawe, n. w. cor. S. 11th.
Hogon Hortense Miss, res. Lawe, n. w. cor. S. 11th.
Hogon Jules, lab., res. Lawe, n. w. cor. S. 11th.
Hogon Lizzie Miss, res. Lawe, n. w. cor. S. 11th.
Holderman Charles, lab., res. Adams House.
Holland Eugene, fireman, res. 646 S. Madison.
Holland Timothy, wiper, res. e. s. 9th av., 3 n. 2d, Ft. H.
Hollingsworth John S., veterinary surgeon and pharmacist, 714 Main, res. 343 S. 11th.
Hollister Annie E., music teacher, res. 902 Mason.
Hollister Ethel, stenog., res. 902 Mason.
Hollister Frank B., engineer, res. e. s. 9th av., 1 n. 3d, Ft. H.
Hollister Russell, fireman, res. 339 8th av., Ft. H.
Hollister Wm. W., lumberman, res. 902 Mason.
Hollman Albert W., clk. The Weise-Hollman Co., res. 309 N. Jefferson.
Hollman Fred. A., v.-pres. The Weise-Hollman Co., res. 309 N. Jefferson.
Hollman Fred H., clk. the Weise-Hollman Co., res. 309 N. Jefferson.
Hollmann Henry A., clk. The A. Spuhler Co., res. 128 S. Jefferson.

**THE A. SPUHLER CO.** *LADIES', MISSES' and CHILDREN'S*
**GREEN BAY** — **CLOAKS, CAPES, JACKETS**

Hollmann Lydia Miss, teacher, res. 128 S. Jefferson.
Hollogne Sidonia (wid. Joseph), res. 1413 Harvey.
Holloway James, lab., res. 227 S. Quincy.
Holloway John, plasterer, res. 400 2d, Ft. H.
Holman Fred G., lab., res. 429 N. Quincy.
Holmes Albert G. E., res. 211 N. Jefferson.
Holmes Albert G. E. Jr., student, res. 211 N. Jefferson.
Holmes Charles H., pres. Fox River Electric Ry., res. 702 S. Monroe av.
Holz Emma Miss, res. 1107 Doty.
Holz Ernst, tailor, res. 434 Walnut.
Holz Fred, car repairer, res. 307 John, Ft. H.
Holz Georgia (wid. Gust.) res. 629 Cherry.
Holz Herman, car repairer, res. s. s. Dousman, 5 w. Willow, Ft. H.
Holz Herman, cigarmkr, res. 307 John, Ft. H.
Holz Herman A., tailor, res. 1107 Doty.
Holz Mathilda (wid. Herman), res. 1107 Doty.
Holz Minnie (wid. Frederick), res. 1237 Walnut.
Holzer John, carp., res. s. s. Mather, fronting Duck Creek rd., Ft. H.
Holzknecht Helena Miss, milliner, res. 233 S. Quincy.
Holzknecht Henry, waiter, res. 233 S. Quincy.
Holzknecht Lena, milliner, res. 233 S. Quincy.
Holzknecht Matthias, res. 233 S. Quincy.
Holzknecht Minnie, dressmkr, res. 233 S. Quincy.
Holzknecht Wm. C., prop. St. John Mineral Water, res. n. s. Stuart, bet. S. Quincy and S. Jackson.
Homme Frederick, carp., res. 108 Cherry, Ft. H.
Hood Alexander J., machinist, res. 708 Cedar, Ft. H.
**HOOD WILLIAM**, Justice of the Peace and Notary Public, 218 Main, Ft. H., res. 708 Cedar, Ft. H.
Hope Wm., bartender The Beaumont, res. same.
Hoppe Albert Sr., tailor, res. 1257 Walnut.
**HOPPE JOSEPHINE F. MRS.** (Robert Hoppe, mngr.), merchant tailor, 219 N. Adams, res. 709 Pine.
Hoppe Otto F., saloon, 116 Broadway, res. 114 Broadway, Ft. H.
**HOPPE ROBERT**, mngr. J. F. Hoppe, res. 709 Pine.
Hoppe Sophie (wid. Albert), res. 734 Walnut.
Hoppe Theodore W. F., tailor, res. 326 S. Quincy.
Horn Annie Mrs., res. 604 St. George.
Horn Henry L., machinist, res. 293 6th av., Ft. H.
Horn Josephine Miss, dressmkr, res. 604 St. George.
Horn Mary Miss, res. 604 St. George.
Horn Theresa Miss, res. 604 St. George.

Horne Theresa, domestic 326 N. Monroe av.
Horton Effie Miss, res. n. e. cor. Kellogg and Chestnut, Ft. H.
Horton Jairus D., marine engineer, res. n. e. cor. Kellogg and Chestnut, Ft. H.
Hoslet Albert, lab., res. 423 N. 11th.
Hoslet Desire (Looze & Hoslet), res. 423 N. 11th.
Hoslet Joseph, carp., res. 423 N. 11th.
Hoslet Mary Miss, clk. Jorgensen Blesch Co., res. 423 N. 11th.
Hossketter Anton, hostler, res. Orphan Asylum, e. s. De Pere rd.
Hottensen Carl, baker, s. w. cor. Broadway and Hubbard. Ft. H., res. same.
Hottensen Elsa, clk., res. s. w. cor. Broadway and Hubbard, Ft. H.
Hottensen Freda Miss, clk., res. s. w. cor. Broadway and Hubbard, Ft. H.
Houart Amand, bkpr. Henry Rahr's Sons, res. 814 Cherry.
Houle Albert, lab., res. 809 Broadway, Ft. H.
Houlihan Catherine, teacher, res. n. e. cor. 2d and 10th av., Ft. H.
Houlihan Ellen (wid. Michael), res. n. e. cor. 2d and 10th av., Ft. H.
Houlihan Frank, boilermkr, res. n. e. cor. 2d and 10th av., Ft. H.
Houlihan James, mach., res. n. e. cor. 2d and 10th av., Ft. H.
Houlihan Mary, teacher, res. n. e. cor. 2d and 10th av., Ft. H.
**HOWARD FOUNDRY AND MACHINE WORKS,** A. M. Duncan, prop., cor. Broadway and John, Ft. H.
Howard House, 205 Dousman, Ft. H.
Howard Nelson M., foreman bridge dept. C., M. & St. P. R. R., res. 1125 Pine.
Howard Rubber Stamp Co., James Kerr & Son, props., 311 Pearl, Ft. H.
Howland Eben W., res. w. s. 6th av., 4 s. Bridge, Ft. H.
Howland Leo, lumberman, res. w. s. 6th av., 4 s. Bridge, Ft. H.
Howlett Edward, fireman, res. 412 Elm.
Howlett Ellen Miss, res. s. w. cor. 2d av. and 8th, Ft. H.
Howlett Frank, lab., res. s. w. cor. 2d av. and 8th, Ft. H.
Howlett George M., warehouseman, res. 304 3d av., Ft. H.
Howlett James, carp., res. s. w. cor. 2d av. and 8th, Ft. H.
**HOWLETT JAMES N.,** grocer, 805 3d av., res. s. w. cor. 2d av. and 8th, Ft. H.
Howlett John, lab., res. 304 3d av., Ft. H.
Howlett John C., clk., res. s. w. cor. 2d av. and 8th, Ft. H.
Howlett Marie, dressmkr, s. w. cor. 2d av. and 8th, Ft. H., res. same.

THE A. SPUHLER CO., Green Bay  CARPETS, RUGS, OIL CLOTHS
Draperies and Window Shades.

HOW 139 HUD

Howlett Nellie L. Miss, milliner, 313 Broadway, Ft. H., res. w. s. 3d av., 3 s. 3d, Ft. H.
Howlett Thomas, clk., res. s. w. cor. 2d av. and 8th, Ft. H.
Howlett William, clk., res. s. w. cor. 2d av. and 8th, Ft. H.
Howley James M., machine opr. steam laundry, res. e. s. Cedar, 2 n. Dousman, Ft. H.
Hubbard Anna Miss, res. s. s. Duck Creek rd., 14 w. Mather, Ft. H.
Hubbard Emilie (wid. Donald J.), res. n. s. Dousman, 2 w. George, Ft. H.
Hubbard Hiram H., sexton cemetery, res. s. s. Duck Creek rd., 14 w. Mather, Ft. H.
Hubbard Hiram L., mill-hand, res. s. s. Duck Creek rd., 14 w. Mather, Ft. H.
Hubbard Kittie Miss, res. s. s. Duck Creek rd., 14 w. Mather, Ft. H.
Hubbard Samuel E., supt. The Little Rescue Brigade, res. n. s. Dousman, 2 w. George, Ft. H.
Huber Annie Miss, res. 1267 Cedar.
Huber Barbara Miss, res. 1267 Cedar.
Huber Frank, machinist, res. 303 6th av., Ft. H.
Huber Harry B., clk. frt. auditing dept. G. B., W. & St. P. R. R., res. 303 6th av., Ft. H.
Huber Louise (wid. Geo. H.), res. 303 6th av., Ft. H.
Hubert Adolph, teamster, res. 520 S. Quincy.
Hubert Charles, lab., res. 1128 Doty.
Hubert Delia Miss, res. 1128 Doty.
Hubert Emil, lab., res. 1128 Doty.
Hubert Ferdinand, lab., res. 1128 Doty.
Hubert Rosie Miss, res. 1128 Doty.
Huck James, lab., res. w. s. Pearl, 4 s. Hubbard, Ft. H.
Hudd Gertrude Miss, res. 202 N. Jefferson.
Hudd May Miss, res. 202 N. Jefferson.
Hudd Nellie Miss, res. 202 N. Jefferson.
**HUDD THOMAS R.**, lawyer, 3 P. O. block, res. 202 N. Jefferson.
Hudel Carl, foreman J. M. Voigt Mnfg. Co., res. 531 S. Van Buren.
Hudson Charlotte (wid. Samuel), res. w. s. Oneida rd., 1 s. Shawano rd., Ft. H.
Hudson David W., mach., res. w. s. Oneida rd., 1 s. Shawano rd., Ft. H.
Hudson Fred, lab., res. 901 Walnut.
Hudson Ida Miss, res. 112 Chestnut, Ft. H.
Hudson Joseph D., teamster, res. 801 Chestnut, Ft. H.

Hudson Roy S., painter, res. 213 Chestnut, Ft. H.
Hudson Timothy, marine engineer, res. 112 Chestnut, Ft. H.
Huebner Conrad, res. 119 S. Monroe av.
Huempfner Frank, shoemkr, res. 232 S. Van Buren.
Huenger Carrie Miss, dressmkr, res. 627 Cherry.
Huenger Dorothea Miss, res. 627 Cherry.
Huenger Emma Miss, res. 627 Cherry.
Huenger Ernestine Miss, teacher, res. 627 Cherry.
Huenger Gustave, res. 627 Cherry.
Hueus Constant, lab., res. 1011 Cedar.
**HUERTH JOHN,** cigar mnfr., 308 N. Washington, res. 1242 Cedar.
Huetter Frederick, teamster, res. 442 S. Quincy.
Huffman Henry P., res. n. e. cor. Dousman and Chestnut, Ft. H.
**HUFFMAN HOUSE,** P. Krouse, prop., cor. Broadway and Kellogg, Ft. H.
Huget Josephine, domestic 345 S. Adams.
Huguet Alphonse M., book agt., res. w. s. De Pere rd., 1 n. Hochgreve brewery.
Hughes James, prop. Eagle Foundry, res. e. s. 10th av., bet. 1st and 2d., Ft. H.
Hughes George, lab., res. Willmar House.
Hugnin Rufus, brakeman, res. 512 Chestnut, Ft. H.
Huilizka Wenzel, carp., res. 713 Shawano rd., Ft. H.
Hull George H., conductor, res. Ferris Hotel, Ft. H.
Hume John W., conductor, res. 923 S. Quincy.
Hummel Johanna Mrs., furrier, 129 N. Adams, res. same.
Hummel John, res. 624 N. Jefferson.
Hummel John, fisherman, res. Willow, foot of Fox River.
Hummel John Jr., cooper, res. 129 N. Adams.
Humpfner E. & Co. (Enoch Humpfner and Lambert Fonder), meatmarket, 544 S. Monroe. av.
Humpfner Enoch (E. Humpfner & Co.), res. 515 Mason.
Hunt Anna, teacher, res. 707 Cedar, Ft. H.
Hunt Marie Ann (wid. Patrick), res. 707 Cedar, Ft. H.
Hunt Susan (wid. Dominic), res. 314 Cedar, Ft. H.
Hunter Albert (Green Bay Mineral Spring Co.), res. 1401 Mason.
Hunter William, well-driller, res. St. James Hotel.
Huntington Howard J., county judge, res. 826 Mason.
Huntington Laura, student, res. 826 Mason.
Huntington Louise, student, res. 826 Mason.
Huntington Paul, student, res. 826 Mason.
Huntington Solomon P. (Cady & Huntington), res. 826 Mason.
Hurckmans Joseph, ry.-hand, res. n. s. Division, 3 e. Fink, Ft. H.

**THE A. SPUHLER CO., GREEN BAY, WIS.** **Fine Dress Goods**
Samples Furnished on Application.

Hurlbut Agnes Miss, res. 428 Cherry.
**HURLBUT FRED.**, pres. Ft. Howard Lumber Co., coal, wood, oils, salt fish and building materials, 201 Cedar, res. 428 Cherry.
Hurlbut Jessie Miss, res. 428 Cherry.
Hurley Henry, mill-hand, res. McDonald, near lumber yard, Ft. H.
Huron James, lab., res. 316 Main.
Hutchinson Sarah E. Mrs., res. s. w. cor. N. Madison and Pine.
Hutchinson William, res. s. w. cor. N. Madison and Pine.
Huth Augusta (wid. August), res. 706 3d, Ft. H.
Huth C. Wm., fish-packer, res. Manitowoc rd.
Huth Christain, carsmith, res. n. w. cor. 10th av. and 3 I, Ft. H.
Huth Emil, gardener, res. w. s. Manitowoc rd, 7 s. Bellevue.
Huth Jacob, res. 706 3d, Ft. H.
Huth Otto, fish-packer, res. Manitowoc rd.
Huth Wm. Rev., pastor St. Paul's Church, res. 226 S. Madison.
Huybrecht Ferdinand, gardener, res. 1263 Harvey.
Huybrecht Lucy, confectionery, 725 Main, res. 1263 Harvey.
Huybrecht Paul, lab., res. Empire House.
Huybrecht Peter, boilermkr, res. 104 Cedar, Ft. H.
Huybrecht William, gardener, res. s. s. Harvey, 1 w. St. George.
Hyke Frances (wid. Peter), res. 114 Cherry, Ft. H.
Hyska Joseph, lab., res. 1300 Crooks.
Hyska Michael, lab., res. 1193 Stuart.

# I

ILG Frederick, cabinetmkr, res. w. s. 6th av., 2 s. 3 I, Ft. H.
Iliff George, blksmith, res. 429 N. Quincy.
Indra Anton, car-smith, res. 309 John, Ft. H.
Indra Clara Miss, tailoress, res. 309 John, Ft. H.
Indra Emelia, teacher 5th Ward School, res. 309 John, Ft. H.
Indra Henry, blksmith, res. 309 John, Ft. H.
Indra Theresa, dressmkr, res. 309 John, Ft. H.
Ingalls George H., bookkpr., res. 730 Main.
Ingalls J. M. Mrs., res. 730 Main.
Irwin Emilie V. Miss, res. 519 Walnut.
Irwin Hattie Miss, res. 402 Main.
Iversen Louis, lab., res. s. s. 5th, 2 w. 3d av., Ft. H.
Iversen Tor, news stand, e. s. 3d av., 2 s. 2 I, Ft. H., res. same.

## J

JABUREK Jacob, res. 1154 Doty.
Jackson Albert, planer, res. Eldred's boarding house, Ft. H.
Jackson Annie, mngr. Eldred's boarding house, w. s. 2d av., cor. 10th, Ft. H.
Jackson James, clk., res. 429 N. Quincy.
Jackson Emma Miss, res. Eldred's boarding house, Ft. H.
Jackson Grace Miss, res. Eldred's boarding house, Ft. H.
Jackson Jacob, mill-wright, res. Eldred's boarding house, Ft. H.
Jackson James H., watchman, res. 911 Main.
Jackson John, lab., res. 307 Pearl, Ft. H.
Jackson Richard D., switchman, res. 706 S. Jefferson.
Jackson Square, bet. S. Martin, S. Monroe, Moravian and School.
Jackson William R., engineer, res. 305 Cedar, Ft. H.
Jacob John, cooper, res. 1214 Cherry.
Jacob Lucy Miss, res. 1214 Cherry.
Jacobi Manfred (Martin & Jacobi), res. 1156 Cherry.
Jacobs John, clk., res. 810 S. Jefferson.
Jacobs Margaret (wid. John B.), res. 312 Lawe.
Jacobs Minnie, domestic 1221 Crooks.
Jacobsen Andrea (wid. Jacob), res. w. s. Webster av., 2 s. city limits.
Jacobsen Andrew, lab., res. w. s. Webster av., 2 s. city limits.
Jacobsen Annie Miss, res. s. s. Shawano rd., 5 w. Hazel, Ft. H.
Jacobsen Emma, domestic 229 S. Washington.
Jacobsen Hans, mill-hand, res. 318 Chestnut, Ft. H.
Jacobsen Hans A., lab., res. w. s. Webster av., 2 s. city limits.
Jacobsen Martin, lab., res. w. s. Webster av., 2 s. city limits.
Jacobsen Mathilda, clk. Jorgensen-Blesch Co., res. 318 Chestnut.
Jacobsen Nellie Miss, dressmkr, res. 318 Chestnut, Ft. H.
Jacobsen Nels, mill-hand, res. 318 Chestnut, Ft. H.
Jacobsen Peter, sexton Woodlawn Cemetery, res. w. s. Webster av., 2 s. city limits.
Jacobson Andrew, lab., res. 1249 Cherry.
Jacobson Andrew, watchman, res. 707 3d av., Ft. H.
Jacobson Andrew M., carp., res. w. s. 4th av., 2 n. 10th, Ft. H.
Jacobson Bernhard, carp., res. s. s. Grignon, near 11th.
Jacobson Hans, ship-carp., res. s. s. Grignon, near 11th.
Jacobson Hans H., fisherman, res. 1249 Cherry.
Jacobson Henry, sailor, res. s. s. Grignon, near 11th.
Jacobson Lillie, dressmkr, res. 1249 Cherry.
Jacobson Louis, carp., res. 703 3d av., Ft. H.

**Headquarters for Boys' Clothing** THE A. SPUHLER CO.
GREEN BAY.

Jacobson Mary Miss, res. 1249 Cherry.
Jacquain Desire, sawyer, res. 420 N. Madison.
Jacqmin Justinian, lab., res. 507 N. Jefferson.
Jacquart Alexander, res. 1281 Walnut.
Jacquart Eugene, cigarmkr, res. 1281 Walnut.
Jacque Charles, mason, res n. s. Willow, 2 w. 12th.
Jahn Albert, barber, res. 1290 Cherry.
Jahn August H., lab., res. 107 Cedar, Ft. H.
Jahn Bertha Miss, tailoress, res. 1123 Crooks.
Jahn Charles, barber, res. 1012 Doty.
Jahn Frederick, carpenter, res. 1200 Cherry.
Jahn Lena Miss, tailoress, res. 1123 Crooks.
Jahn Michael, tailor, res. 1123 Crooks.
Jahn Oscar A., carp., res. 1630 Morrow.
Jahn Raimund F., blksmith, res. 1345 Cedar.
Jahn Ronnie Miss, res. 309 Cherry, Ft. H.
Jahn William, carp., res. 309 Cherry, Ft. H.
Jahn William Jr., mach., res. 309 Cherry, Ft. H.
James Francis (wid. William), res. 307 S. Adams.
James Liggins, lab., res. 1029 Main.
Jamison Jos. M., lab., res. n. w. cor. S. Washington and Stuart.
Janke Amelia, domestic Charles House.
Janke Lizzie, cook Charles House.
Janke Mary, domestic Charles House.
Jansen Amalie Miss, dressmkr, res. 1274 Cherry.
Jansen Annie Miss, res. 217 N. Jefferson.
Jansen Dorothea (wid. Francis C.), res. 1274 Cherry.
Jansen Frank, res. 915 S. Monroe av.
Jansen Fred., engineer, res. 915 S. Monroe av.
Jansen Gustav, lab., res. 1217 Cherry.
Jansen Harry, switchman, res. 920 S. Quincy.
Jansen Julius G., cigarmkr, res. 1274 Cherry.
Jansen Margaret Miss, res. 915 S. Monroe av.
Jansen Martin, switchman, res. 915 S. Monroe av.
Jansen Martin Jr., brakeman, res. 915 S. Monroe av.
Jansen Peter, lab., res. 303 4th, Ft. H.
Jansen Rachel Miss, res. 1274 Cherry.
Jansen William, bridgetender, res. 915 S. Monroe av.
Janssen Charles, lab., res. n. w. cor. 9th av. and 2d, Ft. H.
Janssen Christian, lab., res. 900 3d av., Ft. H.
**JANSSEN JOHN L. F.**, watchmaker and jeweler, 916 Main, res. same.
Janssen John W., carp., res. 1222 S. Monroe av.
Janssen Louis, brakeman, res. e. s. 7th av., 1 s. 5th, Ft. H.

Janssen Wm. C., machine-hand, res. 1222 S. Monroe av.
Janssen, Jansen. See also Jensen and Johnson.
Jaquart Leon, yardman The Beaumont, res. same.
Jaques Charles, sailor, res. s. s. Bridge, cor. Pearl, Ft. H.
Jaques Elizabeth (wid. Anton), res. w. s. 4th av., 4 n. 9th, Ft. H.
Jaques Henry, sailor, res. s. s. Bridge, cor. Pearl, Ft. H.
Jaques Ida May Miss, res. McDonald, near lumber yd., Ft. H.
Jaques John, sailor, res. 309 Pearl, Ft. H.
Jarvy Andrew, brickmkr, res. s. s. Shawano rd., 2 w. R. R. track, Ft. H.
Jaster Anna (wid. Martin), res. s. e. cor. Manitowoc rd. and Charles.
Jaster August, gardener, res. s. w. cor. Manitowoc rd. and Charles.
Jax Peter, res. 132 S. Jackson.
Jeffcott Charles H., fish-packer, res. 1018 Cedar.
Jeffcott Frank, bkpr. C. W. Streckenbach & Co., res. 1018 Cedar.
Jeffers Peter, del.-clk. M. J. Corbett, res. 137 Chestnut, Ft. H.
Jeffrey Maud Miss, dressmkr. res. 815 Stuart.
Jeffrey Robert, sailor, res. 1269 Willow.
Jeffrey Thomas, res. 815 Stuart.
Jeffs Edward, brakeman, res. Cook's Hotel.
Jendrzejewski Vincent, lab., res. 1345 Crooks.
Jenkins Frank M., carp., res. 793 Shawano rd., Ft. H.
Jenkins George R., foreman, res. American House.
Jenkins Josephine, domestic 200 S. Adams.
Jenkins Lucius T., carp.-contr., res. 793 Shawano rd., Ft. H.
Jenkins M. William, harnessmkr, res. 793 Shawano rd., Ft. H.
Jenkins Wyburn C., sec. The Green Bay Advocate Co., res. 410 Walnut.
Jennings John P., attendant, res. n. e. cor. S. Madison and Porlier.
Jensen Annie W., teacher, res. 315 S. Washington.
Jensen Clement E., clk., res. 315 S. Washington.
Jensen Hans, store keeper, res. 118 Broadway, Ft. H.
Jensen Hans, dry goods, 118 3d av., res. 201 3d av., Ft. H.
Jensen Hans, lab., res. Green Bay House.
Jensen Hilga, domestic 308 N. 11th.
Jensen Henry, cigarmkr, res. 314 Pearl, Ft. H.
Jensen James, clk. Hans Jensen, res. 201 3d av.
Jensen Jennie A. (wid. Clement), res. 315 S. Washington.
Jensen Jennie E. Miss, teacher, res. 315 S. Washington.
Jensen Theresa A. Miss, res. 315 S. Washington.
Jensen. See Jansen, Janssen, Johnson.

**THE A. SPUHLER CO.** *LADIES', MISSES' and CHILDREN'S*
**GREEN BAY** — **CLOAKS, CAPES, JACKETS**

Jenson Sophie Miss, domestic 433 S. Monroe av.
Jepner William, lab., res. 322 Willow, Ft. H.
Jepsen Zena, domestic, res. w. s. 2d av., 4 s. 7th, Ft. H.
Jerzyk John, lab., res. 1326 Chicago.
Jirasek Amelia Miss, res. 127 S. Quincy.
Jirasek George F., barber 926 Main, res. 127 S. Quincy.
Jirasek William, cigarmkr, res. 127 S. Quincy.
Joachim Desire, lab., res. No. 8, n. end Monroe av., e. Murphy's mill.
Joachim Ferdinand, lab., No. 8, n. end Monroe av., e. Murphy's mill.
Joachim Gaspard, lab., res. 1120 Day.
Joachim Hubert, lab., res. 1213 Day.
Joachim John, lab., res. 1213 Day.
Joannes Arthur W., res. 325 S. Monroe av.
Joannes Bros. (Charles, Mitchell and Thomas Joannes), whol. grocers, 118-124 S. Washington.
Joannes Charles (Joannes Bros.), res. 328 S. Jefferson.
Joannes Eugene, student, res. 328 S. Jefferson.
Joannes Felix E. (Joannes & Edwards), res. 319 S. Quincy.
Joannes Flora Miss, res. 328 S. Jefferson.
Joannes Frank E. Y., res. 325 S. Monroe av.
Joannes Genevieve Miss, res. 717 S. Monroe av.
Joannes Josephine Miss, res. 520 Doty.
Joannes Mary E. (wid. Eugene), res. 520 Doty.
Joannes Mitchell (Joannes Bros.), res. 344 S. Quincy.
Joannes Ralph, student, res. 328 S. Jefferson.
Joannes Thomas (Joannes Bros.), res. 717 S. Monroe av.
Joannes Wm., salesman 124 S. Washington, res. 325 S. Monroe av.
**JOANNES & EDWARDS** (F. E. Joannes and I. L. Edwards), general roofers and galvanized iron works, 225 N. Adams.
Jobelius Jacob, lab., res. 1181 Crooks.
Jobelius John, saloon, 1301 Main, res. same.
Jobelius Mary Miss, res. 1301 Main.
Jochim Joseph, lab., res. 1319 Walnut.
Jochim Michael, lab., res. 1362 Walnut.
Joergensen Agnes, domestic 801 Broadway, Ft. H.
Joergensen Emma, domestic Junction Hotel, Ft. H.
Joergensen Christian, lab., res. 505 1st, Ft. H.
Joergensen George, carpenter, res. 612 Cherry, Ft. H.
Joergensen.  See Jorgensen.
Johansen Ernest, blksmith, res. 1256 Doty.

Johnson A. Wallace, marble yard, 310 Cherry, res. 207 Chestnut, Ft. H.
Johnson Alexander, carp., res. 306 7th av., Ft. H.
Johnson Amalia Miss, res. 319 7th av., Ft. H.
Johnson Amelia, domestic 420 S. Jefferson.
Johnson Andrew, ship-carp., res. w. s. 2d av., 2 s. 7th, Ft. H.
Johnson Andrew, ship builder, res. 140 Pearl, Ft. H.
Johnson Andrew J., captain, res. 1 w. 623 Mather, Ft. H.
Johnson Annie M. Miss, res. 1303 Cherry.
Johnson Axel, lab., res. w. s. 11th av., cor. 3d, Ft. H.
Johnson Bico, res. e. s. S. Monroe av., nr. city limits.
Johnson Carrie (wid. Charles), res. 113 Chestnut, Ft. H.
Johnson Christian, lab., res. 1243 Walnut.
Johnson Edith, dressmkr, res. 118 Chestnut, Ft. H.
Johnson Elias J., lab., res. 319 7th av., Ft. H.
Johnson Emma, domestic 414 S. Webster av.
Johnson George, lab., res. 404 2d, Ft. H.
Johnson George, mill-hand, res. Eldred's boarding house, Ft. H.
Johnson George A., carp., res. w. s. 2d av., 3 s. 7th, Ft. H.
Johnson Hannah, domestic 412 S. Adams.
Johnson Hans, lab., res. 303 N. Jefferson.
Johnson Harry, carp., res. 1019 Harvey.
Johnson Henry, cigarmkr, res. 314 Pearl, Ft. H.
Johnson Henry, lab., res. 319 7th av., Ft. H.
Johnson James, carp., res. 625 Mather, Ft. H.
Johnson John, lab., res. 306 7th av., Ft. H.
Johnson John, brakeman C., M. & St. P. Ry., res. 303 Lawe.
Johnson John, lake captain, res. 813 Cherry, Ft. H.
Johnson John, stage prop., res. Reis Hotel.
Johnson John, teamster, res. 404 2d, Ft. H.
Johnson John, teamster, res. 132 Chestnut, Ft. H.
Johnson John E., carp., res. 1019 Harvey.
**JOHNSON JOHN S.,** whol. fish dealer and packer, 1234 Main, res. 1303 Cherry.
Johnson Knut, lab., res. 101 Chestnut, Ft. H.
Johnson Louis, lab., res. Junction Hotel, Ft. H.
Johnson Magnus (Johnson & King), res. 1019 Harvey.
Johnson Sena Miss, res. 404 2d, Ft. H.
Johnson Stena, waitress, res. 404 2d, Ft. H.
Johnson Tillie Miss, res. 404 2d, Ft. H.
Johnson William, fireman Hose No. 1., res. 107 S. Washington.
Johnson Xenia, domestic e. s. Willow, 2 n. of Baird, Ft. H.
Johnson & King (Magnus Johnson and John C. King), carp. contrs., 1019 Harvey, and Cedar bet. 10th and 11th.

**THE A. SPUHLER CO., Green Bay** CARPETS, RUGS, OIL CLOTHS
Draperies and Window Shades.

Johnson. See Jansen, Janssen and Jensen.
Johnston Albert, teamster, res. Eldred's boarding house, Ft. H.
Johnston Cora, teacher, res. 1707 Main.
Johnston Eugene R., bkpr. Green Bay **Planing Mill Co.**, res. 1707 Main.
Johnston George, teamster, res. 1707 Main.
Jolka Joseph, lab., res. n. s. St. Clair, 6 e. N. 12th.
Joly Lawrence, carp., res. 521 S. 12th.
Joly Peter, teamster, res. 1282 Chicago.
Joly. See Juley.
Jones Bernhard, mill-hand, res. 117 7th av., Ft. H.
Jones Edward, brakeman, res. Cook's Hotel.
Jones Frank T., salesman, res. 1256 Chicago.
Jones Fred, cigarmkr, res. 117 7th av., Ft. H.
Jones George (Jones & Eggner), res. 213 Broadway, Ft. H.
**JONES GUSTAVE,** house mover and carp.-contr., n. w. cor. 2nd and 10th av., Ft. H., res. same.
Jones Henry, fireman, res. 117 7th av., Ft. H.
Jones John M., com. trav., res. 122 N. Washington.
Jones Peter, lab., res. 117 7th av., Ft. H.
Jones Porter, foreman Green Bay Advocate News **Room, res.** 822 S. Jefferson.
Jones & Eggner (George Jones and Peter Eggner), cigar mnfrs., n. w. cor. Main and Broadway, Ft. H.
Joppe August, beer peddler, res. n. s. Main, 3 e. Forest.
Jordan Carl, carp., res. s. s. Elmore, 5 w. Cedar, Ft. H.
Jordan Henrietta (wid. Christian), res. 1377 Stuart.
Jordan Silver, plumber, res. 444 S. Jefferson.
Jordan Thomas S., foreman press-room The State Gazette, res. 444 S. Jefferson.
**JORGENSEN-BLESCH CO.** (limited), J. L. Jorgensen, pres.; F. T. Blesch, sec. and treas.; whol. and retail dry goods, carpets and house furnishing goods, 303-307 N. Washington.
Jorgensen Gabriel, carp., res. e. s. 3d av., 2 s. 4th, Ft. H.
Jorgensen Gerhard, lab., res. e. s. 3d av., 2 s. 4th, Ft. H.
Jorgensen John L., pres. Jorgensen-Blesch Co., res. n. e. cor. Hubbard and Chestnut, Ft. H.
Jorgensen Rasmus A., grocer, s. w. cor. 3d av. and 4th, res. e. s., 3d, 2 s. 4th, Ft. H.
Jorgenson Charles H., bkpr., res. 105 Broadway, Ft. H.
Jorgenson Ole, ship-carp., res. 105 Broadway, Ft. H.
Jorgenson. See Joergenson.
Joseph Frank, res. 421 S. Washington.
Jossart David Sr., lab., res. 806 Day.

Jossart David Jr., saloon, res. 800 Day.
Jossart Elsie, res. 615 N. 12th.
Jossart Eli, lab., res. 806 Day.
Jourdain William G., carp., res. 932 Smith.
Jubain George, engineer, res. 221 N. Quincy.
Jubert Fred, teamster, res. 415 S. Washington.
Judd Belle Miss, stenog. Hart's Steamboat Line, res. 709 S. Jefferson.
Judd Jane W. (wid. James V. H.), res. 111 N. Van Buren.
Judkins George, lab., res. s. e. cor. Chicago and 11th.
Juenger Catherine Miss, res. 429 Broadway, Ft. H.
Juenger Henry, barkpr. 505 Broadway, Ft. H., res. same.
Juenger John J., mngr. Klaus Hall, res. 429 Broadway, Ft. H.
**JUENGER JOHN P.,** saloon and restaurant, 429 Broadway, s. w. cor. Dousman, Ft. H., res. same.
Juley Matthew, lab., res. cor. 3d av. and 7th, Ft. H.
Juley Minnie Miss, res. 219 3d av., Ft. H.
Juley Nicholas J. (Miller & Juley), res. s. e. cor. 3d av. and 7th, Ft. H.
Juley Peter, res. cor. 3d av. and 7th, Ft. H.
July Gertie Miss, res. 131 S. Van Buren.
July Jacob, res. 333 S. Van Buren.
July. See Joly.
**JUNCTION HOTEL,** J. J. Nelson, prop., s. s. 2d, opp. G. B., W. & St. P. depot, Ft. H.
Jungbluth Fred., lab., res. w. s. 11th av., 2 n. 2d, Ft. H.
Junkel. See Youngle.
Justice Jesse, carp., res. Columbia Hotel.

# K

KAAP Herman, tailor, res. 221 S. 10th.
Kaap William, tailor, res. 221 S. 10th.
Kagmagnska Petroneli, domestic Commercial House, Ft. H.
Kahler Gusta, domestic 127 Chestnut, Ft. H.
Kaiser, see Keyser and DeKeyser.
Kalasinski Anton, lab., res. 702 Cherry, Ft. H.
Kalasinski Stanislaus, lab., res. 702 Cherry, Ft. H.
Kalb Joseph, res. 538 S. Jefferson.
**KALB LOUIS,** meat market and tug office, 107 N. Washington, res. same.
Kalb, see Kolb.
Kaminski Carl, lab., res. 1224 Crooks.
Kane Annie (wid. O. J.), res. n. s. Elmore, 10 w. Cedar, Ft. H.

Kane Catherine Miss, res. n. s. Elmore, 10 w. Cedar, Ft. H.
Kane Francis, lab., res. n. s. Elmore, 10 w. Cedar, Ft. H.
Kane Mary Miss, teacher 5th Ward School, res. n. s. Elmore, 10 w. Cedar, Ft. H.
Kane Michael, tallyman, res. Eldred's boarding house, Ft. H.
Kane Nellie Miss, res. n. s. Elmore, 5 w. Cedar, Ft. H.
Kane Robert A., conductor, res. Cook's Hotel.
Kanter Asrael, butcher, res. 825 Main.
Kapp John, lab., res. s. s. Main, 1 e. city limits, Town Preble.
Kapp Louis E., carp., res. 323 S. Adams.
Kapp Walburga (wid. John), res. s. s. Main nr. Forest.
Kappell Michael, butcher, res. 1468 Mason.
Karlson Alexander, lab., res. Junction Hotel, Ft. H.
Karn William, engineer, res. 525 S. Jackson.
Karsten Matthias, saloon, 204 3d av., res. 402 2d, Ft. H.
Kaeke Annie, domestic Bradley House.
Kaspareck Frank, edge-tool grinder, 1265 Main, res. same.
Kasper Louise, domestic 901 Broadway, Ft. H.
**KASTER CASTOR**, merchant tailor, 209 Pine, res. 408 Howard.
Kaster Frank, cutter C. Kaster, res. 408 Howard.
Kaster Jacob, barkpr. Wm. Seguin, res. 518 Cherry.
Kaster Joseph, bookkpr. Hagemeister Brewing Co., res. 644 S. Quincy.
Kaster Peter, bookkpr. Buengener & Bur, res. 116 N. Quincy.
Katers Wm., lab., res. w. s. Oneida, 2 s. Shawano rd., Ft. H.
Kattner Amelia, domestic 719 Cherry.
Kattner Carl (Brehme & Kattner), res. s. w. cor. Chestnut and Baird, Ft. H.
Kattner Helene, domestic 137 Broadway, Ft. H.
Kattner Rudolph, lab., res. s. w. cor. Chestnut and Baird, Ft. H.
Kauffman Louis, lab., res. n. e. cor. 5th av. and 10th, Ft. H.
Kaufmann Caroline (wid. Gottlieb), res. 1504 Elm.
Kaufmann Herman H., live stock dealer, 1504 Elm, res. same.
Kaufmann John L. butcher, res. 1447 Cedar.
Kaufmann Louis, meatmkt, 1447 Cedar, res. same.
Kaye Alexander, lab., res. 1119 Harvey.
Kaye Edward J., tailor, res. 1119 Harvey.
Kaye Elie, gardener, res. 1301 Day.
Kaye John, cigarmkr, res. 1301 Day.
Kaye John, lab., res. 1116 Cedar.
Kaye John B. butcher, res. 1119 Harvey.
Kaye Joseph V., clk. Weise-Hollman Co., res. 628 S. Jackson.
Kaye Joshua, lab., res. 1228 Day.

Kaye Josie Miss, tailoress, res. 1119 Harvey.
Kaye Julius E. (Krippner & Kaye), res. 1011 Harvey.
Kaye Minnie Miss, res. 1301 Day.
Kaye Selina (wid. Theofil), res. 1119 Harvey.
Kayser Charles, lab., res. 509 Broadway, Ft. H.
Kayser Nicholas, saw-filer, res. 606 Cedar, Ft. H.
Keiper James, switchman, res. 802 Cedar, Ft. H.
Kelbie Joseph, lab., res. 1257 Doty.
Kelleher Annie Miss, dressmkr, res. 121 S. Monroe av.
Kelleher Della Miss, res. 121 S. Monroe av.
Kelleher Edward, fireman, res. 715 S. Jefferson.
Kelleher John, captain, res. 715 S. Jefferson.
Kelleher Julia Miss, res. 121 S. Monroe av.
Kelleher Margaret, teacher, res. 308 S. Quincy.
Kelleher Mary Miss, res. 715 S. Jefferson.
Kelleher Mary (wid. Peter), res. 121 S. Monroe av.
Kelleher Maurice G., bartender, res. 330 Main.
Kelleher Minnie H. Miss, teacher, res. 308 S. Quincy.
Kellner Henry, butcher, res. 112 N. Washington.
Kellogg E. B., com.-trav. Standard Oil Co., res. 607 Main, Ft. H.
Kellogg Katie Miss, teacher, res. 408 Kellogg, Ft. H.
Kellogg Libbie Miss, stenog. Wm. Larsen, res. 607 Main, Ft. H.
**KELLOGG NATIONAL BANK THE**, Wm. J. Fisk, pres.; Fred. Hurlbut, v.-pres.; Henry R. Baker, cashier, 301 N. Washington.
Kellogg Stock Farm, R. B. Kellogg Est., prop., horse breeders. De Pere rd., 2½ miles s. city limits.
Kellogg Thomas Jr., night police, res. 408 Kellogg, Ft. H.
Kellogg Wm. E., mngr. Kellogg Est., res. De Pere rd., 2½ miles s. city limits.
Kelly Bernard, engineer, res. 436 S. Jefferson.
Kelly Clara Miss, res. 436 S. Jefferson.
Kelly Cornelius, mail agt., res. s. w. cor. Willow and Baird, Ft. H.
Kelly Frank, res. 436 S. Jefferson.
Kelly Thomas J., conductor, res. 230 S. Quincy.
Kemnitz August, foreman, res. 130 Broadway, Ft. H.
Kemnitz Ferdinand H., com. trav., res. 806 Pine.
Kemnitz Kate Miss, student, res. n. e. cor. Main and Cedar, Ft. H.
Kemnitz Louis, sec. Theo. Kemnitz Furniture Co., res. 707 Dousman, Ft. H.
Kemnitz Richard, carp., res. 130 Broadway, Ft. H.
**KEMNITZ THEO. FURNITURE CO. THE**, Theodor Kemnitz, pres. and treas.; Louis Kemnitz, sec.; Theodor Kemnitz, Jr., v.-pres., cor. Pearl and Baird, Ft. H.

James Kerr.     Established Sept. 1873.     Chas. J. Kerr.

## James Kerr & Son,
### Publishers of The Ft. Howard Review.
### Steam Job Printing.

109–111 Ewart Street.     Fort Howard Wis.

---

The Review is the Official Paper of City and County.

---

The Best Advertising Medium in N. E. and N. W. Wisconsin.

---

Advertising Specialties in Variety.     Job Printing of all descriptions.

# HOWARD RUBBER STAMP CO.,

MANUFACTURERS OF ALL KINDS OF

## RUBBER STAMPS

—AND DEALERS IN—

### RUBBER STAMP GOODS,

FORT HOWARD, WIS.

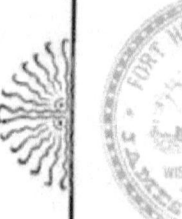

## CHAS. S. KERR,

MANUFACTURERS' AGENT FOR

# BICYCLES

311 Pearl Street, FORT HOWARD, WIS.

### BICYCLES FOR RENT.

BARGAINS in Second-Hand WHEELS.

**Headquarters for Boys' Clothing** THE **A. SPUHLER CO.** GREEN BAY.

Kemnitz Theodor, pres. Theo. Kemnitz Furniture Co., res. 300 Cedar, Ft. H.
Kemnitz Theodor Jr., v.-pres. Theo. Kemnitz Furniture Co., res. 302 Cedar, Ft. H.
Kendall Philo R., sec. and treas. The Land & Abstract Co., res. 415 Crooks.
**KENDALL WM. F.,** civil engineer and architect, 6, 320 N. Washington, res. same.
Kennedy Wm., chief fire dept., res. 123 S. Madison.
Kenney William, fireman, res. Northwestern Hotel, Ft. H.
Kensler Frank, lab., res. 1114 Walnut.
Kensler Rosalie (wid. Frank), res. 1114 Walnut.
Kern Ida, domestic 306 Cherry, Ft. H.
Kern Margaret (wid. John), res. 1267 Cedar.
Kernin Edward J., carp., res. 709 Walnut.
Kernin Wm., clk., res. 709 Walnut.
Kerr Charles S. (James Kerr & Son), res. 340 Broadway, Ft. H.
Kerr James (James Kerr & Son), res 340 Broadway, Ft. H.
**KERR JAMES & SON** (James and Charles S. Kerr), props. and pubs. Fort Howard Review, 309 Pearl, Ft. H.
Kerr William L., city clk. Ft. H., res. 340 Broadway, Ft. H.
Kersten Jacob, carp., res. 1181 Crooks.
Kersten. See Karsten.
Kesselhuth J. William, mach., res. s. s. Shawano rd., 4 w. Hazel, Ft. H.
Kewaunee, Green Bay & Western R. R., W. J. Abrams, pres.; S. W. Champion, gen. mngr.; s. e. cor. Adams and Pine, depot s. e. cor. S. Washington and Crooks.
Keyes Oliver A., train dispatcher C. M. & St. P. Ry., res. 543 S. Jefferson.
Keyser William, lab., res. Eldred's boarding house, Ft. H.
Kiel Caroline (wid. Christian), res. w. s. Monroe av. rd., 2½ miles s. city limits.
Kiernan Laura Miss, res. 820 S. Monroe av.
Kiernan Rose Miss, res. 820 S. Monroe av.
Kiernan Wm., res. 820 S. Monroe av.
Kiernan Wm. Jr., lumberman, res. 820 S. Monroe av.
Kiernan. See Kernin.
Kies Daniel T., mail carrier, res. 320 S. Webster av.
Kies Mary R. (wid. Chas. H.), res. 320 S. Webster av.
Kieylls John, lab., res. 312 5th av., Ft. H.
Kile Mary, cook Bradley House.
Kiley James E., lab., res. 206 Willow, Ft. H.
Kiley William, res. 206 Willow, Ft. H.

Killian John A., notary and insurance, 218 N. Washington, res. 108 S. Monroe av.
Killian John E., loco.-engineer, res. 723 S. Adams.
Killian Michael, engineer, res. 521 Cherry, Ft. H.
Kilmer Abram, sawyer, res. 303 S. Adams.
Kilmer Wilson, com.-trav. Columbian Baking Co., res. Portage, Wis.
**KIMBALL ALONZO,** wholesale and retail hardware, blksmith and mill supplies, 106–110 N. Washington, res. 324 S. Adams.
Kimball Chas. T., mngr. A. Kimball, res. 420 S. Jefferson.
Kimball Charles T. Jr., res. 420 S. Jefferson.
Kimball Gertrude Miss, clk., res. 108 S. Jefferson.
Kimball Mary B. Miss, res. 420 S. Jefferson.
Kimball Myra W. Miss, res. 420 S. Jefferson.
Kimball Newell S., master mechanic C., M. & St. P. Ry., res. 108 S. Jefferson.
Kimball Walter H. Mrs., res. 108 S. Jefferson.
King Adeline Miss, res. 503 Cedar.
King Adolph, cooper, res. 503 Cedar.
King Benjamin, res. 503 Cedar.
King Caroline Miss, res. 319 S. Adams.
**KING EDWARD B.,** druggist, 116 3d av., Ft. H., res. same.
King Frances Miss, domestic 717 S. Monroe.
King John C. (Johnson & King), res. 1205 Cedar.
King Joseph, lab., res. 714 Main.
King Lizzie Miss, res. 116 3d av., Ft. H.
King Wenzel, brewer, res. 1357 Doty.
Kinney Vincent, lab., res. 1357 Doty.
Kipp Annie, domestic 411 Cherry, Ft. H.
Kirbey Charles R., cigar mnfr., 202 Dousman, res. n. w. cor. Broadway and Bond, Ft. H.
Kirby Nellie, domestic 505 Broadway, Ft. H.
Kirkpatrick Alexander, conductor, res. 1116 Cherry.
Kirkpatrick Inez Miss, res. 1116 Cherry.
Kirtland Ida M. Miss, res. 631 N. Madison.
Kirtland Philip W., lake captain, res. 631 N. Madison.
Kitchen Wesley, lather, res. 703 Cherry, Ft. H.
**KITTNER EDWARD C.,** blksmith and wagonmkr, 127 S. Washington, res. 319 S. Washington.
Kittner Emil, lumber scaler, res. 319 S. Washington.
Kittner Ernst, car-painter, res. 319 S. Washington.
Kittner Helen, dressmkr, res. 319 S. Washington.

**THE A. SPUHLER CO.** *LADIES', MISSES' and CHILDREN'S* **CLOAKS, CAPES, JACKETS**
GREEN BAY

Kittner John E., fireman, res. 214 Doty.
Kitts Henry, city police, res. n. s. Elm, cor. Van Buren.
Klaus Andrew, butcher, res. 1035 Main.
Klaus Annie Miss, res. 1035 Main.
Klaus Christine Miss, dressmkr, res. 1035 Main.
Klaus Elizabeth Miss, res. 526 Pine.
Klaus Elizabeth Miss, res. 1035 Main.
Klaus Elizabeth (wid. Philip), res. 526 Pine.
Klaus Henry P., res. 526 Pine.
Klaus Ida Miss, res. 733 Pine.
Klaus Louis C., meat market, 1035 Main, res. same.
Klaus Mary (wid. Charles) res. 733 Pine.
Klaus Mary K. Miss, res. 326 S. Quincy.
**KLAUS OPERA HOUSE**, Sebastian Beuder, mngr., 222-226 Pine.
Klaus William S., cigarmkr, res. 733 Pine.
Kleinschmidt August, barrelmkr, res. 1121 S. Jackson.
Kleinschmidt Wm., carp., res. 1117 S. Monroe av.
Klesges Annie Miss, res. 208 N. Washington.
Klesges John, lab., res. 866 Dousman, Ft. H.
Klesges Nicholas, carp., res. 1300 Walnut.
**KLESGES VALENTINE**, saloon, 208 N. Washington, res. same.
Klesse Bruno (Brossig & Klesse), res. Sturgeon Bay rd., e. city limits.
Kling George, engineer McDonald's planing mill, res. McDonald's boarding house, Ft. H.
Kloepping Fred., lab., res. e. s. Chestnut, 1 n. Kellogg, Ft. H.
Kloepping Henry, confect., res. e. s. Chestnut, 1 n. Kellogg, Ft. H.
Kloepping Sophia (wid. Fred.), res. e. s. Chestnut, 1 n. Kellogg, Ft. H.
Kloskey Alex., lab., No. 6, n. end Monroe av., e. Murphy's mill.
Knaepple John, res. e. s. Oneida, 1 s. Shawano rd., Ft. H.
Knapp Winfield, lab., res. n. w. cor. Cedar and Main, Ft. H.
Knechtel Theodore, lab., res. Champion Hotel.
Knell John, res. 112 S. Monroe av.
Knell Katie Miss, res. 112 S. Monroe av.
Knell Matthew, res. 112 S. Monroe av.
Knoller Godfrey, sawyer, res. 132 S. Jackson.
Knowlton Edward, lab., res. e. s. 4th av., 3 n. 9th, Ft. H.
Knox Andrew T., watchman, res. No. 1, n. end Monroe av., e. Murphy's mill.
Knox Frank L., teamster, res. No. 1, n. end Monroe av., e. Murphy's mill.

Knox W., book agt., res. 213 Chestnut, Ft. H.
Knox & Wilner (Henry D. Wilner), boots and shoes, 200-202 N. Washington.
Knudson Knud, carp., res. 100 Cherry, Ft. H.
Knuth Charles F., farmer, res. 200 S. Jackson.
Knuth Josephine, dressmkr, res. 200 S. Jackson.
Knutson Benjamin, teamster, res. 331 Pearl, Ft. H.
Knutson Mary, cook St. James Hotel.
Knutzon Lorenz, lab., res. 1208 Walnut.
Kobussen Francis W., lab., res. n. e. cor. Cedar and Elmore, Ft. H.
Koch Frank (Spude & Koch), res. 228 S. Jackson
Koch Frank Jr., mason, res. 228 S. Jackson.
Koch Frederick, mason, res 228 S. Jackson.
Koch Lizzie M. Miss, res. 228 S. Jackson.
Koch Louis, farmer, res. s. s. 2d, 6 w. Ry. track, Ft. H.
Koch Oscar, moulder, res. s. s. 2d, 1 w. Ry. track, Ft. H.
Koch Therese Miss, res. 228 S. Jackson.
Kocha James, car-smith, res. w. s. 4th av., 3 s. 8th.
Kocha Joseph, lab., res. w. s. 4th av., 2 n. 9th, Ft. H.
Kocha Peter, lab., res. 812 3d av., Ft. H.
Koeferl Max, mach., res. n. w. cor. Mather and Cherry, Ft. H.
Koenig Charles H., carp. res. n. s. St. Clair, 2 w. N. 11th.
Koenig Edward, watchmkr, res. 122 S. Quincy.
Koenig Esther, domestic 316 Mason.
Koenig Frederick, lab., res. 1012 Cherry.
Koenig Richard, res. 1012 Cherry.
Koenig Sophie Miss, res. 1012 Cherry.
Koerber Henry, railway-band, res. Charles House.
Koetter Matthias, lab., res. 1420 Smith.
Koetter Michael, lab., res. 1420 Smith.
Kofod Christian, lab., res. 304 2d, Ft. H.
Kohler George, lab., res. e. s. 9th av., 2 n. 2d, Ft. H.
Kohls Henry L., foreman carsmith shop, res. w. s. 11th av., 1 n. 2d, Ft. H.
Kolb Peter, teamster, res. 346 S. Jackson.
Kolb.   See Kalb.
Kolbrick Edward, lab., res. e. s. 7th av., 3 s. 2d, Ft. H.
Kolucheske Thomas, prop. Coopertown House, res. same.
Kolodzick Clara Miss, res. 1283 Crooks.
Kolodzick Fred., lab., res. 1283 Crooks.
Kolman John, lab., res. w. s. 4th av., 3 n. 9th, Ft. H.
Kommarlein Henrietta (wid. Caspar), res. 306 3d av., Ft. H.
Konikowski Annie, domestic 333 S. Jefferson.

**THE A. SPUHLER CO., Green Bay** CARPETS, RUGS, OIL CLOTHS
Draperies and Window Shades.

Konowsky Aug., lab., res. e. s. Hazel, 3 s. Shawano rd., Ft. H.
Konowsky William, delivery clk., res. Broadway House, Ft. H.
Kopczynski George, lab., res. 1400 Chicago.
Koppellman Jacob, tailor, res. 1415 Mason.
Koppens Felix, lab , res. s. s. Dousman, 6 w. Willow, Ft. H.
Kornowski Annie Miss, res. 5 w. 929 Dousman, Ft. H.
Kornowski Gustav, lab., res. 5 w. 929 Dousman, Ft. H.
Kornowski William, lab., res. 5 w. 929 Dousman, Ft. H.
Kortebein Amelia, domestic 529 Cherry.
Kortebein Annie, domestic 333 S. Adams.
Koske August, clk. 417 Main, res. Schauer Hotel.
Kosnar Frank, teamster J. P. C. Schmit, res. s. e. cor. Monroe av. and Mason.
Koviak Andrew, lab., res. 1500 Chicago.
Koviak S. Frank, res. 1500 Chicago.
Koviak Stanislaus, lab., res. 1500 Chicago.
Kowski Gustav, mason, res. 202 Chestnut, Ft. H.
Kowski Henry, car repairer, res. 202 Chestnut, Ft. H.
Kox.  See Cox.
Kraemer August, farmer, res. n. e. cor. Preble and Heyrman.
Kraemer Mary Miss, res. n. e. cor. Preble and Heyrman.
Kraemer Matthias, lab., res. 1008 Main.
Kraemer Otto, farmer, res. n. e. cor. Preble and Heyrman.
Kraemer William, farmer, res. n. e. cor. Preble and Heyrman.
Kraemer.  See Cramer.
Kraft Charles, res. 1344 Doty.
Kraft Christine (wid. Louis), res. 1328 Harvey.
Kraft Frank, engineer Henry Rahr's Sons, res. 1344 Doty.
Kraft Frederick, cooper, res. 1328 Harvey.
Kraft Julius, lab., res. 1323 Doty.
Kraft Louis, wheelman, res. 1450 Day.
**KRAKE IRA**, painter, paper hanging, calcimining and mason work, n. e. cor. 5th av. and 10th, Ft. H., res. same.
Kramer Annie, domestic 400 S. Madison.
Kraus Anton, lab., res. w. s. Oneida, 3 s. Shawano rd., Ft. H.
Kraus Bertha, domestic 406 N. Van Buren.
Kraus John, lab., res. w. s. Oneida, 3 s. Shawano rd., Ft. H.
Kraus Rudolph, engineer, res. 1208 Walnut.
Krause Amelia, domestic 516 S. Van Buren.
Krause Frederick, fisherman, res. 611 Cedar, Ft. H.
Krause Otto, lab., res. 611 Cedar, Ft. H.
Krause William, clk., res. Commercial hotel, Ft. H.
Krause.  See Krouse.
Krautsch Berthold, marbleetr., res. St. James hotel.

Kraynik Joseph, lab. res. 513 Cherry, Ft. H.
Krezma Thomas, lab., res. w. s. 2d av., 3 s. 8th, Ft. H.
Kriescher Maggie, domestic 509 Pine.
Kriescher Ottilie, domestic 611 S. Madison.
Krieser Albert W. T., butcher, res. 1274 Cedar.
Krieser Emil L., clk Felix J. Hannon, res. w. s. Chestnut, 5 s. Baird, Ft. H.
Krippner Bernhard J., mach., res. 119 Cherry, Ft. H.
Krippner Edwin M. (Krippner & Kaye), res. 119 Cherry, Ft. H.
Krippner & Kaye (Edwin M. Krippner and Julius E. Kaye), merchant tailors, 313 Main, Ft. H.
Kroening Gustav, lab., res. 1200 Day.
Krouse Fred. A., clk., res. Huffman House, Ft. H.
Krouse Grant N., salesman, res. Huffman House, Ft. H.
Krouse Libbie Miss, res. Huffman House, Ft. H.
**KROUSE PETER,** prop. Huffman House, cor. Broadway and Kellogg, Ft. H., res. same.
Krouse William B., car inspector, res. Huffman House, Ft. H.
Krueger Albert, lab., res. 1239 Doty.
Krueger Carl, lab., res. 625 Baird.
Krueger Carl, photog., res. 128 N. Adams.
Krueger Emma Miss, res. 1239 Doty.
Krueger Fred. W., marble polisher, res. 1239 Doty.
Krueger Lena Miss, res. 1239 Doty.
Krueger Wm., bookbinder, res. 1239 Doty.
Krug Frederick W., conductor G. B., W. & St. P. R. R., res. 307 7th av., Ft. H.
Krug Henry, mason, res. 306 3d av., Ft. H.
Krug Johannes, res. 306 3d av., Ft. H.
Krug Louise Miss, res. 306 3d av., Ft. H.
Kuehl Bros. (Frederick and Herman Kuehl), dairy, s. s. 9th, 2 w. C. & N. W. R. R. track, Ft. H.
Kuehl Frederick (Kuehl Bros.), res. s. s. 9th, 2 w. C. & N. W. Ry. track, Ft. H.
Kuehl Herman (Kuehl Bros.), res. s. s. 9th, 2 w. C. & N. W. Ry. track, Ft. H.
Kuehl Julius, machinist, res. 402 6th av., Ft. H.
Kugel Frank, brewer Hochgreve Brewing Co., res. w. s. Monroe av. rd., 2¼ miles s. city limits.
Kugel Joseph, brewer Hochgreve Brewing Co., res. w. s. Monroe av. rd., 2¼ miles s. city limits.
Kuhaupt Christopher, carp., res. 201 Cherry, Ft. H.
Kuhaupt Henry, barber, 206 Main, res. 201 Cherry, Ft. H.
Kuhn Bruno, res. 1125 Cass.

**THE A. SPUHLER CO., GREEN BAY, WIS.** **Fine Dress Goods**
Samples Furnished on Application.

Kuhn Jacob M., lab., res. 1125 Cass.
Kuipers Mary, domestic 109 N. Webster av.
Kujawa Annie Miss, res. 1220 Stuart.
Kujawa Anton, lab., res. 1220 Stuart.
Kujawa Katie, forewoman, res. 1220 Stuart.
Kujawa Maggie Miss, res. 1220 Stuart.
Kukral Albert, lab., res. 1023 Harvey.
Kukral Joseph, lab., res. 1023 Harvey.
Kukral Mary Miss, res. 1023 Harvey.
Kull Eugene, mason, res. 1257 Chicago.
Kull Fred. Jacob, watchman, res. 304 3 1, Ft. H.
Kull George, watchman, res. 304 3d, Ft. H.
Kull Herman, fireman, res. 505 Willow, Ft. H.
Kull. See Cull.
Kummer Theresa Miss, res. 601 S. Monroe av.
Kupper Annie M. Miss, res. 918 Walnut.
Kupper Appolonia Miss, res. 918 Walnut.
Kupper Jacob, lab., res. 625 S. Jefferson.
Kupper John H., mason, res. 918 Walnut.
Kupper Mary A. (wid. Henry), res. 918 Walnut.
Kupper Nicholas, lab., res. 918 Walnut.
Kurth Ferdinand, lab., res. 201 Baird, Ft. H.
Kurvers Mary, domestic 328 S. Jefferson.
Kurz Albert G., photog., 210-212 Cherry, res. same.
Kurz Gottlieb, marble-ctr., res. e. s. Goodell, n. of Crooks.
Kush Sophie Miss, ironer steam laundry, res. 135 N. Adams.
Küstermann Agnes Miss, res. 415 Walnut.
Küstermann Carl, asst. postmaster, res. 415 Walnut.
**KÜSTERMANN GUSTAV,** postmaster, pianos and organs, books, etc., 217 N. Washington, res. 828 Cherry.
Küstermann Julia Miss, res 415 Walnut.
Küstermann Tillie Miss, bkpr. G. Küstermann, res. 828 Cherry.
Kutzra Anton, teamster, res. 310 N. Quincy.
Kutzra Anton W., 'bus-driver, res. Schauer's Hotel.
**KYBER GEORGE E. T.,** notary public, real estate, foreign passage, mortgage loans and collection office, 214 N. Washington, res. town Allouez.
Kynaston Frank T., carp., res. 113 S. **Adams.**

# L

LABART Euphrosine (wid. Seraphim), res. 421 N. Jefferson.
Laby Julius, res. 1112 Doty.
Laby Peter, res. 1112 Doty.

Lace John, lab., res. 708 S. Madison.
**LACHANCE HENRY E.,** saloon, 225 Cherry, res. same.
La Chapelle Joseph (Brinneman & La Chapelle), res. Reis Hotel.
Lackawanna Transportation Co., foot Pine.
Lacombe Alex., drayman, res. n. s. Bond, 7 w. Cedar, Ft. H.
Lacombe Josephine Miss, res. n. s. Bond, 7 w. Cedar, Ft. H.
La Court Antoine, saloon and boarding house, 425 Main, res. same.
La Court Louis, barkpr, res. 425 Main.
La Crosse Augusta (wid. Caspar), res. 1131 Stuart.
La Crosse Emil, res. 1131 Stuart.
Ladewig William, tallow-renderer, res. 1221 Walnut.
Ladouceur Moses, harnessmkr. res. 135 Chestnut, Ft. H.
La Due Maggie Miss, res. 621 S. Madison.
**LA DUKE GEORGE W.,** blksmith and horseshoer, Broadway, opposite Wm. Larsen Canning Co., res. n. s. Bond, 3 w. Willow, Ft. H.
Lady of Charity Orphan Asylum, n. w. cor. S. Madison and Milwaukee.
Laes Henry, tinsmith, res. 729 Main.
Laes John, cooper, res. 735 Main.
Laes Lambert, saloon, 729 Main, res. same.
Lafave Louis, brakeman, res. Northwestern Hotel, Ft. H.
Lafave Simon, brakeman, res. Northwestern Hotel, Ft. H.
Lafrombois Agnes Miss, domestic 645 S. Monroe av.
Lagers John, mason, res. 426 N. 11th.
Lagers Peter, mason-contr., 426 N. 11th, res. same.
Lahaye Julius, lab., res. 1 w. 874 Dousman, Ft. H.
Lally Patrick, blksmith, res. e. s. 10th av., 3 n. 2d, Ft. H.
Laluzerne Joseph W., blksmith, res. 226 S. Van Buren.
Lamarre Joseph, carp., res. 1315 Day.
Lamarre Joseph L., lab., res. 1315 Day.
Lambeau Marcell, mason, res. 1636 Morrow.
Lambeau Mary Miss, res. 1636 Morrow.
Lambeau Mary A. (wid. Victor), res. 1636 Morrow.
Lambert Joseph, barkpr., res. 615 N. 12th.
Lambrecht Charles Erich, piano tuner, 1244 Cherry, res. same.
Lamont Mary, domestic 515 Cherry.
Lamper Sarah (wid. Joseph), res. 527 School.
**LAND & ABSTRACT CO. THE,** C. E. Vroman, pres.; P. R. Kendall, sec. and treas.; abstracts, real estate and real estate mortgages, 301 N. Washington.
Landberg Malcolm E., res. 403 2d, Ft. H.
Landberg Malcolm J., stonecutter, res. 403 2d, Ft. H.

**Headquarters for Boys' Clothing** THE A. SPUHLER CO.
GREEN BAY.

Lande Charles, lab., res. 416 N. Madison.
Landford A. J., res. Odd Fellows' Home.
**LANDSMANN DER**, Lehman & Robinson, props., 222 N. Adams.
Landwehr Sebastian, real estate, res. e. s. Oneida, 1 s. Shawano rd., Ft. H.
Lang Anna (wid. Joseph), res. 1026 Walnut.
Lang Charles, woodsman, res. 316 Main.
Langlois Edward, lab., res. Howard House, Ft. H.
Langlund Andrew, lab., res. 304 7th av., Ft. H.
Langworthy Albert, res. s. s. Shawano rd., 2 w. Oak, Ft. H.
Langworthy John, conductor C. & N. W. Ry., res. 218 N. Washington.
Lannegan Morris, druggist, res. Huffman House, Ft. H.
Lannoye August, mach., res. e. s. Cedar, 1 n. Dousman, Ft. H.
Lannoye Prosper, lab., res. n. s. Shawano rd., 2 w. 854, Ft. H.
Lantow Charles N., barber, res. 319 Pine.
La Pine Louis, ship-carp., res. 723 S. Jefferson.
La Pine Louis Jr., brakeman, res. 723 S. Jefferson.
Lardinois Arthur, lab., res. 1028 Stuart.
Lardinois Victor, lab., res. 1141 Doty.
Lardinoit Desire Mrs., res. n. s. Shawano rd., 2 w. Fisk, Ft. H.
Lardinoit Joseph, farmer, res. n. s. Shawano rd., 2 w. Fisk, Ft. H.
Lardo James, lab., res. 1108 Cedar.
Larkin Johanna (wid. Nicholas), res. 426 N. 11th.
Larkin Joseph, lab., res. 426 N. 11th.
Larkin Kate Miss, res. 426 N. 11th.
Larkins Nicholas, stage driver, res. Reis Hotel.
La Roche John, fish-packer, res. 825 Main.
Larock John, lab., res. w. s. N. Van Buren, 1 s. of Elm.
Larolle August, lab., res. 147 Pearl, Ft. H.
Larret Anton, lab., res. 711 Pleasant.
Larscheidt Frank, teamster, res. s. s. Charles, 1 e. George.
Larscheidt Frank Jr., lab., res. s. s. Charles, 2 e. George.
Larscheidt John, teamster, res. s. s. Charles, 2 e. George.
Larscheidt John Jr., lab., res. s. s. Charles, 2 e. George.
Larscheidt Julius, lab., res. s. s. Charles, 2 e. George.
Larscheidt Katie Miss, res. Cedar Creek rd., e. city limits.
Larscheidt Lorenz, gardener and saloon, Cedar Creek rd., e. city limits, res. same.
Larsen Andrew, cooper, res. 1137 Cedar.
Larsen Annie Miss, res. 306 4th, Ft. H.
Larsen Austin C., clk. Wm. Larsen, res. 507 Dousman, Ft. H.
Larsen Bart., bridge, carp., res. 304 4th, Ft. H.

Larsen Carl, carp., res. 318 Chestnut, Ft. H.
Larsen Christ, fisherman, res. 617 Main.
Larsen Christ, lab., res. Coopertown House.
Larsen Christopher, painter, res. 407 5th av., Ft. H.
Larsen Christopher, tailor, res. 306 4th. Ft. H.
Larsen George, carp., res. 401 1st, Ft. H.
Larsen Henry, wholesale fruits, res. 127 Chestnut, Ft. H.
Larsen Laura, domestic A. Hagemeister.
Larsen Louis J., foreman Howard Lumber Co., res. 116 Chestnut, Ft. H.
Larsen Mabel Miss, res. s. e. cor. Dousman and Cedar, Ft. H.
Larsen Nellie, domestic s. e. cor. Willow and Baird, Ft. H.
Larsen Olof, res. s. w. cor. 4th av. and 8th, Ft. H.
Larsen Peter, carpenter, res. 113 6th av., Ft. H.
Larsen Peter, captain, res. 1126 Main.
Larsen Sigurd, foreman, res. 116 Chestnut, Ft. H.
Larsen Virgea Miss, res. 407 5th av., Ft. H.
**LARSEN WILLIAM** (Wm. Larsen Canning Co.), mayor of Ft. Howard, res. cor. Dousman and Cedar, Ft. H.
Larsen William, lab., res. s. w. cor. 4th av. and 8th, Ft. H.
Larsen William Canning Co. The (William Larsen), cor. Broadway and Dousman, Ft. H.
Larson Anton, lab., res. 1179 Doty.
Larson Frank, lab., res. w. s. Pearl, 1 s. Hubbard, Ft. H.
Larson John A., clk. Jorgensen Blesch Co., res. n. e. cor. Hubbard and Chestnut, Ft. H.
Larson Severine, carp., res. 715 Harvey.
Last Albert, loco.-fireman, res. 126 6th av., Ft. H.
Last Fannie Miss, res. 413 S. Jefferson.
Last Guy A., clk. C., M. & St. P. Ry., res. 402 S. Jefferson.
Last John, clk. freight auditing dept. G. B., W. & St. P. Ry., res. 402 S. Jefferson.
Last John, lab., res. w. s 7th av., 1 s. 9th, Ft H.
Last John B., gen. freight and pass. agent G. B., W. & St. P. Ry., res. 402 S. Jefferson.
Last Joseph, lab., res. w. s. 7th av., 1 s. 9th, Ft. H.
Last Madeline Miss, res. 402 S. Jefferson.
Last Sarah (wid. John), res. 413 S. Jefferson.
Last Stella Miss, stenog. gen. freight and pass. dept. G. B., W & St. P. Ry., res. 402 S. Jefferson.
Latour Joseph, gardener, res. w. s. Manitowoc rd., 5 s. Bellevue.
Latour Louis, lab., res. s. e. cor. Jackson and Smith.
**LAU CLEMENT REV.**, Rector St. Francis Xavier Cathedral, res. 128 S. Monroe av.

**THE A. SPUHLER CO.** LADIES', MISSES' and CHILDREN'S
**GREEN BAY** — **CLOAKS, CAPES, JACKETS**

Lau Jacob, farmer, res. 42ᵉ Main.
Laudenklos Marie (wid. Peter), res. 321 6th av., Ft. H.
Lauermann Geo., mill-hd., res. Eldred's boarding house, Ft. H.
Lauterbach Christian, lab., res. 1377 Stuart.
Lauterbach Josephine, typesetter, res. 1377 Stuart.
Lavely John, brakeman, res. Northwestern Hotel, Ft. H.
Laverty W. T., com.-trav. Columbian Baking Co.
Lavnow Albert, lab., res. Coopertown House.
Lavoy Mitchel, teamster, res. 319 Pine.
Lawe John D., res. 416 Cherry.
Lawe Leon C., bookkpr. Citizens National Bank, res. 644 S. Monroe av.
Lawrence Anna Mrs., res. e. end Walnut.
Lawrence Helen Miss, res. 339 S. Washington.
Lawrence Michael, carp., res. e. end Walnut.
Lawrence Philip, res. 339 S. Washington.
Leach Ellen Mrs., carpet weaver, 307 8th av., Ft. H., res. same.
Leach Guy, fisherman, res. 307 8th av., Ft. H.
Leach Lucia Miss, res. 307 8th av., Ft. H.
Leach Reuben G., veterinary surgeon, 1125 Main, res. same.
Leanna Ella Miss, res. 319 Pine.
Leanna George, res. 319 Pine.
Leanna Jessie, domestic Bradley House.
Leanna Julia (wid. Comb), res. 319 Pine.
Leanna Louise Miss, res. 319 Pine.
Leanna Napoleon B., res. 319 Pine.
Leanna Tillie Miss, dressmkr, 319 Pine, res. same.
Leathert Catharine (wid. William), res. 106 Cherry, Ft. H.
Leaver Wm., brakeman, res. 632 S. Jefferson.
Lebens-Wasser Mineral Springs, J. J. Handlen, propr., 529 S. Monroe av.
Le Blanc Albert, lab., res. 601 N. 12th.
Le Blanc Jules, engineer, res. 1180 Day.
Le Blanc Paul, clk., res. 1180 Day.
Lechner Valentine, maltster, res. s. s. Main, 2 e. Newhall, Town Preble.
Le Clair Charles G., ice dealer, 519 S. Monroe av., res. same.
Le Clair Charles J., student, res. 420 Howard.
Le Clair Joseph B., electric trimmer, res. 420 Howard.
Le Clair Joseph C., lawyer, res. 420 Howard.
Le Clair Leonard A., student, res. 420 Howard.
Le Clair Louis C., del.-clk. The A. Spuhler Co., res. 420 Howard.
Le Clair Rose, teacher, res. 519 S. Monroe av.
Le Clercq Silvain, mason, res. w. s. Oak, 1 s. Shawano rd., Ft. H.

Le Comte Charles, druggist, 225 Main, res. same.
Le Compte Gustav, mate, res. 1417 Harvey.
Lecoque Anton, musician, res. 416 N. Madison.
Lecoque Joseph, lab., res. 416 N. Madison
Lecoque Mary (wid. Joseph), res. 416 N. Madison.
Lecoque Philomene Miss, clk. The A. Spuhler Co., res. 416 N. Madison.
Leddy George F., cashier C. & N. W. Ry., res. cor. Division and Guesnier, Ft. H.
Lee Anna (wid. Walter P.), nurse, res. 722 Cedar.
Lee Daniel, real estate, res. 900 Walnut.
Lee George D., electrician, res. 900 Walnut.
Lee Lillian M., clk. Brauns & Van, res. 524 S. Monroe av.
Lee Lottie Miss, artist, res. 900 Walnut.
Lee Samuel, porter parlor car, res. 427 N. Madison.
Lee Thomas, night mill boss, res. Eldred's boarding house, Ft. H.
Leeson Emilie J. Miss, res. 704 Dousman, Ft. H.
Leeson James E., cook, res. 704 Dousman, Ft. H.
Leeson Reuben E. delivery clk., res. 208 S. Webster av.
Leeson William N., captain, res. 208 S. Webster av.
Leeson William N. Jr., steward, res. 208 S. Webster av.
Lefebvre Augustine Mrs., grocer, 500 S. Jefferson, res. same.
Lefebvre Charles, lab., res. w. s. 9th, near R. R. crossing, Ft. H.
Lefebvre Edward F. (Lefebvre & Schumacher), res. 314 S. Madison.
Lefebvre Emma Miss, res. 318 S. Madison.
Lefebvre Eugene, mason, res. 1347 Day.
Lefebvre Frank, lab., res. 1101 Harvey.
Lefebvre Gertrude (wid. Joseph), res. 318 S. Madison.
Lefebvre Gilbert (Lefebvre & Schumacher), res. 433 S. Madison.
Lefebvre Henrietta (wid. John B.), res. 115 S. Madison.
Lefebvre John, res. 318 S. Madison.
Lefebvre John B. com.-trav. The Weise-Hollman Co., res. 1310 Elm.
Lefebvre John B., gardener, res. 1101 Harvey.
Lefebvre Joseph, carpenter, res. 1101 Harvey.
Lefebvre Julia Miss, res. 500 S. Jefferson.
Lefebvre Leopold, res. n. s. Shawano rd., 2 w. Fisk.
Lefebvre Mary, domestic 619 Main.
Lefebvre Peter, fisherman, res. 520 N. Madison.
**LEFEBVRE & SCHUMACHER** (Edward F. and Gilbert Lefebvre and John P. Schumacher), furniture and undertakers, 325-327 N. Washington.
Leglise Desire, whitewasher, res. 902 Main.

A. C. LEHMANN.                            A. C. ROBINSON.

# LEHMANN & ROBINSON,

## COMMERCIAL

# JOB PRINTERS

AND PROPRIETORS OF

## ►❊"DER LANDSMANN,"❊◄

Terms:—"Der Landsmann"—$2.00 per year in advance.

"DER LANDSMANN," is the only German Newspaper in the City and County and the only one within a circumference of 250 miles North, 100 miles East and West and 25 miles South and with its rapidly increasing Subscription-list is the best Advertising-Medium in Northern Wisconsin.

222 N. Adams St.,       ➤ GREEN BAY, WISCONSIN.

A. C. LEHMANN.                        A. C. ROBINSON.

# LEHMANN & ROBINSON,

## COMMERCIAL

# JOB PRINTERS

### AND PROPRIETORS OF

## "DER LANDSMANN,"

---

**Terms:—"Der Landsmann"—$2.00 per year in advance.**

"DER LANDSMANN," is the only German Newspaper in the City and County and the only one within a circumference of 250 miles North, 100 miles East and West and 25 miles South and with its rapidly increasing Subscription-list is the best Advertising-Medium in Northern Wisconsin.

222 N. Adams St.,            GREEN BAY, WISCONSIN.

**THE A. SPUHLER CO., Green Bay** CARPETS, RUGS, OIL CLOTHS
Draperies and Window Shades.

Leglise Jerry D., com.-trav. A. Duchateau, res. 1032 Pine.
Leglise Josie C. Miss, printer, res. 902 Main.
Legot Anton, carp., res. 105 S. Van Buren.
Legot Christ, tailor, res. 1337 Cherry.
Legot Joseph, molder, res. 406 3d av., **Ft. H.**
Legot Victor, res. 105 S. Van Buren.
Legrand Jacques, shoemkr, res. 314 S. Webster av.
Legrave John, brickmkr, res. s. s. Shawano rd., 2 **w. ry. track,** Ft. H.
Lehan Mamie Miss, teacher, res. 307 Cherry, Ft. H.
Lehan Patrick, section foreman, res. 307 Cherry, Ft. H.
Lehan. See Lyhane.
Lehman A. & E. (Alfred C. and Eugene **W.** Lehman), books and stationery, 223 N. Washington.
Lehman Alfred C. (A. & E. Lehman), res. 503 S. Monroe av.
Lehman Anton C. (Lehman & Robinson), res. 503 S. Monroe av.
Lehman Eugene W. (A. & E. Lehman), res. 503 S. Monroe av.
Lehman Maria C. Miss, clk., res. 503 S. Monroe av.
Lehman Olga C. Miss, res. 503 S. Monroe av.
**LEHMAN & ROBINSON** (Anton C. Lehman and Albert C. Robinson), props. Der Landsmann, book and job printers, 222 N. Adams.
Leidel Albert, meatmkt., 1149 Main, res. 1273 Main.
Leidel Amanda Miss, res. 1306 Main.
Leidel Augusta (wid. Gottfried), res. 1306 Main.
Leidel Herman L., res. 1149 Main.
Leisch Frank C. (M. Leisch & Son), res. 635 Main.
Leisch Joseph J., res. 635 Main.
**LEISCH M. & SON** (Margaret and Frank C. **Leisch**), grocers and bakery, 635 Main, cor. Quincy.
Leisch Margaret Mrs. (M. Leisch & Son), res. 635 Main.
Leisch Margaretha Miss, res. 635 Main.
Lemanze Anton, farmer, res. s. s. Duck Creek rd., 1 e. Cemetery, Ft. H.
Lemanze **Joseph**, lab., **res. s. s. Duck Creek rd., 1 e. Cemetery,** Ft. H.
Lemanze **Maria Miss, res. s. s. Duck Creek rd., 1 e. Cemetery,** Ft. H.
Lemense Theresa (wid. John), res. 918 Cherry.
Lemere George, carp., res. 1230 Cass.
Lemiux Camill, brakeman, res. St. James Hotel.
Lemieux Elias J., wall-paper, 323 N. Washington, res. 1029 Walnut.
Lemmans August, painter, res. **1115 S. Jackson.**

Lemmans Felix, lab., res. 1115 S. Jackson.
Lemmens Mary Miss, res. 321 Chicago.
Lemrond Caddie Miss, student, res. 310 Cedar, Ft. H.
Lenz Charles (Mohr & Lenz), res. 512 Doty.
Lenz Frank, res. 308 N. Madison.
Lenglund John, gardener, res. s. s. Shawano rd., 6 w. ry. track. Ft. H.
Leonard Frank, paper-hanger, res. 710 Main.
Leonard James H., insurance agent, 105 N. Washington, res. 319 S. Monroe av.
Leonhardt William, lab., res. 311 Cherry, Ft. H.
Leonnis Magloire, fish-packer, res. Waterloo House.
Lepage Theophile, lab., res. 223 S. Jackson.
Leppere Nettie I. Miss, mngr. Postal Tel. Cable Co., res. 211 N. Jefferson.
Lerke Jean Baptiste, lab., res. 1114 Day.
Le Roy Hubbard, stonectr., res. 901 Pine.
**LE ROY J. & CO.** (Joseph Le Roy and Melchior Theisen), props. Cook's Hotel.
Le Roy Joseph (J. Le Roy & Co.) res. Cook's Hotel.
Le Roy Josephine, domestic 607 Main. Ft. H.
Le Sage Aurelia Miss, clk. Jorgensen Blesch Co., res. 530 Moravian.
Le Sage Elizabeth (wid. Joseph), res. 530 Moravian.
Le Sage Frank W., conductor C., M. & St. P. R. R., res. 539 S. Madison.
Le Sage Josephine Miss, res. 530 Moravian.
Le Sage Mary Miss, bookkpr. Columbian Baking Co., res. 530 Moravian.
Le Sage Simeon, wagonmkr, res. 530 Moravian.
Lett George, R. R. police, res. 415 5th, Ft. H.
**LEVEILLE JOSEPH,** fisherman, res. n. e. cor. Elmore and Chestnut, Ft. H.
Leveille Joseph Jr., fisherman, res. n. e. cor. Elmore and Chestnut, Ft. H.
Lewis Adele, domestic, 303 Chestnut, Ft. H.
Lewis Ellen W. Miss, res. 315 Cedar, Ft. H.
Lewis Frank, brewer, res. 1411 Cedar.
Lewis Frank L., physician, 228 N. Washington, res. 315 Cedar, Ft. H.
Lewis George, clk., res. 213 Chestnut, Ft. H.
Lewis Jennie (wid. Charles), res. 402 Willow, Ft. H.
Lewis Martin V., brakeman, res. 225 S. Washington.
Lewis Will D., mngr. W. U. Tel. Co., res. 421 S. Jefferson.

**THE A. SPUHLER CO., GREEN BAY, WIS.** Fine Dress Goods. Samples Furnished on Application.

Lewis Wm. B., ry.-man, res. 402 Willow, Ft. H.
Libbey Oliver, insurance, 209 N. Washington, res. 229 Pine.
Libert Adolph, lab., res. 214 S. 10th.
Libert Frank, clk. Brauns & Van, res. 214 S. 10th.
Libert Isidore, fireman, res. 728 Mason.
Libert Leontine, student, res. 214 S. 10th.
Libert Louis, watchman, res. 728 Mason.
**LIEBENOW JULIUS**, jeweler, 205 N. Washington, res. 1114 Pine.
Liebermann Anna Elizabeth (wid. Richard), res. 417 N. Quincy.
Liebmann Amelia Mrs., res. 227 S. Webster av.
Liebzeit Christian, res. 1349 Stuart.
Liederman Alvina, domestic 212 S. Adams.
Lier Edward, foreman lumber yard, C., M. & St. P. Ry., res. 110 Cedar, Ft. H.
Lier Gilbert, carp., res. 110 Cedar, Ft. H.
Liesse August, res. 425 Main.
Liesse Mathilda (wid. Gustav), res. 421 N. Madison.
Lifort John, lab., res. 1127 Pine.
Limery John, teamster, res. Waterloo House.
Lindenborn Lizzie, waitress Columbia Hotel.
Lindley Samuel, saw-repairer, 313 Cherry, res. 309 Pearl, Ft. H.
Lindner Anna (wid. Gottfried), res. 1315 Cherry.
Lindner Herwarth, tailor, res. w. s. 2d av., 4 s. 8th, Ft. H.
Lindsley Felix, res. e. s. Manitowoc rd., 1 s. Bellevue.
Lindsley Frances A. (wid. Myron P.), res. 102 N. Monroe av.
Lindsley Louis, saloon, 1281 Main, res. same.
Linehan Bridget (wid. Richard), res. 411 Main, Ft. H.
Linehan Bridget Miss, dressmkr. res. 411 Main, Ft. H.
Linehan Maggie, dressmkr. res. 411 Main, Ft. H.
Linenthal Isaac B., dry goods and notions, etc., 112 N. Washington, res. 312 Stuart.
Linford William, foreman D. W. Britton, res. 110 N. Quincy.
Linsday Charles, foreman, res. w. s. 6th av., 1 s. Bridge, Ft. H.
Linsmeyer Joseph, lab., res. 828 Crooks.
Lintelmann August, res. 1034 Cherry.
Lintelmann Bertha Miss, compositor, res. 1034 Cherry.
Lintelmann George, driver U. S. Express, res. 1034 Cherry.
Lintelmann Laura Miss, dressmkr, res. 1034 Cherry.
Lintelmann Lena Miss, bookbinder, res. 1034 Cherry.
Lipski Andrew, lab., res. 1365 Mason.
Lipski Frank, lab., res. 1376 Walnut.
Lison Ernst C., res. 503 N. Jefferson.
Lison Isidore, weighmaster, res. 512 N. Jefferson.

| LIS | 166 | LOO |
|---|---|---|

Lison Isidore, res. 512 N. Jefferson.
Lison Watson, warehouseman, res. n. s. Elmore, 9 w. Cedar, Ft H.
List Albert, lab., res. 1330 Crooks.
List Barbara Miss, res. 1330 Crooks.
List Elizabeth, domestic 416 Lawe.
List Isabelle Miss, res. 1330 Crooks.
List Michael, fisherman, res. 1330 Crooks.
Listle Joseph, lab., res. 314 Pearl, Ft. H.
Listman Charles, express agent, res. 315 N. Jefferson.
Littel Michael, foreman Hochgreve Brew. Co., res. w. s. De Pere rd., 1 s. Hochgreve brewery.
Livingston John, teamster, res. Eldred's boarding house, Ft. H.
Livingston Robert L., student, res. 211 N. Jefferson.
Lobdill Elizabeth (wid. Joseph), res. 1005 Cherry.
Loberg Barbara, domestic, res. Huffman House, Ft. H.
Loberg Marie, domestic, res. Huffman House, Ft. H.
Lochmann August, res. 314 S. Jefferson.
**LOCHMANN PETER J.**, boots and shoes, 1118 Main, res. same.
Lockwood Herman, lab., res. 1313 Doty.
Lodamann Charles, lab., res. n. s. 5th, 3 w. 3d av., Ft. H.
Loewert Fred, machinist, res. 531 Walnut.
Loewert Henry, saloon, 531 Walnut, res. same.
Loewert Henry Jr., carp., res. 531 Walnut.
Loftus Fred, nurse, res. 635 Cherry.
Loftus John, engineer, res. 701 Cherry, Ft. H.
Loftus John F., carp., res. 700 Cherry, Ft. H.
Loftus John Patrick, lab., res. 700 Cherry, Ft. H.
Loftus Joseph, lab., res. 316 Main.
Loftus Joseph, lab., res. 701 Cherry, Ft. H.
Loftus Mary (wid. Thomas), res. 635 Cherry, Ft. H.
Loftus Thomas, lab., res. 635 Cherry, Ft. H.
Loftus Thomas C., asst. train dispatcher C., M. & St. P. R. R., res. 635 Cherry, Ft. H.
Loftus William D., clk. C., M. & St. P. R. R., res. 635 Cherry, Ft. H.
Logan Martin, tailor, res. American House.
Lohfink E. H. Mrs., res. 504 S. Van Buren.
Lohlein Carrie, domestic 100 S. Monroe av.
Lomas Charles W., lawyer, res. 122 Chestnut, Ft. H.
Longneckard Margaret Miss, teacher shorthand and typewriting Green Bay Business College, res. 1021 Crooks.
Longtime Adolph, brakeman, res. St. James Hotel.
Looze Albert, res. 1363 Cedar.

**Headquarters for Boys' Clothing** THE A. SPUHLER CO.
GREEN BAY.

Looze John (Looze & Hoslet), res 1102 Cedar.
Looze Joseph, lab., res. 503 1st, Ft. H.
Looze Joseph, mach., res. 1102 Cedar.
Looze Peter, lab., res. 622 St George.
**LOOZE & HOSLET** (John Looze and Desire Hoslet), flour and feed, 230 Main.
Lopitsch John, cabinetmkr, res. w. s. 6th av, 2 s. 3d, Ft. H.
Loppnow Augusta Miss, res. 302 Willow, Ft. H.
Lorand Desire, lab., res. 1141 Cedar.
Lorenke Annie, domestic 508 S. Monroe av.
**LORENT EUGENE**, carp.-contr., 445 S. Madison, res. same.
Lorenzen Peter L., teacher and organist, res. 114 N. Jackson.
Loukotka Frank, gen. del. clk. P. O. res. 1419 Elm.
Loukotka Joseph, mail carrier, res. 1419 Elm.
Loukotka Wenzel, lab., res. 1419 Elm.
Lucas Abe, city street commissioner, res. 610 Hubbard, Ft. H.
Lucas Abe N., foreman boiler shop C., M. & St. P. Ry., res. 606 Hubbard, Ft. H.
Lucas Alfred, tinner, res. s. e. cor. Dousman and Willow, Ft. H.
Lucas D. & Son (Daniel and Gilbert Lucas), tinware, 317 Broadway, Ft. H.
Lucas Daniel (D. Lucas & Son), res. 1 w. 792 Shawano rd., Ft. H.
Lucas Francis, engineer, res. 518 Cedar, Ft. H.
Lucas Gilbert (D. Lucas & Son), res. n. s. Shawano rd., 2 e. Oak, Ft. H.
Lucas James, engineer, res. 610 Hubbard, Ft. H.
Lucas Violet Miss, res. 1 w. 792 Shawano rd., Ft. H.
Luce William H., filer McDonald lumber yards, res. McDonald's boarding house, Ft. H.
Luckenbach Anna Miss, res. 935 Pine.
Luckenbach John, watchmkr and jeweler, 210 N. Washington, res. 210 S. Jefferson.
Luckenbach Josephine S., principal Park school, res. 935 Pine.
Luckenbach Mary A. (wid. Michael J.), res. 935 Pine.
Luckenbach Myra, compositor, res. 935 Pine.
**LUCKENBACH WILLIAM**, druggist, 212 N. Washington, res. same.
Ludwig Daniel, carp., res. 126 S. Quincy.
Ludwig Emil, lab., res. 305 Cherry, Ft. H.
Ludwig Lena Miss, dressmkr, res. 126 S. Quincy.
Lueck Gustave, lab., res. 1376 Doty.
Lueck Ida Miss, res. 1376 Doty.
Luedke Annie Miss, res. w. s. 5th av., 3 n. 10th, Ft. H.

Luedke Annie, domestic 416 Lawe.
Luedke August, machinist, res. w. s. 5th av., 3 n. 10th, Ft. H.
Luedke John, res. 647 S. Jackson.
Luedke Max, clk., res. w. s. 5th av., 3 n. 10th, Ft. H.
Luedke Otto, fireman, res. w. s. 5th av., 3 n. 10th, Ft. H.
Luedke William, lab., res. 1301 Crooks.
Lueke Florence Miss, res. 544 S. Van Buren.
Lueke William, county treasurer, court house, res. 544 S. Van Buren.
Lumaye Joseph J., tailor, res. 118 S. Van Buren.
Lumaye Julius, merchant tailor, 214 Main, res. 118 S. Van Buren.
Lund Jens, photographer, 1401 Crooks, res. same.
Lund Turina (wid. Jonas), res. 401 2d, Ft. H.
Lureman Jane Mrs., res. 509 S. Monroe av.
Lurquin Felix, gardener, res. 844 Dousman, Ft. H.
Lurquin John B., gardener, res. n. s. Elmore, 11 w. Willow, Ft. H.
Lurquin Joseph, lab., res. s. s. Elmore, 11 w. Cedar, Ft. H.
Lurquin Joseph, lab., res. 844 Dousman, Ft. H.
Luther Charles, res. 1329 Harvey.
Lutyen Michael, lab., res. 1299 Willow.
Lutz Christian, carp., res. s. s. Willow, 1 w. 12th.
Lutz Clara Miss, stenographer, res. 1000 Walnut.
Lye John, section man, res. 1008 Dousman, Ft. H.
Lyhane Daniel, boilermkr, res. 850 Dousman, Ft. H.
Lyhane Michael, flagman, res. 850 Dousman, Ft. H.
Lyman Bart., driver Hose Cart No. 1, res. 216 Walnut.
Lyman Henry, captain, res. 1201 Cherry.
Lynch Cornelius, brakeman, res. Northwestern Hotel, Ft. H.
Lynn Barbara Miss, milliner, res. 219 N. Washington.
Lyon Nettie Miss, dressmkr, 1313 Doty, res. same.
Lyons Charles, traveling agent, res. 319 Chestnut, Ft. H.
Lyons George, lab., res. 316 Main.
Lyons J. B., night clk. Cook's Hotel.
Lyons Orlin D., clk. 212 Main, Ft. H., res. 317 Chestnut, Ft. H.

## Mc.

McALLISTER Hill, scaler, res. Broadway House, Ft. H.
McAnulty Daniel, millwright, res. n. s. Kellogg, 1 w. Chestnut, Ft. H.
McAnulty Lizzie Miss, res. n. s. Kellogg, 1 w. Chestnut, Ft. H.
McArthur Jennie (wid. Daniel) res. 311 3d, Ft. H.
McBride Mary (wid. John), res. 626 Pine.
McBride William, lab., res. 316 Main.

**THE A. SPUHLER CO.** *LADIES', MISSES' and CHILDREN'S*
**GREEN BAY** — **CLOAKS, CAPES, JACKETS**

McCabe Elizabeth, dressmkr, res. 914 S. Van Buren.
McCabe George, res. 614 Cedar.
McCabe Kate Miss, teacher, res. 914 S. Van Buren.
McCabe Kittie Miss, res. 620 Cedar.
McCabe Phoebe Mrs., res. 614 Cedar.
McCabe Susie, res. 914 S. Van Buren.
McCarthy Frank, switchman, res. Broadway House, Ft. H.
McCarthy Jennie (wid. Daniel H.), boarding, res. 202 S. Jefferson.
McCarthy Michael C., reporter, res. Green Bay House.
McCartney David, pres. McCartney National Bank, res. 504 Main, Ft. H.
McCartney David Electric Light Plant, office National Bank, Ft. H.
McCartney Emma Miss, res. 504 Main, Ft. H.
**McCARTNEY NATIONAL BANK,** D. McCartney, pres.; Wm. Larsen, v.-pres.; J. H. Tayler, cashier; 309 Main, Ft. H.
McCarty Nicholas, lab., res. Empire House.
McCauley John, farmer, res. n. s. 2d, 7 w. ry.-track, Ft. H.
McCloskey Aggie Miss, res. 1152 Mason.
McCloskey Mamie Miss, res. 1152 Mason.
McCloskey Philip, lab, res. 1152 Mason.
McCloskey Stephen, lab., res. 1152 Mason.
McClosky Wm. F., clk gen. frt. dept. G. B., W. & St. P. R. R., res. Commercial House, Ft. H.
McClure Agnes (wid. John), nurse, res. 800 Crooks.
McClure Carrie Miss, res. 800 Crooks.
McConnell Henry, telegr. line repairer, res. 402 Howard.
McConnell William J., line repairer, res. 216 S. Quincy.
McCormick Amelia Miss, res. 427 S. Monroe av.
McCormick James, lab., res. w. s. Pearl, 2 s. Hubbard, Ft. H.
McCormick John, clk., res. 621 S. Monroe av.
McCormick Mary (wid. John). res. 427 S. Monroe av.
McCormick May Miss, res. 621 S. Monroe av.
McCormick Michael, lab., res. 306 Willow, Ft. H.
**McCORMICK MICHAEL J.,** agent Goodrich Trans. Co., Lackawanna Trans. Co., Northwestern Fuel Co., foot Pine, res. 427 S. Monroe av.
McCormick Patrick (McCormick & Bates and McCormick & Flatley), res. 621 Monroe av.
McCormick Sarah Miss, res. 427 S. Monroe av.
McCormick William J., messenger Citizens' National Bank, res. 621 S. Monroe av.

22

**McCORMICK & BATES** (Patrick McCormick and Zachary T. Bates), transfer agents, 220 S. Washington.
**McCORMICK & FLATLEY** (Patrick McCormick and Dominick W. Flatley) hay, grain and coal, 220-230 S. Washington.
McCrea Thomas F., engineer, res. 508 S. Jefferson.
McCune Samuel C., res. Cook's Hotel.
**McCUNN JOHN N.,** prop. Green Bay Business College, res. 1021 Crooks.
McDonald Alex., lab., res. 416 N. Madison.
McDonald Alexander, barkpr., res. Adams House.
McDonald Allen, hostler, res. 103 S. Washington.
McDonald Bridget Mrs., res. 706 Cedar.
McDonald Dennis, lab., res. 411 Broadway, Ft. H.
**McDONALD HUGH,** whol. and ret. mnfr. and dlr. in all kinds of lumber, office and yards north end Broadway, res. 901 N. Broadway, Ft. H.
McDonald Kittie Miss, stenog., res. 901 Broadway, Ft. H.
McDonald Margaret S., bookkpr. H. McDonald, res. 901 Broadway, Ft. H.
McDonald Marian Miss, res. 901 Broadway, Ft. H.
McDonald Minnie E. Miss, res. 901 Broadway, Ft. H.
McDonald Ranald, barn boss, res. No. 9, n. end Monroe av., c. Murphy's mill.
McDonald Thomas, res. 626 S. Madison.
McDonald William, assistant McDonald's lumber yard, res. 901 Broadway, Ft. H.
**McDONNELL ANNA H.,** librarian Green Bay Public Library, res. 203 S. Jefferson.
McEachron John A. (A. L. Adams & Co.), res. 621 S. Van Buren.
McEvoy John B., saloon, 320 Main, res. same.
McFayden Findley, real estate, res. 719 Cherry.
McFayden Findley Mrs., milliner, 219 N. Washington, res. 719 Cherry.
McGee Archie, teamster, res. Eldred's boarding house, Ft. H.
McGinnis Hannah (wid. Constantine), res. cor. Dousman and Chestnut, Ft. H.
McGinnis James H., res. cor. Dousman and Chestnut, Ft. H.
McGinnis John E., ins. agent, res. cor. Dousman and Chestnut, Ft. H.
McGinnis William J., barkpr., res. cor. Dousman and Chestnut, Ft. H.
McGowan James H., law student Cady & Huntington, res. 1118 Cedar.

**THE A. SPUHLER CO., Green Bay** CARPETS, RUGS, OIL CLOTHS
Draperies and Window Shades.

McGrath Thomas, conductor, res. 725 S. Adams.
McGrath Thomas J. (McGrath & Anderson), res. 1031 Mason.
McGrath & Anderson (Thomas J. McGrath and William B. Anderson), general contractors, Citizens' National Bank bldg.
McGray Alfred, hostler, res. 112 S. Adams.
McGruer Alexander D., lawyer, 3 P. O. blk, res. 808 Cherry.
McGuire Anna Mrs., res. 217 N. Adams.
McGuire Charles, brakeman, res. St. James Hotel.
McGuire J. F. (Alart & McGuire), res. New York.
McGuire Mary Ann, res. 217 N. Adams.
McGulpin Gussie, domestic, residence 528 12th.
McHugh John, conductor, res. Broadway House, Ft. H.
McHugh Terrence, well digger, 826 Doty, res. same.
McKeague Anna, confectioner, 720 Main, res. same.
McKeague Edward, lab., res. 720 Main.
McKeague Frank, engineer, res. 720 Main.
McKeague Hattie Miss, res. 720 Main.
McKenna, John A., asst. train dispatcher C., M. & St. P. R. R., res. 518 Chicago.
McKenzie Charles, foreman, res. American House.
McKenzie George, conductor, res. 544 S. Jefferson.
McKeough Maggie Miss, dressmkr, res. 635 Cherry.
McKeough Michael, coachman, res. 1045 S. Quincy.
McKevitt Joseph, res. 631 S. Jefferson.
**McKONE JAMES**, livery, 415-417 Main, res. same.
McLean Edward, engineer, res. 510 Cedar, Ft. H.
McLean Fred., engineer, res. Northwestern Hotel, Ft. H.
McLean John, farmer, res. e. s. De Pere rd., 5 s. city limits.
McLean Patrick, res. e. s. De Pere rd., 3 s. city limits.
McLean Thomas, farmer, res. e. s. De Pere rd., 3 s. city limits.
McLean Thomas Jr., baggageman C., M. & St. P. R. R., res. e. s. Monroe av., s. city limits.
McLeish William, boatbldr., res. 300 S. Washington.
**McMAHON MARTIN H.**, superintendent Green Bay pub. schools, res. 115 S. Jackson.
McMillan Mathew, lab., res. 208 Willow, Ft. H.
McMillan Mathew Jr., clk., res. 208 Willow, Ft. H.
McMillin Thomas H., conductor, res. 600 Cedar, Ft. H.
McMillin William, brakeman, res. 317 Chicago.
McNamara John, brakeman, res. 113 2d, Ft. H.
McNamara Katie Miss, res. s. s. Dousman, 4 w. Willow, Ft. H.
McNamara Michael, res. s. s. Dousman, 4 w. Willow, Ft. H.
McNeely Wm. J., lab., res. e. s. Cedar, 2 n. Dousman, Ft. H.
McPartlin J. W., com.-trav. Columbian Baking Co.

McPherson Emma, domestic Broadway House, Ft. H.
McQuade Michael, res. 114 S. Quincy.
**McQUEEN DAN,** boarding house, McDonald st., near H. McDonald Lumber Co., Ft. H.
McQueen John, carp., res. 405 3d av., Ft. H.
McQueen Maggie, domestic 614 Main.

# M

MAAS, Charles, carp., res. 1174 Doty.
    Maas Emma Miss, 1166 Doty.
Maas Frank, res. 1116 Doty.
Maas Ida Miss, res. 1166 Doty.
Maas William, carp., res. 1166 Doty.
Maas. See Maes.
MacGahan Louis, blacksmith, res. 1 w. 832 Shawano rd., Ft. H.
Maccomber John, cooper, res. 223 Cherry.
Maccomber John Mrs., milliner, 223 Cherry, res. same.
Macomber Julio B., salesman Jorgensen Blesch Co., res. 111 S. Madison.
Madden George, cook The Beaumont, res. 318 Main.
Madden George F., fireman, res. 500 S. Madison.
Madden Michael, lab., res. 304 Willow, Ft. H.
Madigan Ann (wid. Edward), res. 635 S. Adams.
Madigan Delia Miss, res. 635 S. Adams.
Madigan John, switchman, res. 635 S. Adams.
Madigan Thomas, res. 635 S. Adams.
Madix Clara Miss, res. 901 Day.
Madix Fred, teamster, res. 901 Day.
Madix Isaac, scavenger, res. 901 Day.
Madsen Anna Miss, res. 806 Pine.
Madsen Frederick, carp., res. 105 4th av., Ft. H.
Madson Nels, lab., res. w. s. 3d av., 1 n. 1st, Ft. H.
Maes Desire, clk., res. 321 S. Jackson.
Maes Frank, baker, res. 635 Main.
Maes John, res. 220 S. Webster av.
Maes Julius, carp., res. 220 S. Webster av.
Maes. See Moes.
Mahn Herman, tailor, res. 1208 Pine.
Mahn Theodore, merchant tailor, 407 Broadway, Ft. H., res. 116 S. Monroe av.
Mahn Theodore, tailor, res. 1208 Pine.
**MAHN WILLIAM C.,** merchant tailor, 228 N. Adams, res. 1200 Pine.

**THE A. SPUHLER CO., GREEN BAY, WIS.** **Fine Dress Goods**
Samples Furnished on Application.

MAH 173 MAN

Mahon Catherine (wid. Christopher) res. n. s. Elmore, 1 w. Cedar, Ft. H.
Mahon John D., bookkpr. 129 S. Washington, res. n. s. Elmore, 1 w. Cedar, Ft. H.
Mahoney Henry J., cashier Oconto station, res. 801 Cedar, Ft. H.
Mahoney Patrick, coachman 425 S. Adams.
Maimow Joseph, lab., res. s. s. Lawe, bet. S. 11th and S. 12th.
**MAIN STREET HOTEL**, P. Robillard, prop., 316 Main.
Malacky William, lab., res. 110 N. Quincy.
Malchow Charles, fisherman, res. Willow, foot Fox River.
Malcorp Emil, lab., res. n. s. Elmore, 8 w. Willow, Ft. H.
Malcorp Joseph, gardener, res. n. s. Elmore, 8 w. Willow, Ft. H.
Malinowski Jacob, lab., res. 1254 Walnut.
Malinowski Michael, miller, res. 427 S. Quincy.
**MALLORY JOHN H.**, city bill poster, paper hanger and cutlery grinder, 108 Walnut, res. 420 Elm.
Maloney Anna, dressmkr. res. 126 S. Webster av.
Maloney Helen Miss, dressmkr. res. 426 Walnut.
Maloney John, drayman, res. 306 Willow, Ft. H.
Maloney John, teamster, res. 126 S. Webster av.
Maloney John, section boss, res. **n. e. cor.** Hubbard and Cedar, Ft. H.
Maloney Patrick W., postal clk., res. 511 Cherry, Ft. H.
Maloney Rose (wid. James), res. 126 S. Webster av.
Maloney William, res. 511 Cherry, Ft. H.
Malotte John, gardener, res. s. s. Duck Creek rd., opposite cemetery, Ft. H.
Malotte Louise **(wid. Frank), res. s. s. Shawano rd., 4 w. ry.-**track.
Malotte Theodor, sawyer, res. 1239 Cedar.
Mangless Albert, lab., res. 1320 Doty.
Mangless Albert Jr., boilermkr., res. 1300 Doty.
Mangless Carl, boilermkr., res. 413 S. Quincy.
Mangless Charles, res. 1300 Doty.
Mangless Emma, dressmkr. 1300 Doty.
Manitowoc House, John Plantikow, prop., 819 Main.
Manley Ella, domestic 128 S. Adams.
Mann Emma Miss, res. 1250 Cedar.
Mann Gustav, carp.-contr, 1250 Cedar, res. same.
Mann James R., asst. foreman J. H. Ebeling, res. 1263 Stuart.
Mann Oscar F., bkpr. The Kellogg Nat. Bank, res. 1250 Cedar.
Mannebach Annie, dressmkr. res. 1119 Cherry.
Mannebach Annie M. (wid. Jacob), res. 1017 Cherry.
Mannebach Barbara Miss, dressmkr. res. 211 Willow, Ft. H.

Mannebach Hubert, boilermkr. res. 211 Willow, Ft. H.
Mannebach Hubert Jr., cigarmkr. res. 1119 Cherry.
Mannebach Jacob, cigarmkr. res. 1119 Cherry.
Mannebach John, shoemkr, 230 N. Adams, res. 1119 Cherry.
Mannebach Maggie, dressmkr. res. 211 Willow, Ft. H.
Mannebach Theodore (Grognet & Mannebach), res. 1017 Cherry.
Mannebach Thomas, shoemkr. res. 1119 Cherry.
Manning Edward B., clk. P. O., Ft. H., res. e. s. Willow, 2 n. Baird, Ft. H.
Manning Mark, tailor, res. e. s. Willow, 2 n. Baird, Ft. H.
Mansart Antoine, res. 1141 Cedar.
Mansart Leopold, res. 1141 Cedar.
Manthei Lena, waitress Bay City House.
**MANTHEY CARL**, marble and granite works, 132 S. Washington, res. 1132 Pine.
Manthey Herman, marble cutter, res. 1132 Pine.
Manthey Otto, porter 124 S. Washington, res. 1132 Pine.
Manville John, carriage-blksmith, res. 520 Cherry.
Mapes Calvin F., fisherman, res. w. s. McDonald, 8 s. lumber yd., Ft. H.
Mapes George L., sailor, res. w. s. McDonald, 8 s. lumber yd., Ft. H.
Marchand Pierre, physician, 222 Cherry, res. 339 S. Washington.
Marchant Charles, lab., res. 929 Dousman, Ft. H.
Marchant Jules, carp., res. e. s. Oak, 1 s. Shawano rd., Ft. H.
Marchant Julia (wid. Telisphore), res. 929 Dousman, Ft. H.
Marchant Maximilian, carp., res. e. s. Oak, 1 s. Shawano rd., Ft. H.
Marchant Nestor, carp., res. e. s. Oak, 1 s. Shawano rd., Ft. H.
Marique Albert, lab., res. 1203 Cedar.
Marique Eli, bookkpr. The State Gazette, res. 514 S. Jefferson.
Marique Florence (wid. Herbert), res. 514 S. Jefferson.
Marique Frank, lab., res. 1203 Cedar.
Marique Mary Miss, res. 1203 Cedar.
Marique Paul, carp., res. 1203 Cedar.
Marique Theophile, lab., res. 514 S. Jefferson.
Markle Elcena Miss, res. 716 Cherry.
Markle Emil G., harnessmkr, res. 716 Cherry.
Markle George, harnessmkr, 327 Main, res. 716 Cherry.
Markle Ida Miss, res. 716 Cherry.
Markusen Mark, clk. H. E. Brehme, res. Shawano av., opp Dr. Lewis' Hospital, Ft. H.
Markusen Mary Miss, domestic 128 N Monroe av.
Markusen Nellie, domestic 609 Main, Ft. H.

**Headquarters for Boys' Clothing** THE A. SPUHLER CO._GREEN BAY._

Marquardt Carl, brewer, res. s. s. Main, 2 e. Forest.
Marquardt William, lab., res. n. s. Main, 1 e. Forest.
Mars Arthur, machinist, res. 215 3d av., Ft. H.
Mars Edward R., clk. Miller & Julev, res. 215 3d av., Ft. H.
Mars Eva Miss, res. 215 3d av., Ft. H.
Mars Julius, barber, 213 3d av., res. 215 3d av., Ft. H.
Marsh Eliza Miss, clk. Theo. Mueller & Co., res. 730 Cherry.
Marshall Abbie Miss, res. 433 S. Van Buren.
Marshall Amanda N. (wid. S. Horatio), res. 433 S. Van Buren.
Marshall Andrew, blksmith, res. 1248 Crooks.
Marshall Carrie Miss, res. e. s. Willow, 2 s. Baird, Ft. H.
Marshall Charles, delivery clk., res 629 Doty.
Marshall Frank C., clk. Thos. H. Burns, res. e. s. Willow, 2 s. Baird, Ft. H.
Marshall Henry H., teamster, res. 2 w. 768 Shawano rd., Ft. H.
Marshall Ida (wid. Ernest), res. 1021 Stuart.
Marshall James A., painter, res. n. s. Dousman, 3 w. George, Ft. H.
Marshall Jules, teamster, res. 1136 Cedar.
Marshall Lilly Miss, cashier Wm. Larsen, res. 501 Main, Ft. H.
Marshall Mary (wid. John), res. 1300 Crooks.
Marshall Theodore, street-sprinkler, res. 620 Doty.
Marshall William T., clk. T. M. Camm, res. 312 Chestnut, Ft. H.
Marshall William T. Mrs., millinery, 309 Main, Ft. H., res. 312 Chestnut, Ft. H.
Marteaux Peter, gardener, res. s. s. Dousman, 3 e. M. & N. R. R. track, Ft. H.
Marteaux Peter Jr., gardener, res. 7 w. 874 Dousman, Ft. H.
Martell Anton, lab., res. n. s. Morrow, at city line, Town Preble.
Martell Frank, lab., res. n. s. Morrow, at city limits, Town Preble.
Martell George, lab., res. 711 Pleasant.
Martell Joseph, teamster, res. 1629 Main.
Martell Lucy Miss, res. n. s. Morrow, at city limits, Town Preble.
Martell Wm., lab., res. n. s. Morrow, at city limits, Town Preble.
Martin Albert, res. 728 Crooks.
Martin Alfred, painter, res. 126 5th av., Ft. H.
Martin Alvin E., clk., res. 426 N. Adams.
Martin Daniel H., county clk., res. 733 S. Webster av.
Martin Deborah B. Miss, res. 1008 S. Monroe av.
Martin Delia Miss, dressmkr, 414 N. Monroe av., res. same.
**MARTIN ELIE**, justice of the peace, real estate, insurance, notary public and collection agent, 302 N. Washington, res. 426 N. Adams.
Martin Elizabeth S. (wid. Morgan L.), res. 1008 S. Monroe av.

Martin Eugene, blacksmith, res. w. s. 3d av., 4 s. 7th, Ft. H.
**MARTIN FREDERICK F.,** prop. Union House, and furniture, 115 3d av., Ft. H., res. same.
Martin Isabelle (wid. Amos), res. 126 5th av., Ft. H.
Martin James C. (Martin & Jacobi), res. 416 S. Monroe. av.
Martin John, res. 733 S. Webster av.
Martin John F., law student, res. 736 S. Madison.
Martin Joseph M., student, res. 704 Cass.
Martin Louis, lab., res. 318 N. Adams.
Martin Mamie Miss, res. 733 S. Webster av.
Martin Mary Miss, domestic 325 S. Monroe av.
Martin Mary L. (wid. Constant), res. 416 S. Monroe av.
Martin Patrick H. (Wigman & Martin), res. 736 S. Madison.
Martin Pauline Miss, res. 728 Crooks.
Martin Rudolph, res. 622 S. 11th.
Martin Sarah G. Miss, res. 1008 S. Monroe av.
Martin Tessie Miss, res. 733 S. Webster av.
Martin Thomas, salesman Jos. Spitz, res. 733 S. Madison.
Martin Toussaint J., clk. B. Fontaine Hardware Co., res. 416 Cedar.
**MARTIN XAVIER,** real estate, insurance and city assessor, 318 N. Washington, res. 728 Crooks.
**MARTIN & JACOBI** (James C. Martin and Manfred Jacobi), insurance and real estate, 218 N. Washington.
Martneck Charles, lab., res. e. s. 4th av., 2 n. 9th, Ft. H.
Marvin Eli, pres. Green Bay & Fort Howard Water Works Co., res. Frankfort, Ind.
Marvin Grace Miss, res. 521 Main.
Marvin Henry H., foreman The State Gazette, res. 307 Cass.
Marvin William H., trunk mnfr. and dealer in paints, oils and glass, 323½ N. Washington, res. 521 Main.
Maslowski Kasimer, lab., res. 407 N. Madison.
Mason F. N., brakeman, res. Cook's Hotel.
Mason Street School, Miss Louise Senn, teacher, n. s. Mason, 1 e. 12th.
Massart Albert, mach., res. 330 S. Van Buren.
Massart George, res. 330 S. Van Buren.
Masse Alphons J. cigarmkr., res. 718 Mason.
Masse Anton G. M., register in probate, court house, res. 319 Lawe.
Masse Birdie Miss, res. 319 Lawe.
Masse Hamilton, res. 319 Lawe.
Masse Henry, carp., res. n. s. Elm, 1 e. Forest, Town Preble.
Masse Joseph, tinsmith, res. 312 Lawe.

MAS 177 MAY

Masse Kittie Miss, res. 319 Lawe.
Massenge August, clk. 207 N. Washington, res. Wilmar House.
Masset Gabriel, plasterer, res. 926 Main.
Massey Annie Miss, res. 502 N. Monroe av.
Massey Arthur, lab., res. 502 N. Monroe av.
Massey Clement, v.-pres. George B. Hess Co., res. 502 N. Monroe av.
Massey Mabel Miss, res. 502 N. Monroe av.
Massey Philip, cooper, res. 1140 Pine.
Massie Josephine, domestic 315 Cedar, Ft. H.
Masson Charles, shoemkr., res. 1316 Elm.
Masson George, clk. Buengener & Bar. res. 1126 Walnut.
**MASSON LOUIS,** saloon, 1101 Main, res. 1126 Walnut.
Massopust Frank, lab., res. 254 Pearl, Ft. H.
Master Joseph, lab., res. 429 N. 12th.
Mathot Arthur, mason, res. 310½ S. Washington.
Mathot Louis, mason, res. 310½ S. Washington.
Mattern Bros. (Henry and Valentine Mattern), meatmkt, 300 S. Quincy.
Mattern Edwin, delivery clk. Mattern Bros., res. 234 S. Quincy.
Mattern Henry (Mattern Bros.), res. 234 S. Quincy.
Mattern Valentine (Mattern Bros.), res. 302 S. Quincy.
Mattheis Victor, lab., res. n. s. Bond, 4 w. Cedar, Ft. H.
Mattheissen Henry, lab., res. 428 Pleasant.
Matthews Florenz, painter, res. 312 Willow, Ft. H.
Matthies Charles, lab., res. e. s. 4th av., 3 s. 8th, Ft. H.
Matthies Florenz, painter, res. e. s. 4th av., 3 s. 8th, Ft. H.
Matthies Robert, tailor, res. e. s. 4th av., 3 s. 8th, Ft. H.
Matthies Thomas, teamster, res. 1121 Pine.
Matty Amelia (wid. Leo), res. n. s. Shawano rd. 5 w. Willow, Ft. H.
Matty Constance Miss, res. n. s. Shawano rd., 5 w. Willow, Ft. H.
Matty Emerence, domestic 308 S. Madison.
Matty Mary Miss, res. 504 Doty.
Matty Virginia Miss, res. n. s. Shawano rd., 5 w. Willow, Ft. H.
Matz William, lab., res. 1351 Doty.
Maus Mary, domestic 831 Main.
May Edgar B. (Case & Co.), res. Commercial House, Ft. H.
May George, mason, res. 1019 Walnut.
**MAY HENRY,** painter, 205 N. Washington, res. 1035 Walnut.
May Hugh, painter, res. 715 Harvey.
**MAY PETER,** mason contractor, 1019 Walnut, res. same.
May William, wagonmkr. res. 414 Broadway, Ft. H.

23

**MAYER HENRY**, upholsterer, furniture repairing, carpet cleaning, 723 Main, res. same.
Mayer Joseph, lab., res. Coopertown House.
Mayhew August, teamster, res. 1136 Crooks.
Mead William C., clk., res. 405 Cherry, Ft. H.
Meagher Catherine Miss, res. 403 S. Jefferson.
Meck Nels, with Green Bay Plumbing & Heating Co., res. Adams House.
Meert John B., gardener, res. s. s. Shawano rd., 1 w. Oneida rd., Ft. H.
Meetz Edward, fireman, res. 118 Cherry, Ft. H.
Meetz John, wiper, res. 120 Cherry, Ft. H.
Meinert Herman Rev., pastor Moravian Church, res. 512 Moravian.
Meinert Herman T., student, res. 512 Moravian.
Meinert Lydia Miss, res. 512 Moravian.
Meinert Martha Miss, res. 512 Moravian.
Meissner Alvina Miss, res. 513 N. Jefferson.
Meister Carrie Miss, res. 1150 Cherry.
**MEISTER CHARLES**, supt. Brown County Fair and Park Association, res. 1273 Cherry.
**MEISTER CHRISTOPH**, carpenter-contractor, 1150 Cherry, res. same.
Meister Emma Miss, res. 1150 Cherry.
Meister Ernst, carp., res. 1150 Cherry.
Meister Fred. W., carp., res. 1150 Cherry.
**MEISTER HERMAN E.**, carp.-contractor, 1128 Cherry, res. same.
Meister Mathilda Miss, dressmkr., res. 1150 Cherry.
Melau Annie, domestic 303 Cedar, Ft. H.
Melchior Peter, shoemkr., res. 310 Cedar.
Mende John, lab., res. 1209 Chicago.
Menne Josephine Miss, domestic 301 S. Monroe av.
Mercer C. A., engineer, res. Cook's Hotel.
Mercey Arthur, lab., res. 835 Day.
Mercey George, lab., res. 835 Day.
Merchent Albert, shingle packr, res. 512 Cherry, Ft. H.
Merchent Louis, carp., res. 1244 Stuart.
Mercier Joseph, lab., res. 622 St. George.
Mercy Nelson, lab., res. s. s. Shawano rd., 5 w. r. r. track, Ft. H.
Merick E. Gerry, student, res. 218 S. Adams.
Merick Maria F. Miss, res. 218 S. Adams.
Merick Mary (wid. Melzas F.), res. 218 S. Adams.
Merita Kate, domestic Ferris Hotel, Ft. H.

**THE A. SPUHLER CO., Green Bay** CARPETS, RUGS, OIL CLOTHS
Draperies and Window Shades.

MER           179           MIC

Merk George, tel. opr. G. B., W. & St. P., res. 213 Chestnut, Ft. H.
Merkel Otto (Theodore Mueller & Co.), bkpr. G. B. & Ft. H. Gas & Electric Light Co., res. 809 Cherry.
Merkx Felix, lab., res. s. s. Duck Creek rd., 16 w. Mather, Ft. H.
Merrick Max, machinist, res. Bay City House.
Merrill Carlton (Ellis & Merrill), res. 645 S. Monroe av.
Merrill Curtis R., res. 724 S. Madison.
Merrill Katherine Miss, res. 724 S. Madison.
Merritt Albert S., printer, res. 633 Walnut.
Merritt Anna B. Miss, res. 633 Walnut.
Merritt Daniel E., cooper, res. 633 Walnut.
Merritt William, broommkr., res. 633 Walnut.
**MESSMER SEBASTIAN G. RIGHT REV.,** bishop of diocese of Green Bay, res. 139 S. Madison.
**METCALF ARTHUR A.,** physician, 326 N. Monroe av., res. same.
Metropolitan Life Ins. Co. of New York, Chas. H. Hess, asst. supt., 9 Parmentier blk.
Metzler Kittie Miss, domestic 910 Cherry.
Meulemans Louis, general store, n. w. cor. 3d av. and 4th, Ft. H., res. same.
Meunier Anton, res. 115 S. Madison.
Meurer John, drug clk., res. 408 N. Webster av.
Meurer Joseph, lab., res. 408 N. Webster av.
Mey Leonard, blksmith, res. 810 Day.
Meyer Annie Miss, domestic 428 Cherry.
Meyer Christian F., res. 1122 Pine.
Meyer Edward, molder, res. 909 Walnut.
Meyer George, cooper, res. 1200 Crooks.
Meyer Gertie Miss, res. 1200 Crooks.
Meyer John, lab., res. 408 Webster av.
Meyer Catherine Mrs., res. s. w. cor. Crooks and S. 10th.
Meyer Katie Miss, res. 1200 Crooks.
Meyer Nicholas, hides and leather, 221 Main, res. 909 Walnut.
Meyer Nicholas A., grocer, 1200 Crooks, res. same.
Meyer William, clk. 221 Main, res. 909 Walnut.
Meyer William, lab., res. 1275 Stuart.
Meyers Julius R., mngr. S. R. Udell & Co., res. 119 S. Monroe av.
Michael Adolf, watchmkr. and jeweler, 216 N. Washington, res. 730 Cherry.
Michael Bertha Miss, res. 730 Cherry.
Michals Felix, yardmaster, res. 1115 S. Jackson.
Michel Frederick, res. 1372 Elm.

Michel Louise, cook Champion Hotel.
Michel Oscar, del. clk. Nejedlo Bros., res. 1372 Elm.
Michelson Edward, farmer, res. s. s. 2d, 4 w. r. r. track, Ft. H.
Michelson Mamie Miss, res. s. s. 2d, 4 w. r. r. track, Ft. H.
Michelson Mathilda Miss, res. s. s. 2d, 4 w. r. r. track, Ft. H.
Michelson Melitta Miss, res. s. s. 2d, 4. w. r. r. track, Ft. H.
Michelson Michael, farmer, res. s. s. 2d, 4 w. r. r. track, Ft. H.
Mickelsen Carrie Miss, domestic 828 Cherry.
Mickelsen Carrie Miss, dressmkr, res. e. s. Rich rd., 2 s. 9th, Ft. H.
Mickelsen Dagmar Miss, res. e. s. Rich rd., 2 s. 9th, Ft. H.
Mickelsen Jacob, dairyman, res. e. s. Rich rd., 2 s. 9th, Ft. H.
Mickelsen Kate Miss, teacher, res. e. s. Rich rd., 2 s. 9th, Ft. H.
Mielke Louis, carp., res. 1300 Cherry.
Mielke Minnie (wid. Gottlieb), res. 1125 Stuart.
Mies John M., res. s. s. Smith, 1 w. 12th.
Mies Joseph, teamster, res. s. s. Smith, 1 w. 12th.
Mies Joseph A., printer, res. s. s. Smith, 1 w. 12th.
Mies Katie Miss, compositor, res. s. s. Smith, 1 w. 12th.
Miesler Gussie Miss, res. 735 Main.
Miesler Vina, domestic n. e. cor. Chestnut and Baird, Ft. H.
Mikolajczek Michael, lab., res. 1343 Walnut.
Miksh James, packer J. H. Ebeling, res. 1265 Main.
Millard Homer R., agent, res 308 Cherry, Ft. H.
Miller Addie Miss, res. 1163 Doty.
Miller C. P. Co. (Charles P. Miller and Pearl S. Young), grocers, 105 Broadway, Ft. H.
Miller Charles, res. 520 S. Jefferson.
Miller Charles, cooper, res. 1163 Doty.
Miller Charles, cooper, res. 1247 Elm.
Miller Charles P. (C. P. Miller Co.), res. 316 Chestnut, Ft. H.
Miller David, peddler, res. 204 Cedar, Ft. H.
Miller Edward, lab., res. 645 S. Jefferson.
Miller Edward M. (Miller & Juley), res. 219 3d av., Ft. H.
Miller Eli, mail carrier, res. 218 N. Madison.
Miller Emanuel F. (Clark & Miller), res. s. e. cor. Elmore and Broadway, Ft. H.
Miller Emory S., mason, res. s. s. Mather, 2 w. Willow, Ft. H.
Miller Ephraim, mach., res. 122 5th av., Ft. H.
Miller Esther Miss, dressmkr, res. 1025 Main.
Miller Frank Mrs., res. 256 Pearl, Ft. H.
Miller Frank, mill-hand, res. 219 3d av., Ft. H.
Miller Frank E., carp., res. 1022 Pine.
Miller George, train dispatcher, res. 520 S. Jefferson.

**THE A. SPUHLER CO., GREEN BAY, WIS. Fine Dress Goods**
Samples Furnished on Application.

**MILLER JASPER W.,** foreman loco. and car dept., C. & N. W. Ry., res. Christiana near Willow, Ft. H.
Miller John, house mover, 520 S. Jefferson, res. same.
Miller John, hack driver, res. 415 Main.
Miller John N., fireman, res. 219 3d av., Ft. H.
Miller Joseph, engineer, res. n. s. Baird, 2 e. Chestnut, Ft. H.
Miller Joseph, lab., res. s. s. 9th, 1 w. C. & N. R. R track, Ft. H.
Miller L. F., setter, res. Eldred's boarding house, Ft. H.
Miller Lizzie, domestic 915 Pine.
Miller Lizzie Miss. res. 517 Walnut.
Miller Louis, res. 645 S. Jefferson.
Miller Maggie (wid. Peter), res. 122 5th av., Ft. H.
Miller Maggie Miss, res. 645 S. Jefferson.
Miller Marguerite (wid. William), res. 118 Cedar, Ft. H.
Miller Margaret Miss, res. 211 N. Jefferson.
Miller Martin, cooper, res. 1163 Doty.
Miller Mary (wid. Baldad), res. 207 S. **Webster** av.
Miller Mary Miss, res. 1214 Cherry.
Miller Mary, domestic n. w. cor. Cedar and Hubbard, Ft. H.
Miller Matt., timberman, res. 645 S. Jefferson.
Miller Matt. Jr., lab., res. 645 S. Jefferson.
Miller Nicholas, res. 219 3d av., Ft. H.
Miller Orville, cooper, res. 1163 Doty.
Miller Peter, carp., res. 526 S. Jefferson.
Miller Sarah Miss, bookpr., res. 645 S. Jefferson.
Miller Sophie (wid. Frank), res. 1025 Main.
Miller Vesta H. Miss. domestic 614 Cherry.
Miller William D., clk. The Beaumont, res. same.
Miller William H., foreman boiler shop G. B., W. & St. P. R. R., res. 118 Cedar, Ft. H.
**MILLER & JULEY** (Edward M. Miller and Nicholas J. Juley), fancy groceries, 214 3d av., **Ft. H**.
Miller. See Mueller and Muller.
Mills Douglas, engineer, res. Cook's Hotel.
Minahan John R., physician, 1 Parmentier blk., **res. 425 S.** Adams.
Minnear Arthur, bartender, res. 507 Main.
Minsart Anton, prin. Dist. School No. 1, **res. n. s. Finger rd.,** Town Preble.
Moberg Andrew, gardener, res. Arlington Hotel, Ft. H.
Moes Frank, lab., res. s. s. Duck Creek rd., 15 w. Mather, Ft. H.
Moes Henry, lab., res. n. s. Mather, 2 w. Cedar, Ft. H.
Moes John, carp., res. n. s. Bond, 4 w. Cedar, Ft. H.
Moes John, lab., res. s. s. Elmore, 11 w. Cedar, Ft. H.

| MOE | 182 | MOR |
|---|---|---|

Moes Peter, carp.-contr., 706 Bond, Ft. H., res. same.
Moffatt John, brakeman, res. Cook's Hotel.
Moger Alberta Miss, res. 719 Mason.
Moger Emma Miss, res. 426 S. Jefferson.
Moger Helen Miss, res. 719 Mason.
Moger Henrietta Miss, res. 426 S. Jefferson.
Moger John J., clk., res. 719 Mason.
Moger William T., confectioner, 230 Pine, res. 538 S. Jackson.
Mohr Anna Miss, res. 925 Main.
Mohr F. Edward, tailor, res. 323 S. Adams.
Mohr Frank, printer, res. 925 Main.
Mohr John (Engels & Mohr), res. 915 Pine.
**MOHR JOHN E.**, saloon, 925 Main, res. same.
Mohr Louis C. (Mohr & Lenz), res. 206 S. Quincy.
Mohr & Lenz (Louis C. Mohr and Charles Lenz), insurance agts., 217 N. Adams.
Molzahn Elizabeth (wid. Gottlieb), res. s. e. cor. 9th av. and 5th, Ft. H.
Molzoff Michael, lab., res. 1377 Elm.
Mommaerts Frank, gardener, res. e. s. Fisk, 1 s. Dousman, Ft. H.
Mommaerts Jerome, lab., res. e. s. Fisk, 1 s. Dousman, Ft. H.
Monahan Mary (wid. William), res. 820 Walnut.
Monahan William J., conductor, res. 441 S. Adams.
**MONASTERY OF OUR LADY OF CHARITY**, Sister Mary St. Anthony Dobmeier, superioress, n. w. cor. Milwaukee and S. Madison.
**MONASTERY OF OUR LADY OF CHARITY, LAUNDRY DEPARTMENT**, n. w. cor. Milwaukee and S. Madison, conducted by sisters of Our Lady of Charity.
Moneau Joseph, lab., res. Bodart House.
Monfils Jule, blksmith, res. Bodart House.
Monski Bertha, dining-room girl Adams House.
Montpas Philip, brakeman, res. 110 N. Washington.
Moody Anson W., mngr. Alart & McGuire, res. s. e. cor. Broadway and Elmore, Ft. H.
Moon Mattie Miss, res. 1149 Cherry.
Mooney Thomas, detective, res. 401 S. Quincy.
Mooney Thomas E., miller, res. 401 S. Quincy.
Mooney William C., lab., res. 401 S. Quincy.
Moore Charles D., carp., 224 Walnut, res. Bay City House.
Moore Earle C., bkpr. W. D. Cooke, res. 418 Cherry.
Moore Kittie, domestic 402 S. Webster av.
Moran James T., register of deeds, res. Bradley House.
Moran Sarah (wid. Edward), res. 513 Chicago.

**Headquarters for Boys' Clothing** THE A. SPUHLER CO.
GREEN BAY.

Morand William, res. s. s. Hubbard, cor. Cedar, Ft. H.
Morns Zoel, brakeman, res. Northwestern Hotel, Ft. H.
Moravetz Michael, lab., res. 402 1st, Ft. H.
Moravian Church (Green Bay), s. s. Moravian near Monroe av.
Moravian Church (Ft. H.), s. e. cor. 5th av. and 4th, Ft. H.
More W. E., lake captain, res. Adams House.
Moreau Felix, lab., res. 709 Pleasant.
Moreau Flora Miss, res. 709 Pleasant.
Moreau Julia Miss, res. 709 Pleasant.
Moreau Mary Miss, res. 709 Pleasant.
Moreau Mary (wid. Victor), res. 709 Pleasant.
Moretag Albert C., engineer, res. 533 S. Jefferson.
Morgan Charles A., engineer, res. 533 S. Jefferson.
Morgan Edward B., plumber, 311 3d av., Ft. H., res. same.
Morgan Frank, motorman, res. 235 S Webster av.
Morgan James, lab., res. Green Bay House.
Morgan Jane Mrs., res. 309 3d av., Ft. H.
Morgan Sabina, domestic, 339 S. Washington.
Morgan William, lab., res. Green Bay House.
Morgenstern Henry, cooper, 514 N. 12th, res. 519 N. 12th.
Morgenstern Louis, cooper, res. s. s. Willow, 2 w. 12th.
Morieux Emanuel, gardener, res. n. s. Smith, 1 e. 12th.
Moritz Conrad, lab., res. s. s. Shawano rd., 2 w. Hazel, Ft. H.
Moritz Herman, lab., res. Shawano rd., 2 w. Hazel, Ft. H.
Mork Swend, lab., res. 837 S. Jackson.
Morley P., lab., res. Junction Hotel, Ft. H.
Mornard Julius, saloon, 501 Main, res. same.
Morrell Burt, driver, res. Adams House.
Morrell Eleazer, watchman, res. s. s. 5th, 3 w. 3d av., Ft. H.
Morrell Frederick, loco.-fireman, res. 506 Baird, Ft. H.
Morrell Josie Miss, clk. The A. Spuhler Co., res. s. s. 5th, 3 w. 3d av., Ft. H.
Morrell Julia Miss, res. s. s. 5th, 3 w. 3d av., Ft. H.
Morris Frank, res. 1545 Morrow.
Morris James, fireman, res. Northwestern Hotel, Ft. H.
Morris Maggie, domestic, res. 314 Cedar, Ft. H.
Morris Susanne Mrs., res. 1545 Morrow.
Morrison Sarah (wid. Peter), res. Odd Fellows' Home.
Morrow Elisha, res. 345 S. Adams.
Morrow Helen Miss, res. 345 S. Adams.
Morrow Jennie Miss, clk., res. 345 S. Adams.
Morrow Joseph, lab., res. 1128 Doty.
Morrow Louis, lab., res. 1247 Elm.
Morrow Louise Miss, res. 345 S. Adams.

Morrow May Miss, res. 345 S. Adams.
Mortensen John, carpet layer Jorgensen Blesch Co., res. Adams House.
Mortenson Henry, lab., res. Green Bay House.
Mortenson James, lab., res. Green Bay House.
Morton Edith Miss, res. n. s. Mather, 1 w. Cherry, Ft. H.
Morton Elmore, mill-hand, res. n. s. Mather, 1 w. Cherry, Ft. H.
Morton U. Samuel, foreman Murphy Lumber Co., res. n. s. Mather, 1 w. Cherry, Ft. H.
Motef Constance, lab., res. 780 Elmore, Ft. H.
Motef Louise (wid. Frank), res. s. s. Elmore, 11 w. Cedar, Ft. H.
Mouford Peter, carp., res. B slart House.
Moussgau Agnes Miss, res. 301 N. Adams.
**MOUSSEAU GEORGE C. REV.**, pastor French Presbyterian church, res. 301 N. Adams.
Moyer Henry, head sawyer H. McDonald, res. 601 Mather, Ft. H.
Moylan Julia, housekeeper Rev. F. M. J. O'Brien, Ft. H.
Mraz Frank, lab., J. H. Ebeling, res. 701 Harvey.
Mraz Joseph, lab., res. 701 Harvey.
Mraz Katie Miss, res. 701 Harvey.
Mrskosch Mary, domestic 203 S. Jefferson.
Mueller August, carp., res. 301 S. Washington.
Mueller Augusta Miss, res. 1280 Doty.
Mueller Bertha, cracker-packer, res. 1280 Doty.
Mueller Bros. & Co. (Ferd. Bierke, William Schmidt, George and William Mueller), props. East River Planing Mill, n. w. cor. Cedar and 10th.
Mueller Catherine, domestic 519 S. Monroe av.
Mueller Carl, saloon, 220 N. Washington, res. 1102 Crooks.
Mueller Carl, foreman Henry Rahr's Sons, res. 424 N. 12th.
Mueller Chas. Jr., barkpr. 220 N. Washington, res. 1102 Crooks.
Mueller Christina (wid. Carl), res. 1280 Doty.
Mueller Emma Miss, clk. The A. Spuhler Co., res. 525 S. Adams.
Mueller Fred., boilermkr., res. 1280 Doty.
Mueller George W. H. (Mueller Bros. & Co.), res. 720 Crooks.
Mueller Gustav, lab., res. 1165 Mason.
Mueller Gussie Miss, res. 301 S. Washington.
Mueller Henry, grocer, 1200 Doty, res. 1202 Doty.
Mueller Laura Miss, clk. Theodore Mueller & Co., res. 700 Pine.
Mueller Louis, fireman, res. 1280 Doty.
Mueller Michael, res. 300 S. Webster av.
Mueller Morris, lab., res. 316 Main.
Mueller Peter, boilermkr., res. 1280 Doty.

**THE A. SPUHLER CO.** LADIES', MISSES' and CHILDREN'S
GREEN BAY — **CLOAKS, CAPES, JACKETS**

MUE        185        MUR

Mueller Theodore (Theodore Mueller & Co.), res. 700 Pine.
Mueller Theodore Jr., clk. Theodore Mueller & Co., res. 700 Pine.
**MUELLER THEODORE & CO.** (Theodore Mueller and Otto Merkel), dry goods, 311 and 313 N. Washington.
Mueller William J. (East River Planing Mill), res. 931 Cherry.
Mueller-Hansen Johann, res. e. s. Hazel, 1 s. Shawano rd., Ft. H.
Mueller-Hansen Ludolf, res. e. s. Hazel, 1 s. Shawano rd., Ft. H.
Mueller. See Miller and Muller.
Mularkey William, blksmith. res. 110 N. Quincy.
Mullen Maurice, res. 138 S. Webster av.
Mullen Thomas E., com.-trav. 124 S. Washington, res. Grand Rapids, Wis.
Muller Henry (Henry Muller & Co.), res. 421 N. Jefferson.
Muller Ida Miss, res. 807 Main.
Muller Henry & Co. (Henry Muller), gen. mdse., 303-305 Main.
Muller Julia, milliner, res. 807 Main.
Muller Mary, clk. 305 Main, res. 807 Main.
Muller Peter, res. 807 Main.
Muller Pheine Miss, res. 807 Main.
Mulqueen Mary, domestic 425 S. Adams.
Mundt Ernst, car repairer, res. 411 Broadway, Ft. H.
Munroe Lydia (wid. Andrew), res. 827 Cherry.
Munroe Medora (wid. Lawrence J.), res. 509 Pine.
Murphy Albert M., director Murphy Lumber Co., res. 843 S. Monroe av.
Murphy Catherine Miss, teacher, res. s. e. cor. Cedar and Elmore, Ft. H.
Murphy Constantine, brakeman, res. s. e. cor. Cedar and Elmore, Ft. H.
Murphy Cornelius H., brakeman, res. Northwestern Hotel, Ft. H.
Murphy Dennis J., res. s. e. cor. Cedar and Elmore, Ft. H.
Murphy Elbridge N., res. 843 S. Monroe av.
Murphy Frank E., sec.-treas. Murphy Lumber Co., res. n. e. cor. Porlier and S. Madison.
Murphy Joseph, blksmith, res. Green Bay House.
Murphy Julia E., teacher, res. s. e. cor. Cedar and Elmore, Ft. H.
**MURPHY LUMBER CO.,** Simon J. Murphy, pres.; William H. Murphy, v.-pres.; Frank E. Murphy, sec.-treas.; lumber manufacturers, mouth of Fox river, n. city limits.
Murphy Nicholas, farmer, res. n. s. 2d, 6 w. R. R. track, Ft. H.
Murphy Patrick, grocer, 206 3d av., Ft. H., res. same.
Murphy Simon J. Sr., pres. Murphy Lumber Co., res. Detroit, Mich.

24

Murphy Simon J. Jr., director Murphy Lumber Co., res. 927 S. Monroe av.
Murphy Thomas, teamster, res. Waterloo House.
Murphy Timothy J., brakeman, res. s. e. cor. Cedar and Elmore, Ft. H.
Murphy William H., v.-pres. Murphy Lumber Co., res. Detroit, Mich.
Murray Charles D., sewing machine agt., res. 421 S. Jefferson.
Murray Thomas, barkpr. The Beaumont, res. 223 N. Jefferson.
Mutza John, fisherman, res. e. s. McDonald, 1 s. lumber yd., Ft. H.
Myers John, conductor, res. 401 Mather, Ft. H.
Myrick William, brakeman, res. Northwestern Hotel, Ft. H.

# N

NADON Peter N., barber, 311 Main, Ft. H., res. same.
Nau Frederick, res. 200 S. Adams.
Nau George D., meat-markt and tug owner, 121 N. Washington, res. 200 S. Adams.
Nau Lambert, butcher, res. 200 S. Adams.
Navarre Simeon, stone-cutter, res. 1364 Cherry.
Nealen John F., lab., res. 705 Cherry, Ft. H.
Nebel Clara Miss, res. 1336 St. Clair.
Nebel Ernst, street commissioner, res. 1336 St. Clair.
Nebel Ida Miss, clk. The A. Spuhler Co., res. 1336 St. Clair.
Nee Coleman, engineer, res. Northwestern Hotel, Ft. H.
Nee David, engineer, res. Northwestern Hotel, Ft. H.
Neenan John W., brakeman, res. Northwestern Hotel, Ft. H.
Nejedlo Albert L., clk., res. 1257 Elm.
**NEJEDLO BROS.** (Louie E., Mitchell R. and Godfrey J. Nejedlo), grocers, 321 N. Adams.
Nejedlo Frank, clk. L. E. Nejedlo, res. n. w. cor. Cedar and Pleasant.
Nejedlo Godfrey J. (Nejedlo Bros.), res. 324 Pine.
Nejedlo James W., clk., res. 1257 Elm.
Nejedlo John, res. 1257 Elm.
Nejedlo Joseph D., clk. L. E. Nejedlo, res. 1257 Elm.
Nejedlo Louis E. (Nejedlo Bros.), grocer, 1374 Main, res. n. w. cor. Cedar and Pleasant.
Nejedlo Mitchell R. (Nejedlo Bros.), res. 324 Pine.
Nejedlo Zephran A., baggageman, res. 832 Pine.
Nelis Max, lab., res. Bodart House.
Nelson Anders, res. n. s. 5th, 2 w. 3d av., Ft. H.

**THE A. SPUHLER CO., Green Bay** CARPETS, RUGS, OIL CLOTHS, Draperies and Window Shades.

Nelson Andrew, carp., res. n. w. cor. 5th and 4th av., Ft. H.
Nelson Andrew, lab., res. e. s. 2d av., 2 s. 8th, Ft. H.
Nelson Annie C., assistant preparatory teacher Green Bay Business College, res. 706 Cedar, Ft. H.
Nelson Annie, domestic 435 S. Webster av.
Nelson Anton, clk. 700 2d, Ft. H., res. s. e. cor. 2d and 7th av., Ft. H.
Nelson Bertha Miss, student, res. 400 2d, Ft. H.
Nelson Edwin C., res. 117 S. Monroe av.
Nelson Emil, lab., res. e. s. 4th av., 3 n. 10th, Ft. H.
Nelson Emilie Miss, res. e. s. 4th av., 3 n. 10th, Ft. H.
Nelson Frank, wagonmkr., res. Hall House, Ft. H.
Nelson G. T. Mrs., groceries, 700 2d, Ft. H., res. s. e. cor. 2d and 7th av.
Nelson Halvor, carp., res. n. s. 5th st., 4 w. 3d av., Ft. H.
Nelson Hans, carp., res. 400 5th av., Ft. H.
Nelson Henry, lab., res. n. s. 5th, 2 w. 3d av., Ft. H.
Nelson Henry, mach., res. n. s. 5th, 4 w. 3d av., Ft. H.
Nelson Holder, clk. 700 2d, res. s. e. cor. 2d and 7th av., **Ft. H.**
Nelson John, lab., res. n. w. cor. 10th and 4th av., Ft. H.
Nelson John C., blksmith, s. s. Charles, 7 w. Manitowoc rd., res. same.
**NELSON JOHN J.**, prop. Junction Hotel, Ft. H. res. same.
Nelson Lizzie, domestic 516 Cedar, Ft. H.
Nelson Lizzie Mrs., res. w. s. Broadway, 4 s. Hubbard, Ft. H.
Nelson Nellie Miss, teacher, res. 706 Cedar, Ft. H.
Nelson Nels, fisherman, res. Coopertown House.
Nelson Nels, mill-hand, res. e. s. 4th av., 3 n. 10th, Ft. H.
Nelson Nels, marblectr, res. Coopertown House.
Nelson Nels, lab., res. n. s. 5th, 2 w. 3d av., Ft. H.
Nelson Ole, lab., res. 400 5th av., Ft. H.
Nelson Ole, lab., res. e. s. 4th av., 3 n. 10th, Ft. H.
Nelson Ole C., live-stock dealer, res. 706 Cedar, Ft. H.
Nelson Severin, lab., res. e. s. 2d av., cor. 8th, Ft. H.
Nelson Stephen, lab., res. e. s. 2d av., cor. 10th, Ft. H.
Netois Henry, lab., res. s. s. Elmore, 8 w. Cedar, Ft. H.
Neufeld Elizabeth M. Miss, res. 100 S. Jefferson.
Neufeld E. A., bookpr. Murphy Lumber Co., res. 102 S. Jefferson.
Neufeld Philipp, tailor, 229 Cherry, res. 100 S. Jefferson.
Neugent Patrick, roadmaster, res. 521 S. Quincy.
Neuman Anna H. (wid. Fred.), res. 1202 Stuart.
Neuman Henry F., lab., res. 1202 Stuart.
Neumann Eliza (wid. Lazarus), confect., 221 S. Monroe av., res. same.

Neumann Sophie, clk., res. 221 S. Monroe av.
Neumann. See Newman.
Neuschwander Edward J., bkpr. E. Boaler, res. cor. Willow and Christiania, Ft. H.
Neville Arthur C. (John C. & A. C. Neville), res. 905 S. Monroe av.
Neville John C. (John C. & A. C. Neville), res. 514 Walnut.
**NEVILLE JOHN C. & A. C.** (John C. and Arthur C. Neville), lawyers, 307 N. Washington.
Neville Jules C., clk. J. Delaporte & Son, res. 308 3d, Ft. H.
Neville Sophie A. Miss, res. 514 Walnut.
Nevins John H., journalist, res. 720 S. Jackson.
Newark Mary, domestic 216 S. Jefferson.
Newell Charles A., carp., res. 524 S. Monroe av.
Newman Edward, tailor, res. 1146 Doty.
Newman Ernst, tailor, res. 1145 Stuart.
Newman Louis, res. 1145 Stuart.
Newman Phenie Miss, dressmkr, res. 1145 Stuart.
Newman William, tailor, res. 1145 Stuart.
Newman William Jr., tailor, res. 1145 Stuart.
Newman. See Neumann.
Newton Porter H., res. 832 Shawano rd., Ft. H.
Ney Michael, com.-trav. J. P. C. Schmit, res. 215 Cherry.
Nichol Grace Miss, dressmkr. res. 1207 Cherry.
Nichol Jennie Miss, cashier Jos. Spitz, res. 1207 Cherry.
Nichol John, cooper, res. 1207 Cherry.
Nichol Robert, machine-hand, res. 1207 Cherry.
Nichols Herbert L., engineer, res. 617 Chestnut, Ft. H.
Nicholson Eugene C., cigar mnfr., 221 Cherry, res. 620 Cherry.
Nicholson Sophie, domestic The Beaumont.
Nicholson Thomas, fireman, res. No. 4, n. end Monroe av., o. Murphy's mill.
Nick George, cooper, res. 415 S. Monroe av.
Nick J. Peter, foreman D. W. Britton, res. 415 S. Monroe av.
Nick Jacob G., clk. Stiller Bros., res. 314 S. Quincy.
**NICK JOHN**, sec. Fox River Soap Co., wood yard foot N. Jackson, res. 1201 Walnut.
Nick John J., barber, res. 1201 Walnut.
Nick Joseph, boots and shoes, 222 Walnut, res. 314 S. Quincy.
Nick Joseph, cooper, res. 630 N. 12th.
Nick Joseph, lab., res. 1201 Walnut.
Nick Kate Miss, dressmkr., res. 1201 Walnut.
Nick Ottilie, dressmkr., res. 314 S. Quincy.
**NICKOLAI JOSEPH**, saloon, 519 Main, res. same.

**THE A. SPUHLER CO., GREEN BAY, WIS. Fine Dress Goods**
Samples Furnished on Application.

Nickolai Jule, barkpr., res. 505 Main.
Nickolai Moses, lab., res. 406 N. Webster av.
Niejahr Clara Miss, res. 928 Doty.
Niejahr Minnie (wid. Adolph), res. 928 Doty.
Niejahr William H. C., clk. Brauns & Van, res. 928 Doty.
Nightingale William H., lab., res. East River, foot of N. Madison.
Niland James, conductor, res. Northwestern Hotel, Ft. H.
Nilson. See Nelson.
Nineway Annie Miss, res. 416 N. Monroe av.
Nineway Eva Miss, res. 416 N. Monroe av.
Nineway Henry, barber, 702 Main, res. 416 N. Monroe av.
Nineway Louise (wid. Henry), res. 416 N. Monroe av.
Nissen Matthias (Streckenbach & Nissen), res. s. s. Shawano rd., 7 w. Willow, Ft. H.
Nitz August, foreman Joannes Bros. spice mills, res. 722 Crooks.
Nitz Gustav, carp.-contr., 315 S. Webster av., res. same.
Nitz Henrietta (wid. Frederick), res. 1361 Doty.
Noehle Theodore, florist, 223 N. Jefferson, res. same.
Noel Alexander, harnessmkr., res. s. s. Smith, 3 e. Jackson.
Noel August, lab., res. s. s. Smith, 3 e. Jackson.
Noel John, lab., res. s. s. 8th, 2 w. 4th av., Ft. H.
Noel Jules, lab., res. s. s. Smith, 3 e. Jackson.
Noel Jules, lab., res. 1401 Day.
Noel Louis, lab., res. Columbia Hotel.
Noel Prosper, lab., res. s. s. Smith, 3 e. Jackson.
Noel Victor, gardener, res. 1371 Crooks.
Noffz John, prop. Green Bay Roller Mills, s. w. cor. S. Washington and Doty, res. 122 S. Madison.
Nolan James, engineer, res. Northwestern Hotel, Ft. H.
Nolan Michael H., chief of police, res. 24 Parmentier blk.
Noland Ellis A., engineer, res. 412 Willow, Ft. H.
Nolet John, bricklayer, res. 1411 Elm.
Nolvin John, lab., res. 1433 Harvey.
Norman Anna J. Miss, res. 514 Walnut.
North George L., merchandise broker and sec. Union Building, Loan & Saving Ass'n., 8 Parmentier blk., res. 333 S. Madison.
North Jerome R. ,lawyer, 301 N. Washington, res. 740 S. Jefferson.
North Ludlow F., yard clk. C., M. & St. P. R. R., res. 333 S. Madison.
Northwestern Fuel Co., M. J. McCormick, agt., foot of Pine.
**NORTHWESTERN HOTEL,** Patrick Shaughnessy & Son, props., w. s. Broadway, 1 n. Kellogg, Ft. H.
Notting John, painter and paperhanger, 1235 Cherry, res. same.
Novak Regina (wid. John), res. n. s. St. Clair, 4 e. N. 12th.

| NOW | 190 | O'NE |
|---|---|---|

Nowitzke Herman, lab., res. w. s. S. 12th, bet. Stuart and Crooks.
Noyens Annie, domestic 302 S. Adams.
Nuss W. Wesley, photographer, 215 N. Washington, res. 513 Pine.
Nydakl Ole, painter, res. 335 Pearl, Ft. H.
Nye David, cigar mnfr., 312½ Cherry, res. 322 N. Webster av.
Nye Johanna Mrs., res. 1306 Elm.
Nye Louis, teamster, res. 1348 Day.
Nye Sam, cigarmkr, res. 1266 Cedar.

## O'

O'BRIEN John, lab., res. 316 Main.

O'Brien Lizzie Miss, dressmkr, res. Broadway House, Ft. H.
O'Brien Michael, lab., res. 1 w. 768 Shawano rd., Ft. H.
**O'BRIEN MICHAEL JOHN REV.**, pastor St. Patrick's Church, res. 401 Cherry, Ft. H.
O'Brien Timothy, saloon, 101 N. Washington, res. 502 Jefferson.
O'Claire Catherine (wid. Isaac), res. 401 Mather, Ft. H.
O'Connor F. Jerry, assistant train dispatcher, C., M. & St. P. Ry., res. 526 S. Madison.
O'Connor Frank, fireman C., M. & St. P. Ry., res. 414 Mason.
O'Connor Mary A. Miss, res. 526 S. Madison.
O'Connor Patrick, roadmaster C., M. & St. P. Ry., res. 526 S. Madison.
O'Connor Philip E., stenog. gen. mngr. G. B., W. & St. P. Ry., res. Commercial House, Ft. H.
O'Connor Timothy C., engineer, res. 530 S. Quincy.
O'Donald Thomas, engineer, res. Bradley House.
O'Keefe John, shoemkr, res. 922 S. Van Buren.
O'Krusch Charles, lab., res. 235 S. Adams.
O'Krusch Meta Miss, res. 235 S. Adams.
O'Krusch Reinhold, res. 235 S. Adams.
O'Leary Bros. (Humphrey, John, Timothy, Michael, Daniel and William O'Leary), boilermkrs, e. s. Pearl, 2 s. Main, Ft. H.
O'Leary Daniel (O'Leary Bros.), res. 120 S. Monroe av.
O'Leary Humphrey (O'Leary Bros.), res. Appleton.
O'Leary John (O'Leary Bros.), res. 120 S. Monroe av.
O'Leary Kate Miss, res. 120 S. Monroe av.
O'Leary Loyal, student, res. 532 Main.
O'Leary Michael (O'Leary Bros.), res. 120 S. Monroe av.
O'Leary Timothy (O'Leary Bros.), res. 120 S. Monroe av.
O'Leary William (O'Leary Bros.), res. 211 Chestnut, Ft. H.
O'Neill Thomas, lab., res. 621 N. 12th.

**Headquarters for Boys' Clothing** THE A. SPUHLER CO. GREEN BAY.

## O

OCKSTADT Peter, butcher, res. 107 N. Washington.
Odd Fellows' Home, William Warren, supt.; Mrs. William Warren, matron, 822 Grignon.
Oldenburg Anton G. (Oldenburg & Co.), res. 320 Chestnut, Ft. H.
Oldenburg Emilie Miss, res. 310 3d, Ft. H.
**OLDENBURG G. & CO.** (Margaret and Otto N. Oldenburg), furniture, 213 Main, Ft. H.
Oldenburg Louis, R. R. hd., res. s. s. Dousman, 2 e. M. & N. R. R. track, Ft. H.
Oldenburg Louis, cabinetmkr., res. 310 3d, Ft. H.
Oldenburg Louise, res. s. a. Dousman, 2 e. M. & N. R. R. track, Ft. H.
Oldenburg Margaret Mrs. (George Oldenburg & Co.) res. 310 3d, Ft. H.
Oldenburg Otto N. (George Oldenburg & Co.), res. 213 Main, Ft. H.
**OLDENBURG & CO.**, A. G. Oldenburg, prop., undertakers, embalmers and dealers in wall paper, room mouldings, curtains and baby carriages, n. w. cor. Pearl and Main, Ft. H.
Olejniczak Jacob, lab., res. 1313 Stuart.
Olejniczak John, lab., res. 1225 Doty.
Olejniczak Joseph P., lab., res. 1329 Stuart.
Oleson Hans, lab., res. 502 5th av., Ft. H.
Oleson Hilda, compositor, res. n. w. cor. 4th av. and 7th, Ft. H.
Oleson John, mach., res. Broadway House, Ft. H.
Oleson Olaf, lab., res. 124 5th av., Ft. H.
Oleson Otto, fireman, res. 902 3d av., Ft. H.
Oliver James (J. Saunders & Co.), res. n. w. cor. 3d and 8th av., Ft. H.
**OLMSTED AUSTIN F.**, physician, P. O. bldg., res. 212 S. Adams.
Olmsted Clara K. Miss, res. 212 S. Adams.
Olmsted Minnie E. Miss, clk., res. 212 S. Adams.
Olmsted Thomas, brakeman, res. Columbia Hotel.
Olsen Albert, res. s. s. Shawano rd., 1 w. Hazel, Ft. H.
Olsen Albert, mach., res. 139 Broadway, Ft. H.
Olsen Bernt, res. s. s. Shawano rd., 1 w. Hazel, Ft. H.
Olsen George, bridge carp., res. 1 n. 514 Chestnut, Ft. H.
Olsen Helena, domestic 505 S. Van Buren.
Olsen Ida A. Miss, res. 139 Broadway, Ft. H.
Olsen Lars, lake captain, res. 139 Broadway, Ft. H.
Olsen Mary Miss, res. s. Shawano rd., 1 w. Hazel, Ft. H.

| OLS | 192 | OWE |
|---|---|---|

Olsen Peter, fireman Hose No. 2, res. 1321 Cherry.
Olsen Peter M., barkpr J. F. Schmitt, res. 303 N. Jefferson.
Olson Hans, lab., res. e. s. 5th av., 1 s. r. r. track, Ft. H.
Olson Hans, lab., res. 307 4th, Ft. H.
Olson Ole, lab., res. Bodart House.
Olson Ole, printer, res. 704 4th av., Ft. H.
Olson Oscar, painter, res. 307 4th, Ft. H.
Olson Thomas, lab., res. 704 4th av., Ft. H.
Onstad Andrew, bkpr. M. J. Corbett, res. 102 3d, Ft. H.
Onstad Martin A., clk. M. J. Corbett, res. 402 3d, Ft. H.
**ONZE STANDAARD**, Edward V. D. Casteele, editor; C. A. Tesselnar, assistant editor, 315 Pine.
Oppen Otto, fireman, res. Huffman House, Ft. H.
Orbert Charles K., res. n. s. Shawano rd., 2 w. Oak, Ft. H.
Orbert Freeman B., postal clk., res. n. s. Shawano rd., 2 w Oak, Ft. H.
Orde Joseph, bellman The Beaumont.
Ording Ada Miss, music teacher, res. 1227 Cherry.
Ording Imogene (wid. Aldrich), res. 1227 Cherry.
Ormsby George W., scaler, res. 302 4th av., Ft. H.
Osmond Christian, lab., res. n. s. Baird, near the slough, Ft. H.
Osmond Daniel, wagonmkr., res. n. s. Baird, 2 w. Willow, Ft. H.
Osmond Peter, res. n. s. Baird, near the slough, Ft. H.
Ostermann Jacob Sr., res. s. w. cor. Main and Newhall.
Ostermann Jacob Jr., carp., res. s. w. cor. Main and Newhall.
Ostermann Lizzie, domestic 927 S. Monroe av.
Ostermann Tillie, domestic 927 S. Monroe av.
Otterson Robert, loco.-eng., res. 406 3d, Ft. H.
Otto Charles, teamster, res. n. e. cor. Day and 11th.
Otto John, lab., res. n. e. cor. Day and 11th.
Otto Joseph, lab., res. n. e. cor. Day and 11th.
Otto William, del.-clk., res. n. e. cor. Day and 11th.
Oudijans Cornelius S., lab., res. s. s. Shawano rd., 8 w. Willow, Ft. H.
Oudijans Lizzie Miss, res. s. s. Shawano rd., 8 w. Willow, Ft. H.
Oudijans Simon, machinist, res. s. s. Shawano rd., 8 w. Willow, Ft. H.
Oudijans Theodore, cigarmkr, res. s. s. Shawano rd., 8 w. Willow, Ft. H.
Outs Joseph, lab., res. 780 Elmore, Ft. H.
Outland Alvin, ship.-clk. 124 S. Washington, res. w. s. S. Quincy, 2 s. Lawe.
Owen Albert H., engineer, res. e. s. Pearl, 1 n. Main, Ft. H.

**THE A. SPUHLER CO.** *LADIES', MISSES' and CHILDREN'S*
**GREEN BAY** — **CLOAKS, CAPES, JACKETS**

## P

PADHAM Frederick, fireman, res. Junction Hotel, Ft. H.
Pachl Paul, carp. res. s. s. Shawano rd., 5 w. Willow, Ft. H.
Page Mary, domestic 332 S. Webster av.
Pahl Louisa (wid. Albert), res. 1100 Main.
Pahr William T., painter, res. s. s. Shawano rd., 6 w. Willow, Ft. H.
Palmer A. Bertram, supt. Green Bay & Ft. Howard Water Works Co., res. 621 S. Adams.
Palmer Bertram, teamster W. D. Cooke, res. 712 S. 10th.
Palmer Etta, teacher, res. 712 S. 10th.
Palmer Jedediah D., carp., res. 712 S. 10th.
Paniewicz Simon, fisherman, res. e. s. Chestnut, 2 s. Elmore, Ft. H.
Pankey Charles, butcher, res. 107 N. Washington.
Panure Desire, lab., res. 1340 Day.
Panure Jeanette (wid. Jean Pierre), res. 1340 Day.
Parent John, res. 1130 Main.
Parenteau Abraham, res. 316 Mason.
Parenteau William H., res. 607 S. Jefferson.
Parish Edwin P. (Ansorge & Parish), res. 542 S. Quincy.
Parish George, res. 224 N. Adams.
Parizek Matt., lab., res. 1128 S. Monroe av.
Park School, n. s. School, bet. S. Madison and S. Monroe.
Parker Barton L., law clk. Greene & Vroman, res. De Pere.
Parker Savin, musician, res. Wilmar House.
Parkes James T., court stenog., res. 100 N. Madison.
Parkes William J., teller Citizens' National Bank, res. 100 N. Madison.
Parkinson Jay A., engineer, res. 720 S. Jackson.
Parkinson Michael, supt. car inspectors C., M. & St. P. R. R., res. 1103 S. Quincy.
Parks Frank, lab., res. 729 S. Adams.
Parks Robert, engineer, res. 726 S. Jackson.
Parmentier Block, s. w. cor. N. Washington and Main.
Parmentier Bros. (Xavier and Nestor Parmentier), grocers, 313 Main.
Parmentier Clara Miss, res. 1375 Main.
Parmentier Jules, real estate and loans, 35 Parmentier blk., res. 302 S. Adams.
Parmentier Jules J., lab., res. 1182 Day.
Parmentier Laura Miss, res. 422 N. Adams.
Parmentier Nestor (Parmentier Bros.), res. 313 Main.

Parmentier Sebastian, lab., res. 310 Cass.
**PARMENTIER XAVIER** (Parmentier Bros.), city clk. Green Bay, res. 422 N. Adams.
Paster Frank, mngr. Platten Bros., res. 209 Chestnut, Ft. H.
Patizek Wenzel, lab., res. 1524 Elm.
Patterson Lucy (wid. John L.), res. 413 Pine.
Patterson Samuel, lab., res. 314 S. Jackson.
Patton John, switchman, res. 207 3d av., Ft. H.
Patton Maurice, section hand, res. 303 Lawe.
Patton Michael, lab., res. 207 3d av., Ft. H.
Patton Thomas, lab., res. 207 3d av., Ft. H.
Patton William, teamster, res. 207 3d av., Ft. H.
Patzer Augusta (wid. John), res. 1361 Doty.
Patzke Otto, mason, res. 1160 Chicago.
Paul Henry, sexton Allouez Cemetery, res. n. s. State rd., 1 blk. e. De Pere rd.
Paul Victor, carp., res. 922 11th.
Paulsen Ole, fisherman, res. s. s. Duck Creek rd., 5 w. Mather, Ft. H.
Paulsen Peter E., bridge carp., res. 117 Chestnut, Ft. H.
Paulson Christian, bridge carp., res. 314 6th av., Ft. H.
Payan Amez, res. 818 Walnut.
Peak Marion Miss, res. 905 S. Monroe av.
Peak William S., painter, res. 319 S. Adams.
Pease Harry E., driver, res. Commercial Hotel, Ft. H.
Pease Loren F., clk. Wm. Hoffman, res. 224 N. Washington.
Peaslee Allen W., beer peddler Henry Rahr's Sons, res. 1335 Cedar.
Pech Domin F., clk. Jorgensen Blesch Co., res. Schauer's Hotel.
Pelkin Alexander, lab., res. 526 N. Jefferson.
Pelkin August, carp., res. 214 S. Jackson.
Pelkin Charles, teamster, res. 1139 Pine.
Pelkin Mary (wid. John), res. 214 S. Jackson.
Pellegrin Joseph, res. 723 Bond, Ft. H.
Pellegrin Theodore J., lab., res. 723 Bond, Ft. H.
Pellogor Fred, lab., res. n. w. cor. Cedar and Main, Ft. H.
Penison Edward, lab., res. 519 Cherry, Ft. H.
Penison John, res. 833 S. Jefferson.
Penison Maud Miss, res. 833 S. Jefferson.
Penison Theresa Miss, res. 406 Hubbard, Ft. H.
Penney Patrick, prop. Green Bay House, res. same.
Pennings Albert, fireman, res. 612 St. George.
Pennings Clara Miss, res. 1328 Elm.
Pennings John, teamster, res. 1328 Elm.

THE A. SPUHLER CO., Green Bay CARPETS, RUGS, OIL CLOTHS
Draperies and Window Shades.

PEN        195        PET

Pennings John Jr., lab., res. 1328 Elm.
Pennings May Miss, dressmkr, 1328 Elm, res. same.
Pennock Frances, domestic, res. 793 Shawano rd., Ft. H.
Peor Joseph, lab., res. 1357 Cherry.
Peot Joseph, clk. Bradley House, res. same.
Perkins Henry J., physician, res. 318 Willow, Ft. H.
Perkins Jennie (wid. Alexander), res. 409 Cherry, Ft. H.
Perrigoue Aggie Miss, res. s. s. Shawano rd., 5 w. r. r. track, Ft. H.
Perrigoue Harriette (wid. Wales), res. s. s. Shawano rd., 5 w. r. r. track, Ft. H.
Perrigoue Joseph, lab., res. 5 w. 854 Shawano rd., Ft. H.
Perry Catherine Mrs., res. Odd Fellows' Home.
Perry George, pipe-fitter, res. 1028 Doty.
Pesichek Vaclav, lab., res. 718 Main.
**PETCKA JAMES**, saloon, 322 Main, res. same.
Peterman Charles (Peterman & Foster), res. 114 S. 12th.
Peterman & Foster (Charles Peterman and Wm. Foster), blacksmiths, 1145 Main.
Peters Alex., lab., res. Empire House.
Peters Constance, lab., res. n. s. Bond, 9 w. Cedar, Ft. H.
Peters Ernst, baker, 322 Pine, res. same.
Peters Ernest, lab., res. 628 Pleasant.
Peters Gertrude L., tel.-opr., res. 408 Willow, Ft. H.
Peters Joseph, lab., res. 1362 Willow.
Peters Joseph, lab., res. 628 Pleasant.
Peters Lizzie Miss, res. 325 S. Adams.
Peters Matthias, res. n. e. cor. St. Clair and N. 12th.
Peters Peter Joseph, res. 628 Pleasant.
Peters Squire W., cooper, res. 408 Willow, Ft. H.
Peters Walter D., student, res. 408 Willow, Ft. H.
Peters William, lab., res. n. s. Bond, 9 w. Cedar, Ft. H.
Peters William, brakeman, res. Northwestern Hotel, Ft. H.
Petersen Anson, cooper, res. 110 N. Quincy.
Petersen August, blksmith, res. e. s. Willow, 1 n. Baird, Ft. H.
Petersen Christian, lab., res. w. s. 3d av., 4 s. 2d, Ft. H.
Petersen Emma, dressmkr, res. 101 Chestnut, Ft. H.
Petersen Fred, foreman pickle factory, res. 102 Hubbard, Ft. H.
Petersen Hans, carp., res. 608 2d, Ft. H.
Petersen Henry N., foreman Green Bay Advocate, res. n. s. Baird, near the slough, Ft. H.
Petersen Millie, domestic 441 S. Adams.
Peterson Adolph Rev., pastor Norwegian Lutheran Church, res. 106 Chestnut, Ft. H.

Peterson Alexander, lab., res. Howard House, Ft. H.
Peterson Anna B. Miss, res. 920 S. Madison.
Peterson August, blksmith, 144 Broadway, Ft. H., res. same.
Peterson August, conductor, res. w. s. McDonald, 9 s. lumber yd., Ft. H.
Peterson Charles, carp., res. 206 3d av., Ft. H.
Peterson Christian, lab., res. 300 7th av., Ft. H.
Peterson Christine, domestic 123 6th av., Ft. H.
Peterson Claus G., motorman, res. w. s. Broadway, 4 s. Hubbard, Ft. H.
Peterson Cornelius E., loco.-eng., res. 426 Howard.
Peterson Edward. mill-hand, res. n. s. St. Clair, 1 e. N. 11th.
Peterson Ida O. Miss, res. 920 S. Madison.
Peterson John, horseshoer, res. Parmentier blk.
Peterson Julia, dressmkr, res. 201 3d av., Ft. H.
Peterson Louis, fireman C., M. & St. P. R. R., res. 920 S. Madison.
Peterson Myron L., night clk. Am. Exp. Co., 224 N. Adams.
Peterson Olava Mrs., carpet-weaver, 807 Cherry, Ft. H., res. same.
Peterson Peter, lake captain, res. 920 S. Madison.
Peterson Peter, lab., res. Hall House, Ft. H.
Peterson Tena B. Miss, res. 920 S. Madison.
Peterson Thomas, horse shoer, 144 Broadway, res. 140 Broadway, Ft. H.
Peterson Willis H., livery, w. end Walnut street bridge, res. 407 Cherry, Ft. H.
Petry Adeline Miss, res. 808 Walnut.
Petry Carrie Miss, res. 808 Walnut.
Petry Frederick, shoemkr, res. 808 Walnut.
Petry Mary, dressmkr, res. 808 Walnut.
Pfeiffer Christian, lab., res. s. s. Main, 1 e. Forest.
Pfeifler William, lab., res. n. s. Main, 1 s. Newhall, Town Preble.
Pfotenhauer Albert, res. 1303 Cedar.
Pfotenhauer Charles, carp., res. s. Cedar Creek rd.
Pfotenhauer Charles W., res. 1303 Cedar.
**PFOTENHAUER CHARLES JR.**, saloon, 216 Cherry, res. 325 S. Adams.
Pfotenhauer Frank, barkpr. Charles Pfotenhauer, res. 325 S. Adams.
Pfotenhauer Herman, teamster, res. s. s. Main, 1 e. Newhall.
Pfotenhauer Louise, teacher, res. 325 S. Adams.
Phelps Charles C., com.-trav. 124 S. Washington, res. 801 Broadway, Ft. H.

**THE A. SPUHLER CO., GREEN BAY, WIS.** **Fine Dress Goods**
Samples Furnished on Application.

Phelps John, foreman, res. Ferris Hotel, Ft. H.
Philipps Frederick, hostler, res. W. H. Peterson's livery.
Philips Peter, lab., res. e. s. Grove, bet. Elm and Willow.
Phillips Charles F., cigarmkr, res. 601 Mather, Ft. H.
Phillips Elisha A., carpenter, res. 803 S. Van Buren.
Phillips Ruth (wid. John), res. 619 S. Quincy.
Philpot Stanton, carp., res. Bradley House.
Piarce Martha (wid. Henry), res. w. s. 2d av., 4 s. 7th, Ft. H.
Piaskowski Joseph, lab., res. 1285 Doty.
Piaskowski Juliana (wid. John), res. 1285 Doty.
Piaskowski Michael, lab., res. 1285 Doty.
Pierrot Frank, lab., res. s. s. Main, 1 e. Grove.
Pigeon Desire, beer peddler, res. 1412 Elm.
Pigeon Desire, lab., res. 1533 Harvey.
Pigeon Desire, lab., res. 1116 Main.
Pigeon Emma Miss, res. 1412 Elm.
Pigeon Frank J., bookpr. Green Bay Plumbing and Heating Co., res. 1116 Main.
Pigeon John, clk. Wm. Hoffman, res. 1116 Main.
Pigeon Joseph, lab., res. 1533 Harvey.
Pigeon Joseph, molder, res. 1412 Elm.
Pigeon Joseph, student, res. 1116 Main.
Pigeon Julia Miss, clk., res. 1412 Elm.
Pigeon Mary Miss, clk. The A. Spuhler Co., res. 1116 Main.
Pigeon Peter J., groceries and crockery, 1114 Main, res. 1116 Main.
Pilligor Charles, hostler Adams House.
Piraux Frank, brick mnfr., cor. Porlier and Goodell, res. 1432 Porlier.
Piraux Henry, brickmr. res. 1528 Main.
Piraux Joseph, grocer, 711 Main, res. same.
Piraux Julia Mrs., res. 425 N. 10th.
Piraux Lucy F. Miss, res. 1432 Porlier.
Piraux Otto, bookkpr. Frank Piraux, res. 1432 Porlier.
Piraux Sarah Miss, res. 1432 Porlier.
Pire Emil, drayman, res. 1114 Stuart.
Pireaux August, with The A. Spuhler Co., res. 915 Crooks.
Pirlet Desire, carp., res. 1120 Walnut.
Piron Sidonia (wid. Fred.), res. 783 Elmore, Ft. H,
**PISKE FRANK**, carp.-contr., 327 S. Webster av., res. same.
Pitt Otto, boilermkr, res. Northwestern Hotel, Ft. H.
Planert August G., boots and shoes, 205 Broadway, Ft. H., res. Hall House.

Planert Frank C., shoemkr, res. 505 Broadway, Ft. H.
Plantikow Christine Miss, res. Manitowoc House.
Plantikow John, prop. Manitowoc House, 819 Main, res. same.
Plashalhart Bruno, mill-hand, res. McDonald st., near lumber yard, Ft. H.
Plato Helen (wid. John B.), res. 320 S. Washington.
Platten Albert L., grocer, 310 Dousman, res. n. e. cor. Dousman and Chestnut, Ft. H.
Platten Annie Miss, clk. J. J. Platten & Son, res. 514 Cherry, Ft. H.
Platten Anton G. (Platten Bros.), res. 406 Willow, Ft. H.
Platten Bros. (Anton G. and Peter Platten), meat-market, 305 Main and s. s. Dousman, 1 w. Broadway, Ft. H.
Platten Hattie Miss, res. 701 Elmore, Ft. H.
Platten Hattie Miss, res. 404 Willow, Ft. H.
Platten Henry J. (J. J. Platten & Sons), res. 514 Cherry, Ft. H.
Platten J. J. & Sons (Joseph J., Joseph M. and Henry J. Platten), grocers, s. s. Dousman, 2 w. Broadway, Ft. H.
Platten John, book seller, res. 701 Elmore, Ft. H.
Platten Joseph, switchman, res. n. s. Elmore, 5 w. Cedar, Ft. H.
Platten Joseph J. (J. J. Platten & Sons), res. 514 Cherry, Ft. H.
Platten Joseph M.(J. J. Platten & Sons), res. 514 Cherry, Ft. H.
Platten Katie Miss, res. 514 Cherry, Ft. H.
Platten Mamie Miss, teacher, res. 701 Elmore, Ft. H.
Platten Matt., bookpr. J. J. Platten & Sons, res. 514 Cherry, Ft. H.
Platten Peter (Platten Bros.), res. 404 Willow, Ft. H.
Pleimling Nicolas Rev., res. s. w. cor. Cass and S. 12th.
Ploeger Mary, domestic 700 Pine.
Plumb Ernest A., weighmaster, res. 106 Cherry, Ft. H.
Plunkett Eliza Miss, res. 600 Pine.
Plunkett Henry, clk., res. 600 Pine.
Plunkett Jennie Miss, res. 600 Pine.
Pocan Addie Miss, res 202 S. Jefferson.
Podore Lillie Miss, res. 615 Cedar.
Pohl Theresa Miss, res. 1200 Doty.
Pohl William, clk., res. 1202 Doty.
Poirys Guillaume, lab., res. 214 Main.
Police Station, 34 Parmentier blk.
Polacheck George, lab., res. Coopertown House.
Polasky Annie, domestic 103 S. Monroe av.
Polasky Gertrude, domestic 806 Crooks.
Polson Annie Miss, res. w. s. 2d av., 4 s. 9th, Ft. H.
Polson Bernt, mill-hand, res. w. s. 2d av., 4 s. 9th, Ft. H.

**Headquarters for Boys' Clothing THE A. SPUHLER CO., GREEN BAY.**

Polson Olivia Miss, res. w. s. 2d av., 4 s. 9th, Ft. H.
Pommier Mary Miss, res. 627 S. Madison.
Pommier Melanie (wid. Francis J.), res. 627 S. Madison.
Poquette Sophie (wid. Louis), res. 721 S. Webster av.
Poquette William, lab., res. 706 2d, Ft. H.
Poquin Thomas, sawyer, res. Columbia Hotel.
Porth Henry (Porth & Harman), res. 401 Willow.
Porth & Harman (Henry Porth and William Harman), coopers, 401 Willow.
Post Michael, barn boss, res. American House.
Postoffice, Ft. Howard, A. E. Elmore, P. M., 109 N. Broadway, Ft. H.
**POSTOFFICE,** Green Bay, Gustave Küstermann, P. M., n. e. cor. N. Adams and Cherry.
Postal Telegraph Cable Co., Nettie I. Leppere, mngr., 322 N. Washington.
Pott Augusta, domestic 309 N. Jefferson.
Potter Augustus E., engineer W.W. Cargill Co., res. 501 Spring.
Potter Elwood A., clk. A. & E. Lehman, res. 501 Spring.
Potts Ena K., milliner, res. 310 S. Washington.
Potts Frank S., student, res. 310 S. Washington.
Potts John, carsmith, res. 421 S. Washington.
Potts May S., bkpr., res. 310 S. Washington.
Potts Samuel G., res. 310 S. Washington.
Potts Samuel G. Mrs., milliner, 209 N. Washington, res. 310 S. Washington.
**POWERS ALBERT W. CAPT.,** prop. The Beaumont, res. same.
Powers Ellen (wid. Thomas), res. 210 Willow, Ft. H.
Praeger Edward, plumber, res. Commercial Hotel, Ft. H.
Prentice William L., well-driller, res. St. James Hotel.
Preston Samuel, watchman, res. 669 Cedar, Ft. H.
Preville Agnes Miss, music teacher, res. 525 S. Quincy.
Preville Albert, tinsmith, res. 525 S. Quincy.
Preville Louis Mrs., res. 525 S. Quincy.
Prevot Adolphine Mrs., res. 1146 Pine.
Prevot Joseph, engineer, res. 1146 Pine.
Prevot Sarah, tailoress, res. 1146 Pine.
Priem Hannah, domestic Arlington Hotel, Ft. H.
Prieve Herman A., grocer, 647 S. Jackson, res. same.
Prieve Herman, lab., res. 1119 Doty.
Prieve William, lab., res. 1119 Doty.
Prince Annie, res. 529 N. 12th.
Prince Fernande (wid. Henry), res. **529 N. 12th.**

Pritchard James, carp., res. 1111 Doty.
Proctor Allen J., fireman, res. s. e. cor. 7th av. and 1st, Ft. H.
Puerner Delphie Miss, res. 122 Broadway, Ft. H.
Puerner Emma (wid. Charles), res. 122 Broadway, Ft. H.
Puerner Otto F. W., barber, 208 3d av., res. 122 Broadway, Ft. H.
Puissaint Clement, lab., res. 325 Willow, Ft. H.
Punge Peter, vet. surgeon, res. Schauer Hotel.
Putnam Paulina (wid. A. G.), res. 119 N. Van Buren.
Putney Clarence, res. 526 S. Jefferson.
Puttmans Thomas, lab., res. 1145 Chicago.
Pymm Lucie Miss, dressmkr, res. 308 Willow.
Pymm Marie E. (wid. Wm.), res. 308 Willow, Ft. H.
Pymm May S. Miss, dressmkr, res. 308 Willow, Ft. H.

## Q

QUATSOE Celia, saloon, 230 Walnut, res. same.
Quatsoe Frank L., bookkpr. Knox & Wilner, res. 110 S. Madison.
Quatsoe John, farmer, res. e. s. De Pere rd., 1 n. Hochgreve brewery.
Quatsoe Silvia Miss, milliner, res. 303 N. Jefferson.
Quenney John, conductor, res. Northwestern Hotel, Ft. H.
Quick Joseph, mngr. St. James Hotel, res. same.
Quigley Bartholomew, plumber, res. 1176 Mason.
Quigley Gussie, dressmkr, res. 1113 Mason.
Quigley Lary, clk., res. 1176 Mason.
Quigley Michael, lab., res. 1113 Mason.
Quigley Michael J., clk. A. Kimball, res. w. s. Quincy, 1 s. Cass.
Quigley Thomas, teamster, res. 1176 Mason.
Quigley Thomas Jr., painter, res. 1176 Mason.
Quinn Bessie (wid. Richard), res. 412 Willow, Ft. H.
Quinn Deliah Miss, nurse, res. 509 S. Monroe av.

## R

RAATZ Amanda, domestic 344 S. Monroe av.
Rabek Adolph, blksmith, res. 407 N. Webster av.
Rabenhorst William, lab., res. 1125 Stuart.
Rabidos Louisa Miss, res. w. s. Pearl, 4 s. Hubbard, Ft. H.
**RADELET GUST,** saloon, 119 N. Adams, res. same.
Radick Anna, domestic, res. 402 2d, Ft. H.
Radue Annie, domestic 315 S. Webster av.
Radue William, lab., res. 227 S. Jackson.

**THE A. SPUHLER CO.** *LADIES', MISSES' and CHILDREN'S*
**GREEN BAY** **CLOAKS, CAPES, JACKETS**

Raduns Ida, domestic Bay City House.
Rahn Anna Miss, res. n. w. cor. Main and Newhall.
Rahn Charles, drayman, res. n. w. cor. Main and Newhall.
Rahn Charles Jr., clk., res. n. w. cor. Main and Newhall.
Rahn Emma Miss, dressmkr, res. n. w. cor. Main and Newhall.
Rahn Ida, domestic 803 Cherry.
Rahn William Jr., res. s. s. Finger rd., 3 e. Manitowoc rd.
Rahr Angeline (wid. Henry), res. 103 S. Monroe av.
Rahr Angeline Miss, res. 103 S. Monroe av.
Rahr Fred A. (Henry Rahr's Sons), res. 103 S. Monroe av.
Rahr Henry (Henry Rahr's Sons), res. 103 S. Monroe av.
**RAHR'S HENRY SONS** (Fred A. and Henry Rahr), props. East River Brewery, 1317-1323 Main.
Raiche Emily Miss, res. 1028 Cedar.
Raiche Frederick, lab., res. 1028 Cedar.
Raiche Ida Miss, res. 1028 Cedar.
Raiche Israel, carpenter, res. 1028 Cedar.
Raiche Magdalene Miss, dressmkr, res. 1028 Cedar.
Raiche Minnie Miss, dressmkr, res. 1028 Cedar.
Raleigh Charles, lab., res. s. s. Bond, 2 w. Willow, Ft. H.
Raleigh Henry, res. s. s. Bond, 2 w. Willow, Ft. H.
Raleigh Josephine Miss, res. s. s. Bond, 2 w. Willow, Ft. H.
Ranard Gertie (wid. Joseph), res. 132 S. Jackson.
Randall Jenny (wid. Sebastian), res. 722 Cedar.
Ranous George E., conductor C. & N. W. R. R., res. 525 Chestnut, Ft. H.
Ranous James E. res. 525 Chestnut, Ft. H.
Rasmussen Andrew, fireman, res. 900 3d av., Ft. H.
Rasmussen Charles, engineer, res. Junction Hotel, Ft. H.
Rasmussen Christian P., fisherman, res. 1281 Cherry.
Rasmussen Edward, engineer, res. 115 5th av., Ft. H.
Rasmussen John, coachman 904 S. Monroe av.
Rasmussen Maggie (wid. Hans), res. 1281 Cherry.
Ratajczak Michael, res. 1320 Stuart.
Ratajczak Peter, blksmith, res. 1320 Stuart.
Ratelle Henry, delivery-clk. Allouez Mineral Spring Co., res. John, Ft. H.
Rathman Emma, teacher, res. 831 Main.
Rathman Natalie (wid. Henry), res. 831 Main.
Rauch Benedict, cooper, res. 418 N. Madison.
Rawley Frank, res. 321 Cass.
Rawley Frank Jr., conductor C. & N. W. Ry., res. 515 S. Madison.
Rawley Jules, clk. 124 S. Washington, res. 317 Cass.

Rawlings Joseph P., general sec. Young Men's Christian Assn. res. 121 Chestnut, Ft. H.
Ray James, teamster, res. 826 S. Jackson.
Raymakers Catherine Miss, res. Town Preble.
Raymakers George (H. Raymakers & Sons), res. Town Preble.
Raymakers H. & Sons (Herman, Leonard, Martin, Henry, John, William, George and Peter Raymakers) grocers, gardeners and produce, 1400-1402 Main.
Raymakers Helena Miss, res. Town Preble.
Raymakers Henry (H. Raymakers & Sons), res. s. e. cor. Cedar and Pleasant.
Raymakers Herman, tailor, res. 1250 Walnut.
Raymakers Herman (H. Raymakers & Sons), res. Town Preble.
Raymakers John (H. Raymakers & Sons), res. Town Preble.
Raymakers John, tailor, res. 1243 Walnut.
Raymakers Leonard (H. Raymakers & Sons), res. Town Preble.
Raymakers Martin (H. Raymakers & Sons), res. Town Preble.
Raymakers Martin, wagonmkr, res. 324 S. 10th.
Raymakers Peter (H. Raymakers & Sons), res. Town Preble.
Raymakers Peter J., tailor, res. 1243 Walnut.
Raymakers Wm. (H. Raymakers & Sons), res. Town Preble.
Raymaster Andree, butcher, res. 311 S. Van Buren.
Raymaster Frank, cigarmkr, res. 311 S. Van Buren.
Raymond Edwin A., engineer, res. 607 Cherry, Ft. H.
Raymond Mariette (wid. Alonzo), res. 607 Cherry, Ft. H.
Reber Annie (wid. Henry C.), res. 717 Cherry.
Reber Hattie Miss, res. 717 Cherry.
Reber Henry C., life ins. agent, res. 331 S. Quincy.
Reber Llewellyn C., sec. and treas. Columbian Baking Co., res. 720 S. Webster av.
**REDEMAN CHARLES W.** (Geo. Haupt & Co.), prop. Charles House, res. same.
Redeman Ella Miss, res. Charles House.
Redeman Otto, clk , res. Charles House.
Redline Benjamin H., clk. U. S. Express Co., res. 412 N. Adams.
Redline Edward T., res. 412 N. Adams.
Redline Harriet M. Miss, res. 412 N. Adams.
Redline Joseph S., sailor, res. 412 N. Adams.
Redman August, tailor, 702 Main, res. same.
Redman Reinhard, tailor, res. 702 Main.
Reed August J., machinist, res. 501 Main, Ft. H.
Reed Edmund, fireman, res. s. s. Elmore. 7 w. Cedar, Ft. H.
Reed James, farmer, res. s. s. Duck Creek rd., 12 w. Mather, Ft. H.

**THE A. SPUHLER CO., Green Bay** CARPETS, RUGS, OIL CLOTHS
Draperies and Window Shades.

Reed James, lab., res. s. s. Elmore, 7 w. Cedar, Ft. H.
Reed Mary Miss, res. s. s. Elmore, 7 w. Cedar, Ft. H.
Reed Michael, boilermkr, res. s. s. Elmore, 7 w. Cedar, Ft. H.
Regnier Lucian, boilermkr, res. Ferris Hotel, Ft. H.
Reinard Katie Miss, res. 724 Pine.
Reinecke Henry M. (Reinecke & Wendorff), supt. **Woodlawn Cemetery**, res. 118 S. Jefferson.
**REINECKE & WENDORFF** (Henry M. Reinecke and Hermann C. Wendorff), florists, 112 S. Jefferson.
Reinhardt Ella Miss, dressmkr, 206 N. Adams, res. same.
Reinhart Ella Miss, teacher, res. 109 Chestnut, Ft. H.
Reinhart Ellen (wid. Caleb), res. 109 Chestnut, Ft. H.
Reinhart Sarah Miss, dressmkr, res. 109 Chestnut, Ft. H.
Reis Andrew, res. 1124 Doty.
**REIS ANDREW JR.**, prop. Reis Hotel, res. same.
Reis Anna M. Miss, res. 531 S. Adams.
Reis Frederick L., delivery-clk., res. 531 S. **Adams**.
Reis George J., butcher, res. 531 S. Adams.
**REIS HOTEL**, Andrew Reis Jr., prop., 1148 Main.
Reis Jacob, cigar mnfr., 1142 Main, res. same.
**REIS LEONHARD L.**, meat market, 210 **N. Adams**, res. 531 S. Adams.
Reis Louis A., butcher, res. 531 S. Adams.
Reis William, butcher, res. 531 S. Adams.
Reiter Dominic, cigarmkr, res. 520 N. Jefferson.
Remich Anton, barber, 211 Pine, res. 221 S. Webster av.
Remich Henry, barber, res. 332 S. Monroe av.
Remich John, barber, res. 332 S. Monroe av.
Remich Mathias, barber, 307 Main, res. 332 S. Monroe av.
Remich Mollie Miss, retoucher, res. 332 S. Monroe av.
Renard Donie, lab., res. 316 S. Van Buren.
Renard Ernst, lab., res. 316 S. Van Buren.
Renard Jerome, photographer, 313 N. Quincy, res. 316 S. **Van Buren**.
Renard Jule, tailor, res. 316 S. Van Buren.
Rene Mary Miss, dressmkr, 36 Parmentier blk., res. same.
Rene Mary (wid. Eugene), res. 36 Parmentier blk.
Renier Emil, lab., res. 1435 Cedar.
Renier Felix, lab., res. w. s. 2d av., 3 s. 9th, Ft. H.
Renier Joseph, lab., res. w. s. 2d av., 3 s. 9th, Ft. H.
Reno Louis, stonectr., res. 2 w. 874 Dousman, Ft. H.
Rentmeester Henry, lab., res. 1255 Doty.
Rentmeester William, lab., res. w. s. Oak, 2 s. **Shawano av.**, Ft. H.

Resch Belle Miss, res. 703 S. Monroe av.
Resch May Miss, res. 703 S. Monroe av.
Resch Nettie Miss, res. 703 S. Monroe av.
Reschke Fred L., carp., res. 1336 Porlier.
Reschke Julius, lab., res. 1124 Mason.
Reschke Mary Miss, res. 1336 Porlier.
Reschke Minnie (wid. William), res. 1336 Porlier.
Reschke Ottilie Miss, res. 1336 Porlier.
Retzlaff Bertha, domestic 1184 N. Washington.
Retzlaff Siegfried, carpenter, res. 425 Main.
Reubel George, sawyer, res. 403 3d av., Ft. H.
Reuter William, clk. G. Küstermann, res. 126 N. Washington.
Reynen Anton, lab., res. e. s. De Pere rd., 6 s. city limits.
Reynen Ella Miss, res. e. s. De Pere rd., 6 s. city limits.
Reynen Martin, lab., res. e. s. De Pere rd., 6 s. city limits.
Reynen Matthias, farmer, res. e. s. De Pere rd., 6 s. city limits.
Reynen Wm., brakeman, res. e. s. De Pere rd., 6 s. city limits.
Reynolds A. Heber, cashier Joannes Bros., res. 435 S. Webster av.
Reynolds Adin H., cook, res. 608 Cherry, Ft. H.
Reynolds Clarence, tel.-operator, res. 832 Shawano rd., Ft. H.
Reynolds Werden, res. 435 S. Webster av.
Rhode Atha, res. 315 N. Jefferson.
Rhode Henry, physician, 226 N. Washington, res. 315 N. Jefferson.
Rhode Henry P., physician, 226 N. Washington, res. 315 N. Jefferson.
Rhode Ida Miss, res. 315 N. Jefferson.
Rhoder August, carp., res. 118 N. Monroe av.
Rice Cyrenus A., brakeman, res. e. s. 4th av., 3 s. 7th, Ft. H.
Rice Margaret (wid. Aaron), res e. s. 4th av., 3 s. 7th, Ft. H.
Rice Thomas H. (Wright Bros. & Rice), res. The Beaumont.
Richard Albert, lab., res. 1263 Main.
Richardson Birdie Miss, res. 1149 Cherry.
Richardson Edward C., conductor, res. 729 S. Adams.
Richardson George, res. 801 Broadway, Ft. H.
Richardson George A., bkpr. McCartney Nat. Bank, res. 801 Broadway, Ft. H.
Richardson John R., bkpr., res. 1149 Cherry.
Richter Alois, tailor, res. Bay City House.
Richter John, butcher, res. s. s. Mather, 1 w. Willow, Ft. H.
Richter John P., coachman, res. 619 S. Quincy.
Richter Julia, domestic 723 Cherry.
Richter Michael, lab., res. 1362 Walnut.

**THE A. SPUHLER CO., GREEN BAY, WIS. Fine Dress Goods**
Samples Furnished on Application

Rickel Joseph, blksmith, res. 114 S. 12th.
**RICKLIN LEO. A. REV.**, pastor St. John's Church, res. 413 Milwaukee.
Riley Joseph, conductor, res. s. w. cor. Dousman and Cedar, Ft. H.
Riley Julia Miss, res. s. w. cor. Dousman and Cedar, Ft. H.
Riley Maggie Mrs., res. w. s. 11th av., near G. B., W. & St. P. shops, Ft. H.
Riley Marie (wid. Terrence), res. s. w. cor. Dousman and Cedar, Ft. H.
Riley Matthew C., res. s. w. cor. Dousman and Cedar, Ft. H.
Riley Thomas, lab., res. n. w. cor. 3d and 10th av., Ft. H.
Riley William, conductor, res. s. w. cor. Dousman and Cedar, Ft. H.
Ringer Desire, lab., res. 1283 Day.
Ringer Emil, lab., res. 1283 Day.
Ringer Jeremias, res. 1283 Day.
Ringer Joseph, sailor, res. 1283 Day.
**RINGSDORF WARREN M.**, dentist, 319 Broadway, Ft. H., res. same.
Riordan Ella, domestic 531 Main, Ft. H.
Rippe Gebhard, confectr, res. Bay City House.
Ritchie Joshua, engineer, res. 820 Walnut.
Ritter Anna M. Miss, res. 1247 Cedar.
Ritter William, res. 113 S. Monroe av.
Ritz Elizabeth (wid. Bonifacius), res. 1354 Stuart.
Ritz John, lab., res. 1354 Stuart.
Roaur Mary, domestic 605 Cherry.
Robb James, sec. and treas. Green Bay Planing Co., res. n. s. Porlier, bet. S. Monroe av. and S. Quincy.
Robert Denis, lab., res. 12th, cor. Smith.
Robert Joseph, lab., res. 415 Cedar.
Robert Spencer, res. 610 Elmore, Ft. H.
Roberts Alexander, mill-hand, res. w. s. 9th, near R. R. crossing, Ft. H.
Roberts Eli, clk. Jos. Spitz, res. 812 Walnut.
Roberts John K., book agt., res. w. s. 5th av., 2 n. 10th, Ft. H.
Roberts Joseph, butcher, res. 812 Walnut.
Roberts Michael, teamster, res. 812 Walnut.
Roberts R. C., agt. windmills, etc., res. Reis Hotel.
Roberts William, bottler Henry Rahr's Sons, res. 1120 Walnut.
Robillard Napoleon, barkpr., res. 316 Main.
**ROBILLARD PETER**, saloon and hotel, 316 Main, res. same.

Robinson Abbie B. Miss, clk. money order dept. P. O., res. 416 Lawe.
Robinson Albert C. (Lehman & Robinson), res. 416 Lawe.
Robinson Alexander, gardener, res. 873 Dousman, Ft. H.
Robinson Belle Miss, music teacher, res. 510 Chestnut, Ft. H.
Robinson Emilie Miss, clk. money order dept. P. O., res. 416 Lawe.
Robinson Erwin, teamster, res. Eldred's boarding house, Ft. H.
Robinson Frank, lumberman, res. 719 Cherry.
Robinson Henry, lab., res. 402 3d av., Ft. H.
Robinson James, barn boss, res. Eldred's boarding house, Ft. H.
Robinson James W., res. 221 N. Madison.
Robinson John, druggist, wholesale and retail, 228 N. Washington, res. 519 Walnut.
Rock Charles T., trunkmkr, res. 215 Main.
Rock John, sawyer, res. Eldred's boarding house, Ft. H.
Rockstroh Charles J. F., ship.-clk., 124 S. Washington, res. 226 Pine.
Rockstroh Edward A., baker, res. 115 N. Adams.
**ROCKSTROH JOHN C.**, bakery and confectionery, 115 N. Adams, res. same.
Rodgers Peter, switchman, res. 736 S. Jefferson.
Roemer Daniel H., salesman 1155 Main, res. Columbia Hotel
Roeser Anna (wid. Simon), res. 1200 Day.
Roeser Philip, maltster Henry Rahr's Sons, res. 1320 Cedar.
Roffus John, sec. and treas. Standard Printing Co., res. West Depere.
Rogalski Albert, porter Cook's Hotel.
Rogalski August, carp., res. 1102 S. Van Buren.
Rogalski August Jr., carp., res. 815 S. Jackson.
Rogalski Augusta Miss, res. 1221 S. Jackson.
Rogalski Edith, domestic, res. 812 Emilie.
Rogalski Emma, dressmkr, res. 1007 Mason.
Rogalski Frederick, lab., res. 1221 S. Jackson.
Rogalski Fred, switchman, res. 321 Chicago.
Rogalski Henry, janitor, res. 1007 Mason.
Rogalski Jennie, head chambermaid Cook's Hotel.
Rogalski Johanna, dressmkr, res. 812 Emilie.
Rogalski John, section hand, res. 812 Emilie.
Rogalski Julia, domestic 312 Lawe.
Rogalski Martha, dressmkr, res. 1102 S. Van Buren.
Rogalski Mathilda Miss, printer, res. 1007 Mason.
Rogalski Minnie, stenographer, res. 1007 Mason.
Rogalski Pauline, domestic 826 Mason.

**Headquarters for Boys' Clothing** THE A. SPUHLER CO. GREEN BAY.

Rogalski Rudolph, lab., res. 1263 Crooks.
Rogalski Rudolph A., marble-cutter, res. 1102 S. Van Buren.
Rohan Ann (wid. John), res. 632 Cherry.
Rohan Ella Miss, teacher, res. 632 Cherry.
Rohan James, res. 632 Cherry.
Rohan Mary Miss, res. 632 Cherry.
Roland Leo, brakeman, res. Commercial Hotel, Ft. H.
Rollin Joseph, carp., res. 1155 Doty.
Rollin Joseph, fireman, res. 302 Stuart.
Rollin Sylvia, domestic American House.
Rollin Victoria, domestic American House.
Romain Frank, res. 117 S. Jackson.
Romain Henry, lab., res. 117 S. Jackson.
Romson Peter A., porter 124 S. Washington, res. 215 S. Van Buren.
Rondou Alphonse, res. s. s. Elmore, 11 w. Cedar, Ft. H.
Rondou Emanuel, clk. A Brauns, res. 1161 Walnut.
Rondou F. Zacharias, notary public and insurance, 220 N. Washington, res. 1161 Walnut.
Rondou Louis, lab., res. 1161 Walnut.
Roohr Charles, lab., res. s. s. Main, 2 e. city limits, Town Preble.
Rooney Libbie (wid John), res. 429 N. Jackson.
Root Andrew J., cooper, res. 801 Main.
Root Erastus, printer, 225 Pine, res. 114 N. Monroe av.
Root Etta Miss, res. 801 Main.
Root Louis, printer, res. 114 N. Monroe av.
Root Marion Miss., res. 114 N. Monroe av.
Ropeik Frank, res. w. s. Pearl, 3 s. Hubbard, Ft. H.
Ropeik Fred., lab., res. w. s. Pearl, 3 s. Hubbard, Ft. H.
Roppel Conrad, lab., res. s. s. Main, 3 e. Forest.
Roppel Louis, lab., res. s. s. Main, 3 e. Forest.
Rose Annie Miss, res. 701 S. Webster av.
Rose Carl, carp., res. 701 S. Webster av.
Rose Charles, lab., res. 1436 Harvey.
Rose Felix, barber, res. 1263 Day.
Rose John, messenger the Kellogg Nat Bank, res 1263 Day.
**ROSE JOHN B.**, mason contractor, 1263 Day, res. same
Rose Jules, lab., res. 1436 Harvey.
Rose Julia Miss, res. 1263 Day.
Rose Pierre, res. 1436 Harvey.
Rose Rocelia Miss, res. 416 Cherry.
Rose Rudolph, carpenter, res. 701 S. Webster av.
Rose Victor, barber, 324 Main, res. 1263 Day.
Rosenberg Albert, peddler, res. 206 Cherry, Ft. H.

Rosenberg Joseph, clk., res. 206 Cherry, Ft. H.
Rosenberg Zacharias, peddler, res. 206 Cherry, Ft. H.
Roskams Catherine (wid. Peter), res. s. s. Elmore, 4 w. Cross rds., Ft. H.
Roskams Felix, gardener, res. s. s. Elmore, 4 w. Cross rds. Ft. H.
Ross John W., saloon, 309 N. Adams, res. same.
Ross William, res. 234 S. Jackson.
Rosse Martin, painter, 445 S. Madison, res. same.
Rossmiller Florian, machinist, res. 202 5th av., Ft. H.
Rost Caroline (wid. Charles), res. 719 Walnut.
Rostock August C., res. 1500 Mason.
Roszkowski John, lab., res. 1316 Stuart.
Roszkowski Peter, lab., res. 1316 Stuart.
Rotelle Henry, lab., res. John, s. e. cor. Broadway, Ft. H.
Rothe Bernard, blksmith, res. s. s. 2d, 2 w. R. R. track, Ft. H.
Rothe Charles B., saloon, 1375 Main, res. same.
Rothe Clara Miss, res. 717 Pine.
Rothe Frank, miller, res. 419 N. 12th.
**ROTHE JOSEPH F.**, prop. Green Bay Iron and Brass Foundry, 318 N. 11th, res. 1174 Cherry.
Rothe Peter, saloon, 1347 Main, res. same.
Rothe William, blksmith and wagonmkr, 312-314 N. Adams. res. 717 Pine.
Rothe William Jr., blksmith, res. 717 Pine.
Rouelle Louis, lab., res. 1270 Day.
Rouiller Annie, domestic 902 Main.
Roulette Alexander, engineer, res. 224 Walnut.
Roulette Alexander, whitewasher, res. 420 Elm.
Roulette Pinkney, lake captain, res. 420 Elm.
Rousseau Frank, lab., res. 1441 Cedar.
Rousseau Louis, grocer, 1021 Main, res. same.
Rouss's Saving Bank, Fred. Schuette, mngr. department store, 320 N. Washington.
Routhieaux John, plasterer, res. 1009 Harvey.
Roy Edward, lather, res. 812 S. Van Buren.
Roy Harriet Miss, res. 812 S. Van Buren.
Roy John, lather, res. 812 S. Van Buren.
Roy Magdalene Miss, res. 812 S. Van Buren.
Roy Napoleon, cutter Wm. Hoffman, res. 14 Parmentier blk.
Roy Thomas, carp.-contr., 812 S. Van Buren, res. same.
Ruby Mary (wid. Benjamin), res. 1122 Cedar.
Ruckum Anton, lab., res. 316 Main.
Ruckum Henry, lab., res. 316 Main.

**THE A. SPUHLER CO.** *LADIES', MISSES' and CHILDREN'S*
**GREEN BAY** — **CLOAKS, CAPES, JACKETS**

Ruckum Joseph, lab., res. 316 Main.
Rueckert Emma Miss, dressmkr, 1236 Cherry, res. same.
Rueckert Mary (wid. Gustav), res. 1236 Cherry.
Ruel Charles, cigarmkr, res. 801 Broadway, Ft. H.
**RUETH WILLIAM**, saloon, s. w. cor. 2d av. and 9th, Ft. H., res. same.
Ruf Annie Miss, dressmkr, res. 1251 Walnut.
Ruf John, painter, 1251 Walnut, res. same.
Ruf Louis, clk., res. 1251 Walnut.
Ruf William, painter, res. 1251 Walnut.
Ruggles Frederick D., foreman planing mill, res. s. w. cor. 7th av. and 1st, Ft. H.
Ruggles Henry M., clk. Hart's Steamboat Line, res. 214 Pine.
Rukamp A., lab., res. Main Street Hotel.
Rukamp Joseph, lab., res. Main Street Hotel.
Rukems Henry, lab., res. 1299 Cedar.
Rummel Eva (wid. Adam), res. 108 S. Quincy.
Rummel Lena Miss, compositor, res. 108 S. Quincy.
Ruppel Magdalene Miss, domestic 139 S. Madison.
Russell Frank, car cleaner, res. e. s. Hazel, 2 s. Shawano rd., Ft. H.
Russell Jennie Mrs., res. 309 3d av., Ft. H.
Rutten Joseph, cigar mnfr., 1111 Crooks, res. same.
Rutten Lucy Miss, res. 1111 Crooks.
Ruziska Frank, watchman, res. 810 3d av., Ft. H.
Ruziska Tony Miss, res. 810 3d av., Ft. H.
Ryan Clarence, brakeman, res. 608 S. Jefferson.
Ryan John, res. Adams House.
Ryan John, switchman, res. Northwestern Hotel, Ft. H.
Ryan John A., tailor, res. 332 S. Quincy.
Ryan Michael, lab., res. 800 Cherry, Ft. H.
Ryan Michael H., clk. C., M. & St. P. Ry., res. 134 S. Jackson.
Ryan Nora A., bookkpr. Annen Candy Co., res. 332 S. Quincy.
Ryan Patrick, res. 332 S. Quincy.
Ryan Patrick Jr., baker, res. 332 S. Quincy.
Ryan Peter J., foreman C., M. St. P. R. R., res. Bradley House.
Ryan Thomas F., clk., res. 332 S. Quincy.
Rymer Charles, ice peddler, res. 509 Broadway, Ft. H.
Rynders Marie (wid. Leonard), res. 1244 Walnut.

## S

SAFFORD Jos. W., printer, res. Broadway House, Ft. H.
Sager Alma Miss, res. 134 S. Jefferson.
Sager George C., printer, res. 134 S. Jefferson.

Sager Nelson L., machinist, res. 134 S. Jefferson.
Sabaroski Katie, domestic The Beaumont.
Saborsky Sadie, domestic 333 S. Webster av.
St. Clair William, saloon, res. w. s. 2d av., 2 s. 8th, Ft. H.
St. Francis Xavier Cathedral, n. w. cor. S. Monroe and Doty.
St. James Hotel, A. Church, prop., 117 S. Washington.
St. John H. H., fireman, res. Northwestern Hotel, Ft. H.
**ST. JOHN MINERAL WATER CO.**, W. C. Holzknecht, prop., n. s. Stuart, bet. S. Quincy and S. Jackson.
St. John's Church, n. s. Milwaukee, bet. S. Jefferson and S. Madison.
St. John's School, n. e. cor. Chicago and S. Jefferson.
St. Joseph's Convent, Sister Herman Joseph, superioress, 307 S. Jefferson.
**ST. JOSEPH'S ORPHAN ASYLUM**, Sister M. Melania, superioress, 403 S. Webster av.; branch house, Allouez Villa.
St. Louis Church (American Catholic), Most Rev. J. Rene Vilatte, archbishop, s. w. cor. Cass and S. 12th.
St. Louis Ethel Miss, res. 812 Crooks.
St. Louis Frank B., clk. 211 N. Washington, res. 614 Cherry.
St. Louis Ida Miss, res. 812 Crooks.
St. Louis Jas. J., hardware. 211 N. Washington, res. 614 Cherry.
St. Louis Mary (wid. Ephraim), res. 812 Crooks.
St. Louis Philip Rev., chaplain Good Shepard, res. 812 Crooks.
St. Patrick's Church, Cherry, n. e. cor. Hubbard, Ft. H.
St. Paul's Church (Luth.), n. w. cor. S. Madison and Stuart.
St. Peter and Paul Church, Rev. M. T. Anderegg, pastor, n. e. cor. Pleasant and Willow.
St. Vincent Hospital, 626 S. Quincy.
St. Vincent's School, in charge of the sisters of Notre Dame, s. s. Doty, bet. Adams and Jefferson.
St. Willebrod's Church, s. e. cor. S. Adams and Doty.
Sale Sarah (wid. Linus B.), res. 702 S. Monroe av.
Salmon Geraldine, domestic 421 N. Jefferson.
Salmon Joseph, carp., res. 1152 Pine.
Salmon Joseph Jr., carp., res. 1152 Pine.
Salmon Octave, lab., res. 1429 Cedar.
Salmon. See Solomon.
Salvas Clarence, salesman Jorgensen Blesch Co., res. 404 Chestnut, Ft. H
Salvas Hattie Mrs., clk. Jorgensen Blesch Co., res. 404 Chestnut, Ft. H.
Salvas May Miss, teacher 5th Ward, res. 404 Chestnut, Ft. H.

**THE A. SPUHLER CO., Green Bay** CARPETS, RUGS, OIL CLOTHS
Draperies and Window Shades.

**SALVATOR MINERAL SPRINGS**, J. P. C. Schmit, prop., s. e. cor. S. Monroe av. and Mason.
Salvo Archibald J., barber, res. 320 Pearl, Ft. H.
Salvo Louise, music teacher, res. 320 Pearl, Ft. H.
Salvo Peter, fisherman, res. 320 Pearl, Ft. H.
Sampson James, carp., res. n. w. cor. 3d and 9th av., Ft. H.
Sanborn Sarah (wid. Levi), res. 508 Walnut.
Sanders Joseph, cooper, res. Schauer Hotel.
Santy May (wid. Hiram), carpet-weaver, res. 300 N. 11th.
Sargent Chase L., engineer C., M. & St. P. R. R., res. 317 Lawe.
Sasse Celia A. Miss, res. s. s. Baird, 1 w. Willow, Ft. H.
Sasse Stanislaus, lab., res. s. s. Baird, 1 w. Willow, Ft. H.
Saunders Frederick, res. 709 2d, Ft. H.
Saunders George, fisherman, res. 709 2d, Ft. H.
Saunders J. & Co. (John Saunders and James Oliver), whol. dlrs. in fish, west approach Mason street bridge, Ft. H.
Saunders John (J. Saunders & Co.), res. 709 2d, Ft. H.
Savage Cornelius, brakeman, res. Ferris Hotel, Ft. H.
Savage James, conductor, res. Ferris Hotel, Ft. H.
Saylor D. May, dressmkr, res. 300 S. Madison.
Saylor Herbert A., lumber-tallier, res. 300 S. Madison.
Saylor Peter H., supt. A. L. Adams Lumber Co., res. 300 S. Madison.
Scannell Joseph, lab., res. 404 3d, Ft. H.
Scanlan Peter, res. 1314 Chicago.
Schaefer George H., clk. 129 S. Washington, res. Bay City House.
Schaefer Joseph, lineman, res. Charles House.
Schaefer Louis, engine-cleaner, res. 1201 S. Quincy.
Schaefer Philip, clk. 129 S. Washington, res. Bay City House.
Schanuel Martin, gardener, res. 1401 Harvey.
Schauer August (Schauer Bros.), res. 225 S. Monroe av.
**SCHAUER BROS.** (Peter J. and August Schauer), props. Schauer Hotel, 401 Main.
**SCHAUER HOTEL**, Schauer Bros. props., 401 Main.
Schauer Peter J. (Schauer Bros.), res. 401 Main.
Schaumberg Fred., music teacher, 831 Walnut, res. same.
Schaus Celia Miss, res. 1132 Walnut.
Schaus Maggie Miss, dressmkr, res. 1132 Walnut.
Schaus Philip, cigarmkr, res. 1132 Walnut.
Schaut Garrett, lab., res. n. s. Elm, 3 e. Forest, Town Preble.
Schaut Henry, lab., res. w. s. Manitowoc rd., 4 s. Bellevue.
Schaut Hubert, saloon, w. s. Manitowoc rd., 4 s. Bellevue, res. same.

Schaut Mary Miss, res. n. s. Elm, 3 e. Forest, Town Preble.
Schauwers Felix, mason-contr., 1120 Walnut, res. same.
Schavet Hattie Miss, dressmkr, res. 309 S. Webster av.
Schavet Julius, lab., res. 309 S. Webster av.
Schefe Fred. T., meat market, 114 3d av., res. 109 9th av., Ft. H.
Schefe Fred. J., blksmith, res. 109 9th av., Ft. H.
Schefe Henry, butcher, res. 109 9th av., Ft. H.
Schellenbeck Ottilie (wid. Jacob), res. 1125 Cedar.
Scheller Albert, del.-clk. The Weise-Hollman Co., res. 1291 Cedar.
Scheller Louise (wid. Albert), res. 210 Stuart.
Scheller Louis, taxidermist, 531 School, res. 535 School.
Scheller.  See Schiller.
Schepeck Frank, broom mnfr., 1258 Main, res. 1252 Main.
Schepeck.  See Shepeck.
Schorf Carl, tinsmith, res. 1101 Doty.
Scheuer Benjamin, mngr. Joseph Spitz, res. 125 S. Quincy.
Scheunert William, carpenter, res. 1308 Doty.
Scheuren Mary, domestic, res. 312 Stuart.
Schifller J. Albert, clk. Clark & Miller, res. s. e. cor. Elmore and Broadway, Ft. H.
Schilke Mary, domestic 317 Cass.
Schilke Otto, butcher, res. 505 Broadway, Ft. H.
Schilke William, farmer, res. e. s. Rich rd., 1 s. 9th, Ft. H.
**SCHILLER CLARA,** Louis G. Schiller, mngr., dlr. in fresh and salt fish, foot of N. Jefferson, res. 815 Cherry.
Schiller Gustav, clk. C. Schiller, res. 815 Cherry.
Schiller Julia Miss, res. 815 Cherry.
**SCHILLER LOUIS G.,** mngr. Clara Schiller, res. 815 Cherry.
**SCHILLING EDMUND,** dlr. butter, eggs and produce, 907 Main, res. Wequiock, Wis.
**SCHILLING FRANK C.,** mngr. E. Schilling, res. 907 Main.
Schilling Louis G. (C. W. Streckenbach & Co.), res. 406 N. Van Buren.
Schittkeker Theodore, lab., res. 1301 Porlier.
Schlag Nicholas, res. 921 Cherry.
Schleis Annie, dressmkr, s. e. cor. 5th av. and 9th, Ft. H., res. same.
Schleis Joseph, baker, res. s. e. cor. 5th av. and 9th, Ft. H.
Schmidt Anna, dressmkr, res. 1214 Chicago.
Schmidt Anna Maggie (wid. Johann George), res. 1344 Walnut.
Schmidt Bertha Miss, res. 619 S. 11th.
Schmidt Carl, lab., res. 1132 Chicago.

**THE A. SPUHLER CO., GREEN BAY, WIS.** **Fine Dress Goods**
Samples Furnished on Application.

SCH 213 SCH

Schmidt Carl, clk. Knox & Wilner, res. 619 Main.
Schmidt Charles F., cigarmkr, res. 1248 Day.
Schmidt Gustav (Wirtz & Schmidt), res. 256 Pearl, Ft. H.
Schmidt Gustave, boilermkr. res. 1356 Doty.
Schmidt Gustave, mason, res. 619 S. 11th.
Schmidt Hans, lab., res. 1132 Chicago.
**SCHMIDT HERMAN**, mason-contr., 619 S. 11th, res. same.
Schmidt John, lab., res. 315 6th av., Ft. H.
Schmidt William, blksmith, res. e. s. Chestnut, 1 n. Kellogg, Ft. H.
Schmidt William Jr., mechanic, res. 1214 Chicago.
Schmidt William C. (Mueller Bros. & Co.), res. 1214 Chicago.
Schmidt. See Schmit, Smits and Smith.
Schmit Catherine Miss, res. 601 S. Monroe av.
**SCHMIT JOHN P. C.**, whol. liquor dlr. and prop. Salvator Mineral Spring Water, 215 N. Washington, res. 601 S. Monroe av.
**SCHMITT JOSEPH F.**, saloon and restaurant, 118½ N. Washington, res. same.
Schmitz Frederick, lab., res. n. s. 2d, 2 w. 12th av., Ft. H.
Schmitz Garret, canvasser, res. 501 Pine.
Schmitz Henry, truss mnfr., 501 Pine, res. same.
Schmitz Henry P., hack driver, res. 215 N. Adams.
Schmitz Joseph, teamster, res. 307 8th av., Ft. H.
Schmitz Joseph J., horseshoer, res. 501 Pine.
**SCHMITZ PAUL N.**, horseshoer, 613 Main, res. 501 Pine.
Schmitz Richard, lab., res. w. s. 10th av., s. w. cor. 1st, Ft. H.
Schmitz Rudolph, carp., res. 307 8th av., Ft. H.
Schneider Charlotte (wid. John), res. w. s. S. Van Buren, het. Eliza and Emilie.
Schneider Frederick, mach., res. s. s. Shawano rd., 2 w. Oak, Ft. H.
Schneider Fred W., photographer, 310 N. Washington, res. 401 S. Monroe av.
Schneider John, lab., res. 1206 S. Jackson.
Schneider John Rev., pastor 1st M. E. Church, res. 403 Chestnut, Ft. H.
Schneider. See Snyder.
Schober Caroline Miss, dressmkr, res. 428 N. Madison.
Schober George, v.-pres. and supt. Hagemeister Brewing Co., res. Manitowoc rd.
Schober Leonard, cooper, 117 S. Quincy, res. 700 Walnut.
Schober Louis H. Jr., bkpr. The Green Bay Carriage Co., res. Manitowoc rd.

| SCH | 214 | SCH |
|---|---|---|

Schoch Benedict, res. 523 Cedar.
Schoch Joseph, cooper, res. 525 Cedar.
Schoch Oswald, cooper, res. 523 Cedar.
Schoellkopf Paul, brakeman, res. Ferris Hotel, Ft. H.
Schoemaker Catherine Miss, teacher, res. 342 S. Jefferson.
Schoemaker Frank W., asst. cashier C., M. & St. P. Ry., res. 342 S. Jefferson.
Schoemaker John A., res. 342 S. Jefferson.
Schoemaker John M., porter 124 S. Washington, res. 342 S. Jefferson.
Schoemaker. See Schumacher.
Schoen Frank, engineer, res. Schauer Hotel.
Schoepp, August, architect, res. 1403 Cedar.
Schoenauer Lorenz, lab., res. 1331 Elm.
Schoenauer Sebastian, lab., res. 1331 Elm.
Scholten John, engineer, res. 711 Chestnut, Ft. H.
Schoonen Alice, domestic The Beaumont.
Schoonen John, res. 1345 Harvey.
Schoonen Julia Miss, res. 1345 Harvey.
Schoonen Mary, laundress The Beaumont.
Schoonenberg Frank, night policeman C., M. & St. P. R. R., res. 1139 Crooks.
Schraa Angeline (wid. Hubert), res. 232 S. Van Buren.
Schraa Annie Miss, res. 932 Cherry.
Schraa Anton, clk. A. & E. Lehman, res. 932 Cherry.
Schraa John, lab., res. 932 Cherry.
Schraa Mary Miss, res. 932 Cherry.
Schraa Peter, clk. Buengener & Bur, res. 932 Cherry.
Schraa Veronica (wid. Joseph), res. 932 Cherry.
Schram Ella Miss, res. 708 Walnut.
Schram Frederick, lab., res. 708 Walnut.
Schram Susan Miss, res. 708 Walnut.
Schramm Henry, cigarmkr, res. 202 Dousman, Ft. H.
Schramm Julius, engineer, res. 105 N. Washington.
Schreck Conrad, carp., res. 1419 Crooks.
Schreiber Bertha, domestic n. e. cor. Dousman and Chestnut, Ft. H.
Schroeder Charles F., photographer, 313 N. Quincy, res. 639 Pine.
Schroeder Charles W., druggist, 930 Main, res. same.
Schroeder Clara, dressmkr, res. 1147 S. Quincy.
Schroeder Conrad, lab., res. 1147 S. Quincy.
Schroeder Emil, ins. agt., res. 1012 Dousman, Ft. H.
Schroeder Emil, lab., res. 1147 S. Quincy.

**Headquarters for Boys' Clothing** THE A. SPUHLER CO.
GREEN BAY.

Schroeder Emil, engineer, res. 1200 Walnut.
Schroeder Emma Miss, res. 639 Pine.
Schroeder Fred, lab., res. 1157 Stuart.
Schroeder Hannah Mrs., res. 1157 Stuart.
Schroeder Herman, brakeman, res. Bradley House.
Schroeder John J., mngr. Wisconsin Telephone Co., res. 106 N. Monroe av.
Schroeder Julius A., foreman Green Bay Planing Mill Co., res. 1147 S. Quincy.
Schroeder Lizzie Miss, res. 1157 Stuart.
Schroeders Frank, fireman, res. 429 N. Madison.
Schroeders Julius, lime, brick and sand, 427 Willow, res. 429 N. Madison.
Schroeders Nettie (wid. Joseph), res. 429 N. Madison.
Schroeders Pauline Miss, res. 429 N. Madison.
Schrubia Martha, domestic 303 S. Adams.
Schuette Clara Miss, music teacher, 621 Main, res. same.
Schuette Fred, mngr. Rouss's Savings Bank, res. 629 Main.
Schuette Joachim H., res. 621 Main.
Schulkowski Julius, lab., res. 1181 Mason.
Schultz Edward, machinist, res. 768 Shawano rd., Ft. H.
Schultz Peter, res. 409 2d, Ft. H.
Schultz. See Shultz.
Schumacher Arthur, res. 700 Cherry.
Schumacher Bros. (Hubert and Quirin Schumacher), meat markets, 314 and 924 Main.
Schumacher Ella Miss, res. 700 Cherry.
Schumacher Frank, res. 321 N. Webster av.
Schumacher Frank Jr., drug clk. R. Soquet, res. 309 N. Webster av.
Schumacher Henrietta (wid. John), res. 1239 Doty.
Schumacher Hubert (Schumacher Bros.), res. 309 N. Webster av.
Schumacher Hubert Q., butcher, res. 321 N. Webster av.
Schumacher John, res. 321 N. Webster av.
Schumacher John P. (Lefebvre & Schumacher), res. 700 Cherry.
Schumacher Josie C. Miss, res. 700 Cherry.
Schumacher Lizzie (wid. Michael), res. 1332 Stuart.
Schumacher Maggie Miss, res. 321 N. Webster av.
Schumacher Nicholas, lab., res. s. w. cor. 10th av. and 3d, Ft. H.
Schumacher Paulina Miss, res. 321 N. Webster av.
Schumacher Peter F., butcher, res. 926 Walnut.
Schumacher Quirin (Schumacher Bros.), res. 321 N. Webster av.

Schumacher. See Schoemaker.
Schumm Henrietta (wid. Wendel), res. w. s. Manitowoc rd., 1 s. Ellis creek.
Schunck Charles, painter, res. 345 S. Quincy.
**SCHUNCK CHARLES JR.**, cigar mnfr. and whol. tobacco, pipes and smokers' articles, 118 N. Washington, res. same.
Schunck Julius, foreman, 132 S. Washington, res. 1236 Stuart.
Schunck Julius S., res. 345 S. Quincy.
Schuplinski Ludwig, res. e. s. Oak, 4. s. Shawano rd., Ft. H.
Schwartz Andrew, machinist, res. w. s. Manitowoc rd., 9 s. Bellevue.
Schwartz Catherine (wid. Michael), res. w. s. Manitowoc rd., 9 s. Bellevue.
Schwartz Eli, boots and shoes, 228 Main, res. Schauer Hotel.
Schwartz Ernest, fireman, res. 707 Cherry, Ft. H.
Schwartz Marie Miss, res. 707 Cherry, Ft. H.
Schwartz Rose (wid. Matthias), res. 211 Crooks.
Schwartz Sebastian, farmer, res. w. s. Manitowoc rd., 9 s. Bellevue.
Schwartz Sylvester, brakeman, res. 707 Cherry, Ft H.
Schwartze C. & Sons (Carl, Herman and Carl Schwartze Jr ), props. East River Foundry and Machine shop, 1205-1207 Main.
Schwartze Carl Sr. (C. Schwartze & Sons), res. w. s. St George, 1 s. Main.
Schwartze Carl Jr. (C. Schwartze & Sons), res. w. s. St. George, 1 s. Main.
Schwartze Herman (C. Schwartze & Sons), res. w. s. St. George, 1 s. Main.
Schwartze William, foundryman, res. w. s. St. George, 1 s. Main.
**SCHWARZ C. & O.** (Christian and Oscar Schwarz), lumber, e. s. Pearl, nr. School pl., Ft. H.
Schwarz Christian (C. & O. Schwarz), pres. Green Bay Planing Mill Co., res. 137 Broadway, Ft. H.
Schwarz Emma A. Miss, res. 137 Broadway, Ft. H.
Schwarz Herman, student, res. 137 Broadway, Ft. H.
Schwarz Oscar (C. & O. Schwarz), res. s. s. 5th, 1 w. 3d av., Ft. H.
Schwechel Michael, lab., res. 1321 Crooks.
Schweger Robert, butcher, res. Commercial Hotel, Ft. H.
Scott Augusta J. Miss, res. 100 N. Madison.
Scott Emma J. Miss, res. 100 N. Madison.
Scott George, res. 932 Main.
Scott George, lab., res. e. s. 8th av., 1 s. 3d, Ft. H.

**THE A. SPUHLER CO.** *LADIES', MISSES' and CHILDREN'S*
**GREEN BAY** — **CLOAKS, CAPES, JACKETS**

Scott Harriett P. (wid. William), res. 109 N. Madison.
Scott John, engineer G. B. & Ft. H. Gas & Electric Light Co., res. Wilmar House.
Scott Mary (wid. William), res. 314 Stuart.
Scott Sylvester V., sawyer, res. 932 Main.
Scott Walter, sawyer, res. 619 Main.
Sebastian Sophie Mrs., res. 818 Cherry.
Seckel Christian, watchman, res. 827 Walnut.
Secord W. E., brakeman, res. 219 Broadway, Ft. H.
Seguin Sophia (wid. Joseph), res. 621 S. Madison.
Seguin William, saloon, 225 Pine, res. 621 S. Madison.
Seibel John, res. Cedar Creek rd., e. city limits.
Seibert Charles, switchman, res. w. s. 9th av., 2 n. 3d, Ft. H.
Seibert John, lab., res. w. s. S. Van Buren, bet. Eliza and Emilie.
Seickle Theodore, hostler, res. Reis Hotel.
Seifert Ernst, carp., res. 1265 Main.
Seifert John, cooper, res. 1601 Elm.
Seifert Minnie (wid. William), res. 1203 Stuart.
Seims Charles, lab., res. 100 5th av., Ft. H.
Seims Christian, carp., res. 100 5th av., Ft. H.
Seims Julia P. (wid. Paul), res. 104 5th av., Ft. H.
Seims Paul, dock foreman, res. 313 6th av., Ft. H.
Selissen Peter, lab., res. 424 Mason.
Sellers Maggie Miss, res. 320 6th av., Ft. H.
**SELLERS MALCOLM,** justice of the peace, notary public, pension agt. and commission mercht., office w. s. 3d av., 2 n. 1st, res. n. w. cor. 6th av. and 5th, Ft. H.
**SELLERS MALCOLM A.,** livery, sale and feed stable, w. s. 3d av., 1 s. the slough, res. 320 6th av., Ft. H.
Selmer Henry, carp., res. 506 Cedar, Ft. H.
Selmer John, lab., res. 506 Cedar, Ft. H.
Servaes Joseph, lab., res. 724 St. George.
Servais Emil, shoemkr, res. 531 N. Madison.
Servais Jerry, fireman, res. 121 Cedar, Ft. H.
Servais John, clk. F. De Cromer, res. Bodart House.
Servis Alexander, teamster, res. Dan McQueen's boarding house, Ft. H.
**SERVOTTE E. W. & JOSEPH H.** (Ernest W. and Joseph H. Servotte), carp.-contrs, 1034 Walnut and 508 S. Monroe av.
Servotte Emily A. Miss, dressmkr, res. 1034 Walnut.
Servotte Ernest W. (E. W. & Joseph H. Servotte), res. 1034 Walnut.

Servotte Frank W., carp., res. 1034 Walnut.
Servotte Joseph H. (E. W. & Joseph H. Servotte), res. 508 S. Monroe av.
Seventh Day Adventists' church, n. s. Main, bet. Willow and Cedar, Ft. H.
Seymour Frank B., supt. G. B., W. & St. P. Ry., res. 333 S. Jefferson.
Seymour Frederick H., clk. G. B., W. & St. P. Ry., res. 408 4th, Ft. H.
Seymour John, ry.-conductor, res. 123 Broadway, Ft. H.
Seymour Mary (wid. Gilbert), res. 333 S. Jefferson.
Shaba Frank, lab., res. e. s. 5th av., 3 s. 9th, Ft. H.
Shannon Timothy, yardmaster G. B., W. & St. P. Ry., res. 322 Chestnut, Ft. H.
Shapiro Ike, junk buyer, res. 1123 Main.
Shapiro Michael, junk buyer, res. 1123 Main.
Shapiro Wolf, junk dealer, 1123 Main. res. same.
Sharkey William, loco.-fireman, res. 317 Mason.
Sharp Agnes (wid. John), res. 305 7th av., Ft. H.
Sharp Alexander, machinist, res. 301 6th av., Ft. H.
Sharp John, boilermkr, res. 305 7th av., Ft. H.
Shaughnessy John E. (Patrick Shaughnessy & Son), res. Northwestern Hotel, Ft. H.
Shaughnessy Margaret Miss, res. Northwestern Hotel, Ft. H.
Shaughnessy Mary Miss, res. Northwestern Hotel, Ft. H.
Shaughnessy Patrick (Patrick Shaughnessy & Son), res. Northwestern Hotel, Ft. H.
**SHAUGHNESSY PATRICK & SON** (Patrick and John E. Shaughnessy), props. Northwestern Hotel, Ft. H.
Shea Patrick, drayman, res. s. s. 2d, 3 w. r. r. track, Ft. H.
Sheady Lizzie, domestic 1008 S. Monroe av.
Shearer Benjamin P. Mrs., res. 542 S. Quincy.
Shearer Blanche, student, res. 542 S. Quincy.
Shearer Sara, bookkpr. Ansorge & Parish, res. 542 S. Quincy.
Sheedy Elizabeth Miss, res. 1124 S. Monroe av.
Sheedy Josephine Miss, res. 1124 S. Monroe av.
Sheedy Margaret Miss, res. 1124 S. Monroe av.
Sheedy Martin, res. 1124 S. Monroe av.
Sheehy Edward M., engineer, res. s. e. cor. Bond and Cherry.
Sheehy Edward W., lab., res. w. s Chestnut, 2 n. Elmore, Ft. H.
Sheehy Martin, fireman, res. 608 Cedar.
Sheehy William W., fireman, res. 604 Chestnut, Ft. H.
Shepeck Edward, res. 1610 Elm.
Shepeck John, res. 1528 Elm.

**THE A. SPUHLER CO., Green Bay** CARPETS, RUGS, OIL CLOTHS
Draperies and Window Shades.

**SHEPECK JOHN JR.**, real estate, insurance **and passage** agency, 314 Main, res. 1610 Elm.
Sheppard Dennis S., messenger U. S. Ex. Co., res. 208 S. Adams.
Shequin George, engineer, res. n. w. cor. Willow and Baird, Ft. H.
Sheridan Emma Miss, teacher, res. 401 Main, Ft. H.
Sheridan Katie Miss, stenog., res. 401 Main, Ft. H.
Sheridan Marie Miss, res. 213 Chestnut, Ft. H.
Sheridan Philip, lawyer, 3 P. O. blk., res. 401 Main, Ft. H.
Sheridan Sarah Miss, student, res. 401 Main, Ft. H.
Sherman Sadie, domestic 432 S. Monroe av.
Shields May Miss, res. 224 S. Van Buren.
Shilbine William, bridge carp., res. Broadway House, Ft. H.
Shimonek Flora, domestic 222 S. Jefferson.
Shimonek Henry, clk., res. 317 N. Adams.
Shimonek Mary Miss, res. 317 N. Adams.
Shimonek Stephen, boots and shoes, 210 **Main, res. 317 N.** Adams.
Shimonek Stephen Jr., shoemkr, res. 317 N. Adams.
Shipling Fred, lab., res s. w. cor. Lawe and S. 10th.
Shire Emil, lab., res. Champion Hotel.
Shire I. & Son (Isaac S. and Philip Shire), hides and **pelts,** 119 N. Washington.
Shire Isaac S, (I. Shire & Son), res. Milwaukee, Wis.
Shire Philip (I. Shire & Son), res. 204 5th av., Ft. H.
Shorkey Marie, domestic Broadway House, Ft. H.
Shounard John, lab., res. 413 2d, Ft. H.
Shounard Tracy Miss, res. 413 2d, Ft. H.
Shreve William J., mach., res. 127 6th av., Ft. H.
Shriber John, brakeman, res. 210 Stuart.
Shuart Katie Miss, clk. The A. Spuhler Co., res. 525 S. Adams.
Shultz Benjamin J., clk. 212 Main, Ft. H., res. 316 Willow, Ft. H.
**SHULTZ C. E.**, **druggist,** 306 Dousman, res. 508 Guesnier, Ft. H.
Shuskie August, carriage driver, res. w. s. 4th av., 2 s. 8th, Ft. H.
Shuskie Charles, saw setter, res. w. s. 4th av., 2 s. 8th, Ft. H.
Shuskie Gustav, lab., res. w. s. 4th av., 2 s. 8th, Ft. H.
Shuskie Minnie Miss, res. w. s. 4th av., 2 s. 8th, Ft. H.
Shuskie Tena Miss, res. w. s. 4th av., 2 s. 8th, Ft. H.
Sickel Jacob, lab., res. n. s. St. Clair, 3 e. N. 12th.
Sickel Louis, butcher, res. 1120 Cedar.
Sieger Amelia, domestic 333 S. Washington.
Siegmund Albert L., carpenter, res. 133 Chestnut, Ft. H.

Siegmund Anna Miss, milliner, res. 133 Chestnut, Ft. H.
Siegmund Christiana (wid. George), res. 204 5th av., Ft. H.
Siegmund Emelie Miss, dressmkr, 405 4th, Ft. H., res. same.
Siegmund Erwin, millwright, res. s. w. cor. Cherry and School pl., Ft. H.
Siegmund Henry, res. 130 Broadway, Ft. H.
Siegmund Lena Miss, dressmkr, 405 4th, Ft. H., res. same.
Siegmund Louis, clk. 119 N. Washington, res. 300 5th av., Ft. H.
Siegmund William, carp., res. 405 4th, Ft. H.
**SIEGRIST JACOB REV.**, pastor Ev. Luth. Church, res. 909 Cherry.
Siegrist Rachael Miss, music teacher, res. 909 Cherry.
Siegrist Raphael, jeweler, res. 909 Cherry.
**SILBERSDORF KONRAD**, prop. Bay City House, res. same.
Silget Emil, cigarmkr, res. 803 Shawano av., Ft. H.
Silget Katie, domestic 318 Stuart.
Silget William, lab., res. 803 Shawano av., Ft. H.
Simaye Jules, lab., res. cor. Kellogg and Broadway, opposite Huffman House, Ft. H.
Simmons Arthur, res. 1143 Pine.
Simmons Charles, painter, res. 1143 Pine.
Simmons James L., fireman, res. 1167 Walnut.
Simmons Maria Mrs., carpet weaver, res. 1143 Pine.
Simoens Henry, lab., res. 509 Broadway, Ft. H.
Simon Anton, blksmith, res. 409 N. Jefferson.
Simon Eugenia Miss, dressmkr, res. 1012 Main.
Simon Fannie Miss, domestic 309 S. Monroe av.
Simon Joseph, cigarmkr, res. 1103 Walnut.
Simon Josephine Miss, dressmkr, res. 1012 Main.
Simon Kate Miss, clk., res. 1103 Walnut.
Simon Mary Miss, res. 409 N. Jefferson.
**SIMON MATTHIAS**, blksmith, 311 Main, res. 409 N. Jefferson.
Simon Peter, lab., res. 1103 Walnut.
Simon Philip (Smits & Simon), res. 1012 Main.
Simonet Hortense, domestic 139 S. Jefferson.
Simonet Paul, lab., res. 1031 Stuart.
Simons Edward, brakeman, res. 812 S. Jefferson.
Sims Daniel, engineer, res. Junction Hotel, Ft. H.
Sinclair William, saloon, 217 3d av., res. 804 2d av., Ft. H.
**SINGER MANUFACTURING CO.**, W. G. Gillespie, mngr., 212 Cherry.
Sinkler Annie, domestic 904 S. Monroe av.

**THE A. SPUHLER CO., GREEN BAY, WIS.** **Fine Dress Goods**
Samples Furnished on Application.

SIP 221 SMI

Sipes Henry, conductor, res. 629 S. Jefferson.
Sissons Ellen Miss, res. n. e. cor. Main and Newhall.
Sissons Jamima, domestic 413 Pine.
Sissons Mary, domestic 1015 S. Monroe av.
Sissons William, res. n. e. cor. Main and Newhall.
Sissons William J., printer, res. n. e. cor. Main and **Newhall**.
Skarda Edward, tailor, res. 1007 Cherry.
Skarda Julia Miss, res. 1007 Cherry.
Skarda Matthias, tailor, res. 1007 Cherry.
Skeels Barlow K., bkpr. Citizens' National Bank, res. 204 S. Madison.
Skeels Laura B. Mrs., res. 416 Walnut.
Skeels William, res. 416 Walnut.
Skelley James A., electrician, res. 412 S. Monroe av.
Skentna Catherine, domestic 129 S. Monroe av.
**SKOGG NELS**, plumber, 313 Cherry, res. 620 S. Van Buren.
Skutlarek Vincenz, lab., res. 1368 Walnut.
Slater Maria (wid. John), res. 344 Pearl, Ft. H.
Slattery Thomas, engineer, res. 109 Broadway, Ft. H.
Slaughter Abbott W., physician, 224 N. Washington, res. 504 S. Van Buren.
Slotala Anton, lab., res. 1301 Chicago.
Slott John, lab., res. 1331 Walnut.
Slupinsky Anton, fisherman, res. 704 Cherry, Ft. H.
Slusser George E., lath mnfr., res. 619 Main.
Small John T., mailing-clk., res. 617 S. Jefferson.
Smeets Jaques, baker, res. 322 Pine.
Smidt Barbara E., domestic Commercial House, Ft. **H**.
Smith Albert, engineer, res. 533 S. Jefferson.
Smith Albert H., res. 208 7th av., Ft. H.
Smith Albert O., loco.-engineer, res. 206 7th av., Ft. H.
Smith Alfleda, bkpr. 212 Cherry, res. 513 Pine.
Smith Alva A., switchman, res. 319 Chestnut, Ft. H.
Smith Alva L., tel.-opr., res. Commercial Hotel, Ft. H.
Smith Annie (wid. Edward), res. 111 Broadway, Ft. H.
Smith Arthur, clk. C. & N. W. Ry., res. 932 Walnut.
Smith Bartholomew Jos., res. w. s. 2d av., 1 s. 7th, Ft. H.
Smith Benjamin N., clk. J. Beth & Son, res. 611 N. Madison.
Smith Bros. (Henry C., George B., Fillmore B. and Silas S. Smith) grocers, Main s. w. cor. Grove.
Smith C. Edward, bookkpr. D. W. Britton, res. 713 Walnut.
Smith Charles H., conductor, res. Ferris Hotel, Ft. H.
**SMITH DAVID G.**, prop. Commercial Hotel, Ft. H., res. same.

**SMITH EDWIN R.**, police justice, 34 Parmentier blk., res. 932 Walnut.
Smith Emily B. (wid. John M.), res. 1535 Morrow.
Smith Essie W. Miss, teacher 4th ward school, res. w. s. 2d av., 1 s. 7th, Ft. H.
Smith Eva B. Miss, res. 105 Broadway, Ft. H.
Smith Fillmore B. (Smith Bros.), res. 1530 Morrow.
Smith Frank C., saloon, 123 N. Washington, res. 219 S. Quincy.
Smith George, gardener, res. n. s. Bellevue, 3 e. Manitowoc rd.
Smith George R. (Smith Bros.), res. Town Preble.
Smith Granger W. Rev., pastor Baptist Church, res. 308 Chestnut, Ft. H.
Smith Harry K., clk. 212 Main, Ft. H., res. Commercial Hotel, Ft. H.
Smith Hattie Miss, res. 932 Walnut.
Smith Henry, gardener, res. n. s. Bellevue, 3 e. Manitowoc rd.
Smith Henry, janitor Kellogg Nat. Bank, res. n. s. Shawano rd., 3 w. Willow, Ft. H.
Smith Henry, lab., res. n. s. Shawano rd., 2 w. Willow, Ft. H.
Smith Henry C. (Smith Bros.), res. Town Preble.
Smith Howard J., gardener, res. 1535 Morrow.
Smith Irving C., gardener, res. 1535 Morrow.
Smith James H., dredging, res. 138 S. Jefferson.
Smith Jennie L. Miss, res. 905 Broadway, Ft. H.
Smith John, foreman Green Bay Planing Mill Co., res. s. w. cor. Porlier and S. 10th.
Smith John, shoemkr, res. 1609 Elm.
Smith John Jr., res. 1609 Elm.
Smith John B., lab., res. s. s. Bond, 1 w. Cedar, Ft. H.
Smith Louis M., night watchman C. & N. W. depot, res. n. e. cor. Kellogg and Chestnut, Ft. H.
**SMITH LUTHER F.**, foreman C. & N. W. round-house, res. 905 Broadway, Ft. H.
Smith Mamie E. Miss, res. 138 S. Jefferson.
Smith Mary E., dressmkr, w. s. 2d av., 1 s. 7th, Ft. H., res. same.
Smith May E. Miss, teacher, res. 231 S. Jefferson.
Smith Nancy (wid. Henry P.), res. e. Newhall, 2 n. Main.
Smith Otis, lab., res. s. s. Duck Creek rd., 1 w. Mather., Ft. H.
Smith Patrick, r. r. hand, res. n. s. Elmore, 6 w. Cedar, Ft. H.
Smith Samuel, postal clk. C. & N. W. R. R., res. 807 Chestnut, Ft. H.
Smith Samuel F., fireman, res. 124 5th av., Ft. H.
Smith Silas S. (Smith Bros.), res. s. e. cor. Forest and Morrow.

**Headquarters for Boys' Clothing** THE A. SPUHLER CO. GREEN BAY.

Smith Theodore, res. 1609 Elm.
Smith Willis E., district carp. C., M. & St. P. R. R., res. 128 S. Adams.
Smith. See Schmidt and Schmitt.
Smits Henry, printer Standaard Printing Co., res. Depere, Wis.
**SMITS HERMAN** (Smits & Simon), blksmith, 931-935 Main, res. 407 N. Webster av.
**SMITS & SIMON** (Herman Smits and Philip Simon), agricultural implts., 1003-1005 Main.
**SNAVELY GEORGE**, prop. Adams House, res. same.
Snavely Georgianna A. Miss, res. Adams House.
Snavely Louis C., clk. Adams House, res. same.
Snyder Charles A., conductor, res. 644 S. Jefferson.
**SNYDER FRANK**, livery, hacks, 'bus and baggage line, 215 N. Adams, res. 139 S. Jefferson.
Snyder. See Schneider.
Sogey Hans, ship-carp., res. 916 3d av., Ft. H.
Sogey Laura Miss, res. 916 3d av., Ft. H.
Solomon Ezekiel, res. w. s. De Pere rd., 3 s. Hochgreve's Brewery.
Solomon Louis, trainman, res. w. s. De Pere rd., 3 s. Hochgreve's Brewery.
Solomon Philip, saloon and dance hall, w. s. Monroe av. rd., 2 s. Hochgreve's Brewery, res. same.
Sommerfeldt Louis, blksmith, res. 1226 Doty.
Sommerfeldt Herman, carpenter, res. 1311 Cedar.
Sommers William A., shoemkr, 108 Walnut, res. same.
Sonneck Ida Miss, res. 725 Main.
Soos Louise (wid. Carl), res. 1300 Doty.
Soos Wilhelmine (wid. Rudolph), res. 1307 Crooks.
Soquet Constant, res. 406 Cherry, Ft. H.
Soquet Ralph, druggist, 324 N. Washington, res. 406 Cherry, Ft. H.
Sorensen Anton E., carp., res. e. s. 4th av., 2 n. 10th, Ft. H.
Sorensen Erick, farmer, res n. e. cor. 10th and 4th av., Ft. H.
Sorensen John A., gen. store, s. s. cor. 3d av. and 9th, res. s. s. 9th, 2 e. 3d av., Ft. H.
Sorensen Katie, cook The Beaumont.
Sorensen Melvin, clk. John A. Sorensen, res. s. s. 9th, 2 e. 3d, av., Ft. H.
Sorensen Selma Miss, clk. John A. Sorensen, res. s. s. 9th, 2 e. 3d av., Ft. H.
Sorensen Sievert, millwright, res. n. e. cor. 10th and 4th av. Ft. H.

Sorenson Hannah, domestic 409 4th, Ft. H.
Sorenson Karen (wid. Hans J.), res. 700 S. Madison.
Sorenson Meta Miss, res. 700 S. Madison.
Sorenson Nealie J., dressmkr, res. 700 S. Madison.
Sowaski Stephen, lab., res. 1350 Cherry.
Spafford A. Daniel, hackdriver 415 Main, res. 735 Main.
Spang Barbara, domestic 415 5th, Ft. H.
Spangler Joseph, woodworker, res. 506 N. Jefferson.
Spear George O., res. 232 S. Jefferson.
Speck John, boilermkr, res. 1163 Crooks.
Speck William, lab., res. 1244 Doty.
Speerschneider Albert, maltster, res. cor. Forest and Main.
Speerschneider Charles, engineer Hagemeister Brew. Co., res. 1624 Cedar.
Spierings Henry, lab., res. 1267 Walnut.
Spierings Peter, lab., res. 1267 Walnut.
**SPITZ JOSEPH**, Ben. Scheuer, mngr., clothing, men's furnishings, hats and caps, s. e. cor. N. Washington and Main.
Spitzer Isaac, engineer, res. 403 2d, Ft. H.
Spohn John, butcher, res. Reis Hotel.
Sponholz Maria (wid. Godfried), res. 706 Cedar.
Sprague Alexander (Sprague Bros.) res. Christiania, Ft. H.
**SPRAGUE BROS.** (Alexander and Milton Sprague), boarding barn, veterinary infirmary, n. w. cor. S. Washington and Stuart.
Sprague Milton (Sprague Bros.), res. 116 Cherry, Ft. H.
Spreedel Felix, lab., 1132 Day.
Sproedels Andrew, gardener, Cedar Creek rd., e. city limits.
Spude August, lamp-trimmer, res. 1336 Doty.
Spude Fred. (Spude & Koch), res. 201 S. Van Buren.
Spude John, lab., res. 1336 Doty.
Spude Laura Miss, domestic 703 S. Monroe av.
Spude Louis, mason, res. 201 S. Van Buren.
Spude Martha Miss, res. 1336 Doty.
Spude & Koch (Fred. Spude and Frank Koch), mason contrs 201 S. Van Buren.
**SPUHLER A. CO. THE,** Adam Spuhler, pres. and treas.; E. A. Arthur, sec.; dry goods, carpets, clothing, fancy goods, etc., 229-231 N. Washington.
Spuhler Adam, pres. the A. Spuhler Co., res. 525 S. Adams.
Spuhler Alice Miss, res. 525 S. Adams.
Spuhler Fritz C., salesman The A. Spuhler Co., res. 525 S. Adams.
Spuhler Mabel Miss, res. 525 S. Adams.

**THE A. SPUHLER CO.** *LADIES', MISSES' and CHILDREN'S*
**GREEN BAY** — **CLOAKS, CAPES, JACKETS**

| SPU | 225 | STE |
|---|---|---|

Spuhler Sarah B. Miss, cashier The A. Spuhler Co., res. 525 S. Adams.
Stachowiak Matthew, lab., res. 1254 Walnut.
Staiger John W., conductor, res. 519 Chestnut, **Ft. H**.
Staley George, brakeman, res. 504 S. Jefferson.
Stalter Michael, farmer, res. w. s. Manitowoc rd., 2 s. Finger rd.
Stalter Peter, farmer, n. e. cor. Manitowoc rd. and Finger rd.
Standard Oil Co., A. L. Dorn, agent, 213 Cedar.
**STANDARD PRINTING CO.**, Edward V. D. Casteele, pres. and treas.; John Raffers, sec.; printers and publishers Onze Standaard, 315 Cherry
Stannard Horace, carpenter, res. 505 S. Adams.
Stannard Jules, engineer McDonald's saw mill, res. Duck Creek.
Starkey Van, woodsman, res. 316 Main.
Stasek Anton, lab., res. w. s. Bellevue, Town Preble.
Stasek Barbara Miss, res. 822 Pine.
Stasek Jacob, gardener, res. w. s. Bellevue, Town Preble.
Stasek Jacob, hostler, res. Bay City House.
Stasek Lizzie Miss, res. w. s. Bellevue, Town Preble.
**STASKA FRANK**, blksmith and wagonmkr, 719 **Main**, res. 718 Cedar.
Staszak Michael, lab., res. 1254 Walnut.
Staszak Eva, domestic 139 S. Van Buren.
**STATE GAZETTE THE**, Walter E. Gardner, prop. and editor, 116 N. Washington.
Stearns Daniel, res. Charles House.
Steenbach James B., com.-trav. Columbian Baking Co., res. Chicago, Ill.
Steffens Herman, lab., res. 505 Chicago.
Steffens Jacob, millwright, res. 505 Chicago.
Steffens Otto, lab., res. 505 Chicago.
Steffens William, lab., res. 505 Chicago.
Stein Albert, bricklayer, res. 1301 Cedar.
Stein Catherine (wid. Nicolns), res 1247 Cedar.
Steinert Julius, engineer, res. McQueen's boarding house, Ft. H.
Steinke Annie, waitress Bradley House.
Steinman Rudolph L., blksmith, res. 122 Broadway, Ft. H.
Stengel George, farmer, res. w. s. Manitowoc rd., 10 s. Bellevue.
Stenger Fred., butcher, res. American House.
**STENGER GEORGE** (George Stenger & Bro.), meat-market and vessel supplies, 321 N. Washington, res. 139 S. Van Buren.
Stenger George Jr., bookkpr., res. 139 S. Van Buren.
Stenger George & Bro. (George and M. R. Stenger), meatmkt. 317 Main, Ft. H.

Stenger M. R. (George Stenger & Bro.), res. Broadway House, Ft. H.
Stephan Anton, res. 318 N. 10th.
Sterling A. Judson, mill-hand, res. 419 N. Monroe av.
Stewart John, engineer, res. Eldred's boarding house, Ft. H.
Stile Conrad, lab., res. Porlier, n. e. cor. 12th.
Stile Constant Miss, res. Porlier, n. e. cor. 12th.
Stile John, brakeman, res. Porlier, n. e. cor. 12th.
Stiller Anton F. (Stiller Bros.), res. 1133 Walnut.
Stiller August, res. Pearl, 2 n. bridge, Ft. H.
Stiller August, painter, res. 1114 Walnut.
Stiller Bros. (Anton F. Stiller), harnessmkrs, 208 N. Adams.
Stimson Burt D., messenger U. S. Ex. Co., res. 1131 Pine.
Stimson Peter, carp., res. w. s. 11th av., 3 n. 2d, Ft. H.
Stiveo Coelestin, lab., res. 531 N. Madison.
Stiveo Desire, cooper, res. 527 N. Madison.
Stiveo Emil, painter, res. 424 Elm.
Stiveo George, fireman, res. 421 Elm.
Stiveo Henry, lab., res. 531 N. Madison.
Stiveo Joseph, harnessmkr, res. 126 S. Jackson.
Stiveo Louis, lab., res. 531 N. Madison.
Stiveo Theodore, lab., res. 531 N. Madison.
Stobbe Gustave, lab., res. 745 S. Webster av.
Stock Frank, foreman C., M. & St. P. Ry., res. 603 S. Jefferson.
Stoll Ernst, butcher, res. 317 Mason.
Stone J. A. Mrs., milliner, 201 3d av., F. H., res. 723 S. Jefferson.
Stone William H., cooper, res. 533 Cedar.
Stone William O., res. 230 Pine.
Stott Frank, lab., res. 246 Pearl, Ft. H.
Straka Joseph, confectioner, 1353 Main, res. same.
Straschewski John, fisherman, res. 828 Cedar.
Stratton William S., electrician, res. Schauer Hotel.
Straubel Brick Co. (Louis A. and Charles F. Straubel), Mary, at Mason st. bridge.
Straubel Chas. F. (Straubel Brick Co.), res. Mary, cor. Bellevue.
Straubel Edward, brickmkr, res. Mary, cor. Bellevue.
Straubel F. Ernst, res. Mary, cor. Bellevue.
Straubel Fred L. G., sec. and treas. The Weise-Hollman Co., res. 318 Stuart.
Straubel Henry A., res. 109 S. Monroe av.
Straubel Louis A. (Straubel Brick Co.), res. n. w. cor. Mary and Bellevue.
Straubel Otto C., bkpr. A. Kimball, res. 110 S. Madison.
Streckenbach C. W. & Co. (Charles W. Streckenbach and Louis G. Schilling), fresh, salt and smoked fish, 833 Cedar.

**THE A. SPUHLER CO., Green Bay** CARPETS, RUGS, OIL CLOTHS
Draperies and Window Shades.

| STR | 227 | SZC |

Streckenbach Charles W. (C. W. Streckenbach & Co.), res. 316 N. Van Buren.
Streckenbach Edward C. (**Streckenbach & Nissen**), **res. 522** Chestnut, Ft. H.
Streckenbach George, shoemkr, res. 522 Chestnut, Ft. H.
Streckenbach Mary Mrs., cook Adams House.
Streckenbach Nellie Miss, dressmkr, res. 522 Chestnut, Ft. H.
**STRECKENBACH & NISSEN** (Edward C. Streckenbach and Matthew Nissen), boots and shoes, 219 Broadway, Ft. H.
Strelow August, carp., res. Reis Hotel.
Strelow William, carp., res. s. w. cor. Crooks and Bond.
Strenski John, lab., res. 1355 Walnut.
Strnad Mary, domestic 322 Main.
Stuart Peter, scaler, res. Eldred's boarding house, Ft. H.
Stuebe Ferdinand, bookbinder, res. 1318 Walnut.
Stuebe Lena (wid. Martin), res. 1318 Walnut.
Stuebe Theodore, hostler, res. 1318 Walnut.
Stullien P. K., section boss, res. Junction Hotel, Ft. **H.**
Stutzke Charles, lab., res. 1271 Crooks.
Suelflohn Hattie Mrs., res. 1272 Walnut.
Suess George, cabinetmkr, res. s. s. Shawano rd., 2. w. Willow, Ft. H.
Sullivan John, motorman, res. Empire House.
Sullivan Philip B., engineer, res. Northwestern Hotel, **Ft. H.**
Sustmann Mary Mrs., res. 305 2d, Ft. H.
Suydam Charles D., clk. county sheriff, res. Court House.
Suydam Jane (wid. John V.), res. 416 Lawe.
Sweeney John, driver truck No. 1, res. 520 N. **Madison.**
Swejda Albert, lab., res. 1376 Walnut.
Swensen Annie, domestic 621 S. Van Buren.
Swetters Benjamin, brakeman, res. s. s. Elmore, 6 w. Cedar, Ft. H.
Swetters Frank, watchman, res. s. s. Elmore, 6 w. Cedar, Ft. H.
Swetters John, ry.-hand, res. n. s. Elmore, 11 w. Cedar, Ft. H.
Swetters Mary Miss, dressmkr, res. s. s. Elmore, 6 w. Cedar, Ft. H.
Swetters **William, ry.-hand, res. n. s. Elmore, 11 w. Cedar,** Ft. H.
Switzer Catherine (wid. Edward), res. 121 S. Monroe av.
Sykes Byron, res. w. s. 6th av., 4 s. Bridge, Ft. H.
Synnas Casper, carp., res. 305 4th, Ft. H.
Synnas Martin, carp., res. 112 Cedar, Ft. H.
Szczechowski Andrew, lab., res. 1401 Chicago.

# T

TAHLIER Desire, gardener, res. n. s. Elmore, 8 w. Willow, Ft. H.
Tahller Marie, domestic 6 w. 874 Dousman, Ft. H.
Taikowski Josephine, domestic 410 Walnut.
Tanner Milton F., carriage trimmer, res. 426 Walnut.
Tanvers Marie, domestic Ferris Hotel, Ft. H.
Tate Thomas, blksmith, res. 316 Main.
Tatowsky Anastasia (wid. Henry), res. 1001 Harvey.
Tayler Caroline Miss, bkpr. Theo. Kemnitz Furniture Co., res. 110 Chestnut, Ft. H.
Tayler Joseph, ins. agt., res. 131 Broadway, Ft. H.
Tayler Joseph H., cashier McCartney National Bank, res. 133 Broadway, Ft. H.
Tayler Mary E. Miss, bkpr., res. 110 Chestnut, Ft. H.
Tayler Nellie Miss, bkpr. William Larsen, res. 110 Chestnut, Ft. H.
Tayler William H., machinist, res. 110 Chestnut, Ft. H.
Taylor Frank W., station agent C. & N. W. Ry., res. 801 Dousman, Ft. H.
Taylor James, lab., res. w. s. 10th av., near G. B., W. & St. P. Ry. track, Ft. H.
Taylor John, farmer, res. w. s. Rich rd., 1 s. 9th, Ft. H.
Taylor John, butcher, res. Manitowoc House.
Tease Henry, lab., res. 1449 Smith.
Tease Victor, gardener, 1449 Smith, res. same.
Tebo Flora, clk. Jorgensen Blesch Co., res. n. e. cor. Bond and Willow, Ft. H.
Tebo Louis, carp.-contr., n. e. cor. Willow and Bond, Ft. H., res. same.
Tees Henry, clk. J. Beth & Son, res. 1237 Walnut.
Tees Martha Miss, res. 1237 Walnut.
Teetshorn Frank E., train dispatcher G. B., W. & St. P. R. R., res. 502 Walnut.
Tellor Carrie Miss, clk., res. n. w. cor. Cherry and N. Adams.
Tellor George, barkpr., res n. w. cor. Cherry and N. Adams.
Tellor Martin, clk., res. n. w. cor. Cherry and N. Adams.
Tellor Tusan, saloon, n. w. cor. Cherry and N. Adams, res. same.
Tenant Dosty, teamster, res. s. s. Duck Creek rd., 7 w. Mather, Ft. H.
Tenant Prosper, lab., res. s. s. Duck Creek rd., 7 w. Mather, Ft. H.
Tenant Prosper Jr., lab., res. s. s. Duck Creek rd., 7 w. Mather, Ft. H.

THE A. SPUHLER CO., GREEN BAY, WIS. **Fine Dress Goods**
Samples Furnished on Application.

Ten Eyck Hattie L., dressmkr, 1133 Cherry, res. same.
Ten Eyck William B., mason-contr., 1133 Cherry, res. same.
Tenner Jacob F. Mrs., res. 714 S. Webster av.
Tennis Alex., saloon, 547 S. Adams, res. 313 Mason.
Tennis Alex. Jr., barkpr., res. 313 Mason.
Tennis Carrie Mrs., grocer, 635 S. Jefferson, res. same.
Tennis Henry, clk. Brauns & Van, res. 1102 Walnut.
Tennis Jennie Miss, dressmkr, res. 1102 Walnut.
Tennis John, res. 635 S. Jefferson.
Tennis John L., saloon, 31 Main, cor. N. Washington, res. same.
Tennis Julia Miss, res. 313 Mason.
Tennis Leonard J., grocer, 1100 Walnut, res. 1102 Walnut.
Tennis Louis, fireman, res. 313 Mason.
Tennis Oliver, grocer, 445 S. Quincy, res. same.
Tennis Phenie Miss, res. 313 Mason.
Tennis Rose Miss, clk., res. 635 S. Jefferson.
Terp Ives J., clk. Goodrich Trans. Co., res. 320 Willow, Ft. H.
Terrien Louis, engineer Hochgreve Brewing Co., res. w. s. Monroe av. rd., 2½ miles s. city limits.
Terrio Alfred W., bkpr., res. 215 S. Monroe av.
Terrio Frank E., res. 215 S. Monroe av.
Terrio Henry P., printer, res. 215 S. Monroe av.
Terrio Mary (wid. Paul), res. 215 S. Monroe av.
Terrio Oliver A., city editor The State Gazette, res. 215 S. Monroe av.
Terry Edward, prop. Hall House, res. n. w. cor. Broadway and Baird, Ft. H.
**TERRY NICHOLAS J.**, prop. Broadway House, n. w. cor. Broadway and Dousman, Ft. H., res. same.
Terry Patrick, lab., res. n. s. Elmore, 3 w. Cedar, Ft. H.
Tesselnar Cornelius A., asst. editor Onze Standaard, res. Depere, Wis.
Tews John, brakeman, res. Ferris Hotel, Ft. H.
Thays George, cooper, res. 909 Main.
Thays Joseph, cooper, res. 909 Main.
Thees Minna (wid. August), res. 1328 Walnut.
Thees Wm., elevator foreman J. H. Ebeling, res. 1328 Walnut.
Theis Frank, lab., res. 1 w. of 874 Dousman, Ft. H.
Theisen John B., dentist, 312 N. Washington, res. 121 S. Madison.
Theisen Lawrence, teamster, res. Waterloo House.
Theisen Lizzie, domestic 526 S. Madison.
**THEISEN MELCHIOR** (J. Le Roy & Co.) res. Cook's Hotel.
Thelen John, blksmith, res. 409 N. Jefferson.

Thelen Wendel, gardener, res. s. s. Charles, 2 w. Manitowoc rd.
Thelen Wendel Jr., gardener, res. s. s. Charles, 2 w. Manitowoc rd.
Therion Nellie, domestic Empire House.
Therion Seraphin, tailor, res. 300 S. 10th.
Thiele Christian, carp., res. 610 S. Webster av.
Thomas Alois, clk. Albert L. Platten, res. n. e. cor. Dousman and Chestnut, Ft. H.
Thomas August, plumber, res. 1117 Cherry.
Thomas Boredri, clk. Brauns & Van, res. 111 S. Madison.
Thomas Caroline E. Miss, res. 318 N. Van Buren.
Thomas Commodore C., engineer, res. 1178 Doty.
Thomas Dolphin Miss, res. 1117 Cherry.
Thomas Edward (Thomas & Anheuser), res. 1137 Cherry.
Thomas Frank, agt. Am. Ex. Co., res. 315 N. Jefferson.
Thomas Frank W., res. 318 N. Van Buren.
Thomas George, lab., res. 1178 Doty.
Thomas Joseph, bookpr Thomas & Anheuser, res. 1117 Cherry.
Thomas Joseph Jr., plumber, res. 1117 Cherry.
Thomas Walter J., frt. and ticket auditor G. B., W. & St. P. R. R., res. 902 Main.
Thomas William E., com.-trav. 124 S. Washington, res. 318 N. Van Buren.
Thomas & Anheuser (Edward Thomas and Matthias Anheuser), plumbers and gunsmiths, 227 Pine.
Thompson Claude, brakeman, res. St. James Hotel.
Thompson David, painter, res. 6th av., s. w. cor. 2d, Ft. H.
Thompson Dora, domestic w. s. Chestnut, 5 s. Baird, Ft. H.
Thompson Foster, boilermkr, res. 6th av., s. w. cor. 2d, Ft. H.
Thompson Henry A., clk. freight auditing dept. G. B., W. & St. P. Ry., res. 509 School.
Thompson Henry W. Rev., pastor 1st M. E. Church, res. 509 School.
Thompson Iver, lab., res. 1306 Elm.
Thompson John, maltster Hochgreve Brewing Co., res. w. s. Monroe av. rd., 2½ miles s. city limits.
Thompson Joseph, bridge tender, res. 1231 Main.
Thompson Maggie, waitress American House.
Thompson Mell A., switchman, res. 101 6th av., Ft. H.
Thompson Nellie B., tel.-opr. W. U. Tel. Co., res. 6th av., s. w. cor. 2d, Ft. H.
Thompson Robert H., engineer, res. 310 7th av. Ft. H.
Thompson William, conductor, res. 107 6th av., Ft. H.
Thompson W. Y., master car builder G. B., W. & St. P. Ry., res. 6th av., s. w. cor. 2d, Ft. H.

**Headquarters for Boys' Clothing** THE A. SPUHLER CO.
GREEN BAY.

Thum Byron P., lab., res. 1272 Walnut.
Thum Edward E., lab., res. 1272 Walnut.
Thunm Herman, lab., res. 1143 Doty.
Thys Nettie, domestic 342 S. Webster av.
Tibau Joseph, harnessmkr, res. 126 S. Jackson.
Tibbitts Ambrose S., res. 799 Shawano av., Ft. H.
Tibbitts B. Frank, ship.-carp., res. 799 Shawano av., Ft. H.
Tibbitts Hyman, teamster, res. Reis Hotel.
Tickler Albert L., carp.-contr., res. 939 S. Quincy.
Tickler Louis, lab., res. 702 3d av., Ft. H.
Tickler Marie Miss, res. 702 3d av., Ft. H.
Tickler Peter L. (Brown & Tickler), res. 702 3d av., Ft. H.
Tickler Theodore J., ship.-clk. The Weise-Hollman Co., res. 222 S. Quincy.
Tiernan Catherine C. Mrs. (wid. John), res. 517 Cherry, Ft. H.
**TIERNAN JAMES**, druggist, 303 Main, res. 304 Cherry, Ft. H.
Tiernan John H., switchman, res. 517 Cherry, Ft. H.
Tilgen Andrew, lab., res. 1435 Harvey.
Tilkins Alphonse, lab., res. 1273 Willow.
Tillimans Frank, mason, res. 1524 Elm.
Tillman Cornelius, fisherman, res. n. s. St. Clair, 2 e. N. 12th.
Tillman Louis, fisherman, res. n. s. St. Clair, 2 e. N. 12th.
Tillmanns Tony, mason, res. 428 Pleasant.
Tilqui Albert, lab., res. n. s. 2d, 1 w. r. r. track, Ft. H.
Tilton Arthur C., student, res. 614 S. Jefferson.
Tilton B. Frank, mail-carrier, res. 526 S. Jackson.
Tilton Carrie M., dressmkr, res. 614 S. Jefferson.
Tilton Charles A., engineer, res. 614 S. Jefferson.
Tilton Frank, editor Green Bay Advocate, res. 614 S. Jefferson.
Timmermann Frank, mason, res. 1209 Day.
Tittner John, freight clk., res. Broadway House, Ft. H.
Toisoul Constance (wid. Desire), res. 3104 S. Washington.
Tols Frank, farmer, res. n. s. 2d, 4 w. r. r. track, Ft. H.
Tols Peter, lab., n. s. Bellevue, 1 e. Manitowoc rd.
Tombal Joseph, lab., res. 1135 Doty.
Tomlinson John, filer, res. Columbia Hotel.
Tonne Adolph, cigarmkr, res. 914 Pine.
Tonne Annie C. Miss, res. 914 Pine.
Tonne Carrie Miss, teacher, res. 914 Pine.
Tonne Fred Jr., tel. messenger, res. 914 Pine.
Tonne Frederick W. G., drayman, res. 914 Pine.
Tonon Jules, gardener, res. 1483 Mason.
Toohey James, lab., res. s. s. Bond, 1 w. Cedar, Ft. H.
Tooker Fred. C., candymkr, res. e. s. Cherry, 2 n. Baird, Ft. H.

Tooker Phebe (wid. Oliver A.), res. e. s. Cherry, 2 n. Baird, Ft. H.
Tooker William A., lab., res. 513 Chestnut, Ft. H.
Toole James, foreman McDonald's saw mill, res. 603 Mather, Ft. H.
Torgersen Christina (wid. Hans), res. 306 5th av., Ft. H.
Toussaint Emil, res. Willmar House.
Toutloff Annie Miss, res. 801 Dousman, Ft. H.
Townsend Edson D., engineer, res. 119 Broadway, Ft. H.
Trassard Cornelius, lab., res. Bodart House.
Travis James, molder, res. 406 Hubbard, Ft. H.
Treanor Kate Miss, res. 619 Cherry.
Treml Rosina, domestic 320 S. Washington.
Tremmel Lena Mrs., res. 1201 Crooks.
Treptow Emma, domestic 434 Walnut.
Trich James, cigarmkr, res. 601 St. George.
**TRICH JOHN,** saloon, 1259 Main, res. same.
Trich Joseph, res. 1259 Main.
Trich Wenzel, res. 1259 Main.
Tricott Jerome, plasterer, res. 214 S. 10th.
Trigloff Edith, domestic 740 S. Jefferson.
Trinkner John, lab., res. 138 S. Webster av.
Trinkner Wm., carp., res. 1324 Cherry.
Troullier Louisa, domestic 1201 Cherry.
Turner Hall, n. w. cor. Walnut and N. Monroe av.
Tush Mary, domestic 210 S. Jefferson.
Tuttle Laura Mrs., res. Reis Hotel.
Tuyls Joan Miss, teacher, res. 1245 Day.
Tuyls John A., carp., res. 1440 Cedar.
Tyler Clifford W., res. 526 S. Van Buren.
Tyler Nancy (wid. Benjamin), res. e. s. 8th av., 3 n. 5th, Ft. H.
Tyler Willis E., trav. and pass. agt. C., M. & St. P. R. R., res. 526 S. Van Buren.
Tyrell Emerson L., watchmkr, 226 N. Washington, res. 732 Main.
Ty River Belle Miss, teacher, res. 1021 Crooks.

## U

UDELL S. R. & Co., Julius R. Meyers, mngr., whol. cheese, 129 S. Washington.
Uhlmann Mary, domestic 100 S. Jefferson.
Uland John, fisherman, res. 316 Pearl, Ft. H.
Umbehaun Gottfried, lab., res. 1106 Stuart.
Umbehaun Hattie Miss, res. 1014 Walnut.
Umbehaun Louis F., sailor, res. 133 S. Quincy.

**THE A. SPUHLER CO.** *LADIES', MISSES' and CHILDREN'S*
**GREEN BAY** — **CLOAKS, CAPES, JACKETS**

Umbehaun William, cigarmkr, res. 1106 Stuart.
Umenthum Henry, brewer, res. 1285 Cedar.
Underhill Adeline E. (wid. William), res. n. e. cor. Hubbard and Cherry, Ft. H.
Underhill Charles W., baggage man, res. n. e. cor. Hubbard and Cherry, Ft. H.
Underhill Frances Miss, res. n. e. cor. Hubbard and Cherry, Ft. H.
Union Building, Loan and Savings Association, D. W. Flatley, pres.; J. S. Chase, v.-pres.; George L. North, sec.; W. P. Wagner, treas.; F. C. Cady, atty., 8 Parmentier blk.
**UNION HOUSE**, Fred Martin, prop., 115 3d av., Ft. H.
United States Express Co., F. H. Fuller, agent, 220 Pine.
United States Weather Bureau, F. W. Conrad, observer, 17 Parmentier blk.
Unruh Abraham C., carpenter, res. 303 6th av., Ft. H.

## V

VALENTINE Ernst, res. 1256 Stuart.
    Valentine Frederick E., brakeman C., M. & St. P. Ry., res. 831 Crooks.
Valentine James W., res. 910 Cherry.
Van Beek George, clk., res. 201 S. Quincy.
Van Beek Gertie Miss, res. 201 S. Quincy.
**VAN BEEK JOHN L.**, general mdse., 201 S. Quincy, res. same.
Van Beek Kittie Miss, res. 201 S. Quincy.
Van Beek Rudolph, clk., res. 201 S. Quincy.
Van Bellingen Peter, gardener, res. 10th, s. e. cor. Emily.
Van Bellingen Rose, domestic Odd Fellows' Home.
Van Benden Anton, res. e. s. George, 1 s. Guesnier.
Van Benden John, lab., res. n. s. Charles, 1 e. Bellevue.
Van Bever John, lab., res. 12th, cor. Smith.
Van Bever Peter, lab., res. 509 Broadway, Ft. H.
Van Boxel Albert, lab., res. 1310 Cedar.
Van Boxel Albert, lab., res. 428 Pleasant.
Van Boxel Albert E., brewer, res. 1339 Cedar.
Van Boxel Martin, lab., res. 318 N. Adams.
Van Dalen William, mason, res. 1261 Walnut.
Van den Berg Albert, gen. store, 408 3d av., Ft. H., res. same.
Van den Berg Albert H., del.-clk., res. 438 S. Quincy.
Van den Berg Annie, domestic 809 Walnut.
Van den Berg Annie Miss, res. 438 S. Quincy.
Van den Berg Carrie A. Miss, res. 408 3d av., Ft. H.

| VAN | 234 | VAN |
|---|---|---|

Van den Berg George, bottler, res. 508 S. Quincy.
Van den Berg Henry A., engineer, res. 438 S. Quincy.
Van den Berg John L., res. 438 S. Quincy.
Van den Berg Katie Miss, res. 408 3d av., Ft. H.
Van den Berg L. R., clk., res. 408 3d av., Ft. H.
Van den Berg Lizzie, domestic 213 N. Monroe.
Vandenboom George L., painter, res. 200 5th av., Ft. H.
Vandenboom John A., carp., res. 200 5th av., Ft. H.
Vandenboom John W., fireman, res. 200 5th av., Ft. H.
Van Den Braak Edwin (Brauns & Van), pres. J. P. Annen Candy Co., res. 222 S. Madison.
Van den Braak Marie Miss, res. 331 S. Adams.
Van den Branden Julius, lab., res. n.s. Mather, 1 w. Cedar, Ft.H.
Van den Brook Anna Miss, res. s. e. cor. Mather and Broadway, Ft. H.
Van den Brook Frank, brakeman, res. 712 Broadway, Ft. H.
Van den Brook Henry, filer, res. 807 Broadway, Ft. H.
Van den Brook Lizzie Miss, res. s. e. cor. Mather and Broadway, Ft. H.
Van den Brook Maggie Miss, res. s. e. cor. **Mather and Broadway, Ft. H.**
Van den Brook Mamie, dressmkr, res. 807 Broadway, Ft. H.
Van den Brook Martin, foreman McDonald Lumber yd., res. s. e. cor. Mather and Broadway, Ft. H.
Van den Brook Nellie Miss, res. 712 Broadway, Ft. H.
Van den Brook Peter, drayman, res. 712 Broadway, Ft. H.
**VAN DEN BROOK WILLIAM,** teaming, 708 Broadway, Ft. H., res. same.
Van den Brook William Jr., switchman, res. 706 Cherry, Ft. H.
Van den Busch Delia Miss, res. n. w. cor. Main and St. George.
Van den Busch Eli, fish-packer, res. n. w. cor. Main and St. George.
Van den **Busch John, painter, res. n. w. cor. Main and St.** George.
Van den **Busch Peter, blksmith, res. n. w. cor. Main and St.** George.
Van den Heuvel Frank, lab., res. 217 Cherry.
Van den Heuvel Henry, barkpr., res. 217 Cherry.
Van den Heuvel John, saloon, 217 Cherry, res. same.
Van den Heuvel Martin, carpenter, res. 1020 Stuart.
Van den Huevel Nic, cook, res. n. w. cor. S. Webster and Stuart.
Van den Langenberg Henry, lab., res. 1315 Harvey.
Van den Mooter Phillmont, barber, res. 336 S. Monroe av.
Van den Plas Frederick, lab., res. s. s. Duck Creek rd., 11 **w.** Mather, Ft. H.

**THE A. SPUHLER CO., Green Bay** CARPETS, RUGS, OIL CLOTHS
Draperies and Window Shades.

Van den Plas John W., lab., res. s. s. Duck Creek rd., 11 w. Mather, Ft. H.
Van den Plas Martin, lab., res. s. s. Duck Creek rd., 9 w. Mather, Ft. H.
Van den Plas Victor, lab., res. n. s. Bond, 9 w. Cedar, Ft. H.
Van den Plas Victor, lab., res. s. s. Duck Creek rd., 11 w. Mather, Ft. H.
Van den Plas William, gardener, res. s. s. Duck Creek rd., 9 w. Mather, Ft. H.
Van den Venn Cornelius, baker, res. 212 N. Adams.
Van den Verran Victor, lab., res. s. s. Bond, 4 w. Willow, Ft. H.
Van der Coeln Theresa, domestic 304 N. Adams.
Van der Elsen Cornell, jeweler, 326 Main, res. 209 S. Quincy.
Van der Geeten Adaline, dressmkr, res. 1019 Main.
Van der Geeten Adolph, plasterer, res. 1019 Main.
Van der Geeten Pierre, lab., res. 1441 Smith.
Van der Kelen Alphonse, fish packer, res. 1434 Day.
Van der Kelen Virginia, domestic 402 Main.
Van der Kellen Theodore, blksmith, w. s. Manitowoc rd., 4 s. Bellevue, res. same.
Van der Kin Annie Miss, res. 1179 Doty.
Van der Kin Gertrude (wid. Jacob), res. 1179 Doty.
Van der Leen Philip, farmer, res. n. s. 2d, 5 w. r. r. track, Ft. H.
Van der Leest Albert, lab., res. 1321 Cherry.
Van der Leest Henry, lab., res. s. s. St. Clair, 1 e. 12th.
Van der Linden Frank, mason, res. 1341 Day.
Van der Mass Eugene, shooting gallery, res. 1275 Stuart.
Van der Meulen Emil, lab., res. 2 w. 874 Dousman, Ft. H.
Van der Meulen Joseph, gardener, res. 3 w. 874 Dousman, Ft. H.
Van der Meulen Joseph Jr., gardener, res. 3 w. 874 Dousman, Ft. H.
Van der Meulen Moses, gardener, res. 2 w. 874 Dousman, Ft. H.
Van der Meulen Victor, lab., res. 2. w. 874 Dousman, Ft. H.
Van der Perren Jos., lab., res. s. s. Duck Creek rd., 2 w. Mather.
Van der Plass Henry, gardener, res. w. s. Manitowoc rd., 6 s. Bellevue.
Van der Plass William, gardener, res. n. e. cor. Shawano rd. and Fisk.
Van der Steen Adrian Albert, printer, res. 1164 Cherry.
Van der Steen Henry (Crone & Van der Steen), res. 1164 Cherry.
Van der Steen Henry, farmer, res. e. s. Bellevue, Town Preble
Van der Steen John, carp., res. 1164 Cherry.
Van der Steen John, farmer, res. e. s. Bellevue, Town Preble.
Van der Steen William, res. e. s. Bellevue, Town Preble.

Van der Wedden Fred., lab., res. e. s. Webster av., 1 s. city limits.
Van der Weg Frank, gardener, res. w. s. Manitowoc rd., 8 s. Bellevue.
Van der Wist William, printer Standard Printing Co., res. Town Preble.
Van der Zanden Jacob, jeweler, 310 Main, res. s. s. Cedar, 2 n. Main, Ft. H.
Van Derzee Frank, land agt., 227 Pine, res. 414 S. Webster av.
Van Deuren Carrie Miss, res. 332 S. Madison.
Van Deuren Henry, lab., res. 1175 Crooks.
Van Deuren Henry, saloon, 203 Dousman, Ft. H., res. same.
Van Deuren John, lab., res. 1175 Crooks.
Van Deuren John B., cigarmkr, res. 1033 Cherry.
Van Deuren Peter J., general store, 323 N. Adams, res. 332 S. Madison.
Van Deuren William J., res. 415 N. Jefferson.
Van Deuren William L., clk. P. J. Van Deuren, res. 332 S. Madison.
Vandewill Frank, lab., res. 1309 Willow.
Van de Zande John, saloon, 231 Main, res. same.
Van de Zande Lizzie, res. 231 Main.
Van Doren Felix, ice peddler, res. 1325 Chicago.
Vandrell Gregoire, lab., res. 414 Elm.
Vandrell Joseph, cooper, res. 414 Elm.
Vandrell Josephine, milliner, res. 414 Elm.
Vandrell Jules, harnessmkr. res. 414 Elm.
Vandunk Cornelius H., electrician, res. s. e. cor. Division and George, Ft. H.
Vandunk Cornelius N., janitor Fourth Ward School, res. s. e. cor. Division and George, Ft. H.
Van Dunsel John, Sr., lab., res. Town Preble, n. Smith.
Van Dunsel John Jr., res. Town Preble, n. Smith.
Van Dycke Alice C. Miss, res. 129 S. Adams.
Van Dycke Constant, res. 129 S. Adams.
Van Dycke Emil C., pres. O. Van Dycke Brewing Co., res. 806 Crooks.
Van Dycke Julius J., bkpr. O. Van Dycke Brewing Co., res. 129 S. Adams.
**VAN DYCKE O. BREWING CO.**, Emil Van Dycke, pres.; Mrs. O. Van Dycke, treas., s. w. cor. Chicago and S. Jackson.
Van Dycke Octavia Mrs., treas. O. Van Dycke Brewing Co., res. 129 S. Adams.
Van Ermen Andrew, lab., res. 1524 Elm.

**THE A. SPUHLER CO., GREEN BAY, WIS.** **Fine Dress Goods**
Samples Furnished on Application.

VAN 237 VAN

Van Ermen Anton, lab., res. Wisconsin House.
Van Ermen Ernst, saloon, 330 Main, res. same.
Van Ermen Frank, harnessmkr, 229 Main, res. 521 S. Madison.
Van Ermen Rosa, domestic 231 Main.
Van Ess Anton, saloon, 318 N. Adams, res. same.
Van Ess Simon, lab., res. 509 Broadway, Ft. H.
Van Evenhoven Alphonse, car repairer, res. 9 w. 874 Dousman, Ft. H.
**Van** Evenhoven Mary (wid. **Alphonse), res. s. s. Shawano rd., 5 w. Willow, Ft. H.**
Van Eyck John, lab., res. s. w. cor. Cass and 14th.
Van Eyden Frank, lab., res. 1530 Morrow.
Van Eyden Peter, lab., res. s. s. Main, 1 w. Forest.
Van Frachem Adrian J., stonecutter, res. e. s. Chestnut, 2 n. Elmore, Ft. H.
Van Frachem Herman, janitor Green Bay Business **College, res.** 408 Cherry, Ft. H.
Van Frachem Nettie Miss, res. 408 Cherry, Ft. H.
Van Garland Louis, barkpr., res. Champion Hotel.
Van Hagen Augusta, domestic 106 S. Adams.
**VAN HALDER JOHN**, com.-trav., res. 1166 Mason.
Van Halder Octavia, music teacher, res. 1166 Mason.
Van Halder Peter, boilermkr, res. 1166 Mason.
Van Hoof Vitel, lab. res. s. s. Elmore, 11 w. Cedar, Ft. H.
Van Hoorebecke Barney, gardener, res. 10th, s. e. cor. Emily.
Van Hoven Anna M. (wid. William), res. 300 S. Jackson.
Van Hoven Louise, domestic 333 S. Madison.
Van Hoven Theodore (Green Bay Mineral Spring Co.) res. 300 S. Jackson.
Van Kaster Joseph, carp., res. 1127 Pine.
**VAN KESSEL FRANK**, prop. American House, res. same.
Van Kessel Frank Jr., res. American House.
Van Kessel Hattie Miss, res. American House.
Van Kessel John, night clk. American House.
Van Kessel John, bridgetndr, res. 1169 Pine.
Van Kessel John, molder, res. 1273 Main.
Van Kessel Mamie Miss, res. American House.
Van Kessel William, day clk. American House.
Van Kessel William, lab., res. 1145 Pine.
Van Laanen Anton, shoemkr Hoeffel Bros. Shoe Co., res. **1531** Cedar.
Van Laanen Edward J., bookpr. J. M. Voigt Mnfg. Co., **res.** American House.
Van Laanen Frank, com. **trav. Hagemeister Brew. Co., res.** 630 S. Jackson.

| VAN | 238 | VER |

Van Laanen George, painter, res. 1531 Cedar.
Van Laanen John, gardener, res. 1531 Cedar.
Van Laanen John Jr., gardener, res. 1531 Cedar
Van Laanen John, lab., res. n. s. Willow, 1 e. Grove.
Van Laanen Martin, painter, res. 1531 Cedar.
Van Lanen Albert, gardener, res. 1476 Mason.
Van Lier Henry, porter Cook's Hotel.
Van Lier Michael, lab., res. 416 Lawe.
Van Loo Anton, beer peddler, res. 415 12th.
Van Nuvenhoven Felix, lab., res. s. s. Duck Creek rd., 6 w. Mather, Ft. H.
Vanmerbeck Louisa, domestic Champion Hotel.
Vannes Mamie, res. 800 Pine.
Van Oss Adrian, switchman, res. s. s. Grignon, near 11th.
Van Oss Charles, lab., res. e. s. Webster av., 2 s. city limits.
Van Oss Delia (wid. K.), res. s. s. Grignon, near 11th.
Van Oss Frank, switchman, res. 632 S. Jefferson.
Van Oss Martin, lab., res. 1240 Cass.
Van Oss William, conductor, res. 213½ S. Quincy.
Van Roosmalen William Rev., pastor St. Willebrod's Church, res. 209 S. Adams.
Van Rosmaulen Addie Miss, res. 432 S. Monroe av.
Van Rosmaulen Edward, bkpr., res. 432 S. Monroe av.
Van Rosmaulen Mayme Miss, clk. The A. Spuhler Co., res. 432 S. Monroe av.
Van Rosmaulen Peter J., com.-trav., res. 432 S. Monroe av.
Van Rossum William, conductor, res. 300 S. Madison.
Van Roy Mary (wid. Theodore), res. 1427 Mason.
Van Ruyden Pauline Miss, res. 906 Walnut.
Van Schyndel Antoinette (wid. John), grocer, 1107 Main, res same.
Van Schyndel Anton P., cigarmkr, res. 1146 Walnut.
Van Schyndel Frank, wood dealer, res. 1329 Walnut.
Van Schyndel Minnie Miss, res. 1107 Main.
Van Schyndel Martin, porter 124 S. Washington, res. 719 S. Van Buren.
Vase Nestor, carp., res. 445 S. Madison.
Verbackel Henry, lab., res. 1280 Cherry.
Verbawckle William, lab., res. 1210 Day.
Verdette Philippe, lab., res. n. s. Duck Creek rd., 1 w. Mather, Ft. H.
Verdoot Frank, res. 1602 Elm.
Ver Hagen John, carp., res. 1361 Day.
Verheyden Annie K., dressmkr, res. 614 S. Madison.
Verheyden George, painter, res. 728 Grignon.

**Headquarters for Boys' Clothing THE A. SPUHLER CO.** GREEN BAY.

Verheyden Henry, engineer, res. 614 S. Madison.
Verheyden Jacob, hostler, res. Manitowoc House.
Verheyden Joseph H., clk. Green Bay & Ft. Howard Water Works Co., res. 728 Grignon.
Verheyden Josephine (wid. Jacob), res. 638 S. Jefferson.
Verheyden Louis, lab., res. 614 S. Madison.
Verhoelsd August, lab., res. 509 Broadway, Ft. H.
Vernon Henry H., carp., res. 1147 Cass.
Verriden Henry, packer, res. 1251 Elm.
Verriden John, lab., res. 324 S. Van Buren.
Verriden Peter, del.-clk. Buengener & Bur, res. 114 S. Webster av.
Versin Edward, lab., res. 879 Dousman, Ft. H.
**VERSIN HUBERT**, gardener, res. 879 Dousman, Ft. H.
Versin John, lab., res. 879 Dousman Ft. H.
Versin Louis, lab., res. 879 Dousman, Ft. H.
Versin Theresa Miss, res. 879 Dousman, Ft. H.
Vervooren Annie, domestic n. w. cor. Willow and Shawano av., Ft. H.
Vervooren Edward, lab., res. w. s. Garfield, 1 s. Shawano av., Ft. H.
Vieau Charles G., lab., res. s. s. 9th, 3 w. C. & N. W. Ry. track, Ft. H.
Vieau David, lab., res. e. s. 5th av., 4 s. 9th, Ft. H.
Vieau Dominik, lab., s. w. cor. 9th and 7th av., Ft. H.
Vieau Eli, lab., res. 925 Dousman Ft. H.
Vieau Felix, lab., res. 925 Dousman, Ft. H.
Vieau Frank, lab., res. 9th av., 1 n. 9th, Ft. H.
Vieau George J., lab., res. 707 S. Adams.
Vieau Georgia Miss, 707 S. Adams.
Vieau John, lab., res. 925 Dousman, Ft. H.
Vieau Joseph, res. 707 S. Adams.
Vieau Joseph, foreman Water Works, res. s. s 9th, 3 w. C. & N. W. Ry. track, Ft. H.
Vieau Louis, lab., res. 925 Dousman, Ft. H.
Vieau Paul, lab., res. 1152 Crooks.
Vieau Rebecca (wid. Andrew), res. 721 S. Webster av.
Vieau Sophronia Mrs., res. 925 Dousman, Ft. H.
**VILATTE J. RENE MOST REV.**, Archbishop American Catholic church, also grand master of the order Cnevaliers of the Crown of Thorns, res. n. w. cor. Cass and S. 12th.
Vilim Frank P., grocer, 124 S. Monroe av., res. same.
Vilim Julia, clk., res. 124 S Monroe av.
Vilim Louis F., cigarmkr, res. 121 S. Monroe av.
Vilim Mary, clk., res. 124 S. Monroe av.
Villarce John, hostler, res. Bodart House.

Villiesse Anton, wheelsman, res. 1288 Main.
Villiesse Delia Miss, res. 1288 Main.
Villiesse George, broommkr, res. 1288 Main.
Villiesse Henry, res. 1288 Main.
Villiesse Jerome, broommkr, res. 1288 Main.
Villiesse Philomena Miss, res. 1288 Main.
Vincent Alphonse, stockdlr, res. 1113 Harvey.
Vincent Alice, domestic 619 Walnut.
Vincent Constant, cabinetmkr. and carver, 328 Main, res. 319 N. Jefferson.
Vincent David, lab., res. 1113 Harvey.
Vincent Eli, lab., res. 212 N. 11th.
Vincent Mary, domestic 103 S. Jefferson.
Vincent Mary (wid. John B.), res. 324 S. Van Buren.
Vincent Rachel Miss, dressmkr, res. 1113 Harvey.
Vincent Raphael, teamster, res. 1121 Pine.
Vitbreau John, night watchman, res. e.s. 4th av., 3 n. 9th, Ft. H.
Voegtar Mary Miss, res. 299 S. Adams.
Voigt Annie, domestic 809 Cherry.
Voigt Edward J., machinist, res. 127 Broadway, Ft. H.
**VOIGT JOHN M. MANUFACTURING CO. THE,** D. J. Davidson, pres.; F. A. Dieckmann, sec. and treas., sash doors and blinds, e. s. Pearl, opp. School pl., Ft. H.
Voigt Minnie (wid. John M.), res. 127 Broadway, Ft. H.
Vonckx Alphonse, lab., res. 6 w. 874 Dousman, Ft. H.
Vonckx Frank, lab., res. n. s. Bond, 9 w. Cedar, Ft. H.
Vonckx Joseph, bartender, res. 217 Main.
Von Goeben Alex., clk. Buengener & Bur, res. 701 Cherry.
Von Goeben Otto, com.-trav. Eckhardt & Schunck, res. 725 Walnut.
Von Goeben Tony Miss, res. 725 Walnut.
Vorpahl Augusta, domestic 122 Chestnut, Ft. H.
Vorpahl Lucie, domestic 309 Chestnut, Ft. H.
Voss Bertha (wid. Julius), res. 224 S. 10th.
Voss Herman, lab., res. 224 S. 10th.
Voss Louise Miss, res. 224 S. 10th.
Voss Paul, lab., res. 224 S. 10th.
Voss Rudolph, res. 224 S. 10th.
Vroman Charles (Greene & Vroman), res. 619 S. Quincy.
Vullengs John, gardener, res. 215 N. 11th.

# W

Wachal Annie, domestic 134 S. Jefferson.
Waeytens Emanuel, gardener, res. 854 Shawano rd., Ft. H.

**THE A. SPUHLER CO.** LADIES', MISSES' and CHILDREN'S
**GREEN BAY** **CLOAKS, CAPES, JACKETS**

Waggoner William H., pass and freight agt. Hart's Steamboat Line, res. 1019 Cherry.
Wagner Bertha, domestic 231 S. Jefferson.
Wagner Frederick A., painter, res. 1333 Mason.
**WAGNER HENRY,** wall paper, paints and oils, 220 Cherry, res. 412 Pine.
Wagner Jennie, clk., res. 412 Pine.
Wagner John G., photographer, n. e. cor. Pearl and Main, Ft. H., res. same.
Wagner John P., clk. The A. Spuhler Co., res. 528 N. Madison.
Wagner Julia (wid. Peter), res. 333 S. Van Buren.
Wagner Mamie Miss, dressmkr, 528 N. Madison, res. same.
Wagner Marie Miss, res. 412 Pine.
Wagner Mary C. Miss, nurse, res. 231 S. Jefferson.
Wagner Mattie Miss, res. 528 N. Madison.
Wagner Nicholas, res. 412 Pine.
**WAGNER WILLIAM P.,** cashier Citizens' Bank, res. 816 S. Madison.
Wagner William P., carpenter, res. 528 N. Madison.
Wah You, laundryman, res. 113 N. Washington.
Wahl Bernhard, butcher, res. 107 N. Washington.
Wakefield John F., millwright, res. 407 Chestnut. Ft. H.
Wakefield Miriam Miss, res. 407 Chestnut, Ft. H.
Walch Francis, land-hunter, res. e. s. McDonald, 9 s. lumber yd., Ft. H.
Walch John J., brakeman, res. w. s. McDonald, 9 s. lumber yd., Ft. H.
Walczak Frank, saloon, 435 Main, res. 1111 Cedar.
Walda Anton, carp., res. 224 Walnut.
Waldo Carl W., fireman, res. 1201 Doty.
Waldo Charles Jr., lab., res. 1201 Doty.
Waldo Frank, lab., res. 1201 Doty.
Waldo Morris A., carp., res. 409 Cherry, Ft. H.
Waldo Nellie J. Miss, teacher, res. 409 Cherry, Ft. H.
Waldo William, lab., res. 1201 Doty.
Walker Edwin E., bookpr. Standard Oil Co., res. 324 S. Adams.
Walker Ella B. (wid. H. A.) res. n. w. cor. 6th av. and 1st, Ft. H.
Walker Katie, cook, res. n. e. cor. S. Madison and Porlier.
Walker Matthew H., civil engineer, res. 324 S. Adams.
Walker William K., bookpr. Fred. Hurlbut, res. 324 S. Adams.
Wall James H., cond. C. & N. W. Ry., res. 129 S. Monroe av.
Wallace Edith Miss, res. 726 S. Jackson.
Wallace George E., fireman, res. 426 S. Monroe av.
Wallace Myra Miss, res. 726 S. Jackson.

| WAL | 242 | WAT |

Wallen John P., general yardmaster C. & N. W. Ry., res. 521 Chestnut, Ft. H.
Wallenfang Frank, lab., res. 102 Hubbard, Ft. H.
Wallenfang Henry, shoemkr, res. 102 Hubbard, Ft. H.
Wallenfang Joseph, saw-filer, res. 102 Hubbard, Ft. H.
Walley Catherine (wid. Joseph), res. 538 S. Monroe av.
Walley Lizzie Miss, dressmkr, res. 538 S. Monroe av.
Walsczinski Frank, lab., res. 1376 Cherry.
Walsczinski Joseph, cigarmkr, res. 1376 Cherry.
Walsczinski Justina Miss, res. 1376 Cherry.
Walt Michael, farmer, res. e. s. Bellevue, Town Preble.
Walters Augusta Miss, res. n. s. Elmore, 10 w. Willow, Ft. H.
Walters Edward, cigarmkr, res. 600 Chestnut, Ft. H.
Walters Felix, gardener, res. n. s. Elmore, 10 w. Willow, Ft. H.
Walers Jacob, gardener, res. 3 w. 854 Shawano rd., Ft. H.
Walters Jacob, lab., res. w. s. Cedar, 3 n. Dousman, Ft. H.
Walters John, city teamster, res. 301 Pearl, Ft. H.
Walters John, farmer, res. w. s. Cedar, 3 n. Dousman, Ft. H.
Walters John, res. s. s. Bond, 5 w. Willow, Ft. H.
Walters Peter, gardener, res. n. s. 3 w. 854 Shawano rd., Ft. H.
Walters William, gardener, res. 866 Dousman, Ft. H.
Walther Gustav, molder, res. e. s. 8th av., 2 s. 2d, Ft. H.
Walther Lena Miss, dressmkr, res. e. s. 8th av., 2 s. 2d, Ft. H.
Walther Louise (wid. William), res. e. s. 8th av., 2 s. 2d, Ft. H.
Warner Peter, clk., res. 1155 Main.
Wanske Frederick, sailor, res. 1221 Mason.
Ward George, fireman, res. Junction Hotel, Ft. H.
Warm Adolph F., barkpr., res. 312 Cherry.
Warm Conrad J., saloon, 312 Cherry, res. same.
Warren Albert A., insurance, real estate and loans, 301 N. Washington, res. 344 S. Monroe av.
Warren Clyde L., student, res. 344 S. Monroe av.
Warren Edgar B., clk. A. A. Warren, res. 344 S. Monroe av.
Warren Edward D., ticket clk. C. & N. W. Ry., res. The Beaumont.
Warren Fred. B., ins. agt., res. 308 S. Madison.
Warren Wm., supt. Odd Fellows' Home, res. 822 Grignon.
Waterloo House, Fabien Goel, prop., 323 Main.
Watermolen Augusta, domestic 103 S. Jefferson.
Watermolen Constant, lab., res. 1159 Walnut.
Watermolen Dora Miss, res. 637 S. Monroe av.
Watermolen F. Adolph, deputy clk. of courts, res. 637 S. Monroe av.
Watermolen Francis, res. 1159 Walnut.
Watermolen Henry, clk. of courts, res. 637 S. Monroe av.

THE A. SPUHLER CO., Green Bay CARPETS, RUGS, OIL CLOTHS
Draperies and Window Shades.

Watermolen Isabelle Miss, teacher, res. 637 S. Monroe av.
**WATERMOLEN JOHN F.**, U. S. Court commissioner and attorney, 300 N. Washington, res. 904 Crooks.
Watermolen Louise Miss, res. 637 S. Monroe av.
Watermolen Philip, lab., res. 1138 Walnut.
Watermolen William, grocer, n. w. cor. Harvey and N. 12th, res. 1366 Elm.
Waters Walter B., cooper, res. 105 S. Adams.
Wauters Charles, lab., res. 1483 Mason.
Wauters Peter, saloon, 507 Main, res. same.
Wavrunek Jacob, lawyer, 326 Main, res. 1415 Day.
Wawls John, grocer, 1610 Willow, res. same.
Webb E. Leolen, ship.-clk. J. P. Annen Candy Co., res. 718 Pine.
Weber Herman Sr., butcher, res. 1424 Elm.
Weber Herman Jr., butcher, res. Willmar House.
Weber John, lab., res. 1127 Pine.
Weber Joseph, hostler, res. Reis Hotel.
Weber Margaret Miss, dressmkr, res. 1424 Elm.
Weber Mathias, teamster, res. 1005 Cedar.
Webster Hubert W., captain, res. 800 Crooks.
Weddigen Arnold, bookkpr. Green Bay Creamery Co., res. 831 Walnut.
Weed Theresa (wid. Stephen), res. 921 S. Monroe av.
Weeks Frank R., sec. and treas. Fort Howard Lumber Co., res. 124 N. Monroe av.
Weeks William, mach., res. n. e. cor. 6th av. and 3d, Ft. H.
Wegner Charles, teamster, res. n. s. Main, 4 e. Forest.
Wegner Julius, teamster, res. n. s. Main, 4 e. Forest.
Weiand. See Wyhand and Weyand.
Weiderman Cora Miss, res. 214 Pine.
Weidner Ernst, mngr. Salvator Mineral Spring, res. 401 Main.
Weiher Otto, tailor, res. Ferris Hotel, Ft. H.
Weiler Michael J., ship.-clk. Theo. Kemnitz Furniture Co., res. 305 Broadway, Ft. H.
Weise Albert, pres. The Weise-Hollman Co., res. 117 S. Jefferson
Weise Albert W., electrician, res. 213 S. Adams.
Weise Charles W., mngr. Weise Furniture Co., res. 630 S. Madison.
Weise Furniture Co., A. Weise, prop., C. W. Weise, mngr., mnfr. of tables and beds, cor. Harvey and Jackson.
Weise George A., blksmith, 130 S. Washington, res. 213 S. Adams.
Weise George A., wagonmkr, res. 213 S. Adams.
Weise John B., mill-hand, res. 932 11th.

Weise Joseph, lab., res. 932 11th.
**WEISE & HOLLMAN CO. THE**, Albert Weise, pres.; Fred. A. Hollman, v.-pres.; Fred L. G. Straubel, sec. and treas.; whol. and retail crockery, 304-306 N. Washington.
Weissmiller A. N., student, res. American House.
Weissmiller Anna Miss, bookpr. J. Beth & Son, res. 119 N. Van Buren.
Weissmiller Edward, tinner, res. 119 N. Van Buren.
Weissmiller Lena, music teacher, res. 802 Doty.
**WEISSMILLER LOUIS P.**, cigarmkr, 110 N. Washington, res. same.
Weissmiller Oscar, drug clk., res. 119 N. Van Buren.
Wellems Anna (wid. Nicolas), res. 1511 Elm.
Wellems Annie, waitress The Beaumont, res. 1511 Elm.
Wellems Joseph, saloon, 215 Pine, res. same.
Wellems Lina, waitress The Beaumont, res. 1511 Elm.
Wellems Maggie Miss, res. 1511 Elm.
Wells Daniel W., lab., res. 103 Hubbard, Ft. H.
Wells Della L. Miss, teacher, res. 111 N. Van Buren.
Wells John, lab., res. s. s. 2d, 1 w. 10th av., Ft. H.
Wells Nellie E. Miss, res. 111 N. Van Buren.
Wendland John, engineer, res. e. s. Willow, 1 n. Baird, Ft. H.
Wendorff H. C. (Reinecke & Wendorff), res. 118 S. Jefferson.
Wenner John, stage driver, res. Reis Hotel.
Wenner Marie Miss, res. 414 Broadway, Ft. H.
Wenner Peter, res. 414 Broadway, Ft. H.
Werner John Peter, lab., res. Reis Hotel.
Wesley James, lab., res. n. e. cor. 5th av. and 9th, Ft. H.
Wesley Joseph, painter, res. n. e. cor. 5th av. and 9th, Ft. H.
Wesley Vincent, lab. res. n. e. cor. 5th av. and 9th, Ft. H.
West George, res. Odd Fellows' Home.
Westberg August, carp., res. n. w. cor. 9th av. and 2d, Ft. H.
Westcott Henry, lab., res. 526 N. Jefferson.
**WESTERN UNION TELEGRAPH CO.**, W. D. Lewis, mngr., 323 N. Washington.
Weston William, baker, res. 318 N. Quincy.
Wets Charles, lab., res. Dan McQueen's boarding house, Ft. H.
Weyand Peter, lab., res. 620 N. 12th.
Whealon Benjamin, barkpr., res. 435 N. 11th.
Wheeler Merritt, motorman, res. 309 Cedar, Ft. H.
Wheeler Merritt N., motorman, res. 311 Cedar, Ft. H.
Wheelock Frances C. (wid. Carleton B.), res. 118 S. Adams.
Wheelock Henry C., engineer, res. 118 S. Adams.
Whelen Lizzie (wid. Thomas C.), res. n. w. cor. Cedar and Hubbard, Ft. H.

**THE A. SPUHLER CO., GREEN BAY, WIS.** **Fine Dress Goods**
Samples Furnished on Application.

WHE 245 WIG

Whelen William H., conductor, res. 441 S. Adams.
Whipple Charles V., sawyer, res. w. s. Cedar, 3 s. Hubbard, Ft. H.
Whipple Edward, machinist, res. 311 Cedar, Ft. H.
Whitcomb Walter S., carp.-contr., 803 Crooks, res. same.
White Cora, domestic 410 Cherry, Ft. H.
White Edward E., teamster, res. Dan McQueen's boarding house, Ft. H.
White Frank, hostler, res. 415 Main.
White Henry J., livery, n. s. Main, near the Bridge, res. 112 S. Adams.
White Horace M., section boss G. B., W. & St. P. R. R., res. 835 Day.
White Nellie Miss, res. 112 S. Adams.
Whitmore Christina (wid. George), res. 308 2d, Ft. H.
Whitney Annie Miss, res. 422 Main.
Whitney Emmeline Miss, res. 422 Main.
Whitney Harriet H. Miss, res. 422 Main.
Whitney Helen D. Miss, res. 737 S. Monroe av.
Whitney Henry E., com.-trav., res. 422 Main.
Whitney Ira G., com.-trav., res. 737 S. Monroe av.
Whitney Ira G. Jr., res. 737 S. Monroe av.
Whitney John, call-boy C., M. & St. P. Ry., res. 422 N. Quincy.
Whitney Joshua, res. 402 Main.
Whitney Kate (wid. Charles), res. 422 N. Quincy.
Whitney Louise A. Miss, res. 737 S. Monroe av.
Whitney Mary Miss, res. 422 Main.
Whitney Mary (wid. William H.), res. 122 S. Van Buren.
Whitney Ruth G. Miss, res. 737 S. Monroe av.
Whittlesey Matthew, student, res. 218 S. Adams.
Widsteen Anna S. Miss, res. 532 Cherry.
Widsteen Gerhard O., res. 532 Cherry.
Widsteen L. F. Mrs., milliner, 204 N. **Washington, res. 532** Cherry.
Widsteen Lafayette F., clk. **Jorgensen Blesch Co., res. 532** Cherry.
Wiedemann Caroline Miss, housekpr 139 S. Madison.
Wierczinski Valentine Rev., res. 139 S. Madison.
Wieting August M. Rev., pastor German M. E. Church, res. 1025 Doty.
Wiggers Peter, grocer, 1400 Mason, res. same.
Wight Albert, res. 130 Chestnut, Ft. H.
Wight Charles, lab., res. 130 Chestnut, Ft. H.
Wight Edward, lab., res. 512 Chestnut, Ft. H.
Wight Joseph, del.-clk. M. J. Corbett, res. 130 Chestnut, Ft. H.

Wight Ralph H., civil engineer G. B., W. & St. P. Ry., res. Bay City House.
Wigman Anna Miss, res. 704 Cass.
Wigman John C., engineer, res. 301 S. Webster av.
Wigman John H. M. (Wigman & Martin), U. S. district attorney Eastern district Wisconsin, res. 704 Cass.
Wigman Josephine, stenographer, res. 704 Cass.
Wigman Lizzie Miss, clk. The A. Spuhler Co., res. 704 Cass.
**WIGMAN & MARTIN** (John H. M. Wigman and Patrick H. Martin), lawyers, 201 N. Washington.
Wilcox John L., harnessmkr, s. e. cor. Main and Chestnut, res. 303 Cedar, Ft. H.
**WILDE WILLIAM H.**, expert accountant, 209 N. Washington, res. 203 S. Jefferson.
Wildfang Addie Miss, res. 306 Cedar, Ft. H.
Wildfang Daniel, cabinetmkr, res. 306 Cedar, Ft. H.
Wiley J. M., teacher Green Bay Business College.
Wilner Henry, res. 121 N. Washington.
Williams Albert, res. 3 w. 929 Dousman, Ft. H.
Williams Caroline E. (wid. I. J.), res. 1227 Walnut.
Williams Charles J., barber, 204 Dousman, res. e. s. Cherry, 1 n. Kellogg, Ft. H.
Williams George S., conductor, res. 539 S. Adams.
Williams Harp, brakeman, res. 1227 Walnut.
Williams Henry, cigarmkr, res. 1329 Cherry.
Williams James A., foreman freight depot C. & N. W. R. R., res. 309 Cedar, Ft. H.
Williams Joseph, blksmith, res. s. s. St. Clair, 1 e. N. 11th.
Williams Matthew, lab., res. 402 1st, Ft. H.
Williquet Deliah Miss, res. 429 N. Jefferson.
Williquet Leola Miss, res. 429 N. Jefferson.
Williquet Pauline (wid. Eugene), res. 429 N. Jefferson.
Wilmar House, Mrs. L. Denis, prop., 433 Cedar and 503 N. Madison.
Wilmet Ernst, res. 1149 Walnut.
Wilmet Julia Miss, res. 1149 Walnut.
Wilmet Rose (wid. Alexander), res. 1149 Walnut.
Wilner Henry (Knox & Wilner), res. N. Washington.
Wilson Agnes Mrs., cashier Jorgensen Blesch Co., res. 134 S. Jefferson.
Wilson Albert, horse-dlr., res. American House.
Wilson Andrew, gardener, res. s. s. 9th, 4 w. C. & N. W. R. R. track, Ft. H.
Wilsing Andrew Jr., tinsmith, res. s. s. 9th, 5 w. ry.-track, Ft. H.
Wilson Arthur, lab., res. s.s. 9th, 5 w. C.& N.W.R.R. track, Ft. H.

**Headquarters for Boys' Clothing** THE A. SPUHLER CO.
GREEN BAY.

Wilson Ellen (wid. Joseph C.), res. 619 Walnut.
Wilson Fred. B. (W. Wilson & Sons), res. n. s. Duck Creek rd., 3 w. Mather, Ft. H.
Wilson George, lab., res. 416 N. Madison.
Wilson Henry E. (W. Wilson & Sons), res. n. s. Duck Creek rd., 3 w. Mather, Ft. H.
Wilson Maggie (wid. John). res. 402 Pine.
**WILSON ROBERT M.,** saloon, 120 3d av., res. 400 4th av., Ft. H.
Wilson William, lab., res. Eldred's boarding house, Ft. H.
Wilson William, agt. International Meat Co. of Chicago, res. 409 Chestnut, Ft. H.
Wilson W. A. (W. Wilson & Sons), res. n. s. Duck Creek rd. 3 w. Mather, Ft. H.
Wilson W. & Sons (W. A., Henry E. and Fred. B. Wilson), milkdlrs., n. s. Duck Creek rd., 3 w. Mather, Ft. H.
Wing Charles S., foreman Columbian Baking Co., res. 416 Cherry.
Wing Joseph B., lighthouse keeper, res. 719 Walnut.
Wing Myron P., res. 719 Walnut.
Wing Sam, laundry, 113 N. Washington, res. same.
Winnekens Henry, lab., res. 1149 Doty.
**WINTER THOMAS,** gunsmith and dealer in sewing machines, repairing of guns, bicycles, and sewing machines, 226 N. Washington, res. 1000 Walnut.
Wirth James, lab., res. 1326 Crooks.
Wirth Philip L., engineer, res. 1147 Pine.
Wirtz Nicholas (Wirtz & Schmidt), res. 301 Pearl, Ft. H.
Wirtz Peter, engineer, res. 424 N. Quincy.
Wirtz & Schmidt (Nicholas Wirtz and Gustav Schmidt), cigar mnfrs., 303 Pearl, Ft. H.
Wisconsin House, Louis Grossen, prop., 315 Main.
Wisconsin Telephone Co., John J. Schroeder, mngr., 202 N. Washington.
Witherill George, lab., res. 1206 S. Jackson.
Witters Frank H., clk., res. 516 Cedar, Ft. H.
Witters William L., flour and feed, w. s. Broadway, 2 s. Hubbard, res. 516 Cedar, Ft. H.
Wittinger John, lab., res. 816 3d av., Ft. H.
Wittinger Joseph, lab., res. 816 3d av., Ft. H.
Woehler Edward T. H., res. 309 Stuart.
Woelz Charles A., res. 421 N. 12th.
Woelz Christian, printer, res. 421 12th.
Woelz Christian A., bookbinder, res. 1291 Main.
Woelz Clara Miss, res. 1291 Main.

Woelz Frederick, clk. Wm Luckenbach, res. 813 Webster av.
Woelz Henry, lab., res. 1296 Main.
Woelz Leonard, jeweler, res. 813 S. Webster av.
Woelz L. Fred, harnessmkr, res. 813 S. Webster av.
Woelz Mary M. (wid. Christian), res. 1291 Main.
Woerpek Herman, messenger U. S. Ex. Co , res. 303 N. Jefferson.
Wohlfarth Frederick, clothing, 312-314 Broadway, Ft. H., res. same.
Wohlfarth Marie Miss, res. 312 Broadway, Ft. H.
Wohlfeil Albert, boilermkr, res. 719 3d av., Ft. H.
Wohlfeil August, machinist. res. 719 3d av., Ft. H.
Wohlfeil Fred, lab., res. 719 3d av., Ft. H.
Wohlfeil Herman, engineer electric light plant, res 321 6th av., Ft. H.
Wohlfeil Louise (wid. Chas.), res. w. s. 4th av., 2 s. 8th, Ft. H.
Wolcott Charles, res. Odd Fellows' Home.
Wolfe John, brakeman, res. 539 S. Adams.
Wolter Herman A., pres. George B. Hess Co., physician, 213 N. Washington, res. same.
Woltring Theodore, lab., res. s. e. cor. 8th and 4th av., Ft. H.
Wondrash Mary, domestic 843 S. Monroe av.
Wood Alice Miss, dressmkr, res. 1256 Cedar.
Wood Frances Miss, res. 1256 Cedar.
Wood Stephen, conductor, res. 720 S. Jefferson.
Wood Walter S., watchman, res. 1256 Cedar.
Woodard Charles, lab., res. 614 N. Jefferson.
Woodard Thomas B., res. 614 N. Jefferson.
Woodlawn Cemetery, w. s. Webster av., s. Derby.
Woodruff Eugene, contractor, res. 212 S. Madison.
Woodruff Laura Miss, res. 212 S. Madison.
Woodruff Mary A. Miss, res. 222 S. Jefferson.
**WOODRUFF WALTER H.**, mngr. Green Bay Creamery Co., res. 214 S. Webster av.
Woods Oscar, mill-hand, res. Eldred's boarding house, Ft. H.
Woodward Arthur D., clk., res. 601 Cedar, Ft. H.
Woodward Ella E. Miss, res. 601 Cedar, Ft. H.
Woodward James C., carp., res. 601 Cedar, Ft. H.
Woolford Eunice Miss, res. 302 S. Jefferson.
Woolford Mary Miss, res. 302 S. Jefferson.
Woolford William B., yardmaster C., M. & St. P. R. R., res. 302 S. Jefferson.
Worts Robert F., com.-trav., res. 222 Pine.
Woulier Joseph, watchman, res. 1345 Cherry.
**WRIGHT ALFRED G.**, pub. Green Bay Directory, 107 Wisconsin St., Milwaukee.

**THE A. SPUHLER CO.** *LADIES', MISSES' and CHILDREN'S*
**GREEN BAY** — **CLOAKS, CAPES, JACKETS**

Wright Anson F. (Wright Bros. & Rice), res. Iron Mountain, Mich.
**WRIGHT BROS. & RICE** (J. K. Wright, A. F. Wright and J. H. Rice), whol. cedar posts, lower Broadway, Ft. H.
Wright David, fireman, res. Northwestern Hotel, Ft. H.
Wright Jason K. (Wright Bros. & Rice), res. Marinette, Wis.
Wright J. F., bkpr. and stenog. Wright Bros., res. 134 Jefferson.
Wright Perry G., bkpr. 124 S. Washington, res. 331 S. Monroe av.
Wright Viola Miss, res. w. s. McDonald, 4 s. lumber yd., Ft. H.
Wright William, mason-contractor, n. s. 3d, 2 w. 8th av., Ft. H., res. same.
Wuertz William (Wuertz & Burkard), res. 718 Cherry.
**WUERTZ & BURKARD** (William Wuertz and John Burkard), decorators, fresco, sign and house painters, 718 and 927 Cherry.
Wyhand Sophie (wid. Joseph), res. 1421 Elm.
Wynen Bertha Miss, res. 1282 Chicago.

## Y

YOLKEY Alvina, domestic Commercial House, Ft. H.
Young Henry, conductor, res. 944 S. Jackson.
Young James F. Rev., res. 103 Cherry, Ft. H.
Young Pearl S. (C. P. Miller & Co.), res. 609 Main, Ft. H.
Young Wallie, grocer, wall paper and toys, 1100 Main, res. same.
Younkle Charles, lab., res. 728 St. George.
Younkle Wm., barn boss, res. Champion Hotel.
Ysebaert August, lab., res. s. s. Elmore, 1 w. Cross rds., Ft. H.

## Z

ZAHORIK Martin, watchman Henry Rahr's Sons, res. 300 N. 11th.
Zahorik Mary Miss, res. 300 N. 11th.
Zahorik Joseph, res. 300 N. 11th.
Zapfe Austin F., boilermkr., res. 200 7th av., Ft. H.
Zapfe Emil M., carp., res. 200 7th av., Ft. H.
Zapfe Fred. C., carp., res. 200 7th av., Ft. H.
Zapfe Herman G., carp., res. 200 7th av., Ft. H.
Zapfe Ida L. Miss, res. 200 7th av., Ft. H.
Zapfe Laura L. Miss, res. 200 7th av., Ft. H.
Zarinski Stephen, res. 1270 Stuart.
Zegers Dominic J. H., clk. Brauns & Van, res. 708 Walnut.
Zegers John, saloon, w. s. Webster av., 1 s. city limits, res. same.
Zegers Peter, lab., res. 708 Walnut.

| ZEL | 250 | ZIN |

Zeller Peter, engineer, res. 408 N. Adams.
Zellner Henry, clk. J. Beth & Son, res. 308 N. Quincy.
Zemanek Joseph, watchman, res. n. s. Main, 5 e. Forest.
Zens Joseph, hack driver, res. Adams House.
Zenz Frank, beer peddler, res. 235 S. Jackson.
Zenz Nicolas, malster, res. 235 S. Jackson.
Zeutzius Andrew, farmer, res. Schauer Hotel.
**ZEUTZIUS JOSEPH**, saloon, 1000 Main, res. Columbia Hotel.
Zeutzius Lorenz, beer peddler, res. 1278 Cedar.
Zicot Gustav, lab., res. Bodart House.
Ziebart Herman, lab., res. s. s. Shawano rd., 1 w. r. r. track, Ft. H.
Ziebell Ludwig, brewer, res. 1274 Cedar.
Zieger Bertha, domestic Schauer Hotel.
Ziehm Albert, printer, res. s. e. cor. 2d and 11th av., Ft. H.
Ziehm Edward, carp., res. s. e. cor. 2d and 11th av., Ft. H.
Ziehm William, fireman, res. s. e. cor. 2d and 11th av., Ft. H.
Zilke Minna, domestic 109 S. Monroe av.
Zilkoski Clara Miss, res. 1214 Walnut.
Zilkoski Emily Miss, dressmkr, res. 1214 Walnut.
Zilkoski Katie Miss, clk., res. 1214 Walnut.
Zilkoski Louis P., barber shop, 221 N. Adams, res. 1214 Walnut.
Zilkoski Maximilian, carp., res. 1214 Walnut.
Zilkoski Walter W., barkpr., res. Bradley House.
Zilles John, saloon and boarding, 428 Pleasant, res. same.
Zilles Matthias, saloon, 1247 Main, res. same.
Zimmer Anna Miss, teacher, res. 111 N. Van Buren.
Zimmer Herman, lab., res. 1148 Chicago.
Zimmermann Mary, chambermaid Adams House.
Zindel Bernhard, machinist, res. 108 5th av., Ft. H.
Zindel Lizzie, domestic 136 Chestnut, Ft. H.
Zindel Lottie Miss, res. 108 5th av., Ft. H.
Zingsheim Godfried, tinsmith, res. s. e. cor. N. Washington and Main.
Zingsheim John, tinsmith, res. 317 S. Van Buren.

# WRIGHT'S DIRECTORY
## OF
# GREEN BAY & FT. HOWARD,
## 1894.

### CLASSIFIED BUSINESS DIRECTORY.

| ABS | 251 | BAK |

### Abstracts of Title.
Land and Abstract Co. The, 301 N. Washington.

### Accountants.
**WILDE WILLIAM H.,** 209 N. Washington.

### Agricultural Implements.
Gonion N. H., 413 Main.
Smits & Simon, 1003-1005 Main.

### Architects.
Buck Carlos C., Citizens' National Bank bldg.
Clancy James E., 231 Pine.
Harteau David M., 505 Main.
**KENDALL WILLIAM F.,** 320 N. Washington.
Shultz C. E., 306 Dousman, Ft. H.

### Artists.
Lee Lottie Miss, 900 Walnut.

### Bakers.
Daems August, 212 N. Adams.
**COLUMBIAN BAKING CO.,** 401-411 Walnut.
Gass Louis, 219 Cherry.
Hottensen Carl, s. w. cor. Broadway and Hubbard, Ft. H.
Leisch M. & Son, 635 Main.
Peters Ernst, 322 Pine.
Rockstroh J. C., 115 N. Adams.

## Bands.

Fort Howard Cornet Band, H. C. Buenger, leader, e. s. Cedar, bet. Main and Hubbard.
Star Trombone Band, L. P. Weissmiller, mngr., 110 N. Washington.

## Banks.

**CITIZENS' NATIONAL BANK**, s. e. cor. N. Washington and Cherry.
**KELLOGG NATIONAL BANK THE**, 301 N. Washington.
McCartney National Bank, 309 Main, Ft. H.

## Barbers.

Beach George, 1119 Main.
Boileau Joseph, n. e. cor. S. Washington and Stuart.
Dietz George, 111 N. Washington.
Erdmann & Galineau, 210 Main.
First & Erdmann, 213 Cherry.
Gagnon M., 120 N. Washington.
Hogan Spencer, The Beaumont.
Jirssek George, 926 Main.
Kuhaupt Henry, 206 Main, Ft. H.
Mars Julius, 213 3d av., Ft. H.
Nadon Peter N., 311 Main.
Nineway Henry, 702 Main.
Puerner Otto F. W., 208 3d av., Ft. H.
Remich Anton, 216 Pine.
Remich Mathias, 307 Main.
Rose Vic, 324 Main.
Williams Charles J., 204 Dousman, Ft. H.
Zilkoski Louis P., 221 N. Adams.

## Bicycles.

Kerr Chas. S., 311 Pearl, Ft. H.

## Bill Posters.

**MALLORY J. H.**, 108 Walnut.

## Blacksmiths.

See also Horseshoers and Wagonmakers.

De Groot John, 1357 Main.
Heidgen Mathias, 212-214 Broadway, Ft. H.

**THE A. SPUHLER CO., GREEN BAY, WIS.** **Fine Dress Goods**
Samples Furnished on Application.

BOA 253 BOO

Kittner Edward C., 127 S. Washington.
La Duke George W., Broadway near Dousman, Ft. H.
Nelson John C., s. s. Charles, 7 w. Manitowoc rd.
Peterman & Foster, 1145 Main.
Peterson August, 144 Broadway, Ft. H.
Rothe William, 312 N. Adams.
**SIMON MATTHIAS,** 311 Main.
Smits Herman, 931-935 Main.
Staska Frank, 719 Main.
Van der Kellen Theod., w. s. Manitowoc rd., 4 s. Bellevue.
Weise George A., 130 S. Washington.

### Boarding Houses.
See also Hotels.

Absileus Frank, 418 N. Adams.
Alberts Katie, 110 S. Madison.
Catlin Margaret, 204 S. Madison.
De Vroey D. Mrs., 303 N. Jefferson.
Eldred's boarding-house, n. s. 2d av., cor. 10th, Ft. H.
Forrer Edward W., 229 S. Washington.
Hanrahan Michael, 505 Broadway, Ft. H
La Court Antoine, 425 Main.
McCarthey Jennie Mrs., 202 S. Jefferson.
McQueen Don, McDonald St., nr. McDonald Lumber Co., Ft. H.
Wilmar House, 433 Cedar.

### Boat Builders.

Conley Horace J., foot Stuart.

### Boiler Makers.

Burns D. M. & Son, e. s. Pearl, 1st and 3d s. Main, Ft. H.
O'Leary Bros., e. s. Pearl, 2 s. Main, Ft. H.

### Bookbinders.

Clark & Fiedler, 214 N. Washington.
Green Bay Advocate Co. The, 216 Pine.
Herrmann John & Son, 229 Pine.

### Books and Stationery.

**KUSTERMANN G.,** 217 N. Washington.
Lehman A. & E., 223 N. Washington.

## Boots and Shoes.

Aschenbrenner John, 1253 Main.
Brevig Peter E., 401 2d, Ft. H.
De Forest L. B., 210 Main, Ft. H.
Dittmer William, 1008 Main.
**ENGELS & MOHR**, 206 N. Washington.
**HAGEMEISTER LOUIS A.**, 312 N. Washington.
Hansen Bernard Nels P., 310 3d av., Ft. H.
Hoeffel Bros. Shoe Co., 302 N. Washington.
Knox & Wilner, 200-202 N. Washington.
**LOCHMANN PETER J.**, 1118 Main.
Mannebach John, 230 N. Adams.
Nick Joseph, 222 Walnut.
Planert August, 205 Broadway, Ft. H.
Schwartz Eli, 228 Main.
Shimonek Stephen, 210 Main.
Sommers William A., 108 Walnut.
Streckenbach & Nissen, 219 Broadway, Ft. H.
Summers William A., 108 Walnut.

## Brewers.

**HAGEMEISTER BREWING CO.**, 310 N. Adams.
**HOCHGREVE BREWING CO.**, w. s. Monroe av. rd., 2½ miles s. city.
**RAHR'S HENRY SONS**, 1317-1323 Main.
**VAN DYCKE O. BREWING CO.**, s. w. cor. Chicago and S. Jackson.

## Brick Yards.

Finnegan's Brickyard, e. s. 2d av., s. 10th.
Piraux Frank, cor. Porlier and Goodell.
Straubel Brick Co., Mary, at Mason st. bridge.

## Brokers—Merchandise.

North George L., 8 Parmentier blk.

## Broom Manufacturers.

Shepeck Frank, 1258 Main.

## Building Material.

Hurlbut Fred., 201 Cedar.

**Headquarters for Boys' Clothing THE A. SPUHLER CO. GREEN BAY.**

BUI 255 CAR

### Building and Loan Societies.
Union Building, Loan and Savings Assn., 8 Parmentier blk.

### Business Colleges.
**GREEN BAY BUSINESS COLLEGE,** n. e. cor. N. Adams and Walnut.

### Cabinetmakers.
See also Furniture.

Vincent Constant, 328 Main.

### Calciminers.
**WUERTZ & BURKARD,** 718 and 927 Cherry.

### Carpenters and Builders.
Anderson Martin, 606 1st, Ft. H.
Beerntsen William, n. s. Emilie, nr. Baird.
**CRONE & VAN DER STEEN,** 1707 Cedar.
Daggett Charles M., 118 6th av.
Dandoy Ferdinand, 701 S. Jefferson.
Davidson David J., 120 6th av., Ft. H.
De Groat Peter, 1020 Stuart.
Delloye Anton, 1111 Walnut.
Geniesse Jule H., 322 S. Van Buren.
**GREEN ADOLPH,** 1019 Pine.
Hansen Nels, 105 Chestnut, Ft. H.
Jenkins Lucius T., 793 Shawano rd., Ft. H.
Johnson & King, 1019 Harvey, and Cedar bet. 11th and 12th.
Jones Gustave, n. w. cor. 2d and 10th av., Ft. H.
**LORENT EUGENE,** 445 S. Madison.
Mann Gustav, 1250 Cedar.
Meister Christoph, 1150 Cherry.
Meister Herman E., 1128 Cherry.
Moes Peter, 706 Bond, Ft. H.
Moore Charles D., 224 Walnut.
Nitz Gustav, 315 S. Webster av.
Pinskowski Joseph, 1285 Doty.
Piska Frank, 327 S. Webster av.
Roy Thomas, 812 S. Van Buren.
Schmidt William C., 1214 Chicago.
**SERVOTTE E. W. & JOSEPH H.,** 508 S. Monroe av., and 1034 Walnut.
Tebo Louis, n. e. cor. Willow and Bond, Ft. H.
Tickler Albert J., 939 S. Quincy.
Whitcomb Walter S., 803 Crooks.

### Carpets.

**JORGENSEN-BLESCH CO.** (Limited), 303-307 N. Washington.
**SPUHLER A. CO. THE,** 229-231 N. Washington.

### Carpet Weavers.

Crary Mary, 514 Cedar, Ft. H.
Leach Ellen Mrs., 307 8th av., Ft. H.
Peterson Olava Mrs., 807 Cherry, Ft. H.
Santy May, 300 N. 11th.
Simmons Maria, 11-13 Pine.

### Carriage Manufacturers.

See also Wagonmakers.

Green Bay Carriage Co. The, 419 N. Adams.

### Cedar Ties and Posts.

Elmore J. H. & Co., 227 Pine.
Fisk W. J. & H. W., C. & N. W. depot, Ft. H.

### Cheese Dealers—Whol.

Udell S. R. & Co., 129 S. Washington.

### China and Glassware.

**BAUM JOHN,** 521 Main.
Weise & Hollman Co. The, 304-306 N. Washington.

### Cigar Mnfrs.

Barth Alois Jr., 1109 Cherry.
Eckhardt Oswald, 200 S. Quincy.
Gigler Jacob, 517 Main.
**HUERTH JOHN,** 308 N. Washington.
Jones & Eggner, n. w. cor. Main and Broadway, Ft. H.
Kirbey Charles R., 202 Dousman, Ft. H.
Nicholson E. C., 221 Cherry.
Nys David, 312½ Cherry.
Reis Jacob, 1142 Main.
Rutten Joseph, 1111 Crooks.
Schunck Charles Jr., 118 N. Washington.
**WEISSMILLER LOUIS P.,** 110 N. Washington.
Wirtz & Schmidt, 303 Pearl, Ft. H.

**THE A. SPUHLER CO.** LADIES', MISSES and CHILDREN'S
GREEN BAY — **CLOAKS, CAPES, JACKETS**

CIG    257    CON

### Cigars and Tobacco.
Schunck Charles Jr., 118 N. Washington.

### Cistern Manufacturers.
Gaffney L. H., 224 S. Van Buren.

### Civil Engineers.
Gayton D. C., 216 N. Washington.
**KENDALL WM. F.**, 6, 320 N. Washington.

### Clothing.
**BAUM JOHN**, 521 Main.
Coel F. & Son, 310 N. Washington.
Cohen Louis, 207 N. Washington.
Cohn & Gotto, 300 N. Washington.
Delaporte J. & Son, 218 N. Washington.
Hoffman William, 224 N. Washington.
Spitz Joseph, s. e. cor. N. Washington and Main.
Wohlfarth Frederick, 312–314 Broadway.

### Coal and Wood.
Bardouche J. B., foot N. Madison.
Barkhausen & Hathaway, w. end Walnut-st. bridge, Ft. H.
Hurlbut Fred, 201 Cedar.
McCormick & Flatley, 220–230 S. Washington.
**NICK JOHN**, foot N. Jackson.
Northwestern Fuel Co., foot Pine.
Van Schyndel Frank, 1329 Walnut.

### Coffee and Spice Mills.
Champion Coffee & Spice Mills, 118–124 S. Washington.

### Collection Agents.
**BRICE O. J. B.**, 35 Parmentier blk.
Martin Elie, 302 N. Washington.

### Commission Merchants.
Blesch Andrew, 717 Main.
**SELLERS MALCOLM**, w. s. 3d av., 2 n. 1st, Ft. H.

### Confectioners—Whol.
Annen J. P. Candy Co., 109-111 N. Washington.

### Confectioners—Retail.
Bodoh Agnes, 207 Chicago.
Cincick Mathias, 204 N. Adams.

33

Cody Delia, 201 3d av., Ft. H.
Huybrecht Lucy, 725 Main.
Lambrecht C. E. Mrs., 1248 Cherry.
McKeague Anna, 720 Main.
Mozer William T., 230 Pine.
Neumann Eliza, 221 S. Monroe av.
Straka Joseph, 1353 Main.

### Consuls.

**BRICE O. J. B.** (Belgian), 35 Parmentier blk.

### Contractors—General.

Basche Michael, 539 S. Jefferson.
Delanoy James K., 531 Main, Ft. H.
English Mark, 518 Walnut.
**GREEN ADOLPH,** 1119 Pine.
Greiling Bros., P. O. box 1356.
McGrath & Anderson, Citizens' National Bank bldg.

### Coopers.

Britton D. W., n. end N. Monroe av.
Morgenstern Henry, 514 N. 12th.
Porth & Harman, 401 Willow.
Schober Leonard, 117 S. Quincy.

### Cracker Mnfrs.

**COLUMBIAN BAKING CO.,** 401-411 Walnut.

### Creameries.

**GREEN BAY CREAMERY CO.,** n. e. cor. S. Adams and Doty.

### Decorators.

**WUERTZ & BURKARD,** 718 and 927 Cherry.

### Dentists.

Baldwin H. Walter, Citizens' National Bank bldg.
Ellsworth A. H., 206 N. Washington.
Gage C. O., 221 N. Washington.
Ringsdorf Warren N., 319 Broadway, Ft. H.
Theisen John B., 312 N. Washington.

### Draymen.

Armstrong Robert, 1030 Doty.
Shea Patrick, s. s. 2d, 3 w. r. r. track, Ft. H.
Van den Brook Peter, 708 Broadway, Ft. H.
Van den Brook William, 706 Broadway, Ft. H.

THE A. SPUHLER CO., Green Bay CARPETS, RUGS, OIL CLOTHS Draperies and Window Shades.

### Dredging Cos.

Green Bay Dredging and Pile Driving Co., 218 N. Jefferson.

### Dressmakers.

Anderson Anna Miss, 207 7th av., Ft. H.
Basten Gertrude, 521 Main.
Beahan Kate, 715 Pine.
Beneng Josie, 1115 Main.
Bentheimer Auguste Mrs., 1403 Cedar.
Berger Elizabeth, 528 St. George.
Blackman Hattie, 504 Moravian.
Bourden Georgianna, 418 Cedar.
Bowes Tessie, 1200 Walnut.
Bruner Barbara Miss, 409 S. Madison.
Burkard Anna, 927 Cherry.
Cannard Victoria, 1364 Elm.
Casper Lizzie Miss, 228 Pine.
Condon Maggie, 309 2d, Ft. H.
Cox Josephine, 327 S. Jackson.
Curran Anna, 231 S. Adams.
Curran Minnie, 231 S. Adams.
Daniel Katie Miss, 120 N. Adams.
Dean Olive, 527 S. Jefferson.
Dietrichson Catherine, 829 Pine.
Deuster Lizzie, 1251 Day.
Devillers Mary Miss, 1118 Cedar.
Du Chateau Alice, 401 S. Madison.
Friedel Rose, 1234 Chicago.
Geniesse Flora, 1244 Stuart.
Gerpin Lizzie, 708 3d av., Ft. H.
Grose Marie, s. w. cor. 9th av. and 5th, Ft. H.
Hammer Minnie, 301 Main.
Hansen Charlotte A., 1303 Cherry.
Hansen Hannah, 733 Pine.
Hansen Martha, 733 Pine.
Hanson Hanna, 320 S. Jackson.
Hanson Kittie, 320 S. Jackson.
Hanson Mary, 320 S. Jackson.
Haran Sarah, 621 S. Monroe av.
Hills Lizzie, 316 Pine.
Hinks Katie Mrs., 328 Pine.
Holzknecht Menne, 233 S. Quincy.
Horn Josephine, 604 St. George.

### Dressmakers—Continued.

Howlett Marie, s. w. cor. 2d av. and 8th, Ft. H.
Huenger Carrie, 627 Cherry.
Jacobson Lillie, 1249 Cherry.
Jansen Amalia Miss, 1274 Cherry.
Jeffrey Maud, 815 Stuart.
Kelleher Annie Miss, 121 S. Monroe av.
Klaus Christine, 1035 Main.
Knuth Josephine, 200 S. Jackson.
Leanna Tillie, 319 Pine.
Lemense Theresa, 918 Cherry.
Lintelmann Laura Miss, 1034 Cherry.
Ludwig Lena, 126 S. Quincy.
Lyon Nettie Miss, 1313 Doty.
McCabe Elizabeth, 914 S. Van Buren.
McKeough Maggie, 635 Cherry.
Maloney Anna, 126 S. Webster av.
Maloney Helen, 126 S. Webster av.
Mangless Emma, 1300 Doty.
Mannebach Annie, 1119 Cherry.
Martin Delia, 414 N. Monroe av.
Meister Mathilda Miss, 1150 Cherry.
Mickelsen Carrie, e. s. Rich rd., 2 s. 9th, Ft. H.
Miller Esther, 1025 Main.
Nichol Grace, 1207 Cherry.
Pennings May Miss, 1328 Elm.
Petry Mary, 808 Walnut.
Quigley Gussie, 1113 Mason.
Reinhardt Ella Miss, 206 N. Adams.
Rene Mary Miss, 36 Parmentier blk.
Rueckert Emma Miss, 1236 Cherry.
Saylor, D. May, 300 S. Madison.
Schaus Maggie Miss, 1132 Walnut.
Schleis Annie, s. e. cor. 5th av. and 9th, Ft. H.
Schmidt Anna, 1214 Chicago.
Servotte Emily A. Miss, 1034 Walnut.
Siegmund Emily Miss, 405 4th, Ft. H.
Siegmund Lena Miss, 405 4th, Ft. H.
Simon Eugenia, 1012 Main.
Simon Josephine, 1012 Main.
Smith Marie E., w. s. 2d av., 1 s. 7th, Ft. H.
Sorenson Nealie J., 700 S. Madison.
Ten Eyck Hattie L., 1133 Cherry.
Tennis Jennie Miss, 1102 Walnut.

**THE A. SPUHLER CO., GREEN BAY, WIS.** Fine Dress Goods. Samples Furnished on Application.

Tilton Carrie M., 614 S. Jefferson.
Verheyden Annie K., 614 S. Madison.
Wagner Mamie Miss, 528 N. Madison.
Walley Lizzie M., 538 S. Monroe av.
Wood Alice, 1256 Cedar.
Zilkoeki Emily Miss, 1214 Walnut.

### Druggists.

Bliedung Carl, 215 Cherry.
Cauwenbergh Bros., 213 N. Washington.
Hannon Felix J., n. w. cor. Broadway and Main, Ft. H.
King Edward B., 116 3d av., Ft. H.
Le Comte Charles, 225 Main.
Luckenbach William, 212 N. Washington.
Robinson John, 228 N. Washington.
Schroeder Charles W., 930 Main.
Shultz C. E., 306 Dousman, Ft. H.
Soquet Ralph, 324 N. Washington.
Tiernan James, 305 Main, s. w. cor. Broadway, Ft. H.

### Dry Goods.

See also General Stores.

**BAUM JOHN,** 521 Main.
Clark & Miller, cor. Main and Broadway, Ft. H.
Cohen Isaac, 124 N. Washington.
Gray Albert L., 217 Main, Ft. H.
Hoffman Robert, 125-127 N. Washington.
Jensen Hans, 118 3d av., Ft. H.
**JORGENSEN-BLESCH CO.,** 303-307 N. Washington.
Linenthal I. B., 112 N. Washington.
Mueller Theodore & Co., 311-313 N. Washington.
**SPUHLER A, CO., THE,** 229-231 N. Washington.

### Dyers.

**BUSCHER JOSUA,** 330 S. Washington.

### Electric Light Cos.

Green Bay & Ft. Howard Gas & Electric Light Co., 415 Elm.

### Electric Railways.

Fox River Electric Railway Co., 312-318 S. Washington.

### Elevators.

Ebeling John H., n. w. cor. S. Washington and Doty.
Cargill W. W. Co., Fox river, n. Dousman, Ft. H.

## Express Cos.

American Express Co., 224 N. Adams.
United States Express Co., 220 Pine.

## Fish—Wholesale.

Boaler Edwin, n. s. Willow, bet. Jefferson and Madison.
Hermes Arnold, e. s. McDonald, 2 s. lumber yd., Ft. H.
Hermes Henry, w. s. McDonald, 2 s. lumber yd., Ft. H.
Johnson John S., 1234 Main.
Leveille Joseph, n. w. cor. Elmore and Chestnut, Ft. H.
Saunders John, 709 2d, Ft. H.
**SCHILLER C.,** foot N. Jefferson.
Streckenbach C. W. & Co., 833 Cedar.

## Florists.

Noehle Theodore, 223 N. Jefferson.
Reinecke & Wendorf, 112 S. Jefferson.

## Flour Mills.

Ebeling John H., n. w. cor. S. Washington and Doty.
**HESS GEO. B. CO.,** n. w. cor. Cedar and N. Quincy.
Noffz John, s. w. cor. S. Washington and Doty.

## Flour and Feed Dealers.

See also General Stores, also Grocers.

Looze & Hoslet, 230 Main.
Witters William L., w. s. Broadway, 2 s. Hubbard, Ft. H.

## Fresco Painters.

**ERICKSEN MARTIN,** 335 Broadway, Ft. H.
**WUERTZ & BURKARD,** 718 and 927 Cherry.

## Fruit—Whol.

Larsen William, 103 Dousman, Ft. H.

## Furniture Dealers.

Dewan Eugene J., 226 Main.
Haupt George & Co., 109 S. Washington.
Lefebvre & Schumacher, 325-327 N. Washington.
Martin Fred., 115 3d av., Ft. H.
Mayer Henry, 725 Main.
Oldenburg G. & Co., 213 Main, Ft. H.

## Furniture Mnfrs.

Kemnitz Theo. Furniture Co., cor. Pearl and Baird, Ft. H.
Weise Furniture Co., cor. Harvey and Jackson.

**Headquarters for Boys' Clothing** THE A. SPUHLER CO. GREEN BAY.

### Furriers.
Hummel Johanna Mrs., 129 N. Adams.

### Galvanized Iron Works.
Joannes & Edwards, 225 N. Adams.

### Gardeners.
Adams Nicholas, 922 N. 12th.
De Roost Frank, 1 w. 854 Shawano rd., Ft. H.
De Witt Martin, 1161 Cherry.
Dunk Joseph, e. s. Goodell, cor. Eliza.
Huybrecht Ferdinand, 1120 Harvey.
Larscheid Lorenz, Cedar Creek rd., e. city limits.
Meert John B., s. s. Shawano rd., 1 w. Oneida rd., Ft. H.
Raymakers H. & Sons, 1400-1402 Main.
Sproedel Andrew, Cedar Creek rd., e. city limits.
Tease Victor, 1449 Smith.
Waeytens Emanuel, 854 Shawano rd., Ft. H.
Walters Jacob, n. s. Shawano rd., 3 w. 854, Ft. H.
Wilson Andrew, e. s. 9th, 4 w. C. & N. W. R. R. track, Ft. H.

### Gas Companies.
Green Bay & Ft. Howard Gas & Electric Light Co., 415 Elm.

### General Stores.
Alsteens Peter J., 1299 Main.
**BAUM JOHN,** 521 Main.
Berens Fred, 933-935 Walnut.
Meulemans Louis, n. w. cor. 3d av. and 4th, Ft. H.
Muller Henry & Co., 303-305 Main.
Rouse's Savings Bank, 320 N. Washington.
Sorensen J. A., s. e. cor. 3d av. and 9th, Ft. H.
Smith Bros., s. w. cor. Grove and Main.
Van Beek John L., 201 S. Quincy.
Vandenberg Albert, 408 3d av., Ft. H.
Van Deuren Peter J., 323 N. Adams.

### Grain Dealers.
Cargill W. W. Co., Fox River, n. Dousman, Ft. H.

### Grinders—Tool.
Kaspareck Frank, 1265 Main.

### Grocers—Whol.
Joannes Bros., 118-124 S. Washington.
**CORBETT MICHAEL J.,** 214-216 Main, Ft. H.

## Grocers—Retail.

Baerman Otto, 300 S. Webster av.
Beerntsen Henry, 1221 Crooks.
Beth John & Son, 315-319 N. Washington.
Beth Joseph, 1303 Walnut.
Bomber Joseph, 801 Harvey.
Bonlet Charles J., 431 Mason.
Brauns & Van, 203 N. Washington.
Brehme Herman E., 215 Main, Ft. H.
Bruyere Joseph, 1132 Cherry.
Buengener & Bur, 117-119 N. Washington.
Callaghan Bros., 212 Main, Ft. H.
Camm Thomas M., 221 Main, Ft. H.
Cathersol Frank, 513 Cedar, Ft. H.
Christman & Du Bois, 932-934 Main.
Coppersmith Theodore, 820 Crooks.
**CORBETT MICHAEL J.,** 214-216 Main, Ft. H.
Crimmins Jim, 1138 Main.
De Cremer Florian, 316 N. Washington.
Devroy Peter, 308 Dousman, Ft. H.
Derwae Arnold C., 1300 Cherry.
Gibson William H., 503 Main.
Gothe Fred, s. s. Shawano av., nr. city limits, Ft. H.
Hartmann Sylvester, 301 Willow, Ft. H.
Howlett James N., 805 3d av., Ft. H.
Jorgensen Rasmus A., s. w. cor. 3d av. and 4th, Ft. H.
Lefebvre Augustine, 500 S. Jefferson.
Leisch M. & Son, 635 Main.
Meyer Nicholas, 1200 Crooks.
Miller C. P. Co., 105 Broadway, Ft. H.
Miller & Juley, 214 3d av., Ft. H.
Mueller Henry, 1200 Doty.
Murphy Patrick, 206 3d av., Ft. H.
Nejedlo Bros., 321 N. Adams.
Nejedlo Louis E., 1374 Main.
Nelson G. T. Mrs., 700 2d, Ft. H.
Parmentier Bros., 313 Main.
Pigeon Peter J., 1114 Main.
Piraux Joseph, 711 Main.
Plotten Albert L., 310 Dousman, Ft. H.
Plotten J. J. & Sons, s. s. Dousman, 2 w. Broadway, Ft. H.
Prieve Herman A., 647 S. Jackson.
Raymakers H. & Sons, 1400-1402 Main.
Rousseau Louis, 1021 Main.

**THE A. SPUHLER CO.** LADIES', MISSES' and CHILDREN'S
GREEN BAY **CLOAKS, CAPES, JACKETS**

GUN 265 HID

Tennis Carrie, 635 S. Jefferson.
Tennis Leonard, 1100 Walnut.
Tennis Oliver, 445 S. Quincy.
Van Schyndel Antoinette, 1107 Main.
Vilim Frank P., 124 S. Monroe av.
Wawls John, 1610 Willow.
Watermolen George, 801 N. 12th.
Wiggers Peter, 1400 Mason.
Young Wallie, 1100 Main.

### Gunsmiths.
Hickok T. A., 401 Willow.
Thomas & Anheuser, 227 Pine.

### Hair Goods.
Caron Frank, 400 Broadway, Ft. H.
Gagnon M., 120 N. Washington.

### Hair Tonic Mnfrs.
Dietz George, 111 N. Washington.

### Hardware, Stoves and Tinware.
Brown & Tickler, 208 3d av., Ft. H.
Burns Thomas H., 109 Broadway, Ft. H.
Cooke William D., 201 N. Washington.
Danz Hillmar, 318 Main.
Findeisen Bros., 309 N. Washington.
Follett George B., 1234 Main.
Fontaine B. Hardware Co., 218 Main.
Gotfredson Bros., 1155-1157 Main.
Hambitzer Joseph, 218 Cherry.
Hartung Charles, 105 N. Washington.
Kimball Alonzo, 106-110 N. Washington.
Lucas D. & Son, 317 Broadway, Ft. H.
St. Louis J. J., 211 N. Washington.

### Harnessmakers.
Franssens John M., 223 Main.
Green Bay Leather & Harness Co., 208 N. Adams.
Hills L., 210 Cherry.
Markle George, 327 Main.
Van Ermen Frank, 229 Main.
Wilcox John L., s. e. cor. Main and Chestnut, Ft. H.

### Hides and Pelts.
Shire I. & Son, 119 N. Washington.

### Horse Breeders.

Desnoyers & Du Chateau, 329 N. Washington.
Kellogg Stock Farm, De Pere rd., 2½ miles s. city.

### Horseshoers.

See also Blacksmiths.

Brinneman & La Chapelle, 509 Main.
Peterson Thomas, 144 Broadway, Ft. H.
Schmitz Paul N., 613 Main.

### Hotels.

**ADAMS HOUSE,** 209-213 N. Adams.
American House, n. e. cor. N. Washington and Walnut.
Arlington Hotel, 419 Broadway, Ft. H.
Bay City House, 100-104 S. Washington.
Beaumont The, n. e. cor. Main and N. Washington.
Bodart House, 319 Main.
**BRADLEY HOUSE,** 411 S. Washington.
Broadway House, n. w. cor. Broadway and Dousman, Ft. H.
Champion Hotel, 215 Main.
Charles House, 108-110 S. Washington.
Columbia Hotel, 1106 Main.
Commercial Hotel, D. J. Smith, prop., 105 Broadway, Ft. H.
**COOK'S HOTEL,** s. w. cor. N. Washington and Cherry.
Coopertown House, 617 Main.
East River Hotel, 1273 Main.
**EMPIRE HOUSE,** 203 S. Washington.
Ferris Hotel, 216-218 3d av., Ft. H.
Green Bay House, 328 N. Adams.
Hall House, n. w. cor. Broadway and Baird, Ft. H.
Howard House, 205 Dousman, Ft. H.
Huffman House, cor. Broadway and Kellogg, Ft. H.
**JUNCTION HOTEL,** J. J. Nelson, prop., s. s. 2d, opp G. B., W. & St. P. depot, Ft. H.
**MAIN STREET HOTEL,** P. Robillard, prop., 316 Main.
Manitowoc House, 819 Main.
Northwestern Hotel, w. s. Broadway, 1 n. Kellogg, Ft. H.
**REIS HOTEL,** 1148 Main.
St. James Hotel, 117 S. Washington.
**SCHAUER HOTEL,** 401 Main.
**UNION HOUSE,** Fred. Martin, prop., 115 3d av., Ft. H.
Waterloo House, 323 Main.
Wisconsin House, 315 Main.

**THE A. SPUHLER CO., Green Bay** CARPETS, RUGS, OIL CLOTHS, Draperies and Window Shades.

### House Furnishing Goods.
Gotto Joseph, 231 Pine.

### House Movers.
Gravy John, n. e. cor. Division and Fink, Ft. H.
Jones Gustave, n. w. cor. 2d and 10th av., Ft. H.
Miller John, 520 S. Jefferson.

### Ice Dealers.
Duchateau Fred, s. s. Mather, 3 w. Willow, Ft. H.
Glass John, ft. N. Jefferson.
Le Clair Charles G., 519 S. Monroe av.

### Insurance Agents.
Ansorge & Parish, 126 N. Washington.
Brauns August, 220 N. Washington.
**BRICE O. J. B.,** 35 Parmentier blk.
Burdon Rowland T., 207 N. Washington.
Camm & Erbe, 312 Main, Ft. H.
Forrer Edward W., 229 S. Washington.
Hess Charles H., 9 Parmentier blk.
Killian John A., 218 N. Washington.
Leonard J. H., 105 N. Washington.
Libbey Oliver, 209 N. Washington.
Martin Elie, 302 N. Washington.
Martin Xavier, 318 N. Washington.
Martin & Jacobi, 218 N. Washington.
Mohr & Lenz, 217 N. Adams.
Reber Henry C., 331 S. Quincy.
Rondou F. Z., 220 N. Washington.
**SHEPECK JOHN JR.,** 314 Main.
Tayler Joseph, 131 Broadway, Ft. H.
Warren Albert A., 301 N. Washington.

### Iron Foundries.
**DUNCAN A. M.,** Broadway and John, Ft. H.
Eagle Foundry, n. w. cor. Pearl and Baird, Ft. H.
**GREEN BAY IRON AND BRASS FOUNDRY,** 318 N. 11th.
Schwartze C. & Sons, 1205-1207 Main.

### Jewelers.
**JANSSEN JOHN L. F.,** 916 Main.
**LIEBENOW JULIUS,** 205 N. Washington.

### Jewelers—Mnfg.

**JANSSEN JOHN L. F.**, 916 Main.
**LIEBENOW JULIUS**, 205 N. Washington.

### Junk Dealers.

Shapiro Wolf, 1123 Main.

### Justices of the Peace.

Grignon D. H., 112 N. Washington.
Hood William, 218 Main, Ft. H.
Martin Elie, 302 N. Washington.
**SELLERS MALCOLM**, w. s. 3d av., 2 n. 1st, Ft. H

### Land Agents.

Van Derzee Frank, 227 Pine.
Fisk Land & Lumber Co., C. & N. W. depot, Ft. H.

### Laundries.

Conradsen Nels P., 303 3d av., Ft. H.
Green Bay Steam Laundry No. 1, 408 N. Adams.
Monastery of Our Lady of Charity, laundry department. n. w. cor. Milwaukee and S. Madison.
Wing Sam, 113 N. Washington.

### Lawyers.

Cady & Huntington, 205 N. Washington.
Calkins Lafayette A., 218 Main, Ft. H.
Ellis & Merrill, 4-7 Parmentier blk.
Greene & Vroman, 301 N. Washington.
Grignon David H., 112 N. Washington.
Hudd Thomas R., 3 P. O. blk.
Huntington Howard J., Court House.
Le Clair Joseph C., 420 Howard.
Lomas Charles W., n. e. cor. Broadway and Main, Ft H.
McGruer Alexander D., 3 P. O. blk.
North Jerome R., 301 N. Washington.
Sheridan Philip, 3 P. O. blk.
Watermolen John F., 300 N. Washington.
Neville John C. & A. C., 307 N. Washington.
Wavrunek Jacob, 326 Main.
Wigman & Martin, 201 N. Washington.

### Leather and Findings.

Meyer Nicholas, 221 Main.

### Lime Dealers.

Champeau Joseph, 216 Cedar.
Schroeders Jules, 427 Willow.

### Live Stock Dealers.

Kaufmann Herman, 1504 Elm.

### Livery Stables.

**BLACK J. J.**, 3d av., near Broadway bridge, Ft. H.
Bowser Frederick A., w. s. Broadway, 3 s. Hubbard, Ft. H.
**CARLIN PATRICK H.**, 103-105 S. Washington.
Crocker Ephraim, 208 Broadway, Ft. H.
**FLATLEY DOMINIC**, 220 N. Adams.
**McKONE JAMES**, 415-417 Main.
Peterson Willis H., w. end Walnut-st. bridge, Ft. H.
**REIS ANDREW JR.**, 1148 Main.
**SELLERS MALCOLM A.**, w. s. 3d av., 1 s. the slough, Ft. H.
**SNYDER FRANK**, 215 N. Adams.
White Henry J., n. s. Main, near the Bridge.

### Lumber Mnfrs. and Dealers.

**ADAMS A. L. & CO.**, n. w. cor. 2d av. and 10th, Ft. H.
Brown-Chapin Lumber Co., s. w. cor. 2d av. and 10th, Ft. H.
Dobry Josephine, cor. Cedar and N. Van Buren.
Eldred Anson & Son, e. s. 2d av., s. 10th, Ft. H.
Fort Howard Lumber Co., w. s. 2d av., cor. 10th, Ft. H.
Green Bay Planing Mill Co., N. Adams, n. e. cor. Cedar.
**McDONALD H.**, n. end Broadway, Ft. H.
Murphy Lumber Co., mouth of Fox river, n. city limits.
Schwarz C. & O., e. s. Pearl, s. School place.
Wright Bros. & Rice, lower Broadway, Ft. H.

### Machine Shops.

Burns D. M. & Son, cor. Pearl and Main, Ft. H.
Halbach Albert, w. s. Pearl, 2 s. Main, Ft. H.
Howard Foundry and Machine Works, cor. Broadway and John, Ft. H.
Schwartze C. & Sons, 1207 Main.

### Marble Works.

Johnson Ambrose W., 310 Cherry.
**MANTHEY CARL**, 132 S. Washington.

## Mason Contractors.

Destree Frank, 729 Harvey.
**FABRY & HENKELMANN**, 330 S. Jackson.
**GOLUEKE CHARLES**, 921 Cherry.
Krake Ira, n. e. 5th av. and 10th, Ft. H.
Lagers Peter, 426 N. 11th.
**MAY PETER**, 1019 Walnut.
**ROSE JOHN B.**, 1263 Day.
Schauwers Felix, 1120 Walnut.
**SCHMIDT HERMAN**, 619 S. 11th.
Spude & Koch, 201 S. Van Buren.
Ten Eyck William B., 1133 Cherry.
Wright William, n. s. 3d, 2 w. 8th av., Ft. H.
Rose John B., 1263 Day.

## Meat Markets.

Burghardt & Duchateau, 505 Main.
Busch Louis, 1249 Main.
Humpfner E. & Co., 544 S. Monroe av.
Kalb Louis, 107 N. Washington.
Kaufmann Louis, 1447 Cedar.
Klaus Louis C., 1035 Main.
Leidel Albert, 1149 Main.
Mattern Bros., 300 S. Quincy.
Nau George D., 121 N. Washington.
Platten Bros., 305 Main and s. s. Dousman, nr. Broadway, Ft. H.
Reis L. L., 210 N. Adams.
Schefe Fred. T., 114 3d av., Ft. H.
Schumacher Bros., 314 and 924 Main.
Stenger George, 321 N. Washington.
Stenger George & Bro., 317 Main, Ft. H.

## Merchant Tailors.

Brandenstein W. A., 311 Cherry.
Delaney J. Henry, 122 N. Washington.
Delmarcelle Bros., 1117 Walnut.
Detienne Bros., 126 N. Washington.
**FRISQUE FLORENTIN**, 222 Main.
**HOFFMANN WILLIAM**, 224 N. Washington.
**HOPPE JOSEPHINE F. MRS.**, 219 N. Adams.
Kaster Castor, 209 Pine.
Krippner & Kaye, 313 Main, Ft. H.
Larsen Christopher, 306 4th, Ft. H.
Lumaye Julius, 214 Main.

**Headquarters for Boys' Clothing** THE A. SPUHLER CO.
GREEN BAY.

Mahn Theodore, 407 Broadway, Ft. H.
**MAHN WILLIAM C.**, s. e. cor. Pine and Adams.
Neufeld Philip, 229 Cherry.
Redman August, 702 Main.

### Midwives.
Bitter Mary, 203 Baird, Ft. H.

### Milkmen.
Dielen Jacob, 1400 Baird.
Kuehl Bros., s. s. 9th, 2 w. C. & N. W. R. R. track, Ft. H.
Mickelsen Jacob, e. s. Rich rd., 2 s. 9th, Ft. H.
Wilson W. & Sons, n. s. Duck Creek rd., 3 w. Mather, Ft. H.

### Mill Supplies.
Kimball Alonzo, 106-110 N. Washington.

### Milliners.
De Both Mary V. Mrs., 311 N. Adams.
Howlett Nellie L., 313 Broadway, Ft. H.
McComber John Mrs., 223 Cherry.
McFayden Finley Mrs., 219 N. Washington.
Marshall William, 309 Main, Ft. H.
Potts S. G. Mrs., 209 Washington.
**SPUHLER A. CO. THE**, 229-231 N. Washington.
Stone J. A. Mrs., 201 3d av., Ft. H.
Widsteen L. F. Mrs., 204 N. Washington.

### Mineral Water.
Allouez Mineral Spring Co., s. e. cor. Chicago and S. Jackson.
Green Bay Mineral Spring Co., 300 S. Jackson.
**LEBENS WASSER MINERAL SPRINGS**, 529 S. Monroe av.
**ST. JOHN MINERAL WATER**, n. s. Stuart, bet. S. Quincy and S. Jackson.
**SALVATOR MINERAL SPRINGS**, s. e. cor. S. Monroe av. and Mason.

### Ministers.
Anderegg Martin T. Rev. (Cath.), 710 Pleasant.
Erpling Frederick Rev. (Luth.), 1026 Cherry.
Fox J. J. Very Rev. (Cath.), 139 S. Madison.
Gronfeld John J. (Moravian), 409 4th, Ft. H.
Haff Franklin R. (Epis.), 419 Cherry.
Hewitt John L. (Pres.), 417 S. Adams.
Huth William (Luth.), 226 S. Madison.

### Ministers—Continued.

Lau Clement (Cath.), 128 S. Monroe av.
Meinert Herman (Mor.), 512 Moravian.
Messmer S. G. Right Rev. (Cath.), 139 S. Madison.
Mousseau George C. Rev. (Pres.), 218 N. Madison.
O'Brien Michael John (Cath.), 401 Cherry, Ft. H.
Peterson Adolph (Luth.), 106 Chestnut, Ft. H.
Pleimling Nicolaus Rev. (Am. Cath.), s. w. cor. Cass and S. 12th.
Ricklin Leo A. (Cath.), 413 Milwaukee.
St. Louis Philip (Cath.), 812 Crooks.
Schneider John (Method.), 403 Chestnut, Ft. H.
Siegrist Jacob (Ev. Luth.), 909 Cherry.
Smith Granger W. (Bap.), 308 Chestnut.
Thompson Henry W. (M. E.), 509 School.
Van Roosmalen Wm. F. (Cath.), 209 S. Adams.
Vilatte J. Rene Most Rev. (Am. Cath.), n. w. cor. Cass and S. 12th.
Wieting August M. Rev. (M. E.), 1025 Doty.
Young J. Frank (Presb.), 103 Cherry, Ft. H.

### Mortgage Loans.

Kyber George E. T., 214 N. Washington.

### Mouldings.

**OLDENBURG & CO.**, n. w. cor. Pearl and Main, Ft. H.

### Musical Mdse.

Dickinson Music Co., 206 N. Adams.
**KÜSTERMANN GUSTAV,** 217 N. Washington.

### Music Teachers.

Ansorge Wm. K., 1001 Walnut.
Austin Thirsa, 309 Cedar, Ft. H.
Babcock Stella Miss, 315 S. Jackson.
Blesch Louise Miss, 325 Willow, Ft. H.
Camm Edith M., 318 Main.
Hollister Annie E., 902 Mason.
Ording Ada, 1227 Cherry.
Preville Agnes, 525 S. Quincy.
Robinson Belle Miss, 510 Chestnut, Ft. H.
Salvo Louise Miss, 320 Pearl, Ft. H.
Schaumberg Fred., 831 Walnut.
Schuette Clara, 621 Main.
Siegrist Rachael, 909 Cherry.
Van Halder Octavia, 1166 Mason.
Weissmiller Lena, 802 Doty.

**THE A. SPUHLER CO.** GREEN BAY — LADIES', MISSES' and CHILDREN'S **CLOAKS, CAPES, JACKETS**

### News Depots.

Carlisle James H., 315 Broadway, Ft. H.
Dickinson Edwin M., 206 N. Adams.
Iversen Tor, e. s. 3d av., 2 s. 2d, Ft. H.

### Newspapers.

Fort Howard Review, 309 Pearl, Ft. H.
Green Bay Advocate, 216 Pine.
Landsmann Der, 222 N. Adams.
Onze Standaard, 315 Pine.
State Gazette The, 116 N. Washington.

### Notaries Public

Abrams Winfred, 402 S. Webster av.
Ansorge E. K., 126 N. Washington.
Baker H. B., 301 N. Washington.
Bartran W. H., 307 Broadway, Ft. H.
Beaumont Sophie, 301 N. Washington.
Bong Gerhard, 301 S. Quincy.
Brauns August, 220 N. Washington.
Brett Fred. N., 231 S. Jefferson.
Brice O. J. B., 35 Parmentier blk.
Cady F. C., 205 N. Washington.
Calkins L. A., 218 Main, Ft. H.
Ellis E. H., 4-7 Parmentier blk.
Greene George G., 301 N. Washington.
Hart Peter C., s. e. cor. Cedar and Hubbard, Ft. H.
Hawley Alice M., 408 Kellogg, Ft. H.
Hood William, 218 Main, Ft. H.
Hudd T. R., 3 P. O. blk.
Huntington S. P., 205 N. Washington.
Jacobi Manfred, 218 N. Washington.
Kaster Joseph, 310 N. Adams.
Kendall P. R., 301 N. Washington.
Kerr James, 309 Pearl, Ft. H.
Killian J. A , 218 N. Washington.
Kyber George E. T., 214 N. Washington.
Lenz Charles, 512 Doty.
Lomas Charles W., 122 Chestnut, Ft. H.
McGruer A. D., 3 P. O. blk.
Marique Eli, 116 N. Washington.
Martin Elie, 302 N. Washington.
Martin J. F., 736 S. Madison.
Martin P. H., 201 N. Washington.

### Notaries Public—Continued.

Martin Xavier, 318 N. Washington.
Masse A. G. M., 319 Lawe.
Merrill Carlton, 4-7 Parmentier blk.
North Jerome R., 301 N. Washington.
Parish E. P., 126 N. Washington.
Parker B. L., 301 N. Washington.
Parkes J. T., 100 N. Madison.
Ranolds Warden, 435 S. Webster av.
Reber H. C., 331 S. Quincy.
Rondou F. Z., 220 N. Washington.
Sellers M. A., 3d av., s. the slough, Ft. H.
Sellers Maggie J. Miss, 320 6th av., Ft. H.
Sellers Malcolm, w. s. 3d av., 2 n. 1st, Ft. H.
Shepeck John, 314 Main.
Tayler J. H., 309 Main, Ft. H.
Vroman Chas. E., 301 N. Washington.
Wagner W. P., Citizens' Bank.
Watermolen F. A., 637 S. Monroe av.
Watermolen J. F., 300 N. Washington.
Wavrunek Jacob, 326 Main.
Weeks Frank R., Ft. Howard Lumber Co., Ft. H.

### Nurserymen.

Drake James, 912 S. Jackson.

### Nurses.

Lee Anna Mrs., 722 Cedar.
Quinn Delia Miss, 509 S. Monroe av.

### Oculists.

Beaupre William, 121 N. Washington.
Hagen W. T., 217 N. Washington.

### Oil Dealers.

Hurlbut Fred., 201 Cedar.
Standard Oil Co., 213 Cedar.

### Opera Houses.

Klaus Opera House, 222-226 Pine.

### Opticians.

**LIEBENOW JULIUS**, 205 N. Washington.

**THE A. SPUHLER CO., Green Bay** CARPETS, RUGS, OIL CLOTHS, Draperies and Window Shades.

### Paint Mnfrs.

Cointe Aristide J., n. e. cor. 5th av., n. G. B., W. & St. P. R. R. track, Ft. H.
Henderson Robert & Co., 202 Broadway, Ft. H.

### Painters.

Brice Louis C., 1253 Stuart.
Crikelair Frank, 120 N. Adams.
De Moore John B., 327 Main.
Dessain Louis, n. e. cor. Guesnier and Dousman, Ft. H.
Detienne Victor, 336 S. Jackson.
**ERICKSEN MARTIN**, 335 Broadway, Ft. H.
Haworth John, 508 S. Quincy.
**KRAKE IRA**, n. e. cor. 5th av. and 10th, Ft. H.
May Henry, 205 N. Washington.
Notting John, 1235 Cherry.
Pahr William T., s. s. Shawano rd., 6 w. Willow, Ft. H.
Rosse Martin, 445 S. Madison.
Ruf John, 1251 Walnut.
Wagner Henry, 220 Cherry.
**WUERTZ & BURKARD**, 718 and 927 Cherry.

### Paints and Oils.

Marvin William H., 323½ N. Washington.

### Paperhangers.

**MALLORY JOHN H.**, 108 Walnut.
**OLDENBURG & CO.**, n. w. cor. Pearl and Main, Ft. H.
**WUERTZ & BURKARD**, 719 and 927 Cherry.

### Pension Agents.

Sellers Malcolm, 110 3d av., Ft. H.

### Photographers.

Kurz Albert G., 210-212 Cherry.
Lund Jens, 1401 Crooks.
Nuss W. Wesley, 215 N. Washington.
Schneider Fred. W., 310 N. Washington.
Schroeder Charles F., 313 N. Quincy.
Wagner John G., n. e. cor. Main and Pearl, Ft. H.

### Physicians.

Bartran William H., 307 Broadway, Ft. H.
Beck H. M., 205 N. Washington.
Brett B. C., 124 N. Adams.

### Physicians—Continued.

Coffeen W. B., 313 Cherry.
Crane C. E., 207 N. Washington.
Fairfield William E., Citizen's National Bank bldg.
Hittner Henry M., 10 Parmentier blk.
Lewis Frank L., 228 N. Washington.
Marchand Pierre, 222 Cherry.
Metcalf Arthur A., 326 N. Monroe av.
Minnehan J. R., 1 Parmentier blk.
Olmsted A. F., P. O. bldg.
Rhode Henry, 226 N. Washington.
Rhode H. P., 226 N. Washington.
Slaughter A. W., 224 N. Washington.
Wolter Herman A., 213 N. Washington.

### Pianos and Organs.

**KÜSTERMANN GUSTAV**, 217 N. Washington.

### Piano Tuners.

Lambrecht Charles Erich, 1244 Cherry.

### Pickle Mnfrs.

Alart & McGuire, Broadway, between Bond and Mather, Ft. H.

### Planing Mills.

Green Bay Planing Mill Co., N. Adams, n. e. cor. Cedar.
Mueller Bros. & Co., Cedar, n. w. cor. 10th.

### Platers—Gold and Silver.

**JANSSEN JOHN L. F.**, 916 Main.

### Plumbers.

Brehme Anton, 217 Broadway, Ft. H.
Case & Co., 217 N. Adams.
Green Bay Plumbing & Heating Co., 224 Pine.
Morgan Edward B., 311 3d av., Ft. H.
Skogg Nels, 313 Cherry.
Thomas & Anheuser, 227 Pine.

### Police Justices.

Smith Edwin R., 34 Parmentier blk.

### Potash Mnfrs.

Brossig & Klesse, Sturgeon Bay rd., e. city limits.

THE A. SPUHLER CO., GREEN BAY, WIS. **Fine Dress Goods** Samples Furnished on Application.

### Printers.

Clark & Fiedler, 214 N. Washington.
Fort Howard Review, 313 Pearl, Ft. H.
Green Bay Advocate Co., 216 Pine.
**LEHMAN & ROBINSON,** 222 N. Adams.
Root Erastus, 225 Pine.
Standard Printing Co., 315 Cherry.
State Gazette The, 116 N. Washington.

### Produce Dealers—Whol.

Larsen William, s. e. cor. Pearl and Dousman, Ft. H.
Dorschel L. D. & Bro., 114-116 S. Washington.
**SCHILLING EDMUND,** 907 Main.

### Railroads.

Chicago, Milwaukee & St. Paul Ry., James H. Flatley, station agent, depot Washington, s. w. cor. Crooks.
Chicago & Northwestern Ry., depot Broadway, near Dousman, Ft. H.
Green Bay, Winona & St. Paul Ry., gen. offices s. e. cor. Adams and Pine, depot n. e. cor. Pearl and 3d, Ft. H.
Kewaunee, Green Bay & Western R. R., offices s.e. cor. Adams and Pine, depot s. e. cor. Washington and Crooks.

### Real Estate Dealers.

Boland Edmund P., P. O. blk.
**BRICE O. J. B.,** 35 Parmentier blk.
Kyber George E. T., 214 N. Washington.
Landwehr Sebastian, e. s. Oneida, 1 s. Shawano rd, Ft. H.
Martin Xavier, 318 N. Washington.
Martin & Jacobi, 218 Washington.
Parmentier Jules, 35 Parmentier blk.
**SHEPECK JOHN JR.,** 314 Main.

### Restaurants.

Blandin Frank, 222 Pine.

### Rubber Stamps.

Howard Rubber Stamp Co., James Kerr & Sons, props., 311 Pearl, Ft. H.

### Saloons.

Allen William B., 216 N. Washington.
Bader Victor, 301 Main.
Bahan Patrick, 227 Main.
Barth Edward, 103 N. Washington.

### Saloons—Continued.

Barth Martin, 214 Pine.
Basten Joseph, 225 N. Washington.
**BENDER SEBASTIAN,** 226 Pine.
Bhirdo Peter, 1106 Main.
Bibel Frank, n. w. cor. Manitowoc rd. and Charles.
Bidoul John, 705 Main.
Birmingham William, 322 N. Washington.
Bodart August, 319 Main.
Bodart Henry, 702 Main.
Boggs Samuel, s. w. cor. Manitowoc rd. and Finger rd.
**BOUCHARD A. H.,** 203 S. Washington.
**BRADLEY D. P.,** 409 S. Washington.
Brown County Fair and Park Assn., e. end Walnut.
Bunker A. C., 224 Main.
Champagne Joseph, 217 Main.
Church A., 117 S. Washington.
Coal Fabien, 323 Main.
Cook James McG., 323 N. Washington.
**COOK'S HOTEL,** s. w. cor. N. Washington and Cherry.
Deaisch Joseph, 1129 Main.
Dittmer Ludwig, 319 N. Adams.
Engels William, 215 Main.
Fastry William, 329 N. Washington.
Freimann Michael, 347 S. Washington.
Garner William, 222 N. Washington.
Gehr Frederick, 318 N. Washington.
Gothe Frederick, s. s. Shawano rd., near city limits, Ft. H.
Gregor Frank, 718 Main.
Grognet & Mannebach, 231 Cherry.
Gronnert Fred, 1273 Main.
Gross Frederick P. Jr., 215 Broadway, Ft. H.
Gross John G., s. w. cor. Pearl and Main, Ft. H.
Grossen Louie, 315 Main.
Hochgreve August, 320 Main.
Hoppe Otto F., 116 Broadway, Ft. H.
Jobelius John, 1301 Main.
**JUENGER JOHN P.,** 429 Broadway, Ft. H.
Karsten Mathias A., 204 3d av., Ft. H.
Klesges Valentine, 208 N. Washington.
Kolocheske Thomas, 617 Main.
Lachance Henry E., 225 Cherry.
La Court Antoine, 425 Main.

**Headquarters for Boys' Clothing** THE A. SPUHLER CO. GREEN BAY.

Laes Lambert, 729 Main.
Larscheid Lorenz, Cedar Creek, e. city limits.
Lindsley Louis, 1281 Main.
Loewert Henry, 531 Walnut.
McEvoy John B., 320 Main.
Masson Louis, 1101 Main.
Mohr John E., 925 Main.
Mornard Julius, 501 Main.
Mueller Carl, 220 N. Washington.
Nickolai Joseph, 519 Main.
O'Brien Timothy, 101 N Washington.
Penney Patrick, 328 N. Adams.
**PETCKA JAMES,** 322 Main.
Pfotenhauer Charles, 216 Cherry.
Plantikow John, 819 Main.
Quatsoe Celia, 230 Walnut.
Radclet Gust, 119 N. Adams.
Redeman Charles W., 108–110 S. Washington.
**REIS ANDREW JR.,** 1148 Main.
**ROBILLARD PETER,** 316 Main.
Ross John W., 309 N. Adams.
Rothe Charles B., 1375 Main.
Rothe Peter, 1347 Main.
Rueth William, s. w. cor. 2d av. and 9th, Ft. H.
St. Clair William, e. s. 3d av., 1 n. the slough, Ft. H.
Schauer Bros., 401 Main.
Schaut Hubert, w. s. Manitowoc rd., 4 s. Bellevue.
Schmitt J. F., 118½ N. Washington.
Seguin William, 225 Pine.
Shaughnessy Patrick & Son, Northwestern Hotel, Ft. H.
Silbersdorf Konrad, 100–104 S. Washington.
Sinclair William, 217 3d av., Ft. H.
Smith Frank C., 123 N. Washington.
Snavely George, 209–213 N. Adams.
Solomon Phil., Monroe av. rd., near Brewery.
Tellor Tusan, n. w. cor. Cherry and N. Adams.
Tennis Alex., 5117 S. Adams.
Tennis John L., 31 Main.
Trich John, 1259 Main.
Van den Heuvel John, 217 Cherry.
Van Deuren Henry, 203 Dousman, Ft. H.
Van de Zande John, 231 Main.
Van Dorn Henry, 203 Dousman, Ft. H.
Van Ermen Ernest, 330 Main.

### Saloons—Continued.

Van Ess Anton, 318 N. Adams.
Van Kessel Frank, American House.
Walczak Frank, 435 Main.
Warm Conrad J., 312 Cherry.
Wauters Peter, 507 Main.
Wellems Joseph, 215 Pine.
Wilson Robert M., 120 3d av., Ft. H.
Zegus John, w. s. Webster av., 1 s. city limits.
Zeutzius Joseph, 100 Main.
Zilles John, 428 Pleasant.
Zilles Mathias, 1247 Main.

### Sash, Doors and Blinds.

Cook Wm. D., 221 S. Washington.
Voigt John M. Mnfg. Co., Pearl, opp. Shawano, Ft. H.

### Saw Repairers.

Harder O. L., 227 Cherry.
Lindley Samuel, 313 Cherry.

### Sewing Machines.

Bertles John F., 107 S. Washington.
Singer Manufacturing Co., 212 Cherry.
Winter Thomas, 226 N. Washington.

### Ship Yards.

Fowles Carlton, e. s. McDonald, nr. James.

### Soap Mnfrs.

Fox River Soap Co., 219 Main.

### Sporting Goods.

Winter Thomas, 226 N. Washington.

### Stave and Heading Mnfrs.

Britton D. W., n. end N. Monroe av.

### Steamship Agents.

**ANSORGE & PARISH,** 126 N. Washington.
**BRICE O. J. B.,** 35 Parmentier blk.
**SHEPECK JOHN JR.,** 314 Main.

### Stone Quarries.

Hagen Frank A., 217 N. Adams.

**THE A. SPUHLER CO.** LADIES', MISSES' and CHILDREN'S
GREEN BAY — **CLOAKS, CAPES, JACKETS**

STO     281     VES

### Stoves.
See Hardware.

### Surveyors.
Brauns August, 220 N. Washington.

### Tailors.
See Merchant Tailors.

### Taxidermists.
Scheller Louis, 531 School.

### Telegraph Cos.
Postal Telegraph Cable Co., 322 N. Washington.
Western Union Telegraph Co., 323 N. Washington.

### Telephone Cos.
Wisconsin Telephone Co., 202 N. Washington.

### Tinware.
See Hardware.

### Transfer Agents.
**McCORMICK & BATES**, 220 S. Washington.

### Transportation Cos.
Goodrich Transportation Co., ft. Pine.
Hart's Steamboat Line, foot Cherry.
Lackawanna Transportation Co., ft. Pine.

### Trunk Mnfrs.
Marvin William H., 323½ N. Washington.

### Truss Mnfrs.
Schmitz Henry, 501 Pine.

### Tug Owners.
Kalb Louis, 107 N. Washington.
Nau George D. (tug C. M. Charnley), 121 N. Washington.

### Undertakers.
**HAUPT GEORGE & CO.**, 109 S. Washington.
Lefebvre & Schumacher, 325-327 N. Washington.
**OLDENBURG & CO.**, n. w. cor. Pearl and Main, Ft. H.

### Upholsterers.
Evans Thomas O., w. s. Cedar, 2 s. Dousman, Ft. H.

### Vessel Supplies.
Stenger George, 321 N. Washington.

### Veterinary Surgeons.

Braasch Casper N., 608 S. Madison.
Hollingsworth John S., 716 Main.
Leach Reuben G., 1125 Main.
Sprague Bros., n. w. cor. S. Washington and Stuart.

### Wagonmakers.

Brehme & Kattner, 207-209 Broadway, Ft. H.
Hansen Jorgen, 128 Broadway, Ft. H.
**KITTNER EDWARD C.,** 127 S. Washington.
**SIMON MATHIAS,** 311 Main.
**SMITS HERMAN,** 931-935 Main.

### Wall Paper.

Basche Fred. W., 221 N. Washington.
Le Mieux E. J., 323 N. Washington.
Wagner Henry, 220 Cherry.

### Watchmakers and Jewelers.

Frank George, e. s. Broadway, 2 n. Main, Ft. H.
**JANSSEN JOHN L. F.,** 916 Main.
**LIEBENOW JULIUS,** 205 N. Washington.
Luckenbach John, 210 N. Washington.
Michael Adolf, 216 N. Washington.
Tyrell Emerson L., 226 N. Washington.
Van der Elsen Cornelius, 326 Main.
Van der Zande Jacob, 310 Main, Ft. H.

### Water Works.

**Green Bay** and Ft. Howard Water Works Co., P. O. blk.

### Well Contractors.

Gleason Michael, 1233 Stuart.
**GREEN BROS. & CO.,** 1215 Stuart.
McHugh Terrence, 826 Doty.

### Whitewashers.

De Vroey Daniel, 303 N. Jefferson.

### Wines and Liquors—Whol.

Barth Edward, 103 N. Washington.
Bening Charles, 1115 Main.
Duchateau A., 329 N. Washington.
**SCHMIT JOHN P. C.,** 215 N. Washington.

### Yeast Dealers.

Forrer Edward W., 229 S. Washington.

# King-Fowle-McGee Co.

## Printers,
## Engravers,
## Binders,

**342, 344 and 346 Broadway,**

## MILWAUKEE.

**CATALOGUE WORK A SPECIALTY.**

**SEND FOR ESTIMATES.**

# PAUL N. SCHMITZ,
## Practical Horseshoer

INTERFERING HORSES SHOD WITH SUCCESS.

Shoes Made to Order and Shipped to any Point.
Fine Shoeing a Specialty.

613 Main Street, - - GREEN BAY, WIS.

## MATHIAS SIMON,
### HORSE SHOEING

And General Blacksmithing.

313 MAIN STREET, GREEN BAY, WIS.

———— MANUFACTURER OF ————

Wagons, Buggies, Carriages, Cutters, Sleighs, Etc.

## EDW. C. KITTNER,
MANUFACTURER OF
### Wagons, Carriages, Sleighs.

GENERAL BLACKSMITHING AND PAINTING, IN FIRST-CLASS STYLE.

127 South Washington Street,

GREEN BAY, - - WISCONSIN.

### HERMAN SMITS,
MANUFACTURER OF
### Wagons, Carriages,
### SLEIGHS, ETC.

ALL KINDS OF FARMERS' IMPLEMENTS.

SHOPS: 931-935 Main St.,
Corner Webster.

Green Bay, Wis.

―――― Natural Mineral Spring. ――――
## LEBENS WASSER.

The following is the official analysis of this celebrated water by Prof. W. W. Daniells, the noted chemist of the University of Wisconsin:

| | Grains | | Grains |
|---|---|---|---|
| Sodium Chloride | 0.4997 | Calcium Bicarbonate | 17.4561 |
| Potassium Sulphate | 0.0836 | Magnesium Bicarbonate | 10.5565 |
| Sodium Sulphate | 1.0812 | Oxide of Aluminum | 0.0025 |
| Calcium Sulphate | 0.1799 | Silica and insoluble residue | 1.2815 |
| Sodium Phosphate | trace | | |
| Iron Bicarbonate | 0.0583 | Total grains per gallon | 31.2235 |

## J. J. HANDLEN,

DEALER IN

## MINERAL WATER,

GREEN BAY, * * * * WISCONSIN.

## St. John Mineral Water,

North East Corner S. Quincy and Stuart St.

### ANALYSIS.

PROF. W. W. DANIELLS, OF THE UNIVERSITY OF WISCONSIN CHEMICAL LABORATORIES

MADISON, WIS., JAN. 22d, 1891.

| Sodium Chloride | ... | Magnesium Bicarbonate | 3.444 |
|---|---|---|---|
| Sodium Sulphate | ... | Iron Bicarbonate | 2.164 |
| Potassium Sulphate | ... | Aluminum Oxide | 0.140 |
| Calcium Sulphate | ... | Silica and insoluble residue | 3.018 |
| Calcium Bicarbonate | ... | | |
| Magnesium Chloride | ... | Total grains per gallon | 17.996 |

W. W. DANIELLS,
Professor of Chemistry, Pharmacy and Toxicology, University of Wisconsin.

RECOMMENDED BY PHYSICIANS FOR DYSPEPSIA, KIDNEY AND LIVER COMPLAINT, RHUEMATISM, ETC

### GREEN BAY, WIS.

## STEAM DYE WORKS,

JOSUA BUSCHER, Proprietor.

330 S. WASHINGTON ST., GREEN BAY, WIS.

Cloths, Ribbons, Shawls, Laces, etc., will be carefully Dyed or Washed. Gent's Garments Neatly Cleaned and Repaired.

## Dampf=Färberei von Joſua Buſcher,

330 S. Waſhington=Straße, Green Bay, Wis.

### Kleider, Bänder, Shawls, Decken, Schnüre, u ſ w.

werden nach Wunſch gefärbt oder gereinigt.—Herren Kleider werden hübſch gereinigt und reparirt.—Billige, ſchnelle und gute Ausführung wird garantirt.

EDW. ENGELS.   JOHN MOHR.
## ENGELS & MOHR,
DEALERS IN
## BOOTS AND SHOES.
ALSO BOOTS AND SHOES MADE TO ORDER.

**REPAIRING PROMPTLY DONE.**

206 N. WASHINGTON ST.
### GREEN BAY, WIS.

---

## PETER J. LOCHMANN,
DEALER IN
## BOOTS, SHOES,
ETC., ETC.

General Repairing Neatly Done.

1118 Main Street.          GREEN BAY, WIS.

---

## OLDENBURG & CO.
A. C. OLDENBURG, Proprietor.

## UNDERTAKERS, EMBALMERS
And Dealers in

WALL PAPER, ROOM-MOULDINGS, CURTAINS, ETC.

N. W. Cor. Pearl and Main Streets,

FORT HOWARD,   -   -   WISCONSIN.

---

## GEO. HAUPT & CO.,
## Furniture AND Undertaking

109 S. WASHINGTON ST.,
GREEN BAY,   -   WISCONSIN.

www.ingramcontent.com/pod-product-compliance
Lightning Source LLC
Chambersburg PA
CBHW031331230426
43670CB00006B/306